The Moral Psychology of Guilt

Moral Psychology of the Emotions

Series Editor: Mark Alfano, Associate Professor, Department of Philosophy, Delft University of Technology

How do our emotions influence our other mental states (perceptions, beliefs, motivations, intentions) and our behavior? How are they influenced by our other mental states, our environments, and our cultures? What is the moral value of a particular emotion in a particular context? This series explores the causes, consequences, and value of the emotions from an interdisciplinary perspective. Emotions are diverse, with components at various levels (biological, neural, psychological, social), so each book in this series is devoted to a distinct emotion. This focus allows the author and reader to delve into a specific mental state, rather than trying to sum up emotions en masse. Authors approach a particular emotion from their own disciplinary angle (e.g., conceptual analysis, feminist philosophy, critical race theory, phenomenology, social psychology, personality psychology, neuroscience) while connecting with other fields. In so doing, they build a mosaic for each emotion, evaluating both its nature and its moral properties.

Other titles in this series:
The Moral Psychology of Forgiveness, edited by Kathryn J. Norlock
The Moral Psychology of Pride, edited by Adam J. Carter and Emma C. Gordon
The Moral Psychology of Sadness, edited by Anna Gotlib
The Moral Psychology of Anger, edited by Myisha Cherry and Owen Flanagan
The Moral Psychology of Contempt, edited by Michelle Mason
The Moral Psychology of Compassion, edited by Justin Caouette and Carolyn Price
The Moral Psychology of Disgust, edited by Nina Strohminger and Victor Kumar
The Moral Psychology of Gratitude, edited by Robert Roberts and Daniel Telech
The Moral Psychology of Admiration, edited by Alfred Archer and André Grahle

Forthcoming titles in the series:
The Moral Psychology of Regret, edited by Anna Gotlib
The Moral Psychology of Hope, edited by Claudia Blöser and Titus Stahl

The Moral Psychology of Guilt

Edited by
Bradford Cokelet and Corey J. Maley

ROWMAN &
LITTLEFIELD
———INTERNATIONAL———
London • New York

Published by Rowman & Littlefield International Ltd.
6 Tinworth Street, London, SE11 5AL, UK
www.rowmaninternational.com

Rowman & Littlefield International Ltd. is an affiliate of Rowman & Littlefield
4501 Forbes Boulevard, Suite 200, Lanham, Maryland 20706, USA
With additional offices in Boulder, New York, Toronto (Canada), and Plymouth (UK)
www.rowman.com

Selection and editorial matter © 2019 by Bradford Cokelet and Corey J. Maley
Copyright in individual chapters is held by the respective chapter authors.

All rights reserved. No part of this book may be reproduced in any form or by any electronic or mechanical means, including information storage and retrieval systems, without written permission from the publisher, except by a reviewer who may quote passages in a review.

British Library Cataloguing in Publication Data
A catalogue record for this book is available from the British Library

ISBN: HB 978-1-78660-965-6

Library of Congress Cataloging-in-Publication Data Available

ISBN: 978-1-78660-965-6 (cloth : alk. paper)
ISBN: 978-1-5381-6547-8 (pbk : alk. paper)
ISBN: 978-1-78660-966-3 (electronic)

Contents

Acknowledgments   vii

Introduction   1
Bradford Cokelet and Corey J. Maley

SECTION 1: THE NATURE AND MEASUREMENT OF GUILT   11

1   The Feeling of Guilt   13
    Corey J. Maley and Gilbert Harman

2   On the Distinction between Shame and Guilt   37
    Heidi L. Maibom

3   Empathy and Conscience: An Essay on Guilt   53
    John Deigh

4   Against Exclusively Retrospective Guilt   71
    Heidy Meriste

5   Anticipatory Guilt   95
    Alison Duncan Kerr

SECTION 2: UNDERSTANDING GUILT AND ITS FUNCTIONS   111

6   The Evolution of Guilt and Its Non-Instrumental Enactments   113
    Blaine J. Fowers

7   Improving Our Understanding of Guilt by Focusing on Its (Inter)Personal Consequences   131
    Ilona E. De Hooge

8	How Guilt Serves Social Functions from Within *Darren McGee and Roger Giner-Sorolla*	149
9	One Reactive Attitude to Rule Them All *Nicholas Sars*	171

SECTION 3: EVALUATING GUILT — 193

10	Darker Sides of Guilt: The Case of Obsessive-Compulsive Disorder *Juliette Vazard and Julien Deonna*	195
11	Nietzsche's Repudiation of Guilt *Reid Blackman*	211
12	Conscience and Guilt from St. Paul to Nietzsche *Sophie-Grace Chappell*	227
13	A Thomistic View of Conscience and Guilt *Anne Jeffrey*	243
14	Kant and Williams on Guilt, Shame, and the Morality System *Laura Papish*	269
15	Moral Autonomy and Relationality of Confucian Shame: Beyond Western Guilt and Shame *Bongrae Seok*	289

Index	319
About the Contributors	327

Acknowledgments

It has been easier than expected to bring this volume to completion, and that is in good part due to the wonderful help and support we have received from colleagues, friends, and family. Mark Alfano was enthusiastic about the project and provided essential help and encouragement at the early stages, and of course the volume would not exist if he had not founded the wonderful series to which it contributes. Natalie Linh Bolderston and Isobel Cowper-Coles at Rowman & Littlefield International have been uniformly helpful, encouraging, and patient. We could not ask for a better experience with a press. The Department of Philosophy at Kansas, as usual, offered an ideal environment in which to pursue our project, and we also benefited from encouragement from our colleagues. Finally, we thank all the contributors, from whom we have learned a lot and who worked hard to produce excellent chapters.

Brad also wishes to thank his wife, Sarah, and his sons, Eli and Henry, who matter the most.

Corey wishes to thank his former advisors Gil Harman and Sarah-Jane Leslie, both of whom encouraged him to write a dissertation on guilt and shame. Additionally, he thanks audiences at the 2017 meeting of the International Society for Research on Emotion and at the 2018 Consortium of European Research on Emotion. Last, and most importantly, Sarah and Max, who make everything worth doing.

Introduction

Bradford Cokelet and Corey J. Maley

In most Western societies, guilt is widely regarded as a vital moral emotion. In addition to playing a central role in moral development and progress, many take the capacity to feel guilt as a defining feature of morality itself: No truly moral person escapes the pang of guilt when she has done something wrong. But proponents of guilt's importance face important challenges, such as distinguishing healthy from pathological forms of guilt, and accounting for the fact that not all cultures value guilt in the same way, if at all. In this volume, philosophers and psychologists come together to think about the nature and value of guilt. The first section of the book concerns the nature of guilt and questions about how to measure it. The second section focuses on the function (or functions) of guilt and questions about why human beings feel guilt. Finally, the third section turns to how we should evaluate guilt and its varieties. This introduction will lay out some of the main issues discussed in the individual chapters so that readers can better choose which to study, as well as highlight links between the chapters and interdisciplinary connections and tensions that the volume brings to light.

THE NATURE AND MEASUREMENT OF GUILT

Section I contains five papers on the nature and measurement of guilt. The different authors—all philosophers—assume that guilt is a negative response to a bad feature of the self (where this can include a bad thing that one has done). They help us dig deeper by thinking about the relevant forms of response and the relevant bad features. While charting out the subtle conceptual contours of guilt, they also raise questions about how psychologists do and should study guilt and effects; they point to ways in which psychologists have overlooked conceptual distinctions and nuance, and explain how this kind of oversight can raise worries about the validity of psychological results and explanations. By the same token, they offer conceptual material that psychologists can appropriate to build better scales, studies, and theories, and they offer arguments that psychologists might fruitfully contest on methodological grounds.

To get a sense of the conceptual work that our authors do in the first section, consider the kind of response to past bad action that guilt often involves. We can agree that it is a negative response to bad action, but is guilt an *emotion* or a *feeling*? In "The Feeling of Guilt," Corey J. Maley and Gilbert Harman explore this difference, argue that guilt is not an emotion, and offer an account of it as a feeling that avoids the problems that beset emotional accounts. If Maley and Harman are right, psychologists should pay attention to the distinction between emotions and feelings and make sure that their scales and constructs reflect the various ways in which people can feel bad about being guilty.

One might notice that shame, like guilt, often arises as a negative response to some bad feature of the self or what one has done. Are guilt and shame responses of the same kind? Or are they different forms of response to the same or different objects? In her chapter, "On the Distinction between Shame and Guilt," Heidi L. Maibom shows us how to think in a responsible, interdisciplinary way about these questions. She identifies and critically discusses the assumptions about guilt and shame that are found in the extant psychological and philosophic literatures and argues that shame and guilt are different forms of response, with distinct phenomenologies and motivational components.

Next, consider the object of guilt. We know that guilt is a negative response, but to what *kind* of bad features does it characteristically respond? Here again, our first five chapters help to chart out the options. In their chapter, Maley and Harman argue that guilt involves bad feelings about *being guilty*. Maibom contrasts guilt, which "focuses on the effects on another of what one has done or failed to do," with shame, which "focuses on the self as the origin of failure or transgression." This question of guilt's object is more thoroughly explored in John Deigh's chapter, "Empathy and Conscience: An Essay on Guilt." He carefully distinguishes between, on the one hand, feeling bad because one (believes one) is guilty of wrongdoing, and on the other, feeling bad that one has done something wrong. Deigh argues that the former is the correct way to understand guilt. On his view, guilt requires feeling bad that *we are guilty of wrongdoing*, which is marked by the "bite of conscience" and feeling unsettled with ourselves. Of course, it may be morally or prudentially good to feel bad when we harm others or wrong them, but unless we also believe we are guilty and feel bad or anxious about that,

Deigh argues, our responsiveness to having harmed or wronged another is not itself an instance of guilt.

While arguing for their subtle theses about the nature of guilt, Maley and Harman, Maibom, and Deigh also raise worries about psychological studies and theories that do not attend to the conceptual or psychological nuances. Deigh targets Martin Hoffman's empathy-based account of moral development and argues that Hoffman's purported explanations of guilt and its development are hobbled because he does not distinguish between feeling bad that one has harmed someone—for example, someone one cares about and with whom one empathizes—and feeling bad about being *guilty* of harming someone when one should not. Maley and Harman and Maibom also raise worries about psychological research, but they target the scales and theoretical constructs that empirical psychologists have deployed to measure guilt, shame, and their (moral and prudential) effects. For example, they each argue that some scales build pro-social behavior into the criteria that are supposed to indicate the presence of guilt and that this casts doubt on claims that studies using these scales can help establish that guilt explains or predicts pro-social behavior. Put together, these three chapters provide us with material to use when we critically scrutinize psychological studies. For example, although he does not discuss scales or constructs used in empirical studies, Deigh's chapter encourages us to be on the lookout for studies that run together evidence that people feel bad for harming others with evidence that people feel bad *because* they believe they are guilty of wrongfully harming others.

To be sure, psychologists have different methodological aims and standards than philosophers. They might admit that their scales or explanations lack the conceptual subtly and precision that philosophers bring out when they discuss the nature of a moral emotion or feeling like guilt, but still question the utility of introducing greater nuance into their work. Psychologists want scales, constructs, and theories that have explanatory and predictive power that can be used fruitfully in empirical studies, and they should work to incorporate the nuances philosophers bring to light only to the extent that it will help them achieve those goals. Given the aims of psychological research, it seems that at least some conceptual and psychological precision can and must be sacrificed. This is plausible as a general line of response, but the chapters by Maley and Harman, Maibom, and Deigh, clearly suggest that sometimes psychologists can run into trouble, by their own lights, because their scales and constructs do not reflect enough of the philosophic nuances. Thus, they can help psychologists establish better methodological standards, press psychologists to defend assumptions that have been made, and help various scholars critically examine and assess the theories and results that psychologists report.

The discussions of guilt in the first three chapters tend to focus—as most discussions do—on guilt as response to a bad thing *in the past*. In "Against Exclusively Retrospective Guilt," and "Anticipatory Guilt," Heidy Meriste and Alison Duncan Kerr (respectively) expand our focus and suggest that present and future actions can be the objects of legitimate guilt as well.

Meriste argues that present-focused guilt is possible and more widespread than one might think, but her main argument concerns future-directed guilt. She argues that this kind of guilt has the same kind of core evaluation, action tendency, and phenomenological feel that retrospective guilt has, but that it is nonetheless irreducible to past- or present-focused guilt. Moreover, she argues that future-directed guilt is especially interesting because it involves "a peculiar kind of tension between caring about morality and nevertheless acting, or intending to act, against it." She argues that while this tension can be problematic, there are situations, for example, ones involving weakness of will and value pluralism, in which future-oriented guilt is "stable."

In her chapter, Kerr discusses the nature of anticipatory guilt, defends an interesting account of its fittingness conditions, and responds to a worry about the value of anticipatory guilt. Kerr begins by introducing some general views on the nature of emotions and their fittingness conditions, which she then uses to explore the nature and fittingness conditions of anticipatory guilt. Kerr's chapter nicely distinguishes various views one might adopt about its fittingness conditions, so even those who do not accept her specific view are likely to find the discussion and argument helpful. In addition, her discussion raises questions about the fittingness conditions for *retrospective* guilt that are of independent interest. Finally, Kerr discusses empirical evidence suggesting that we systematically overestimate how much guilt we would feel in a given situation, and addresses worries that humans might be prone to feel too much anticipatory guilt. Like Meriste, Kerr thereby helps us pick out and carefully evaluate the reasons that people might have for doubting the value of anticipatory guilt.

Together, the chapters by Meriste and Kerr chart out some of the main questions future researchers will want to answer to give a full account of anticipatory guilt and its (rational, moral, and prudential) value. They give us strong reasons for thinking that anticipatory guilt cannot be reduced to retrospective guilt, and for thinking that it gives rise to new and interesting puzzles.

UNDERSTANDING GUILT AND ITS FUNCTIONS

The second section has four chapters: three by psychologists and one by a philosopher. All four discuss guilt and its various functions in human life.

Broadly speaking, we can distinguish three functions that guilt might be thought serve: an *evolutionary* function, promoting individual or group fitness; a *prudential* function, promoting personal well-being, integrity, or flourishing; and a *moral* function, promoting moral action or relationships. These authors help us think more concretely about these functions, about how guilt might serve one or more at the same time, and about whether shame could serve the same function that guilt does (just as well and in different cultures). In addition, the first three papers, by psychologists, helpfully survey the vast empirical literature on guilt and its consequences.

In "The Evolution of Guilt and Its Non-Instrumental Enactments," Blaine J. Fowers surveys empirical work on human guilt and evolutionary explanations for its existence. This provides us with resources to understand the ways in which guilt can promote individual or group fitness, but it also forces us to question whether guilt has a truly moral function. Guilt motivates us to repair relationships, but if these feelings and behaviors exist only because they increase individual genetic fitness, then it will be tempting to conclude that guilt-motivated behavior is not in any fundamental sense moral (or even prudential). Fowers helpfully raises and sharpens this worry for us and then argues that we can avoid such a conclusion. He offers a constituent-end account of guilt that contrasts with means-ends accounts, and uses that account to explain how guilt is "as much a manifestation of a breach in one's identity and internalized standards as it is a matter avoiding aversive relationship consequences."

In "Improving Our Understanding of Guilt by Focusing on Its (Inter)Personal Consequences," Ilona E. De Hooge surveys the empirical literature on the consequences of guilt in human beings. She helpfully distinguishes between the ways in which guilt can lead to good or bad consequences for the transgressor, for the victim of the transgression, and for unrelated people. After looking at the empirical evidence with those distinctions in mind, De Hooge argues that guilt functions to repair *only* damaged social relationships. However, she also argues that because guilt functions to repair damaged relationships in the most efficient ways possible (from the transgressor's point of view), there is a "self-focused touch even to this moral, other-focused emotion."

In "How Guilt Serves Social Functions from Within," Darren McGee and Roger Giner-Sorolla discuss empirical studies that contrast guilt with shame and that suggest that guilt has more individualistic characteristics. For example, guilt seems to better promote self-control and it is less influenced by public exposure manipulations, so it seems to serve valuable prudential functions. In line with the previous two chapters, McGee and Giner-Sorolla demonstrate that there is strong evidence that humans feel guilt because it promotes socially valuable relationships; however, they note that this leads to a puzzle about how guilt develops and serves *both* individualistic and social functions. Moreover, there is evidence that shame is less individualist than guilt, and we might wonder whether this impacts its ability to serve social or moral functions. With these questions in mind, McGee and Giner-Sorolla offer us a model of internalization for both guilt and shame. They identify a form of guilt internalization in which the self is treated as a social object and argue that their studies "bridge the gap between the social context and the function of guilt" and its individualist functions. In addition, they offer a model of shame internalization and suggest that more cross-cultural work needs to be done in order to determine whether and how shame can serve the same functions that guilt does.

Finally, in "One Reactive Attitude to Rule Them All," Nicholas Sars discusses the individual and interpersonal functions of guilt and shame in the context of P. F. Strawson's influential philosophical work on responsibility and reactive attitudes. Philosophers influenced by Strawson often discuss various personal, moral, and self-focused moral or ethical attitudes (e.g., resentment, indignation, and guilt); it is difficult to see how such seemingly different attitudes are unified. As his title suggests, Sars helps us see the need for a unifying explanation of these attitudes, and then proposes an answer that focuses on the central role of guilt. Specifically, Sars argues that guilt plays both prudential and ethical-moral functions in our lives and that we can explain how it unifies the personal, moral, and self-focused moral or ethical attitudes by attending to these functions. In making his case, Sars points to specific functions of guilt—that it enables us to hold ourselves responsible for living up to our personal ideals and that our feelings of guilt can indicate and communicate how much we (comparatively) value various relationships with others—that, he argues, shame cannot have.

EVALUATING GUILT

The chapters just discussed in the second section of the volume provide us with a survey of the vast empirical literature on guilt; collectively, they suggest that guilt is valuable because it serves various evolutionary, prudential, and moral goals. For example, all of the authors in section 2 would presumably agree that guilt is good because it normally or often helps us repair prudentially and morally valuable relationships. They might also agree that it promotes personal integrity—for example, by enabling us to better live up to our personal ideals, our internalized social expectations, or our identity-defining commitments. On the whole, the papers in section 2 encourage us to embrace *guilt optimism*: the view that guilt is usually good and that if human beings did not feel guilt, life would be (morally or prudentially) much worse.

Part III opens with two papers that question the wisdom of guilt optimism. In "Darker Sides of Guilt: The Case of Obsessive-Compulsive Disorder," Juliette Vazard and Julien Deonna provide us with an empirically informed account that shows how guilt can, at least in some individuals, be bad from both a prudential and moral point of view. They argue that guilt in OCD cases is bad in part because the guilty agents take their feelings to be indicative of a defective self that cannot possibly be repaired. Besides being inherently interesting, this chapter may also ground more general worries about guilt optimism. Vazard and Deonna argue that "the severe patterning of negative emotions characteristic of OCD is familiar, perhaps in lighter forms, to many who do not have the disorder."

Next, Reid Blackman offers Nietzschean reasons to reject guilt optimism and to accept guilt pessimism. In "Nietzsche's Repudiation of Guilt," Blackman provides a new interpretation of Nietzsche's negative views about guilt and argues that we could live better lives (individually and relationally) if we left guilt behind. The chapter offers a bracing challenge to those who think that guilt is a vital source of prudential or moral goods and also raises questions about whether Nietzsche's target is some culturally specific form of guilt or guilt in all its forms. In thinking through that question, readers might find it useful to revisit the chapters in sections 1 and 2 on the nature and functions of guilt. For example, Blackman's case against guilt and his vision of a positive way of life without it challenges Sars's view that guilt, and not other reactions such as regret or shame, can play certain valuable prudential and ethical-moral functional roles.

Sophie-Grace Chappell's "Conscience and Guilt from St. Paul to Nietzsche" also has connections to earlier chapters in this volume, and it offers a strong counterpoint to Blackman's case for guilt pessimism. Chappell highlights the connection between guilt and conscience, which was explored in Deigh's chapter, and insightfully contrasts influential Christian, Kantian, and Nietzschean accounts of conscience. She offer criticisms of all three and then argues in favor of a revised Christian conception that promises to make better sense of conscience and guilt than either Kant or Nietzsche. In the course of her argument, this chapter raises interesting questions about the Nietzschean interpretation of guilt, such as Blackman's mentioned above. In addition, she shows that guilt optimists face questions about how to choose between various competing conceptions of conscience and guilt, and that to do that they can usefully engage with guilt pessimists.

Anne Jeffrey's chapter, "A Thomistic View of Conscience and Guilt," offers readers just what the title would lead them to expect. Jeffrey explains Aquinas's account of conscience and guilt and defends a feature of that account that guilt pessimists would likely target. Like other human feelings and emotions, guilt is sometimes mistaken. For example, we sometimes feel guilty for doing things that are not, in fact, wrong or harmful. Given how bad guilt feels and the possibility that we will take guilt to be indicative of a defective self that cannot possibly be repaired (as Vazard and Deonna point out), guilt pessimists might question the value of guilt and reject the idea that guilt and conscience have some kind of normative authority that we should recognize in our deliberations and self-assessments. Jeffrey faces this worry head-on and defends the normative authority of conscience *even when it errs*. She argues that the guilt of conscience always signals a kind of moral failure in the will, and can be instrumental in the process of moral improvement, whether or not the judgments of conscience are correct.

The final two chapters in the volume broaden the cultural scope of the discussion and consider the possibility that guilt is absent or plays a lesser role in the lives of people in some non-European or historically distant cultures. In "Kant and Williams on Guilt, Shame, and the Morality System," Laura Papish engages with Bernard Williams's attack on the morality system and the positive attitudes he expresses toward ancient Greek cultures that may have emphasized shame over guilt. Williams's views on these topics are provocative and influential but also obscure. Papish works to charitably understand Williams's views and then discusses how Kant and Kantian philosophers might fruitfully learn from Williams's attacks. As McGee and Giner-Sorolla emphasize in their chapter, guilt has a more individualistic focus than shame, and philosophers such as Williams worry that this can be a defect rather than a benefit; insofar as guilt encourages us to focus on our relation to our own conscience rather than the others with whom we live in the actual social world, it can encourage a sort of moral egoism. This might lead one to think that a shame-based morality would be more relational and therefore better. Papish thinks this is a deep worry about guilt and the Kantian conception of morality, but she also thinks it is one that the Kantian conception can rebut. To show how, she argues that Kant can—and does—make room for caring about other people and how one's actions matter from their point of view, and that he does that while rightly insisting that guilt and conscience have a central kind of normative authority in our deliberations and self-assessments.

Finally, Bongrae Seok shows how Confucian moral thought and culture can challenge guilt optimism or at least the assumption that guilt is an essential moral and prudential good. His chapter, "Moral Autonomy and Relationality of Confucian Shame: Beyond Western Guilt and Shame," draws on both psychology and philosophy to elucidate various Confucian concepts that are related, but not reducible, to Western concepts of guilt and shame. This interpretive and philosophic work raises questions about the nature of guilt and the distinction between guilt and shame that will take readers back to the chapters in the first section. Seok's central concern, however, is to question Western assumptions about the importance of guilt and shame. Specifically, he helpfully contrasts Aristotelian shame with Confucian relational shame, and then argues that individual and relational life shaped by Confucian relational shame instead of guilt has some underappreciated appeal. In making his case, he differentiates his argument from Williams's argument (discussed in the chapter by Papish), and responds to various empirical and philosophical worries that Westerners have raised about shame moralities and cultures. In the end, Seok argues that humans can live well without guilt, and he makes his argument without defending guilt pessimism; however, his positive account of Confucian shame certainly invites comparison with Blackman's positive Nietzschean vision of life without guilt and the defenses of guilt's importance that we find in the chapters by Sars, Chappell, and Jeffrey.

Seok's chapter is a fitting end to the volume because it encourages readers to think about what guilt is, why guilt—or some kinds of guilt—are valuable, what human life without guilt would look like, and whether we should welcome or resist the idea of leaving guilt behind. In other words, Seok's chapter shows how cross-cultural philosophy can call on us to tackle a wide variety of philosophical and psychological questions, and opens up questions that might otherwise seem closed.

Section 1

THE NATURE AND MEASUREMENT OF GUILT

Chapter 1

The Feeling of Guilt

Corey J. Maley and Gilbert Harman

INTRODUCTION

One of us (Harman, 2009) has argued that people can be moral—even morally excellent—without experiencing guilt. However, while completing the work of (Maley, 2015), we came to believe that there was a significant confusion between guilt and shame in philosophy, including how each relates to morality. At first, looking to the psychological literature on guilt and shame seemed to offer a useful distinction between the two. Furthermore, empirical studies relying on this distinction seem to answer some questions about whether it was good or bad for people to feel guilt or shame.

But that was not the end of the story. Careful examination of how psychologists understood guilt and shame—that is, how they were operationalized—revealed problems with how guilt was being measured. In what follows, we will discuss these problems, and how they led to the view that guilt may not be an emotion at all, or at least not in some "proper" sense. Rather, we will argue along lines originally pursued in Elison's work (2005) that guilt is what we tentatively call a feeling, rather than an emotion. This distinction makes sense of why many different accounts of guilt exist in a way that has no parallel for other emotions: Philosophers and psychologists generally agree about the nature of sadness, anger, or joy; not so for guilt. We conclude by offering some implications this account has for debates about guilt and its relation to morality.

SOME CONCEPTIONS OF GUILT

Given that we are, after all, morally imperfect, it is no surprise that philosophical investigation of morality extends beyond what we are morally obligated to do, to what happens (or should happen) when we do what we ought not to have done. Guilt is a component of such investigations, although what guilt is and how it relates to our transgressions is not obvious. We do not always feel guilt over transgressions: We may not know we have done something wrong, or we may not care. In this section, we will sketch a few of the major philosophical views on guilt. Our aim is not to argue for any particular view, but to illustrate both the variety of positions regarding the extent to which we should feel guilt, plus the variety of conceptions of guilt on offer. It may be surprising that there are such different conceptions of this so-called emotion, and philosophers are not always precise about what they take guilt to be. Perhaps the thought is that guilt is not in need of clarification or explication: Like other emotions, such as joy and sadness, guilt is supposed to be self-evident. Nevertheless, it will become clear that philosophers do not agree on what counts as guilt, making the need for an account of guilt particularly pressing.

OPPONENTS OF GUILT

A number of writers have argued that guilt is basically bad: It is an emotion that is harmful, in one way or another, and something we should try to excise from our emotional lives. Nietzsche is an early proponent of this view. In the second essay of his *On the Genealogy of Morals*, Nietzsche is concerned with (among other things) articulating the origin of guilt, including its supposed intimate connection to punishment:

Punishment is supposed to possess the value of awakening the feeling of guilt in the guilty person; one seeks in it the actual *instrumentum* of that psychical reaction called "bad conscience," "sting of conscience" (Nietzsche, 1995, p. 517).

Nietzsche goes on to claim that punishment does not, in fact, foster feelings of guilt, but does the opposite: Those punished "suffered no 'inward pain'" (Nietzsche, 1995, p. 518). In a complicated exposition that we cannot do justice to here, Nietzsche claims[1] that guilt (or "bad conscience") is a kind of sickness resulting from our turning certain instincts inward as society and culture have developed. As a sickness, it is undesirable: We are less "cheerful" than those ancients who felt no guilt. Although it is something we cannot realistically hope to rid ourselves of (at least not now), it is nevertheless an illness "as pregnancy is an illness," suggesting that the conditions allowing us to feel guilt are a necessary step to something greater (Nietzsche, 1995, p. 524). Nietzsche's discussion of slave and master moralities in the first essay of *On the Genealogy of Morals* is in the background of his analysis of guilt, which includes views about the connection between guilt and religious belief. As mentioned, we cannot do justice to the complete Nietzschean picture, but note what will be a common theme: that guilt is painful, and that is ultimately something that we should—in some sense or another—banish from our psychological lives (see Blackman, this volume).

Freud engages in a similar project, although rather than explaining the historical or cultural origins of guilt, Freud offers an account of how guilt develops within the individual. Without getting enmeshed in the details of Freud's view of our psychological architecture, we can say that Freud views guilt as a kind of anxiety about being punished by an internalized representation of a parental figure (i.e., the superego) that threatens to punish when the person violates societal norms (see [Freud, 1961], especially chapter VII). Making sense of precisely how this process could work, given the capacities of the various components within Freud's theory—as well as their relations among themselves—is itself an interesting philosophical project (taken on admirably by [Velleman, 2003]). It is sufficient to note here that like Nietzsche, Freud has a dim view of guilt, but without Nietzsche's optimism: Freud sees guilt as an illness lacking even the "pregnant" possibilities that Nietzsche sees in this emotion.

Walter Kaufmann has a particularly negative critique of guilt. We will not spell out his overall project of how we should overhaul morality; a few quotations will suffice to provide an idea of Kaufmann's view of guilt. "Guilt feelings are a contagious disease that harms those who harbor them and endangers those who live close to them. . . . Typically, guilt feelings make those who harbor them feel wretched" (Kaufmann, 1973, p. 114). And further, "as a rule, guilt feelings make men vindictive and inhibit the development of generosity. . . . If guilt feelings were at least of some help to those whom we feel we have wronged, it might still be argued that self-punishment served some purpose. But generally guilt feelings have the opposite effect" (Kaufmann, 1973, p. 115).

As mentioned above, one of us took guilt to be a pernicious emotion that should have no place in our moral lives (Harman, 2009). For every positive role that one might think guilt plays in our behavior, Harman argued that we can imagine either replacing guilt with something else, or eliminating the emotion outright. Thus, where some see anticipatory guilt as playing a role in guiding moral behavior, there are other (and better) reasons to act morally. And while some see those who feel no guilt as psychopathic (perhaps even by definition), Harman offers himself and some of his colleagues as proof of the existence of people who are moral (i.e., not psychopaths) but nevertheless feel no guilt. More generally, it was argued that for any person P normally judged to be moral, we can imagine her counterpart P* who does not feel guilt, and who would be as moral as P. Intuitions to the contrary are simply not shared by others, such as Harman, who remarks that "the proposed necessary connections between morality and guilt are arrived at through introspection and are accepted merely because they seem plausible to the authors, presumably, because of their own experiences of guilt" (Harman, 2009, p. 206).

One might think that these intuitions should not have any more weight than the intuitions of those who disagree: One side intuits that guilt is necessary for morality, the other that it is not. But on Harman's view, the burden of proof is on those who take guilt as necessary. Given the painful nature of guilt, involving "feelings of remorse, involving deep regret, painful humiliation, distress, self-punishment, and/or self-flagellation" (Harman, 2009, p. 206) and the possibility of morality without this painful emotion, Harman concluded that we ought to eliminate guilt from our emotional repertoire. As he put it, "guilt is not needed for moral motivation, that it is incorrect to define moral standards as those standards it is appropriate to feel guilt for violating, that people can lack susceptibility to guilt without being psychopaths, that it would be a good thing to try to bring up children in such a way that they are not susceptible to such guilt, and that it would be a good thing for those moral people who feel guilt to try to eliminate it" (Harman, 2009, p. 212).

PROPONENTS OF GUILT

Philosophers are (unsurprisingly) not unanimously opposed to guilt. Of course, given its unpleasant character, nobody takes guilt to be inherently good, but a number of authors have argued that guilt is instrumentally good insofar as it informs us about what is moral, or provides motivation to do the right thing (or at least avoid doing the wrong thing). For example, guilt plays an important role in Gibbard's view of what it is for something to be morally wrong (Gibbard, 1990; 1992). According to Gibbard, what it is for someone to have done something morally wrong is for that person to be blameworthy; blameworthiness, in turn, is explained in terms of warranted guilt (from the first-person point of view) or impartial resentment (from the third-person point of view). Guilt itself, or at least the prospect of warranted guilt, is an instrument used to guide us to what is moral, and in that sense, is quite desirable (insofar as being moral is desirable, an assumption I will not question here).

In a similar vein, Brandt takes the feeling of guilt to be partially definitive of wrong actions (in light of an ideal moral code, the details about which need not concern us here): "What is it, then, for someone to think sincerely that any action of the kind F is wrong? . . . If he thinks he has just performed an F-action, he feels guilty or remorseful or uncomfortable about it, unless he thinks he has some excuse—unless, for instance, he knows that at the time of action he did not think his action would be an F-action" (Brandt, 1992, p. 121). Brandt leaves open precisely what guilt amounts to (although he does mention that just any feeling of anxiety about punishment or anticipated consequences should not count as guilt). Nevertheless, it is clear that although he views it as a painful emotion, Brandt sees guilt as necessary for explaining morality.

Patricia Greenspan develops an account of guilt in her discussion of moral dilemmas, according to which guilt is an important identificatory mechanism in which the individual feels self-directed anger, and that provides motivation to repair damage done to others (Greenspan, 1995). Greenspan's view is that the core of guilt is the uncomfortable feeling that one is at fault. According to Greenspan, when compared to shame, regret, remorse, moral anguish, and compunction, guilt "is the best candidate among these negative emotional reactions for supplying the motivational force of moral 'ought'" (Greenspan, 1995, p. 135).

Velleman argues that, contrary to most other views (with the exception of Greenspan's), it can be rational to feel guilt when one has not done anything morally wrong. For Velleman, guilt involves anxiety about the possible forfeiture of trust: trust others may have, and the trust that a person has in herself (Velleman, 2003). This withdrawal of trust is a particular form of punishment, and Velleman's position is thus a refinement of Freud's conception. Interestingly, Velleman argues that different anxieties are involved in different kinds of guilt: Survivor's guilt, for example, does not seem to involve anxiety about forfeiture of trust; instead, it involves anxiety about causing resentment. Other occurrences of guilt might involve anxiety about causing envy. As such, "guilt is a family of emotions, including anxiety about having warranted not only distrust but also angry or envious resentment and perhaps other, related reactions as well" (Velleman, 2003, p. 247).

PROBLEMS FOR PHILOSOPHICAL ACCOUNTS OF GUILT

This brief overview of some of the previous philosophical views on guilt makes it clear that the nature of guilt is not obvious (nor settled), that different accounts of guilt are not merely minor variations of one another, and that the precise relationship between guilt and morality is far from clear. The accounts of guilt I have mentioned provide different answers to key questions. For example, does guilt essentially involve anxiety, or feeling that one must be punished? Does feeling guilt make one feel terrible? Does guilt lead people to repair the damages they have caused, or even want to do so in the first place? When should we feel guilt, or expect others to feel guilt, or recommend that they do?

To be clear, we are not suggesting that we should be surprised that different philosophers have different views about guilt; disagreement, after all, is part and parcel of the discipline. Rather, we are suggesting that it is not clear precisely when the various views are in conflict because it is not clear that philosophers are all on the same conceptual page regarding what guilt is. If we had a settled picture of guilt, we would still expect philosophers to disagree about its proper role in our moral psychology. For example, there is virtually no disagreement about what anger is, although there is disagreement about, say, whether anger can play a justificatory role in positive retributivism (Rodogno, 2010).

Now, one might hope that if we look to psychology, we could find some much-needed clarity regarding what, precisely, guilt is. And while, on the surface, this may seem to be the case, we believe there are also some deep concerns about approaches to measuring guilt. Later, we suggest that there can be no settled picture, because guilt is not an emotion in the first place. Before articulating that point, we will first mention a few key studies, and then discuss some issues in the psychological literature.

EMPIRICAL RESEARCH ON GUILT

Contemporary discussions of guilt in the psychological literature are often explicitly contrasted with shame; these most often begin with a conception drawn from psychiatry (Lewis, 1971). Put simply, on this conception an instance of emotional guilt is an instance of feeling bad about something that one has done, whereas an instance of feeling shame is an instance of feeling that one's self is bad (the behavior-self distinction). Other distinctions have been proposed, but have found little support when tested empirically (reviewed in Tangney et al. [2007]). For example, one involves shame as an experience essentially involving public (or perceived public) exposure, contrasted with guilt as the more private emotion (the public-private distinction). Alternatively (and more broadly), some have thought that certain types of situations or experiences might tend to elicit guilt, whereas others elicit shame (e.g., perhaps unintentionally hurting someone elicits guilt, whereas stealing elicits shame). But these ways of distinguishing guilt and shame have been abandoned in favor of Lewis's, and numerous studies have based their findings on this conception.

POSITIVE FINDINGS REGARDING GUILT

First, let us look at some of those studies that explicitly contrast guilt with shame. June Price Tangney and her collaborators have been influential in arguing for the behavior-self distinction between guilt and shame and demonstrating a number of ways in which guilt is beneficial, particularly when compared with shame. In an early study (Tangney, 1991), participants' proneness to guilt, shame, and empathy were measured using a questionnaire, asking these participants about how they would respond to various transgressions. Although guilt-proneness and shame-proneness were correlated (as one might expect, given their near synonymy in everyday language), the two were separable (according to comparisons with prior measures of guilt and shame), and were found to have differential correlations with empathy. Specifically, guilt was found to be positively correlated with empathy (more specifically: other-oriented empathic responsiveness), while shame was negatively correlated. Thus, those people more prone to feeling guilt in response to moral transgressions are also more likely to feel empathy toward others. Similar results were reported in a series of studies by (Leith et al., 1998). Here, guilt-prone participants were more likely than those who were shame-prone to be able to take the perspective of others in stories. Additionally, these researchers found that, when asking participants to recall a situation in which they had experienced an interpersonal conflict, those who were identified as being guilt-prone were more likely—and better able—to take the perspective of the other participant in the conflict. Furthermore, those who were guilt-prone tended to report that the conflict had been resolved positively; shame-prone participants were more likely to report that their conflict had ended badly.

Empirical results regarding the seemingly positive effects of guilt and negative effects of shame are not limited to adults. A number of studies show how children benefit from guilt over shame in various ways. A study by Kochanska and her colleagues videotaped children interacting with an object rigged to break, and studied these children over several years (Kochanska et al. 2002). Independent coders rated the degree to which children displayed various expressions such as gaze aversion, positive and negative affect, and various bodily signals. A stable pattern of behaviors emerged for some of these children, which the researchers argue is nascent guilt. These guilt-prone children were found to be more moral, meaning that later assessments showed that they were less likely to violate moral rules.

It is not just that children experiencing guilt have better outcomes: Their parents' use of guilt, as opposed to shame, is beneficial as well. For instance, Krevans and Gibbs (1998) found that parents who taught their children to feel guilty about moral transgressions involving other people—as opposed to those mothers who used other forms of discipline, such as shame-induction, power-assertion, or love-withdrawal—had children rated to be the most moral and empathetic in later years. Scarnier et al. (2009) studied the ways in which mothers reacted to their children's moral transgressions. One study focused on real scenarios, in which mothers were asked to recall how they felt about their children's wrongdoings, as well as how they dealt with or disciplined their children. Another study focused on hypothetical situations, asking mothers to predict how they would respond to their children. Those mothers who felt guilt about their children's behavior were more likely to use beneficial, adaptive parenting strategies, whereas those who felt shame about their children's behavior were more likely to use maladaptive strategies.

Another set of results that focus solely on guilt suggest that guilt-proneness is correlated with cooperation and other pro-social behaviors. Ketelaar et al. (2003) asked participants to play repeated rounds of a prisoner's dilemma game, and after a prescribed set of these rounds, had one group of participants recall an event in which they had felt guilt (the guilt-induction group), while another control group described a neutral event. Participants in the guilt-induction group were then found to play more cooperatively than those in the control group. Furthermore, those in the guilt-induction group who had previously been least cooperative were most likely to play more cooperatively. A follow-up study investigated the role of naturally-occurring guilt, rather than guilt induced from memory of a past experience. Here, each participant was asked to propose how to divide money between himself and a partner, and the partner is then asked to accept or reject this offer (an ultimatum game). Directly after writing down their offer, participants were asked to rate how they felt about their offer (but before learning whether their partner had accepted or rejected it). Those participants who made selfish offers and who tended to feel guilty about those offers tended to make generous offers on the next round of play (with the same partner).

Results from Wubben et al. (2009) examined the effect of *others'* perception of guilt in a cooperation context. In this study, participants played a so-called public good dilemma game,[2] after which they were asked to report how they felt about their decision on a piece of paper. These answers were recorded, and the participants were given back what were supposed to be their own answers, but were actually the "answers" produced by the experimenters. Participants were thus led to believe that they had mistakenly gotten to see how someone else participating in the experiment felt about their decisions. As expected, participants reported that they expected these other "participants" who reported feeling guilty to cooperate more in future rounds of the game. More interestingly, though, these same participants themselves were then more likely to cooperate than those participants who had read faux-participant reports that expressed no guilt. So merely learning that others—others who these participants had no contact with—felt guilty about their past behavior in this game increased the degree to which they cooperated.

It would seem that the psychological research on guilt—both contrasted with shame and studied in isolation—paints a clear picture: Guilt is, on balance, an emotion with positive effects, particularly relative to shame. Other chapters in this volume, including De Hooge, and McGee and Giner-Sorolla, discuss these and related results that support such a view. It is difficult to avoid the conclusion that we should teach our children to feel guilt (but not shame), and we should encourage other people to feel guilt (but not shame). As Tangney et al. (2007) put it:

> In sum, empirical results converge, indicating that guilt but not shame is most effective in motivating people to choose the moral paths in life. The capacity for guilt is more apt to foster a lifelong pattern of moral behavior, motivating individuals to accept responsibility and take reparative action in the wake of the occasional failure or transgression. . . . Thus, when considering the welfare of the individual, his or her close relationships, or society, feelings of guilt represent the moral emotion of choice. (p. 355)

On the surface, this seems like a remarkable bit of progress toward resolving some of the philosophical disputes mentioned above. Unfortunately, there are unresolved questions about this empirical research that need to be answered before we can conclude that the nature and value of guilt has been settled. First, there are reasons to doubt that guilt and shame are the same kind of thing; thus, the utility of comparing the two is dubious. We will argue in the next section that guilt is not an emotion in the same way that shame is (if guilt is an emotion at all), and so comparing the two is akin to comparing sadness (a genuine emotion) with feeling disappointed (a complex state that has different feelings depending on cooccurring thoughts). Additionally, there are purely methodological worries about how guilt has been conceptualized in much of the psychological research. Elsewhere in this volume, Maibom mentions similar concerns; here we will focus on one particularly influential example.

Researchers interested in the empirical study of guilt face a difficulty. Because there is no instrument for directly detecting guilt (i.e., guiltometers do not exist), one has to somehow operationalize the emotion, then use a questionnaire (or other instrument) to infer its presence in study participants. In the case of guilt, one of the prominent early measures is the Test of Self-Conscious Affect (TOSCA) and its revisions, initially developed by Tangney. Ideally, this measure would reliably detect guilt (as opposed to shame), which would then allow one to observe (or infer) concomitant phenomena in subjects experiencing guilt (or prone to experience guilt, as the case may be).

The difficulty with this approach is that it is very sensitive to the initial operationalization of guilt used to construct the measure. Problematic assumptions can lead one to think that what seems to be a discovery about guilt is actually just a feature of guilt that has been built into the criteria for detecting it in the first place. This is the situation in the TOSCA.

For example, consider the following questions from the TOSCA (Tangney & Dearing, 2002):

1. You have recently moved away from your family, and everyone has been very helpful. A few times you needed to borrow money, but you paid it back as soon as you could.
   (a) You would feel immature.
   (b) You would think: "I sure ran into some bad luck."
   (c) You would return the favor as quickly as you could.
   (d) You would think: "I am a trustworthy person."
   (e) You would be proud that you repaid your debts.
2. You attend your coworker's housewarming party and you spill red wine on a new cream-colored carpet, but you think no one notices.
   (a) You think your coworker should have expected some accidents at such a big party.
   (b) You would stay late to help clean up the stain after the party.
   (c) You would wish you were anywhere but the party.
   (d) You would wonder why your coworker chose to serve red wine with the new light carpet.
3. You break something at work and then hide it.
   (a) You would think: "This is making me anxious. I need to either fix it or get someone else to."
   (b) You would think about quitting.
   (c) You would think: "A lot of things aren't made very well these days."
   (d) You would think: "It was only an accident."

For each answer choice, participants are to rate how likely they are to agree with the statements on a 5-point Likert scale (from 1: not likely, to 5: very likely). Each answer choice corresponds to a different category: shame, guilt, externalization, detachment, and pride, which is sometimes divided into two types (which need not be distinguished for present purposes). For example, in the first question, (a) corresponds to shame, (b) to externalization, (c) to guilt, (d) to alpha-pride, and (e) to beta-pride. In the second, (a) corresponds to externalization, (b) to guilt, (c) to shame, and (d) to detachment. In the third, (a) is guilt, (b) is shame, (c) is externalization, and (d) is detachment. Depending on the particular answers given, researchers can characterize the extent to which a particular participant is guilt-prone, shame-prone, etc.

If we look closely at these answer choices, there is a significant problem. In the questions above (which are representative of others in the TOSCA), the guilt-indicating answer choices consist of a thought or desire to engage in some kind of pro-social behavior (returning a favor, helping clean up, thinking one needs to fix a broken item). This poses a problem for claims about the supposed pro-social nature of guilt: The very instrument used to measure whether a person is prone to guilt does so by operationalizing guilt as the tendency to engage in pro-social behavior. Thus, it is not surprising—and perhaps impossible—for one to measure someone as prone to feeling guilty and subsequently discover that they are relatively more likely to engage in pro-social behavior than others. In the questions above, guilt is measured as the propensity to engage in pro-social behavior (and to also feel anxious, as in question 3).

Some of the other answer choices on other questions differ slightly from this pattern, but the main problem remains. Some guilt-indicating answer choices mention other feelings, such as feeling bad or unhappy. Others consist of concerns about desert, such as feeling that one deserves punishment, or that one should decline an individual award for a group effort. Still others consist of what might constitute mere regret, without mentioning any feelings whatsoever. Examples include vowing to be more careful, or to study harder next time. Thus, this measure of guilt has it that what counts as guilt is some admixture of propensities to engage in pro-social behavior, feel some negative emotion, feel that one deserves punishment, and regret the thing done wrong. Furthermore, the things about which one can feel guilt include being late for appointments, doing poorly on a test, having second thoughts about remaining with a volunteer project, and having a friend's dog run away while one is taking care of it. In other words, this measure of guilt has it that one can feel guilty for arguably non-moral failings, including those involving no other person as a victim.

While many studies rely on the TOSCA, there are other measures of guilt and shame. However, these are sometimes derived from the TOSCA, or share its conceptual commitments, and thus share similar problems. One example comes from Cohen, Panter, & Turan (2012), who developed a measure of guilt derived from (and checked for validity against) the TOSCA. In another example, the parental discipline method known as "guilt-induction" is essentially "discipline which directs the child to attend to his or her victims' perspectives" (Krevans, 1996, p. 3266). Thus, inducing guilt is inducing an empathic orientation. It is then no wonder that parents who "induce guilt" in their children have children who are more "moral."

To be clear, we should not overstate the case: It is at least intuitively obvious that guilt is associated with feelings that involve reparation, apology, and pro-sociality. However, that is not the point. It is certainly not the case that guilt necessarily involves such feelings: One can imagine a case in which a person both feels guilty but does not feel that she needs to repair whatever damage she's done. Thus, it should be a real discovery that guilt, for example, leads to pro-social feelings, and not a defining characteristic of the emotion in the first place. But this cannot be determined if guilt is simply defined to include those very feelings, and thus it is unclear what studies that begin with assumptions like these can demonstrate. As such, until they are fixed, studies that use the TOSCA and similar measures do not provide evidence that guilt is linked to pro-sociality.

One might think—as we do—that this is not an accurate conception of guilt, and that whatever is being measured is too disjointed to count as a single emotion. This is exactly what we will argue for in the next section. We will use this problematically multifaceted view of guilt to motivate the idea that guilt is not an emotion in the first place, but something entirely different.

WHY GUILT IS NOT AN EMOTION

Virtually all of the philosophical and psychological literature on guilt assumes that it is an emotion, just like any other. However, one difficulty for any account of guilt is that the cases in which people describe feeling guilt form a rather diverse class, with a general lack of emotional congruity among those cases. After examining this difficulty, we will argue that guilt is not an emotion at all (an idea first proposed by Ortony [1987], picked up again in Elison [2005], and subsequently ignored). By looking at the various experiences of guilt, we will argue that guilt is best conceived as what we call a feeling, rather than an emotion, a difference we will explain. We then argue that understanding this difference undermines some claims about the desirability of guilt, particularly as opposed to shame. The evidence comes from several sources, and while none of these considerations are conclusive, taken together, they cast doubt on guilt's status as an emotion, moral or otherwise.

VARIETIES OF GUILT

Occasions in which people describe themselves as feeling guilt show that there are several types of guilt, at least as guilt is ordinarily understood. There are four types that we will mention. First, there is guilt directed at harm caused to others, such as accidentally breaking a friend's vase. There is also self-directed guilt, felt when we a person does something that harms only herself, such as eating a piece of cake while on a diet (Wollheim, 1999). Third, there is religious guilt, felt by people of certain faiths (e.g., so-called Catholic and Jewish guilt), involving feelings of being sinful or inadequate relative to religious standards. Finally, there is survivor's guilt, felt by those who have survived some kind of tragedy while others have not. There may be other types, of course, but these alone will suffice to make our point.

Accounts of guilt can be roughly classified as being narrow, emotional, or cognitive, depending on how they understand the types of guilt just mentioned.[3] Narrow accounts offer a single specification of guilt that leaves out others. Examples include the accounts given in (Freud, 1961) and (Harman, 2009): Neither of their conceptions of guilt cover religious or survivor's guilt. Others, such as Velleman (2003), are emotion-based: Guilt is taken to be a family of related emotions, each member of which is captured by different thoughts, but where these are similar enough to warrant their all being called "guilt" (in Velleman's case, that family resemblance is based on anxiety, where the anxiety is about being punished, resented, or feeling anger). In other words, there are different kinds of guilt, but they are unified by the emotional experience of guilt, and not by what one is feeling guilty about. Finally, there are cognitive accounts, such as Prinz & Nichols (2010). In this type of account, guilt is distinguished by what one is feeling guilty about: i.e., the thought that underlies the emotion of guilt.

The primary problem with narrow accounts is, well, their narrowness. While a narrow account may provide a satisfactory picture of one kind of guilt, proponents of these accounts then owe us an explanation of why other types of guilt are not worthy of the name. Perhaps the thought is that only certain kinds of guilt are philosophically interesting, or that certain kinds of so-called guilt are not really instances of guilt at all. While there are some plausible possibilities, most accounts simply do not acknowledge these other types of guilt at all. For example, one might claim that religious guilt is not guilt at all, but a type of shame. Or a supporter of Tangney's account, discussed above, might believe that guilt, understood as the emotion resulting from doing a bad action, is the only conception of the emotion worthy of our consideration, because it is the only conception reliably detected by empirical means (that is, if her account did not have the flaws that it does). As things stand, discounting different types of guilt would require arguments that are just not on offer on narrow accounts.

Emotion-based accounts acknowledge different varieties of guilt, but then have the problem of explaining why these different types count as guilt on the basis of the underlying emotion, but others do not. For example, Velleman conceives of guilt as a family of emotions, united by anxiety. So although one can feel guilty about many different things, what makes those different experiences all count as instances of guilt is the underlying anxiety: Sometimes the anxiety may be fear of punishment, sometimes fear of resentment, sometimes anxiety about being angry. But why do only these types of anxiety count as guilt? For example, why would other anxieties, such as anxiety about fear of failure, not count as a species of guilt? And why should we accept that self-directed guilt essentially involves anxiety about the forfeiture of trust to ourselves, as it does on Velleman's account? It seems dubious to attribute such anxiety to every instance in which a person might feel guilty. I might feel guilty for failing to make it to the gym this week without thereby being anxious about the possibility of being unable to trust myself to ever make it! To be sure, there may be a fix: Perhaps some self-directed guilt is not actually guilt at all. Recall Zeelenberg & Breugelmans (2008), which found that people tend to report feeling guilt when they do something that results in an interpersonal harm, as opposed to feeling regret when the same act results in harm only to oneself. Thus, Velleman could deny that all self-directed guilt is guilt, properly understood. But the more general point remains: It is not obvious that anxiety is always involved in guilt. To take another example, consider a person who is the sole survivor of a plane crash on a desert island for which she bore no responsibility (a fact of which she is perfectly aware). Would she only be able to feel survivor's guilt if there were witnesses, or the potential for rescue? It seems quite reasonable to imagine her feeling survivor's guilt (among many other things, of course) even if she was completely alone and believed she had no hope of being rescued, and thus having no possibility to be anxious about the fear of being resented, as Velleman's account would have it. Perhaps other mixed emotional accounts could fare better, but it is difficult to see precisely what could unify all of these varieties of guilt. Let us turn instead to cognitive accounts.

A good example of a cognitive account is the one mentioned above (Prinz & Nichols, 2010), which attempts to account for all types of guilt by identifying the constitutive thought underlying guilt. The idea here is that the core of guilt is the thought that "someone I am concerned about has been harmed and I have responsibility for that in virtue of what I have done or failed to do" (Prinz & Nichols, 2010, p. 134), where "concern" and "responsibility" are construed broadly enough to account for many types of guilt. For example, "someone I am concerned about" can certainly include oneself as well as others, so both other-directed and self-directed guilt is covered. Perhaps some instances of religious guilt could be covered, but once again, survivor's guilt poses a problem. There may well be some cases of survivor's guilt in which one mistakenly believes she is responsible, but certainly many cases do not involve any such beliefs. Take the example mentioned above: Being the sole survivor of a plane crash may well engender survivor's guilt, even if one believes (rightly) that, as a passenger, she had nothing to do with the tragedy. Another problem with wide accounts is their ability to distinguish guilt from related emotions like shame. Imagine that one feels bad because of his inability to stick up for a friend who is being taunted. Insofar as the thought here is that the person in question is responsible for the harm done to her friend, the case fits this criterion for guilt just mentioned perfectly; but we can easily imagine the person feeling shame, or embarrassment, rather than guilt. The problem for cognitive accounts is to both capture different types of guilt while not capturing other emotions or feelings, such as shame or embarrassment. Perhaps this can be done, but it is difficult to see how.

In general, any account of guilt faces a competing pair of desiderata. On the one hand, an account of guilt should accommodate different types of guilt (or explain why, in a principled manner, certain things that seem to be guilt are not guilt after all). On the other hand, an account of guilt should explain why these different types of guilt really deserve the same label "guilt," yet be able to distinguish these various types of guilt from closely related emotions such as shame. The simplest way to solve this conundrum is to think of guilt not as an emotion, but as a feeling.

FEELING AND BEING

It may seem completely obvious that guilt is an emotion: We speak of feeling guilt, or feeling guilty, in much the same way we speak of feeling angry or sad. Further, as mentioned previously, the mere ability to feel guilt is what separates us from the psychopaths. But talking about a feeling does not necessarily (and not even often) mean that one is talking about an emotion. Consider the wide variety of terms that can be substituted for X into the schema "I feel X." Members of this set include "anxious," "betrayed," "cranky," "discouraged," "empty," "frustrated," "giddy," "happy," "irritated," and many more. It is exceedingly unlikely that each of these deserves to be called an emotion: "Feeling happy" is quite likely to coincide with an instance of happiness, which is an emotion if anything is; but "feeling empty" or "feeling betrayed" are not.[4] While there is often a variety of emotions that people can and do experience when they feel empty or betrayed (as well as a variety of accompanying, and likely necessary, beliefs), these are simply not emotions in any full-blooded sense. Thus, the mere fact that we can speak of feeling something does not necessitate that that something is an emotion.

Our proposal is that guilt is a feeling, and not an emotion. As such, we should not expect guilt to play the role that genuine emotions do in our moral and scientific theories. This idea is perhaps best illustrated by an analogy. Consider betrayal (or abandonment, suggested by Ortony [1987]). Suppose you have, in fact, been betrayed by Jones, but do not care.[5] You might express this fact by saying, "Jones has betrayed me, but it does not bother me. I do not feel betrayed." Now suppose that you do care: You might say "I feel betrayed by Jones." But what do you experience? Perhaps sadness, perhaps anger, perhaps some combination; undoubtedly, some negative emotion seems appropriate (it would be baffling for the feeling of being betrayed to consist of happiness). There is a wide range of appropriate emotions: One instance of betrayal might include anger as the dominant emotion, while in another instance, the dominant emotion might be sadness. The work done when one speaks of "feeling betrayed" is the conveyance that the speaker has a feeling that normally accompanies the belief that one has, in fact, been betrayed, often along with that very belief. That feeling, however, can include any number of emotions.

It is worth belaboring the importance of the difference between being guilty and feeling guilty. The subject of this chapter is the so-called feeling of guilt, but simply being guilty is, by itself, of considerable importance, both philosophically and in everyday life. One can be guilty of all sorts of things, some of which are obviously morally wrong (e.g., murder), some of which are not obviously so (e.g., jaywalking). One can be guilty of things for which one is completely aware (e.g., premeditated murder), and others about which one might be completely unaware (e.g., failing to put money in an unnoticed parking meter). But note: To be sad and to feel sad are virtually identical, and a philosophical treatment of being sad would probably include (or simply be) a philosophical treatment of feeling sad. But to be alone and to feel alone—or to feel lonely—are not the same thing, and the state of merely being alone does not seem to be of any particular philosophical importance. But to be guilty—distinct from feeling guilty—is to be in a state central to philosophical discussions of moral and legal culpability. Guilt in this sense is a rich concept, and of course we cannot take up the nature of being guilty in this chapter.

GUILT AS A FEELING

The proposal we offer is that the so-called emotion of guilt is not an emotion at all, but a feeling—variable across different people and different occurrences—that normally accompanies the (possibly mistaken) belief that one is guilty. There is no single emotion that is guilt: Some occurrences of feeling guilty might involve anxiety, others might involve anger, and still others might involve sadness. And surely there will be cases in which there is a complex combination of these emotions. But just as there is no one emotion of betrayal or abandonment, there is no one emotion of guilt. Of course, there are constraints on what one could reasonably be expected to experience in feelings of these types: Feeling guilt might include feelings of anxiety, or anger, or sadness, but it would certainly not include happiness.

Understanding guilt as a feeling, rather than an emotion, solves many of the problems mentioned above. First, it solves the problem of the plurality of "types" of guilt. Any occasion in which one feels as if she is guilty of some transgression is an occasion in which she feels guilt. Harming another person is one example of such an occasion (i.e., other-directed guilt), but so is eating food forbidden by one's diet (i.e., self-directed guilt). Additionally, the thought that one is constantly sinning, or that one is constantly not living up to certain standards, are both occasions for feeling that one is guilty of religious transgressions (i.e., religious guilt). Finally, we can understand survivor's guilt, in which one feels as if she is guilty of a transgression, even when she is not. On our proposal, this would be similar to feeling alone, even when one is surrounded by friends and is not alone in any sense, even by one's own admission (similar analogies can be made with feeling appreciated, betrayed, neglected, and perhaps many others). The feeling is as if one is alone, just as the feeling in survivor's guilt is as if one is guilty.

This proposal also solves the problem of how to account for the unity of guilt in light of the fact that there seem to be a diversity of types of guilt. Very simply, different types of guilt are just different occasions in which one feels as if one is guilty of a transgression. These occasions need not consist in the same emotions: Again, some instances of guilt might be marked by sadness, others anger. Some instances in which one feels guilty may engender further thoughts, such as that one deserves punishment; others may motivate further behaviors, such as that one ought to try to repair whatever damage has been done. Again, there are constraints: The emotion felt as part of feeling guilt ought not be elation, and the thoughts engendered by feeling guilt ought not motivate one to repeat whatever actions caused the guilt feeling. But what unifies guilt is the thought that one is guilty, rather than any particular emotion.

Finally, this account avoids the problem of counting other related emotions and feelings, such as shame or remorse, as instances of guilt. Feeling guilt is simply feeling as if one is guilty for a transgression, even if one knows that one is not. One of the emotions that might accompany that feeling is shame (as many of the psychological studies on guilt and shame have discovered, guilt and shame are highly correlated); but one can certainly feel shame for things that involve no transgressions at all, such as one's appearance or poor performance. Similarly, many instances in which one feels guilty will involve remorse, but not all: Feeling guilty for intentionally hurting someone might often result in remorse, but feeling guilty for surviving an accident might involve no remorse whatsoever, because there is no action for which one could feel remorseful about.

FEELINGS AND EMOTIONS

The proposal we offer here—that guilt is a feeling, and not an emotion—requires a story about what this difference is and why it's important. A full account of the difference must wait for another occasion, which is in no small part due to the unresolved status of what emotions are in the first place; in the words of Mulligan and Scherer, "There is no commonly agreed-upon definition of emotion in any of the disciplines that study this phenomenon. This fact leads to endless debates and hampers the cumulative progress of research. It also constitutes a major impediment to interdisciplinary dialogue and research collaboration" (Mulligan & Scherer, 2012, p. 345). Nevertheless, there are some preliminary points to make about how feelings differ from emotions, and I will sketch some of those relevant to understanding guilt, particularly with an eye toward distinguishing it from shame.

First, we understand the term "emotion" in an occurrent, episodic sense. Emotions have beginnings and endings: Whatever emotions are, we experience them, and experiences begin and end. Although emotions may be long-lasting, they differ from propensities or dispositions to experience emotions, moods, and so on. Thus, we break company with emotion theorists who take emotions to have intentional objects necessarily. Many emotions do have intentional objects, of course: One can be sad about many things. However, sadness can (and does) occur without that sadness being about anything at all. One might simply be sad, or have sadness induced as the side effect of a medication. A similar point can be made about anxiety.

The term "feeling" can also be understood in a number of ways, and we note only a few relevant points here. First, we take feelings to be distinct from sensations: Although the grammatical similarity of "feeling hungry" and "feeling alone" might suggest that these are similar, the first is an instance of a sensation. We cannot offer a full account of the difference, but one notable difference is that sensations seem to be cognitively impenetrable in a way that proper feelings are not. Although I can distract myself from my hunger pangs, a change in my beliefs will not change the sensation. However, if a person meets up with some friends, and then forms the belief that she has, indeed, met up with these friends, her feeling of being alone should be alleviated. In fact, it seems that feelings—distinct from sensations in this sense—are precisely those things that can only be alleviated by a change in beliefs.[6]

In everyday discourse, feelings are not always distinguished from emotions. However, with careful consideration we find differences, and these differences have important consequences for how we think about these two categories of affective states. Feelings have a cognitive component that emotions may not, and this cognitive component is a belief about what typically causes the state in which one finds oneself. Thus, people are necessarily aware of their feelings in a way that they may not be of their emotions. Consider the emotion of sadness: One may not know why he is sad, or one may even know that she has no reason for being sad (in the case of a medication's side effect). In some cases, one may not even know that he is sad: there are certainly instances of non-conscious emotions. But feelings are not like this:

If someone feels abandoned, she necessarily knows what it is that she feels. And part of what she knows is that this is the state that is normally caused by situations in which she has been abandoned. In other words, what makes it the case that the feeling is abandonment, rather than sadness, or jealousy, or betrayal, is her belief about what made it the case that she is experiencing a negative emotion.

The rough idea, then, is that feelings are conscious emotions plus a belief about the typical cause of the emotion. Two points are important to mention here. First, any particular feeling may consist of some variety of emotions, or even more than one emotion.[7] Feeling betrayed, for example, might include sadness in some instances, anger in others, or both in still others. The second point is that the belief one has about one's emotional state in a feeling is not a belief about its actual cause, but about the typical cause. Thus, when one feels guilt, one does not necessarily believe that one is guilty of anything, although one does believe that the emotional state she finds herself in is of the kind typically caused by being guilty. Survivor's guilt is an example of this: One may truly feel guilty, which may mean that one experiences intense sadness, coupled with the belief that this is the kind of emotional state that is normally caused by being guilty, even though there is absolutely no belief that one actually is guilty of anything. Of course, in many instances, the feeling of guilt will include a belief that one is actually guilty, but this is not necessary, just as it is possible to feel alone without believing that you are, in fact, alone.

Understood this way, feelings and emotions play different roles in explanations of behavior. In our everyday discourse, telling someone that you feel betrayed (or annoyed, or abandoned, or alone, etc.) functions in part to inform others about your emotional state, but more so to convey a certain amount of explanatory information about why you believe you are in the kind of state that you are in. So, for example, suppose that Adam prepares his favorite dish for Brian, but it does not come out well. Adam might say that he feels annoyed with himself, or disappointed, or angry (or Adam might simply say that he is annoyed, disappointed, or angry). Each of these might have a subtly different phenomenology (e.g., annoyance seems closer to anger, whereas disappointment seems closer to sadness), but they might not; in any case, the primary value of these different feelings is that they (or their expression to another person) convey information about their perceived typical cause. In this case, the perceived cause (i.e., the substandard preparation of the dish) is identical to the actual cause. Adam's feeling annoyed with himself suggests that he is unhappy (and perhaps angry) about, say, his own incompetence as a chef, or something else that he may think he could have controlled. Annoyance with oneself conveys that one failed to live up to some standard. On the other hand, if Adam is simply disappointed, this does not suggest that Adam believes that he failed to live up to a standard, but that things just did not work out as he wanted them to (perhaps the recipe is a new one that Adam simply does not like). These observations are in line with recent theories of emotion that emphasize the function of emotions in communication (Scarantino, 2018).

This is a controversial point, and some may object that different feelings do have distinct phenomenal characters, which is how we distinguish them. It is difficult to tell with any precision whether or not this is true. However, the important point is that different feelings do convey distinct kinds of information about their perceived causes. Consider another example, one that many parents have had with their children (and children have had with their parents). Suppose a child does something bad, and the parent finds out, causing the parent to be upset. The parent reacts with a frown, and the child can tell she is in trouble. Two typical (of many possible) responses are that the parent feels angry, or that the parent feels disappointed (or both). Now it may be difficult to separate how these different feelings feel to the parent: Of course they are both unpleasant, and, again, perhaps disappointment has something like sadness as a component. But what is conveyed when expressing these different feelings is obvious, as is the difference between what is conveyed. As many parents and children know, making a parent feel angry is far preferable to making them feel disappointed, and this is not because making a parent feel angry is less painful or less hurtful than making a parent feel disappointed. The "magnitude" of the negative feeling, and even the feeling itself, may, in fact, be identical. However, when a child learns that her actions caused her parent to feel disappointed in her, she learns that her parent's esteem for her has decreased (or something along these lines), but when she learns that her actions caused her parent to feel angry, she does not worry about the decrease in esteem. Even a very angry parent is often preferable to a slightly disappointed one!

Emotions, then, are components of feelings, and thus more basic. As mentioned earlier, we cannot provide a full theory of emotions here. But the idea that emotions are basic is largely uncontroversial. Some, such as Ekman (1992), argue that the only things that really count as emotions are the basic emotions; others, such as Griffiths (1997), argue for distinct lower-level and higher-level emotions. Other animals, such as non-human primates and social mammals such as dogs, seem to have emotions, whereas they do not have feelings (neither in the sense articulated above, nor in everyday discourse, unless one takes emotions and feelings to be synonymous). This is because emotions need not—and often do not—have belief as a component. In any case, whatever precisely emotions are, they are more primitive than feelings.

The view of guilt we have offered in this section is that guilt is a feeling, and not an emotion. Feelings, on our view, are more complex states than mere emotions: Feelings include a belief about what typically causes the emotion one is feeling. In particular, the feeling of guilt is the feeling one has which one normally attributes to being guilty of a violation, although one need not believe that she actually is guilty of such a violation (as in the case of survivor's guilt). Different people will—because of culture and upbringing—feel guilty about different kinds of things; furthermore, the emotion that is part of this feeling may also differ. Thus, some people may feel guilty about putting on weight, and people who feel guilty about this may experience different emotions as part of that feeling (e.g., feeling guilty about gaining a few pounds may be composed of anger in one person, sadness in another). This kind of variation makes generalizations about guilt very difficult to come by: One person's guilt about hitting a friend might involve remorse, whereas another's guilt about not giving to charity might involve shame or sadness. Rather than explaining the kind of mental state that one is in, or what that mental state feels like, describing a state as a feeling of guilt explains what it is that the person having that feeling normally attributes that feeling to.

CONCLUSION

In this chapter, we have outlined some of the accounts that philosophers have given of guilt and discussed some of the seemingly promising findings about guilt that psychologists have discovered. But, we argue, the initial methodology developed to measure guilt builds into guilt many of the features that have then been touted as reasons to favor guilt as a moral emotion, particularly relative to shame. These various features point toward the view that it is a mistake to think of guilt as a single emotion in the first place. Rather, guilt is a feeling, and in particular, to feel guilt is to feel the way that one has learned one typically feels when one is guilty. But the emotional component of that feeling may involve anger, sadness, anxiety, or some combination of these. We suspect that the explanation of this emotional diversity lies in individual learning histories about which violations are the ones one should feel bad about, what the constitutes the appropriate way to feel bad, and how to communicate this to others. Exploring this issue must wait for another day.

We think this distinction is important for understanding the role of affective states in our moral psychology. In order for us to become more moral, for example, it is important that we understand which parts of our psychology are under our control, and to what extent. While many authors have realized the division between cognition and emotion is at best simplistic for some time now (Damasio [1994], for example, offered an early popular exposition), the best way to understand how to proceed with a more sophisticated division of mental processes related to our moral psychology is very much in flux. We hope that our proposal contributes to the effort better understand human moral psychology.

NOTES

1. We say claims, rather than argues, because Nietzsche relies on a story about the historical evolution of guilt that may or may not be true.
2. Public goods dilemma games involve a decision about how much of one's own resources (often money or tokens) to contribute to a public "fund." If the level of the fund reaches some threshold, then that fund, plus some additional bonus, is distributed equally among the players, even those who contributed nothing.
3. These accounts are not meant to cover cases of group-based guilt, where one feels guilt for, or on behalf of, the members of one's group.
4. I deliberately omit terms such as "tired," "cold," and "hungry" that are also obviously feelings, but only in a somatic sense (which it may be better to call sensations). Similarly, I omit talk of feeling that is merely synonymous with believing, as in "He feels that externalism about mental content is crazy."
5. We grant that there is a strong negative connotation to betrayal, such that one might not actually call a betrayal that one did not care about a "betrayal" in the first place. Nevertheless, it is possible to imagine such an occurrence, and difficult to succinctly describe such a scenario without using the word "betrayal." We set this concern aside in what follows.
6. Of course, it may not be psychologically possible for one to have the belief that might alleviate a negative emotion: One's religious guilt might require alterations to beliefs fundamental to one's worldview.
7. Presumably there are limits, including the positive or negative valences of the feelings as they are typically understood. A self-hating person who believes she deserves to suffer might be happy that her friend betrayed her, but "feeling betrayed" would not normally consist of the belief that one has been betrayed, coupled with happiness about that fact. Feeling betrayed should include a negatively valenced, rather than positively valenced, emotion.

BIBLIOGRAPHY

Brandt, R. B. (1992). *Morality, Utilitarianism, and Rights.* Cambridge, UK: Cambridge University Press.

Cohen, T. R., Panter, A. T., & Turan, N. (2012). Guilt Proneness and Moral Character. *Current Directions in Psychological Science, 21*(5), 355–59. http://doi.org/10.1177/0963721412454874.

Damasio, A. (1994). *Descartes' Error.* New York, NY: Penguin Books.

Ekman, P. (1992). An Argument for Basic Emotions. *Cognition and Emotion, 6*(3), 169–200. http://doi.org/10.1080/02699939208411068.

Elison, J. (2005). Shame and Guilt: A Hundred Years of Apples and Oranges. *New Ideas in Psychology, 23,* 5–32.

Freud, S. (1961). *Civilization and Its Discontents.* (J. Strachey, Trans.). New York, NY: W. W. Norton.

Gibbard, A. (1990). *Wise Choices, Apt Feelings*. Cambridge, MA: Harvard University Press.

Gibbard, A. (1992). Moral Concepts: Substance and Sentiment. *Philosophical Perspectives, 6*, 199–221.

Greenspan, P. S. (1995). *Practical Guilt*. Oxford, UK: Oxford University Press.

Griffiths, P. E. (1997). *What Emotions Really Are: The Problem of Psychological Categories*. Chicago, IL: University of Chicago Press.

Harman, G. (2009). Guilt-Free Morality. In R. Shafer-Landau (Ed.), *Oxford Studies in Metaethics, Volume 4* (pp. 203–14). Oxford University Press.

Kaufmann, W. A. (1973). *Without Guilt and Justice*. New York, NY: P. H. Wyden.

Ketelaar, T., & Au, W. T. (2003). Effects of Feeling Guilt on the Behaviour of Uncooperative Individuals in Repeated Social Bargaining Games. *Cognition and Emotion, 17*(3), 429–453. http://doi.org/10.1080/02699930143000662.

Krevans, J., & Gibbs, J. C. (1996). Parents' Use of Inductive Discipline: Relations to Children's Empathy and Prosocial Behavior. *Child Development, 67*(6), 3263–77.

Kochanska, G., Gross, J. N., Lin, M.-H., & Nichols, K. E. (2002). Guilt in Young Children: Development, Determinants, and Relations with a Broader System of Standards. *Child Development, 73*(2), 461–82.

Leith, K. P., & Baumeister, R. F. (1998). Empathy, Shame, Guilt, and Narratives of Interpersonal Conflicts: Guilt-Prone People Are Better at Perspective Taking. *Journal of Personality, 66*(1), 1–37. http://doi.org/10.1111/1467-6494.00001.

Lewis, H. B. (1971). *Shame and Guilt in Neurosis*. New York: International Universities Press.

Maley, C. J. (2015). *On the Nature of Guilt and Shame*. Ph.D. Dissertation. (G. Harman & S.-J. Leslie, Eds.). Princeton University, Princeton, NJ. Retrieved from http://arks.princeton.edu/ark:/88435/dsp010k225d44v.

Mulligan, K., & Scherer, K. R. (2012). Toward a Working Definition of Emotion. *Emotion Review, 4*(4), 345–57.

Nietzsche, F. (1995). On the Geneaology of Morals. In W. A. Kaufmann (Trans.), *Basic Writings of Nietzsche* (pp. 437–599). New York, NY: The Modern Library.

Ortony, A. (1987). Is Guilt an Emotion? *Cognition and Emotion, 1*(3), 283–98. http://doi.org/10.1080/02699938708408052.

Prinz, J. J., & Nichols, S. (2010). Moral Emotions. In J. M. Doris & The Moral Psychology Research Group (Eds.), *The Moral Psychology Handbook*. New York, NY: Oxford University Press.

Rodogno, R. (2010). Guilt, Anger, and Retribution. *Legal Theory, 16*(1), 59–76. http://doi.org/10.1017/S1352325210000066.

Scarantino, A. (2018). Emotional Expressions as Speech Act Analogs. *Philosophy of Science, 85*(5), 1038–53. http://doi.org/10.1086/699667.

Scarnier, M., Schamder, T., & Lickel, B. (2009). Parental Shame and Guilt: Distinguishing Emotional Responses to a Child's Wrongdoings. *Personal Relationships, 16*(2), 205–20.

Tangney, J. P. (1991). Moral Affect: The Good, the Bad, and the Ugly. *Journal of Personality and Social Psychology, 61*(4), 598–607.

Tangney, J. P., & Dearing, R. L. (2002). *Shame and Guilt*. New York, NY: Guilford Press.

Tangney, J. P., Stuewig, J., & Mashek, D. J. (2007). Moral Emotions and Moral Behavior. *Annual Review of Psychology*, *58*, 345–72. http://doi.org/10.1146/annurev.psych.56.091103.070145.

Velleman, J. D. (2003). Don't Worry, Feel Guilty. *Royal Institute of Philosophy Supplement*, *52*, 235–48. http://doi.org/10.1017/S1358246100007992.

Wollheim, R. (1999). *On the Emotions*. New Haven, CT: Yale University Press.

Wubben, M. J. J., Cremer, D. D., & Dijk, E. V. (2009). When and How Communicated Guilt Affects Contributions in Public Good Dilemmas. *Journal of Experimental Social Psychology*, *45*(1), 15–23. http://doi.org/10.1016/j.jesp.2008.07.015.

Zeelenberg, M., & Breugelmans, S. M. (2008). The Role of Interpersonal Harm in Distinguishing Regret from Guilt. *Emotion*, *8*(5), 589–96. http://doi.org/10.1037/a0012894.

Chapter 2

On the Distinction between Shame and Guilt

Heidi L. Maibom

What is the difference between shame and guilt? A near consensus has arisen that guilt concerns what we do, is morally relevant, and quite possibly useful, whereas shame concerns us as persons, is morally irrelevant, and is largely unhelpful. Yet people usually report feeling both at the same time. And, like guilt, shame plays a relatively large role in morality across time and geographical locations. This suggests that a reexamination of the difference between the two emotions is in order. After presenting "the standard picture," I turn to the psychological evidence. The problem with much of that evidence is that it relies on a biased measure. Less biased evidence reveals a close connection between shame and guilt. Moving to philosophy, I deal with two critiques of shame: It is morally irrelevant, and it is heteronomous. I show that guilt shares those very same features. We then look at dysfunctional manifestations of guilt, and find that they, too, seem to mirror dysfunctional manifestations of shame. In their extreme versions, then, both guilt and shame are problematic. I am therefore led to conclude that the two emotions are much closer related than the literature suggests. Nonetheless, there are differences between guilt and shame. These concern their intentional objects, their phenomenology, and their motivational components. When it comes to their moral qualities, I argue that we are not yet in a position to be able to prefer one to the other.

GUILT AND SHAME: THE STANDARD PICTURE

Guilt and shame are two emotions we often experience as the result of having performed actions that, in retrospect, we wish we had not. Such actions might be inactions, such as failing to help a person in need. Both emotions are called "negative emotions" because they make us feel bad, and we often go to extraordinary lengths not to feel them. And both express some sort of failure on the part of the person experiencing them. Shame and guilt are also dubbed "social emotions," because they relate to our life with other people and are usually responses to actions within the social sphere, and "self-conscious emotions," because they are thought to require the ability to be aware of the self and reflect on it. In addition, shame and guilt are also known as "higher emotions" because they involve cognitive evaluations of a type often thought to require sophisticated mental machinery. Philosophers think of one or both of these emotions as prototypical "moral emotions," alongside emotions like "compassion," "gratitude," and "resentment."

Guilt and shame are distinguished in terms of what causes them, their formal objects, the aspects of the self that they index, how socio-moral they are, and their associated motivations to act. Fabrice Terroni and Julien Deonna (2008), for instance, argue that guilt is caused by transgressions, its focus is a behavior, its formal object is a flouted norm, and its typical action-tendency (motivation) is reparation. By contrast, shame is caused by situations where one's reputation is on the line, one's self is the focus, and an undermined value is the formal object. According to June Tangney, shame motivates retreat or aggression, by contrast to guilt, which motivates reparation.

If guilt concerns one's action, it is connected to something one has intentional control over, something that is momentary, and something that is at least partly dissociable from one's identity. Conversely, if shame has to do with the person one is, it seems much less controllable. And it is certainly true that people are often ashamed of features of themselves they have little power to change, such as being short, ugly, or victimized. What is supposed to be particularly debilitating about shame is that it marks one as a person, and so it cannot be escaped unless one changes as a person. That is a great deal more arduous than to apologize, or otherwise make amends, to someone affected by one's actions.

The recent philosophical and psychological literature does not put much stock in shame as a useful emotion. June Tangney (1991) has called it "the ugly emotion" because she found that it was associated with social retreat or aggression, along with a whole list of psychopathologies, most notably depression in women. Philosophers tend to dislike the emotion because of its tenuous connection with autonomy, and its connection to shame cultures, which are typically dismissed as morally backwards, if not explicitly, then implicitly. By contrast, guilt tends to be regarded as an adaptive emotion, one that heals ruptured social bonds, that demonstrates responsiveness to moral norms, and whose affective qualities are less disruptive to individual well-being. Guilt cultures, such as our own, are often regarded as being morally superior, in part because they are thought to be more just. Because guilt is about action and actions can be controlled, holding someone responsible for what they do seems fair. By contrast, we are all familiar with rape victims being killed by their relatives because they have brought shame on the family. Here the victim is doubly victimized: They are exposed to violence and humiliation and are subsequently killed for it. The practice of honor killing in response to someone being shamed is hard to justify in any reasonable moral system.

The problem with this view of guilt and shame is that it is biased. On the side of philosophy, shame is condemned because it does not fit with the prevailing construal of "true" morality. Guilt does. In psychology, the problem is that the most commonly used measures of guilt and shame, the Test of Self-Conscious Affect, or TOSCA for short, is so biased that it is near impossible for shame to come out as positive or guilt to come out as negative.

TOSCA-SHAME, TOSCA-GUILT

June Tangney, the driving force behind TOSCA, says this about the difference between guilt and shame:

> [S]hame is an extremely painful and ugly feeling that has a negative impact on interpersonal behavior. Shame-prone individuals appear relatively more likely to blame others (as well as themselves) for negative events, more prone to a seething, bitter, resentful kind of anger and hostility, and less able to empathize with others in general. Guilt, on the other hand, may not be that bad after all. Guilt-prone individuals appear better able to empathize with others and to accept responsibility for negative interpersonal events. They are relatively less prone to anger than their shame-prone peers—but when angry, these individuals appear more likely to express their anger in a fairly direct (and one might speculate, more constructive) manner. (Tangney & Dearing 2002, 3)

Moreover, Tangney and her colleague Ronda Dearing reference a range of studies that connects shame, but not so-called shame-free guilt, to depression, anxiety, eating disorders, subclinical sociopathy, and low self-esteem (Tangney & Dearing 2002, 120).[1] Things look bad for shame, indeed, but quite rosy for guilt. Guilt may feel bad, but it plays an essential role in interpersonal relationships and appears to have no lasting ill effects.

This is a nice story, to be sure, but there are several problems with it. First, most measures of shame and guilt are dispositional; that is, they measure *tendencies* to feel guilt and shame. Moreover, the few studies that consider the behavioral effects of situational shame suggest that situational shame motivates approach behavior more than avoidance behaviors, contrary to the standard story (e.g., Tangney et al. 1996, de Hooge et al. 2008a and 2010). There is some reason to think that chronic shame motivates retreat, but it is likely that chronic guilt does too (Bybee, Ziegler, Berliner, and Merisca 1996). I have more to say about this in section 4.

Second, the TOSCA appears to be biased toward measuring reasonable and functional amounts of guilt and excessive and dysfunctional amounts of shame. The measure consists of a list of different scenarios in which you are asked to imagine you did something unfortunate, and it gives you four options of how to respond. Based on your responses, you classify as guilt or shame prone. Now, guilt is assumed to characterize actions where you take responsibility ("I should have studied harder"), where you make amends ("You would apologize and talk about that person's good points"), or where you feel bad, but not terribly so ("You'd feel bad you hadn't been more alert driving down the road"). By contrast, shame is supposed to be true of very strong negative reactions to things ("You would feel small . . . like a rat"), strong negative views of the self (You would think, "I am irresponsible and incompetent"), and avoidant behavior ("You would feel as though you want to hide"). Fontaine and colleagues (2001) found that TOSCA-guilt measures "a tendency to reparation associated with guilt" and TOSCA-shame measures "a tendency to global negative self-evaluation." In a later study, the same group designed an alternative measure of reparative behavior and negative self-esteem and found that they functioned just like TOSCA (Luyten, Fontaine, and Corveleyn 2002). These studies used the original TOSCA, but Giner-Sorolla, Piazza, and Espinosa (2011) find that TOSCA-3 is biased in pretty much the same way. TOSCA-guilt measures a tendency toward reparation, but not negative affect, whereas TOSCA-shame measures a tendency to experience negative affect—but here guilt and shame are not distinguished—and not a tendency to repair. This combination of studies lends further support to the idea that TOSCA, as it stands, is fundamentally biased.

If this is right, we also ought to take results from studies that use TOSCA as a measure with a grain of salt. It is worth noting that in a big study that did not use TOSCA, but simply asked students to write down stories about when they felt shame, guilt, and embarrassment, Tangney and her colleagues (1996) found few differences between the two emotions. First, there was little audience effect: Both shame and guilt were more likely to be felt with liked or loved ones than with strangers and disliked others, although shame was more likely than guilt to be felt with mere acquaintances. Both shame and guilt were more likely to be experienced with authority figures or equals than with subordinates, though guilt is more likely with subordinates than is shame. Second, there were comparatively few differences in the emotional experience itself. There was no difference in: (1) the degree to which the emotions were anticipated, (2) how long they lasted, (3) the degree to which they involved feeling disgusted with self, or angry with oneself or others, (4) whether a moral standard was violated, (5) the seriousness of the act, (6) felt responsibility and control, (7) self or other blame, (8) whether the focus was on the self or the other, (9) feeling exposed, and (10) the desire to make amends. Differences were found in a few areas, however. Shame is slightly more intense as a feeling and more sudden, and feels slightly worse than guilt. Shame is associated with feeling more bodily changes, physically smaller, more isolated, and inferior. The biggest difference between the two emotions is in the sense of isolation from others. Compared to guilt, shame causes a greater desire to have acted differently and a greater desire to hide the self and the wrong compared to guilt. Lastly, shame is more connected with feeling that others are angrier than is guilt.

Most of the differences that this study found were subtle. People's responses were measured on a 1–5 scale, and there are no cases where the distance between shame and guilt exceeds 1 point on that scale. For instance, both guilty and shamed individuals wish they had acted differently, only the latter feel it more (4.3) than the former (4.0), and shame feels more intense (4.1) than guilt (3.8). These are differences, to be sure, but they are not big. Because guilt and shame are similar in so many ways, distinguishing them is difficult, and so there is a tendency to focus exclusively on the small differences. I suspect this is how TOSCA came about. But in the attempt to differentiate one emotion from the other, Tangney has created a scale that no longer addresses ordinary shame and guilt, but only dysfunctional versions of the former, and adaptive examples of the latter.

Now, it is easy to see that if shame is *defined* as an unconstructive and negative way of seeing yourself that leads to not dealing with the offending situation, then shame cannot fail to be bad. It is therefore hardly surprising that shame is found to correlate with all sorts of maladaptive reactions, such as other-blaming, aggression, and social retreat. Similarly, if guilt is *defined* as a reaction to a failure where you are motivated to make amends, it cannot fail to be a relatively positive emotion. Apart from being biased, the view also has difficulties accounting for cross-cultural differences and for why so many studies show shame associated with pro-social behaviors, including a desire to make amends. For instance, Bear et al. (2009) found that Japanese children generally felt more shame and guilt than children from the United States. Interestingly, though, they externalized blame less than did American children. And whereas American children reacted to shame with more anger, there was no such relation between the two emotions in Japanese children. Mosquera et al. (2000) also found more positive attitudes toward shame and an increased likelihood of sharing shame experiences in such so-called shame cultures (Japan counts as one). And a whole range of studies show that shame is associated with prosocial actions of various kinds (Berndsen & McGarty 2012; Berndsen & Gausel 2015; Fessler 2004; De Hooge, Breugelmans, and Zeelenberg 2008; De Hooge, Zeelenberg, and Breugelmans 2010; Tangney et al. 1996).

WHAT'S SO BAD ABOUT SHAME?

Whereas psychologists have tended to focus on the negative psychological consequences of experiencing shame, such as depression, anxiety, anger, low self-esteem, externalization of blame, and social retreat, philosophers have criticized shame specifically for its value as a moral emotion. First, it is thought not to be a truly moral emotion because we can feel it about things that are morally irrelevant, e.g., the clothes we are wearing or our ability to sing in tune. Guilt, it is supposed, is a moral emotion because we feel guilt about having performed actions that have moral relevance. Second, shame is called a heteronomous emotion because it is uniquely sensitive to what others think of us, whereas guilt is an autonomous emotion because it reflects our own moral standards. As it turns out, both of those assumptions are false.

If we go by self-report, people feel guilty about all sorts of non-moral actions or events. For example, they feel guilty about overeating, not setting aside more time for cooking for the people invited for dinner, not calling a friend who is feeling down, watching a television show instead of reading a good book, and so on. Clearly, none of these are moral transgressions. Social psychology, too, is clear that if there is a difference in the frequency with which shame concerns moral actions compared to guilt, it is very slight. Moreover, guilt is often reported with respect to failing to do homework, not putting enough effort into a sporting activity, and so on (e.g., Tangney et al. 1996). We ought to conclude, then, that both shame and guilt concern morally relevant and irrelevant actions.

It may be objected that perhaps the real difference is that we often feel shame about things we ought not feel ashamed about. People feel ashamed about the way they look or about what someone has done to them, for instance. Tragic as this might be, guilt also dogs people who ought not feel guilty. People who survive disasters or persecutions, during which many others perished, often report feeling guilty. There is a name for this, in fact: "survivor guilt." People who survive abuse also often report feeling ashamed in addition to feeling guilty. The guilt pertains to the feeling that they must have done something wrong to bring upon themselves that abuse. Usually, this guilt is as unreasonable as the attendant shame. It would seem, therefore, that shame and guilt are very much in the same boat when it comes to sometimes being morally relevant, sometimes not; sometimes being reasonable, sometimes not.

What about autonomy? Is it not a problem that shame is so often indexed to what others think of us? Absolutely. Other people are often not very kind, particularly if they are teenagers, and can make us feel terrible about our pimples, large feet, or gangly gait. On the other hand, what others think of us and what we do is rather important, so being sensitive to it is a good thing.

This is not simply a matter of fitting in. It is often also a moral matter. Much of morality concerns how we treat others. Figuring out what counts as good behavior is not a mere matter of sitting back and reflecting on what values we want to adopt, as if we were the only people in the world. It is a matter of figuring out how what we do impacts others. And so their opinions are of crucial importance to our moral standing. The importance and centrality of others in morality has been obscured by a fixation with moral autonomy. As Chesire Calhoun puts it:

> To attempt to make oneself invulnerable to all shaming criticisms except those that mirror one's own autonomous judgments or that invoke ethical standards one respects is to refuse to take seriously the social practice of morality. (2004, p. 145)

One can make the same point by considering guilt. We are meant to only feel guilt over transgressions that we ourselves recognize to be moral transgressions. Pushing this to the extreme, we ought to be morally indifferent to whether or not what we do makes others upset, as long as we have already determined that there is nothing to be upset about. Certainly there are cases where this seems right; if people are upset about my wearing pants as a woman or failing to go to church on a Sunday, I ought to disregard their opinion. But generalizing this attitude seems absurd. Moral autonomy has to be bounded in the right way by sensitivity to the plight of others, the norms and values that people in our community endorse, and what others think of our actions and our values. In some cases, perhaps others' values should trump our own, because we may be mistaken about what is right and wrong. At the end of the day, we cannot flourish if we live in a society that shuns us because our values are significantly opposed to those of others.

It may be here that proponents of autonomous morality see the shortcoming of shame, for shaming audiences trump our own sense of moral right and wrong, and make our judgment fly with the prevailing winds. Those winds may be unfriendly or superficial. It is common for people who are homosexual to say that they are tired of having been made ashamed of themselves. But it is important to remember that shaming practices also concern the flouting of more generally accepted norms, such as rudeness, lying, cheating, and so on—right down to being homophobic, in fact. And so shaming practices, to the extent that they make people act more morally, clearly have positive functions also. Turning to guilt, people also complain about being "guilted" into doing things they would not otherwise do. Some of those actions may be morally better. Nonetheless, people report being made to do things they do not believe they are required to do, and that they may actually disagree with, such as going to mass or a strip bar. To this we might add assault survivors being guilted by their assailants and their posse because the event has come to light and they fear that it might affect the perpetrators' lives. When it comes to heteronomy—being influenced by the opinion of others when it comes to the moral value of what we do—guilt and shame are hardly polar opposites.

The long and short of it is that we are all, to some extent, held hostage to the prevailing norms of the society in which we operate. People will have a tendency to react to our unconventional actions in ways that are meant to induce guilt or shame, and if we are normally socialized people, we will react accordingly. This is an opportunity for us to learn about the operative norms and to reevaluate our own. It does not mean that we will, or should, automatically change those norms. And so guilt and shame do not differ by guilt being exclusively about moral transgressions and shame being heteronomous. If there is a difference, it is one of degree.

PROBLEMS WITH GUILT

Contrary to the positive picture of guilt that we have been presented with, guilt is itself associated with psychopathologies, such as depression and eating disorders. The DSM-V diagnosis of Major Depressive Disorder includes "feelings of worthlessness or excessive or inappropriate guilt (which may be delusional) nearly every day (not merely self-reproach or guilt about being sick)" (American Psychological Association 2013, 161). An exaggerated sense of responsibility for events is thought to be part of the problem, along with an unrealistically negative evaluation of one's own worth. This association between guilt and depression is pretty commonplace in the psychological literature (e.g., Shafran, Watkins, and Charman 1996; Bybee, Ziegler, Berliner, and Merisca 1996; O'Connor et al. 2002). A recent study found that so-called pathological guilt is significantly associated with depression (Belden et al. 2015). What is pathological guilt? It is a continued tendency to reflect on one's blameworthiness for minor and past misbehaviors or wrongs, blaming oneself excessively, blaming oneself for things that are not one's fault, and feeling globally bad about oneself. Moreover, these thoughts and feelings should be relatively unmodifiable. Jane Bybee and colleagues warn that so-called chronic guilt can "become virulent, providing an ongoing source of self-degradation and an endless reminder of the failing that evoked the guilt" (Bybee, Ziegler, Berliner, and Merisca 1996, 114). They also argue that it is not an excessive predisposition to experience guilt that is the problem, but failure to deal appropriately with the emotion. As they say, "[i]ndividuals faced with guilt-producing situations often ruminate over the event, thinking about what happened over and over again, often with an eye toward wanting to undo the act or with thoughts of how the situation might have been avoided" (Bybee, Merisca, and Velasco 1998, 114).

An association between so-called trait guilt and obsessional disorders, such as obsessive-compulsive disorder, has also been found (e.g., Shafran, Watkins, and Charman 1996), except if you use TOSCA to measure guilt, in which case shame becomes the culprit (Fergus et al. 2010; Hedman et al. 2013). But the reasoning seems strained. We are told that there is no general correlation between guilt proneness and depression because women (their subject group), who were able to get over their guilt about failing to do homework, overeating, and under-exercising by talking to others about it, rationalizing their behavior, or distracting themselves, were not depressed and did not punish themselves. Only women who failed to do so (i.e., continued to feel guilty) experienced more depression, self-hatred, and self-destructiveness. It is hard to understand how this is taken to be a vindication of the harmlessness of guilt and the noxious nature of shame. For is it not possible that people can resolve their shame just like they can their guilt?

Let me mention one other study in the case against guilt, as it were. De Hooge and colleagues (2011) tested whether or not reparative behavior subsequent to guilt could itself be morally problematic. In a series of studies, they offered perpetrators who felt guilty the option to reallocate resources from themselves, or others in need, toward their victim. They found that people tended to reallocate resources, but almost entirely from others, and not from themselves, to their victim. In other words, by compensating for a previous wrong, they created a new victim. Because they could have allocated of their own resources, this new victimization was entirely avoidable. To top it all off, when the subjects were later given the opportunity to make amends to these new victims, they ignored it. In other words, guilt can itself give rise to morally problematic behaviors, just as shame can.

GUILT AND SHAME: A MORE COMPLEX STORY

Where does this leave us? First, we must conclude that shame and guilt are more similar than the picture we started out with would lead us to suppose. There is no principled difference in the sorts of things that can lead a person to feel guilt or shame. It could be a moral transgression, an event that the subject has no control over (a disaster, a rape), or a failure to perform better at some activity. Both emotions feel bad, and people try to avoid feeling them. Shame and guilt can both be dysfunctional, and both are associated with neurosis, if not more severe psychopathologies. Both play an important role in moral conduct and are used liberally in moral education. In support of this idea, we can point out that people who experience little or no guilt or shame, such as psychopaths, are basically amoral. This is unlikely to be a coincidence.

The fact that shame and guilt cannot be differentiated by the simple formula that shame is about failure to live up to an ideal, and guilt is about transgressing norms does not mean that there is no difference between them, however. But the empirical research is of surprisingly little help here, since most of it relies on TOSCA, which, we have seen, is biased. However, we may make some tentative suggestions.

The standard picture of shame and guilt says guilt is more focused on the actions and its consequences *for others*, and that shame has more to do with the self (the person who feels shame). This is a theme one sees running through the literature, although Tangney et al. (1996) actually found no difference here. I am inclined to disregard this result as a bit of a fluke. The idea is supported by many studies and self-reports. The phenomenology is also revealing. In shame, people report feeling small or diminished. The focus in shame, then, is in one's own involvement in creating the unfortunate action, event, or situation. By contrast, in guilt the focus tends to be on the action and/or the person affected by the action, event, or situation. In some cases, that can be oneself, although in these cases, regret is felt more frequently than is shame (Zeelenberg & Breugelsman 2008). The reason it is better to think of guilt and shame less in terms of their eliciting conditions—is it an action, a situation, etc.?—and more in terms of their intentional objects is that both emotions are reliable evoked by the same situations. People often report feeling *both* guilt and shame. This makes a lot of sense if we think of the complexity of action. If, for instance, I hurt someone's feelings, I can focus on the action and the person whom I have hurt, but I can also think of what kind of person I have revealed myself to be. As my focus shifts back and forth, my feelings of guilt and shame should intensify and weaken as a result.

Another reason to suppose that shame is more strongly connected with thoughts about the self than is guilt is that it appears to have evolved from submission or appeasement (Keltner, Young, and Buswell 1997; Keltner & Buswell 1997). Submission is more tightly connected with a social hierarchy than with norms, although attacks will most often track what we can interpret as normative infractions. However, in certain social structures, norms differ according to where you are in the hierarchy, and so are more indexed to who you are than what you have done. This goes some way toward making sense of the fact that shame, more than guilt, is associated with the regard of others, status, and being exposed (Maibom 2010, see also McGee & Giner-Sorolla, this volume).

Many studies, not using TOSCA as a measure, show that shame often causes reparation or other pro-social actions toward relevant others when possible (Berndsen & McGarty 2012; Berndsen & Gausel 2015; Fessler 2004; De Hooge, Breugelmans, & Zeelenberg 2008; De Hooge, Zeelenberg, & Breugelmans 2010; Tangney et al. 1996). It is therefore a misleading simplification to claim, as Tangney does, that guilt gives rise to approach behaviors whereas shame causes retreat. A more nuanced approach is to acknowledge that shame is *more* associated with retreat than is guilt, but may nonetheless cause more reparations, pro-social actions, and commitment to do good, than retreat and rumination. We should note that at least one study found that guilt was as likely to cause desire to escape as was shame (Pivetti, Camodeca, and Rapino 2016), so we should not conclude that guilt does not have this component. However, since shame concerns stable features of the self that were involved in the situation or action that is now regretted, it should motivate some deeper-going change for the better. This does not exclude reparative actions in the here and now, of course, if possible. And that is in fact what we observe. By contrast, guilt can be associated with a one-off action, which one can simply resolve not to perform again. In such cases, the solution to the problem may seem more straightforward than it does if the problem pertains to some deeper, permanent features of the self. This fits with a least one study that found that guilt is more associated with apologies than is shame (Pivetti, Camodeca, and Rapino 2016). And so we might expect that guilt is *more likely* to lead to reparative behaviors than is shame (even though some sort of reparation is the more common reaction to shame). We can also hypothesize that guilt is *less likely* to lead to more thoroughgoing changes than is shame. The evidence that reduced recidivism correlates more with shame than with guilt lends some support to this hypothesis (Tangney, Steuwig, and Martinez 2014).

When it comes to the phenomenology of the two emotions, shame is liable to make us feel small and inferior because of its connection with submission. It is also associated with gaze aversion (Keltner & Buswell 1997; Pivetti, Camodeca, & Rapino 2016). This is very much what submission or appeasement looks like in many nonhuman animals (Keltner & Buswell 1997; Maibom 2010). In humans, it is not too far-fetched to interpret it as an acceptance of one's reduced social or moral standing, even if temporary (Deigh 1983; Gilbert & McGuire 1988; and McGee & Giner-Sorolla, this volume). Guilt, by contrast, is associated more with simply feeling bad about the transgression or situation in question, not necessarily with feeling inferior.

It is important, however, to explain the sort of social standing that is involved in shame. Social status is affected by many things that have limited, or no, interpersonal or moral import, such as income. It is therefore too simple, and potentially misleading, to say that the appraisal in shame involves social status, as Darren McGee and Roger Giner-Sorolla appear to do (this volume). The point is that one's lower social standing is the result of failure to live up to norms or ideals of the group that one belongs to, often of a moral nature. It is worth stressing that McGee and Giner-Sorolla themselves find that statements like "my conscience would be hurt" load equally on guilt and shame, mirroring an earlier finding by Smith, Webster, Parrott, and Eyre (2002) that degree of moral belief affects shame and guilt equally. This brings us to the question of the moral quality of the two emotions.

Guilt is typically preferred to shame because people are often ashamed of morally irrelevant actions or features. But we have seen that guilt *also* concerns morally irrelevant actions and can be induced by the disapproval of others, just like shame. One should not, therefore, prefer guilt to shame on this basis. Might there be other reasons to prefer guilt to shame? Perhaps. But without less biased measures in psychology and less biased views about what matters in morality in philosophy, we are unlikely to make much progress. My own hunch is that the main difference between the two emotions morally speaking is their focus. In shame, the focus is on oneself as someone who has transgressed or failed to live up to certain norms, whereas in guilt the focus is on other persons and how they are affected by what one has done or failed to live up to. If that is right, both are of obvious value. Focusing on others and their well-being is obviously of moral value. But is it not also morally relevant to keep in mind what kind of person one is and wants to become? For instance, when Luke stops himself from killing the emperor in *The Return of the Jedi*, it is out of concern for what *he* will become, not out of concern for the well-being of the emperor.

To conclude, I have argued that shame and guilt are more similar on a number of different dimensions than is standardly acknowledged to be the case. A lot of the psychological evidence at our disposal uses a measure that is so biased that it is unlikely to be of much help in understanding either guilt or shame. It is not true that shame is unhelpful, leads to social retreat, and mental disorder, whereas guilt is useful, leads to reparative action, and is associated with good social functioning. Moreover, although shame is more sensitive to an audience than is guilt, it is not a morally shallow emotion mainly concerned with what others think *tout court*. It is deeply connected with a failure to live up to norms and standards, often of a moral kind. And although guilt is less sensitive to an audience, it is often felt in morally irrelevant situations, as is shame. What distinguishes the two, I have argued, is something much more subtle. The primary factor here is the locus of attention: the self or the other. Shame focuses on the self as the origin of failure or transgression, whereas guilt focuses on the effects on another of what one has done or failed to do. Both types of foci have moral importance. And, lastly, shame is more likely to lead to retreat than is guilt, but this is merely a matter of degree. Very often, shame leads to reparative behaviors too.

NOTE

1. They reference no less than fifteen papers in support of these claims.

BIBLIOGRAPHY

American Psychological Association. 2013. *Diagnostic and statistical manual of mental disorders, fifth edition (DSM-V)*. Washington, DC: The American Psychological Association.

Arimitsu, Kohki. 2006. Guilt, shame/embarrassment, and empathy. *Japanese Journal of Psychology*, 77, 97–104.

Bear, George G., Uribe-Zarain, Ximena, Manning, Maureen A., and Shiomi, Kunio. 2009. Shame, guilt, blaming, and anger: Differences between children in Japan and the US. *Motivation and Emotion*, 33, 229–38.

Belden, Andy C., Barch, Deanna M., Oakberg, Timothy J., April, Laura M., Harms, Michael P., Botteron, Kelly N., and Luby, Joan L. 2015. Anterior insula volume and guilt: Neurobehavioral markers of recurrence after early childhood depressive disorder. *JAMA Psychiatry*, 72, 40–48.

Berndsen, Mariëtte, and McGarty, Craig. 2012. Perspective taking and opinions about forms of reparation for victims of historical harm. *Personality and Social Psychology Bulletin*, 38, 1316–28.

Berndsen, Mariëtte, and Gausel, Nicolay. 2015. When majority members exclude ethnic minorities: The impact of shame on the desire to object to immoral acts. *European Journal of Psychology*, 45, 728–41.

Bybee, Jane, Zigler, Edward, Berliner, Dana, and Merisca, Rolande. 1996. Guilt, guilt-evoking events, depression, and eating disorders. *Current Psychology*, 15, 113–27.

Bybee, Jane, Merisca, Rolande, and Velasco, Rashid. 1998. The development of reactions to guilt-producing events. In J. Bybee: (Ed.) *Guilt and Children*. New York: Academic Press, 3–38.

Calhoun, Cheshire. 2004. An apology for moral shame. *Journal of Political Philosophy*, 11, 1–20.

De Hooge, Ilona E., Breugelmans, Seger M., and Zeelenberg, Marcel. 2008. Not so ugly after all: When shame acts as a commitment device. *Journal of Personality and Social Psychology*, 95, 933–43.

De Hooge, Ilona E., Zeelenberg, Marcel, and Breugelmans, Seger M. 2010. Restore and protect motivations following shame. *Cognition and Emotion*, 24, 111–27.

De Hooge, Ilona E., Nelissen, Rob M.A., Breugelmans, Seger M., and Zeelenberg, Marcel. 2011. What is moral about guilt? Acting "prosocially" at the disadvantage of others. *Journal of Personality and Social Psychology*, 100, 462–73.

Deigh, J. 1983. Shame and self-esteem: A critique. *Ethics*, 93, 225–45.

Fergus, Thomas A., Valentiner, David P., McGrath, Patrick B., and Jencius, S. 2010. Shame- and guilt-proneness: Relationship with anxiety symptoms in a clinical sample. *Journal of Anxiety Disorders*, 24, 811–15.

Fessler, Daniel M. 2004. Shame in two cultures: Implications for evolutionary approaches. *Journal of Cognition and Culture*, 4, 207–62.

Fontaine, Johnny R.J., Luyten, Patrick, de Boeck, Paul, and Corveleyn, Jozef. 2001. The Test of Self-Conscious Affect: Internal structure, differential scales and relationship with long-term affects. *European Journal of Personality*, 15, 449–63.

Giner-Sorolla, Roger, Piazza, Jared, and Espinosa, Pablo. 2011. What do the TOSCA guilt and shame scales really measure: Affect or action? *Personality and Individual Differences*, 51, 445–50.

Gilbert, P. & McGuire, M. 1998. Shame, status, and social roles: Psychobiology and evolution. In P. Gilbert & B. Andrews: (Eds.) *Shame: Interpersonal Behavior, Psychopathology, and Culture*. Oxford: Oxford University Press, 99–125.

Hedman, Erik, Ström, Peter, Stünkel, Angela, and Mörtberg, Ewa. 2013. Shame and guilt in social anxiety disorder: Effect of cognitive behavior therapy and association with social anxiety and depressive symptoms. *PLoS One*, April 19, 2013.

Keltner, D., and Buswell, D.N. 2007. Embarrassment: Its distinct forms and appeasement functions. *Psychological Bulletin*, 122, 250–70.

Keltner, Dacher, and Harker, Lee Anne. 1998. The forms and functions of the nonverbal signal of shame. In P. Gilbert & B. Andrews: (Eds.) *Shame: Interpersonal Behavior, Psychopathology, and Culture*. Oxford: Oxford University Press, 78–98.

Keltner, Dacher, Young, Randall, C., and Buswell, Brenda N. 1997. Appeasement in human emotion, social practice, and personality. *Aggressive Behavior*, 23, 359–74.

Luyten, Patrick, Fontaine, Johnny R.J., and Corveleyn, Jozef. 2002. Does the Test of Self-Conscious Affect (TOSCA) measure maladaptive aspects of guilt and adaptive aspects of shame? An empirical investigation. *Personality and Individual Differences*, 33, 1373–87.

Maibom, Heidi L. 2010. The descent of shame. *Philosophy and Phenomenological Research*, LXXX, 566–94.

McGee, D. & Giner-Sorolla, R. Forthcoming. How guilt serves social functions from within. In B. Cokelet & C. Maley: (Eds.) *The Moral Psychology of Guilt*. Lanham, MD: Rowman & Littlefield.

Mosquera, P.M.R., Manstead, A.S.R., and Fischer, A.H. 2000. The role of honour-related values in the elicitation, experience, and communication of pride, shame, and anger: Spain and the Netherlands compared. *Personality and Social Psychology Bulletin*, 26, 833–44.

O'Connor, Lynn E., Berry, Jack W., Weiss, Joseph, and Gilbert, Paul. 2002. Guilt, fear, empathy, and submission in depression. *Journal of Affective Disorders*, 71, 19–27.

Pivetti, Monica, Camodeca, Marian, and Rapino, Maria. 2016. Shame, guilt, and anger: Their cognitive, physiological, and behavioral correlates. *Current Psychology*, 35, 690–99.

Shafran, Roz, Watkins, Elizabeth, and Charman, Tony. 1996. Guilt in obsessive-compulsive disorder. *Journal of Anxiety Disorders*, 10, 509–16.

Smith, R. H., Webster, J. M., Parrott, W. G., & Eyre, H. L. 2002. The role of public exposure in moral and nonmoral shame and guilt. *Journal of Personality and Social Psychology*, 83, 138–59.

Tangney, June P. 1990. Assessing individual differences in proneness to shame and guilt: Development of the Self-Conscious Affect and Attribution Inventory. *Journal of Personality and Social Psychology*, 59, 102–111.

Tangney, June P. 1991. Moral affect: The good, the bad, and the ugly. *Journal of Personality and Social Psychology*, 61, 590–607.

Tangney, June P., Miller, Rowland S., Flicker, Laura, and Barlow, Deborah H. 1996. Are shame, guilt, and embarrassment distinct emotions? *Journal of Personality and Social Psychology*, 70, 1256–69.

Tangney, June P., Wagner, Patricia E., Dearing, Ronda L., and Gramzow, Richard. 2000. *The Test of Self-Conscious Affect-3 (TOSCA-3)*. George Mason University: Fairfax, VA.

Tangney, June P., and Dearing, Ronda L. 2002. *Shame and guilt*. New York: Guilford Press.

Tangney, June P., Steuwig, Jeffrey, and Martinez, Andres G. 2014. Two faces of shame: The roles of shame and guilt in predicting recidivism. *Psychological Science*, 25, 799–805.

Terroni, Fabrice, and Deonna, Julien A. 2008. Differentiating shame from guilt. *Consciousness and Cognition*, 17, 725–40.

Zeelenberg, M., and Breugelmans, S.M., 2008. The role of interpersonal harm in distinguishing regret from guilt. *Emotion*, 8(5), 589–96.

Chapter 3

Empathy and Conscience
An Essay on Guilt
John Deigh, University of Texas at Austin

Freud used the German expressions *schuldbewusstein* and *schuldgefühl* to refer to an emotion he saw manifested in many of the neurotic symptoms he observed in his patients.[1] This emotion is now popularly known as guilt. As Freud understood it, the emotion not only went with a wrongdoer's consciousness of being guilty of wrongdoing but could also be felt over innocent behavior that nonetheless discomfited its subject and over malicious thoughts and feelings that its subject neither acted on nor betrayed to others. And most important in Freud's theory was its presence in the subject's mind and influence on his or her behavior even though the subject had no conscious sense of guilt. Freud used the expression *unbewusstes schuldgefühl* to refer to this last case of the emotion when the subject's lack of a conscious sense of guilt was due to repression.[2] He believed that this condition of a repressed emotion, the unconscious sense of guilt, explained the neuroses he treated.

The first case, that of an emotion that goes with a wrongdoer's consciousness of guilt, sets the standard. It serves, that is, as the model for understanding the other cases. A prime example is the emotional turmoil that Raskolnikov, the protagonist of Dostoyevski's *Crime and Punishment*, experiences after murdering a pawnbroker whom he despised and her simpleton stepsister. Accordingly, let us refer to the first case as "the Raskolnikov model." Raskolnikov's emotions, the course of which provides the novel's narrative structure, have at their core his knowledge of his horrific crimes. Indeed, Raskolnikov could not have been conscious of his guilt if he did not know that he had committed the crimes of which he was guilty. Nonetheless, a person could experience such emotions even though his apparent consciousness of guilt was an illusion. Think here of the guilt that James Stewart's character in Hitchcock's *Vertigo*[3] experiences after he fails to prevent what he falsely believes is the suicide of the woman with whom he has fallen in love.

The Raskolnikov model, then, does not require knowledge of one's being guilty of wrongdoing. It requires only belief or conviction.

At the same time, such belief or conviction is not a sufficient condition of having the emotion. Someone can know that he is guilty of a crime, even a very grave crime, and still be completely untroubled by this knowledge. The Raskolnikov model then requires that the subject's consciousness of guilt, his belief or conviction that he is guilty of wrongdoing, troubles him in some way. The belief or conviction must unsettle or disquiet the mind. One way, of course, in which consciousness of guilt does trouble the mind is by arousing fear of being found out. "Suspicion always haunts the guilty mind," declares the future Richard III, perhaps the guiltiest of Shakespeare's creations, as he prepares to murder Henry VI.[4] Such suspicion definitely haunts Raskolnikov's mind as he seeks to elude capture by the St. Petersburg police. Dostoyevski portrays his protagonist as tormented by fear and anxiety in the immediate aftermath of the murders and continually so until he confesses to the police. Yet fear of being found out is not the definitive way in which guilt is an emotion of a mind that is troubled by consciousness of being guilty of wrongdoing.

Someone who has committed a crime may live in fear of being found out and be ever wary about what others may suspect without feeling bad about what he did. There need be no hint in him of self-condemnation. Again, Hitchcock provides us with a memorable example. Joseph Cotton's character in *Shadow of a Doubt* is a man of great charm and urbanity who lethally preys on women and is running from the police and federal agents, who suspect him of having murdered several widows.[5] Although fearful of being discovered by his pursuers and leery of the suspicions of his niece, he gives no indication of feeling bad about what he did or of wishing that he had not committed these crimes. He is concerned solely with "saving his skin" and desperate to avoid capture. His lack of guilt is unmistakable. On the Raskolnikov model, then, the emotion of guilt involves feeling bad about the wrongdoing of which one believes one is guilty, and the troubled mind one has on account of this belief thus consists partly in feeling bad about what one did.

The source of the feeling, moreover, must be the belief that one is guilty of wrongdoing. Merely believing that one has done something wrong and thereby feeling bad about it is insufficient. After all, regret over having done something wrong does not require belief that one is guilty, yet it does entail feeling bad about what one has done and wishing that one had not done it. It is possible, in other words, to regard oneself as blameless at the same time as one acknowledges that what one did was wrong, and in that case regret and not guilt would be the apt emotion. Collecting your baggage after a flight, you mistake a stranger's suitcase for your own and start toward the exit with the wrong suitcase in hand. It's an honest mistake, as we say, about which you may, nonetheless, once it comes to light, feel bad for having made and for whatever distress you may have thereby caused the owner of the suitcase to suffer. And if you think that it was an honest mistake, then, though you feel bad about having made it and wish you had not, you need not feel any guilt, nor would there be anything untoward if you didn't. Guilt, on the Raskolnikov model, is an emotion in which the subject's mind is troubled by a belief that he is guilty of wrongdoing and in which the disquiet consists partly in feeling bad about being guilty of wrongdoing as well as about having done something wrong.

What is the difference between feeling bad about being guilty of wrongdoing and merely feeling bad about having done something wrong?[6] It is that one feels uneasy with oneself in the former but not in the latter. Feeling uneasy with oneself is something more than feeling unhappy or sorrow about what one has done. One cannot, in feeling uneasy with oneself, rest until the facture the feeling represents has been repaired. No similar spur is a necessary ingredient in unhappiness or sorrow. Dostoyevski dramatizes this aspect of guilt by portraying Raskolnikov as delirious and stricken with fever in the first few days after the murders and, once his delirium and fever pass and he regains enough strength and acuity to resume daily life, plagued by conflict between the urge to confess and the fear of being found out. The conflict represents the division in Raskolnikov's soul between his conscience and his ego, and only when he does confess and submit to the punishment the state imposes on him does he begin to heal and feel once again whole.

Freud used the term *gewissenangst* to refer to this aspect of the emotion.[7] A natural translation would be "qualms of conscience." Freud, however, used the term to bring the phenomenon under the general account of anxiety he gave in the late stages of his career.[8] Specifically, he used it to denote a kind of anxiety the source of which are the reproaches of a harsh conscience. As such, it is distinct from the kind of anxiety he referred to as "realistic." Following the practice of his English translators, I will refer to it as moral anxiety. On Freud's general account, anxiety is a signal of danger. Accordingly, different kinds correspond to different sources of danger. Realistic anxiety signals danger the source of which is external to or judged to be external by its subject. An example would be anxiety that an employee experiences in advance of a meeting with the boss concerning his or her job performance. Another example would be anxiety a homeowner experiences on hearing a strange sound in the middle of the night that alerts him or her to an intruder. Moral anxiety, by contrast, signals danger that the voice of conscience intimates when it admonishes or condemns, for to go against one's conscience is a breach that destroys one's peace of mind, and the inner agitation that follows threatens to last until one takes steps to repair the breach.

Freud understood conscience to be an authoritative force in the human personality.[9] Specifically, he characterized it as an internal authority that gets installed in a person's mind at an early age as the result of processes by which the person comes to introject the authority of his or her parents. As Freud liked to say, a child acquires a conscience when the external authority of its parents becomes internal.[10] This transformation, he wrote, brings about a "great change" in the child's emotional life.[11] Before the change, Freud observed, the anxiety a child feels when it disobeys its parents is entirely realistic. It fears their discovering its misbehavior and the unpleasant consequences that it imagines such a discovery will bring. After the change, a child becomes liable to moral as well as realistic anxiety, since it now must deal with a harsh and disapproving conscience when it acts disobediently. The lacerations of its conscience, moreover, unlike the punishment the child's parents inflict, are inescapable. Consequently, while the child can avoid the latter, if only temporarily, by taking evasive action, action designed to keep its parents ignorant either of its disobedience or its whereabouts, it must deal with the former by doing whatever will quiet its conscience. That is, while realistic anxiety signals danger its subject will seek to escape if he can, moral anxiety, because the danger it signals is inescapable, will prompt its subject to do what he can to placate the authority that is the source of the danger. Specifically, such anxiety prompts its subject to do what he can to set things right with his conscience. By setting things right, he expiates the guilt he believes he incurred. Thus, relief from moral anxiety requires expiation of guilt. On Freud's account, expiatory acts or their equivalent are the means to healing the division in oneself that gives rise to such anxiety.

Disobedience brings parental discipline when a child's attempts to keep its parents ignorant of its misbehavior or its whereabouts fail. The child sees in its parents' displeasure with or anger at what it did a sign of its having damaged its relations with them, and it may, as a result, be afraid of losing their love and goodwill. The punishment the child receives then serves to repair the damage, for it assuages their anger and restores to the relations, at least in the child's mind, the love and amicability the loss of which it feared. When the child introjects its parents' authority and thus acquires a conscience, Freud theorized, this interpersonal dynamic is reproduced in the child's relations to its conscience. And because any attempt to hide one's actions and, indeed, one's thoughts and feelings from one's conscience is bound to be futile, one necessarily seeks ways to appease it whenever one's actions, thoughts, or feelings spark its ire. What one seeks, then, on Freud's theory, are substitutes for parental punishment. Accordingly, Freud held that moral anxiety, the aspect of the emotion of guilt that consists in feeling uneasy with oneself, manifests a need for punishment. The term he used for this need was *Strafbedürfnis*.[12] As he put it, the emotion is the expression of such a need.

Freud's identification of the emotion with a need for punishment served well his interest in explaining physical distress and illness from which many of his patients suffered that one could not explain as the effects of some organic disorder. These conditions, he hypothesized, satisfied a need for punishment that the patients who suffered from them had as a result of repressed memories of wrongdoing or, alternatively, repressed fantasies of the same that originated in the first few years of their lives and became implanted in their minds as false memories. In other words, the patients who suffered from these conditions, he hypothesized, unconsciously made themselves sick as a way to appease their conscience. Freud also applied the same explanation to masochism and to self-inflicted injuries that fit a pattern of self-abuse. These behaviors, he held, manifested an unconscious sense of guilt. They, too, satisfied a need for punishment that resulted from repressed memories or fantasies that originated in early childhood.[13]

In addition, Freud's theory covers the aforementioned cases of guilt in which the object of the emotion is not an act of wrongdoing. Freud himself emphasized, as part of the great change in a child's emotional life, that the installation in its mind of an internal authority brings about, that thoughts and feelings as well as actions become subject to the surveillance and judgment of this authority. The theory, then, readily explains feelings of guilt over malicious thoughts and feelings that one neither acts on nor betrays to others.[14] And it explains, too, guilt that one feels over wholly innocent actions. One can, that is, following Freud's theory, explain these feelings as the residual effects of parental strictures that were the original dictates of one's conscience but that one had long ago abandoned in the course of forging an identity around a different set of values from those of one's parents. Like old, once ingrained habits of thought and feeling that one no longer embraces, they, too, can be difficult to extinguish.

Thus Freud, by first setting up conscience as the internal representation of parental authority and then explaining feelings of guilt as products of an interpersonal dynamic between oneself and one's conscience that reproduces the dynamic that existed between oneself, when a small child, and one's parents, developed the Raskolnikov model into a rich source of psychological insight. By doing so he illuminated a variety of otherwise puzzling emotional and behavioral phenomena including mysterious illnesses and gratuitously self-defeating and self-injurious conduct as well as feelings of guilt over inappropriate objects. At the same time, because Freud's account of the emotion grew out of his clinical interest in understanding the root causes of these puzzling phenomena and, more generally, the psycho-neurotic conditions from which his patients suffered, it is narrowly constructed to explain suffering that people either induce in themselves or seek out to quiet their conscience. His point, after all, of identifying a sense of guilt with a need for punishment was to render such suffering meaningful. As a result, his account does not explain, except perhaps indirectly, other means than suffering that people take to quiet their consciences and relieve the uneasiness with themselves that is the hallmark of guilt. For this reason it is incomplete.

Think again of the emotional turmoil that Raskolnikov experiences following the murders he committed. As the horror of his crimes takes over his thoughts and weighs heavily on his mind, Raskolnikov increasingly feels the need to lift the weight of his guilt through confession. And when he does confess, first to Sonia, the young prostitute who befriends him, and finally to the police, the thoughts that had tormented him for days begin to recede and the denunciations of his conscience subside. Confession, however, is not punishment. It lifts the weight of guilt, not by inducing suffering in oneself or having others inflict it on one, but rather by ending one's efforts to keep others ignorant of what one did or to maintain falsely one's innocence in the face of suspicions or accusations to the contrary. These efforts require constant vigilance over one's words and actions lest one either be found out or unmasked. Hence, a need for punishment does not explain the pressures to confess to wrongdoing that the emotion of guilt can generate.

Of course, confessing to wrongdoing is not the result of such pressures if it is done merely because one can no longer keep up the vigilance over one's words and actions that is required to hide from others what one did or to maintain falsely one's innocence in the face of suspicions or accusations to the contrary. Guilt is no more the driving force behind such a confession than it is the driving force behind a wanted man's turning himself in out of sheer exhaustion from being on the run for years as a fugitive from justice. Rather, guilt moves one to confess to wrongdoing when one makes the confession as a prelude to asking for forgiveness or receiving absolution and in an attempt to make again whole the relations one's wrongdoing ruptured. It moves one, in other words, to confess from a desire to end the estrangement from those whom one wronged or disobeyed, for the estrangement from them that results from the rupture will persist as long as one continues to hide from them what one did or to deny that one did it. The first step, then, in repairing one's relations with them is to come clean.[15]

Still, one may wonder how a wrongdoer's conscience is quieted by his being forgiven or receiving absolution. Why should his self-condemnation cease just because others, whose condemnation would be warranted, openly forswear it and invite resumption of good relations? In point of fact it may not. A wrongdoer's conscience may continue to torment him even though the victims of his actions forgive him or the authority he disobeyed absolves him, and even though he is punished by others who either have the authority to punish him or take it upon themselves to do so. The lesson to draw from the relief from his tormenting conscience that Raskolnikov's confession brings is not that in the standard case of the emotion the wrongdoer's acknowledging his action and his being responsible for it to those relations with whom it ruptured or their representatives is sufficient for quieting his conscience. Rather, it is that it is necessary, for in the standard case, the estrangement from others' relations with whom one's wrongdoing ruptured feeds the uneasiness with oneself that is the hallmark of guilt. And wanting an end to the pain and anxiety of this uneasiness means wanting to do what is necessary to end the estrangement, to make one's relations with them whole. This social dimension of guilt is an element of the Raskolnikov model that Freud's identification of the emotion with the need for punishment excises.

The reason for the excision is not hard to see. Freud understood guilt to be an emotion to which a person develops a liability when at an early age he acquires a conscience. Before that time the only authorities to which the person is subject are external. The acquisition of a conscience, on Freud's theory, significantly changes the situation, for it consists in the installation in the mind of an internal authority. After explaining the processes by which such an authority is installed in the mind, Freud then narrowed his account of guilt to the relations within that mind between its possessor—more exactly, his ego, the part of the mind that bears his identity and carries out executive functions—and his conscience. Specifically, Freud defined guilt as tension that arises between a person's ego and his conscience. The emotion therefore moves its subject to do things or bring about in himself conditions that alleviate the tension. In principle, this account can comprehend the emotion's social dimension. But Freud's interest lay in using it to explain cases of the emotion in which the social dimension is at best remote and the means for alleviating the tension that is guilt do not intelligibly include making a confession as a way to gain the forgiveness or absolution of those whom one believes one has wronged or disobeyed. Indeed, on Freud's account, once an internal authority is installed in a person's mind, it eclipses the external authorities from which it derives so that the only relations that matter to explaining the nature of the emotion are those between a person—more exactly his ego—and his conscience. And since one's conscience is not an authority to whom it would make sense to confess in an attempt to heal the division one caused in disobeying it, only acquiescing in or inducing in oneself suffering as punishment makes sense, on Freud's account, as a way to quiet one's conscience and heal the division. Hence, Freud's identification of guilt with a need for punishment and his omission of the emotion's social dimension.

Some writers take the social dimension of guilt as the basis for understanding the emotion.[16] In their view, guilt is an emotion the liability to which is inherent in human sociability. Human beings, being social by nature, are sensitive to the joys and sufferings of others as well as to their own joys and sufferings and are thus prone to feeling both pleasure at another's good fortune and pain at his or her misfortune. Hume highlighted this feature of human nature in his account of our moral sensibilities. He attributed it to our capacity for sympathy with others, which he understood to be a capacity to reproduce in one's mind the feelings that one observes in others.[17] A cyclist hits a skid and crashes. Witnessing the accident, you see her struggling to stand, and in realizing that she has been hurt, you cannot help but feel imaginatively the pain that she is in. For Hume, your sympathy with the cyclist is shown in your feeling pain that matches the pain the cyclist is feeling. The preferred term, nowadays, for this phenomenon is *empathy*. Many of those writers who base their understanding of guilt on the emotion's social dimension explain the liability to the emotion as being rooted in the capacity for empathy. Accordingly, they take the liability to be inherent in human sociability.

Contemporary studies of empathy in experimental social psychology attribute the capacity for it to children at a very early age. These studies yield evidence of the role of the capacity's exercise in the emergence in young children of an ability to differentiate themselves as distinct individuals from others. The evidence consists of observations of the reactions of small children to seeing or hearing other children or grown-ups in distress. The observations are made at different stages of a child's social development. Infancy is the earliest stage. At this stage infants as young as a few days old exhibit the capacity that Hume had highlighted. They react to the crying of other infants by crying as well, and this reaction shows the contagiousness among infants of the feelings of distress that their crying expresses. At the next stage, small children are observed to react to another's distress, the distress of a playmate, say, not only with feelings of distress that match their playmate's, but also with attempts to ease their own distress as if it had been caused directly rather than empathically and despite their being aware of its origins in their playmate's condition. At a still later stage, however, small children turn their efforts at dealing with their empathic feelings of distress toward comforting the child or grown-up whose distress is its origin. They do this at first by offering the child or grown-up remedies that make sense as remedies for their own distress but not as remedies for the distress of the person they are trying to comfort. One example is that of a child who turned to its mother as someone who could soothe a playmate's distress when the playmate's own mother was equally close at hand. Eventually, though, small children come to offer to others in distress remedies that make sense as remedies for the distress of those they are trying to comfort. At this point, one can say that they fully recognize others as distinct individuals from themselves.

One of the leading writers on the role of empathy in children's social development, Martin Hoffman, describes the course of these advances in a child's development of a capacity for empathy, after the earliest stage, as a progression from empathy that has an egocentric character to empathy characterized by concern for another's well-being. Hoffman calls the latter "veridical empathy" in view of the appropriateness of the remedies the child offers to the person to whose distress it is responding.[18] Their appropriateness shows that the child grasps the difference between the distress the person is feeling and its own empathic distress. "Veridical empathy," Hoffman writes, "is an important stage because, unlike the preceding stages which are short-lived and disappear as they give way to subsequent stages, this stage has all the basic elements of mature empathy. . . ."[19] He then goes on to explain how children become at this stage, or not long after, liable to what he calls "empathy-based guilt."[20] His explanation reflects his understanding of the emotion as based on its social dimension. This understanding has been widely influential.

Hoffman understands guilt to be, in the first instance, an emotion one feels over one's having either harmed someone or allowed someone to be harmed. The object of the emotion, again in the first instance, is not, on his understanding, an act of wrongdoing or disobedience to authority. Rather it is an act that causes harm to another or an omission that results in another's being harmed. Acts of wrongdoing and disobedience to authority become, according to the scheme of social development that Hoffman constructs, objects of the emotion only after a child has internalized moral standards and norms. At this stage in Hoffman's scheme, the stage at which moral standards and norms are internalized, the child has already acquired a liability to empathy-based guilt. Let us assume that the internalization of moral standards and norms that Hoffman places at this later stage of social development is the process by which the child acquires a conscience. Accordingly, on Hoffman's understanding of guilt, one can be liable to the emotion even though one lacks a conscience. His understanding, therefore, flatly contradicts Freud's. Indeed, it contradicts any understanding of guilt as a species of bad conscience.

Hoffman locates the development of a liability to guilt at this earlier stage in his scheme because he takes the emergence in a child of the ability to differentiate itself as a distinct individual from others as the catalyst of this development. Not until a child is able to realize that other people are distinct individuals capable of feeling joy and sorrow, pleasure and pain that are independent of its feelings of joy and sorrow, pleasure and pain, can it grasp the idea of other people's being benefited or harmed by events that have an impact on them. A child, in other words, cannot, until it comes to this realization, fully distinguish the well-being of another person from its own well-being and therefore cannot fully understand how its actions can affect another for better or worse independently of those actions' affecting its own well-being. Once a child reaches the stage at which it does realize that other people are distinct individuals capable of feeling joy and sorrow, pleasure and pain, that are independent of its feelings of joy and sorrow, pleasure and pain, it is then able to recognize, when something happens to another person that results in his or her feeling pain, anguish, sorrow, or the like, that this other person has been hurt and that it has not been hurt. For the child, when it feels empathically distress that matches the distress another person feels, is able to recognize that the distress it feels is not due to its having been hurt. Consequently, when its own actions cause another pain, anguish, sorrow, or the like, and it feels empathically the distress that matches the distress the other feels, it realizes that it has hurt this other person but not itself. It realizes that it is responsible for hurting the other person. The realization that one is responsible for hurting another to which one comes through veridical empathy with the distress that the latter feels, Hoffman maintains, triggers empathy-based guilt.

Hoffman takes as evidence of such guilt in small children the actions of a child who has hurt another the purposes of which are to comfort the latter, to acknowledge responsibility for having caused the latter distress, and to express sorrow for having done so. He characterizes these actions as reparative. Commenting on observations that other researchers made of infant development in interpersonal relations, he writes, "Spontaneous helping by infants became more frequent in the second year as did reparative acts accompanied by guiltlike expressions of concern when they caused another's distress."[21] He then offers two examples of such acts and expressions: "an 18-month-old who accidentally hit a baby-sitter and said, 'Sorry Sally,' and patted the sitter's forehead; and a 2-year-old who pulled her cousin's hair and having been told not to do that by her mother crawled to the cousin, said 'I hurt your hair, please don't cry,' and gave her a kiss."[22] Later he describes how a child's reactions to another's distress develop from a simple feeling of empathic distress to a combination of empathic distress and feelings of guilt when the child's own actions are the cause of the other's distress. The former reactions are exhibited in a child's first year; the latter appear in the second year. And the behavior he cites as signs of the feelings of guilt that are among the latter reactions consists of things a child says after hurting another, a playmate, say, or a babysitter, that show the child's awareness of its having hurt the playmate or sitter and that express its feeling bad about having done so.

Hoffman is not alone in taking reparative actions as signs of feelings of guilt in small children. Some psychoanalysts, notably, Melanie Klein, who hold that children become liable to guilt at a much earlier age than the age at which Freud fixed the acquisition of a conscience, attribute the emotion to very young children and even infants in view of reparative actions they take after having acted aggressively toward someone to whom they are attached, typically and primarily, their mother.[23] While these psychoanalysts agree with Freud in thinking that the dynamic of the relations between a child and its parents is crucial to explaining a child's developing a liability to guilt, they disagree with him about which feature of those relations is crucial. For them the crucial feature is the child's being the recipient of its parents' care and nurture and not its being subject to their authority. On their explanation, children, being the recipients of their parents' care and nurture, form in return strong attachments to their parents that define the love they have of their parents and also dispose them to guilt when they behave aggressively toward their parents. They are so disposed because aggression against a parent, in a small child's mind, is an attack on something or someone they deeply value, and imagining that they have seriously damaged what they deeply value, they act to repair the damage and to restore things to good order. On these psychoanalysts' explanation, the motive behind these reparative actions is guilt, just as older children and adults act out of guilt, when, having treated others with whom they enjoy good relations badly, they act to set things right with them.

Reparative actions, however, are not always signs of guilt. To the contrary, in many cases they are not. When one harms another with whom one enjoys good relations and feels bad about what happened as a result, one naturally responds in a conciliatory way. One expresses sorrow for the harm and regret for having caused it. One asks, "How can I make it up to you?" And one implies through such expressions of regret and offers of compensation that, despite what happened, one's goodwill toward the person continues undiminished, that one's action does not signify any ill will toward him or her or indifference to his or her well-being. And if one thinks the person has some doubt about one's being well-disposed toward him or her, one is concerned to reassure the person one harmed that one is so disposed and may offer to make good any loss he or she suffered. Such conciliatory actions are meant to be reparative of any damage to the relations one may have caused as well as supportive of the person one harmed. They are, at the same time, entirely consistent with the absence in one's mind of any sense of guilt about what one did. One can, in other words, feel badly about having harmed someone, convey how badly one feels to that person with expressions of sorrow and regret, and offer recompense for his or her losses without thinking that one is guilty of anything. One can, in short, say and do things meant to be reparative without being in the least uneasy with oneself. Indeed, the spontaneity of the reparative actions of the two-year-olds whom Hoffman cites as evidence of empathy-based guilt argues against these children's being uneasy with themselves when they engaged in those actions. The division within oneself that such uneasiness reflects and the restlessness it generates is not at all evident in the behavior of the two-year-olds that Hoffman describes.

Hoffman's error in taking reparative actions to be evidence of guilt represents a conflation of feeling bad about having done something wrong with feeling bad about being guilty of wrongdoing. When you do something wrong and the victims of your wrongdoing are aware of it, you are liable to lose their trust. Wrongdoing alone, in other words, can cause a rupture in your relations with others. When it does, the burden of repairing those relations, the burden of restoring the trust on which good relations are built, rests with you as the wrongdoer. Having taken the wrong suitcase when picking up your baggage after a flight and then realizing your mistake, to recur to an earlier example, you go back to the baggage area, return the suitcase to its owner, and offer her an apology and an explanation. The apology is an expression of how you feel bad about your mistake, and your explanation is a way of reassuring the owner of your respect and goodwill toward her, of your not being someone who disregards the property rights of others. These reparative acts serve to allay any suspicions and assuage any hard feelings that your action may have provoked, and thus they serve to restore the trust that you may have lost. You may do them sincerely without at all thinking that you are guilty of anything. Indeed, if the explanation is meant to be exculpatory, then the thought that you are guilty of wrongdoing would be out of place.

What distinguishes such reparative actions from the reparative actions that spring from guilt? Either may be done in the interest of regaining the trust of others that one lost as a result of having acted wrongly, but the reparative actions that spring from guilt are done to meet the heavier burden of regaining the trust of others who, in one's mind, rightly regard one as untrustworthy. Guilt, that is, moves a wrongdoer to take reparative actions in an effort to redeem himself in the eyes of those whom he wronged or disobeyed. And because success in this effort requires that the wrongdoer gain their forgiveness, given that they harbor hard feelings toward him, the reparative actions that spring from guilt are aimed then at softening the hearts of those whom he or she wronged or disobeyed. Such actions include, not only apologies and expressions of sorrow, but also open acknowledgment of one's being at fault in acting wrongly and submission to punishment or the sacrificing of something of value that those from whom one seeks forgiveness demand of one as evidence of one's contrition and commitment to not repeating what one did. The open acknowledgment of being at fault in acting wrongly conveys a promise that it won't happen again, and submission to punishment or the sacrifice of something of value serves as a surety that backs up this promise. Submitting to punishment and making a sacrifice, because the suffering that typically goes with either is suffering that one accepts rather than resists, signify the sincerity with which one commits to reforming one's behavior.

The social dimension of guilt does not, then, imply that children develop a liability to the emotion before they internalize moral standards and norms. And if such internalization is the process by which a child acquires a conscience, then it does not imply that children develop a liability to guilt before they acquire a conscience. To make out a case for children's developing the liability to guilt before they acquire a conscience one would have to explain how a child came both to regard itself as at fault for its bad behavior or disobedience and to believe that others whom it had hurt or disobeyed would be right to regard it as untrustworthy on account of its having behaved badly or disobediently. To be sure, one can explain how a child, before it acquires a conscience, comes to be able to recognize that it has lost the trust of others on account of its having behaved badly or disobediently, for such loss would be evident in the reactions of those whom it hurt or disobeyed. But to believe that others are right to cease to trust one on account of one's bad or disobedient behavior, one must have some notion of oneself as answerable to them for that behavior and as subject to their demands that one accept punishment or make some sacrifice to earn back their trust. Clearly, one would have such a notion if one had a conscience, but it is far from clear how one could have it if one didn't. People who have a conscience are answerable to their conscience and, accordingly, understand that they are answerable to others for acting wrongly or disobediently. How someone who lacked a conscience could have that same understanding, however, is, as I said, hard to see. At most, it seems that such a person could understand that others will make him answer for his wrongdoing or disobedience, but understanding that one can be made to answer for one's actions is not the same as understanding that one is answerable to others for them.

Conscience and empathy are therefore distinct elements of the human personality. The capacity for the latter belongs to the social nature of human beings. The former, by contrast, is a precipitate of processes by which a child internalizes the moral standards and norms of its culture. Exercises of the capacity for empathy may inform the workings of conscience, or they may inspire actions that go against the dictates of conscience. A person, moreover, may have a strict conscience and only a limited capacity for empathy. Indeed, some people may be sufficiently awkward or imperceptive in their social relations as to raise questions about their even having a capacity for empathy, yet such people can be impeccably conscientious in upholding moral standards and norms in how they live their lives. A common example is someone who has a mild form of autism. People who have such autism are sometimes described as high functioning. That is, their autism is not so severe as to prevent them from living productive and fulfilling lives. Their condition is entirely compatible with their being both subject to compunctions of conscience and liable to guilt over actions that violate moral standards and norms. Their liability to guilt is readily explained by their having a conscience. By contrast, explaining it as being based in empathy would seem to be a much harder proposition to sustain.

Could the reverse be true of someone who grew up in modern society? That is, could someone who grew up in modern society lack a conscience and nonetheless have a developed capacity for empathy? In the abstract such a person is imaginable. Consider, for example, the character, Hannibal Lecter, in Jonathan Demme's *The Silence of the Lambs*.[24] Lecter is a highly accomplished psychiatrist who is also a serial killer with a proclivity for eating his victims. His cannibalism speaks to his lack of a conscience; his skills as a psychiatrist speak to his capacity for empathy. The latter is evident in the film in his interactions with the FBI agent, Clarice Starling, who interviews him in the prison where he is being held in hopes that he will help her track down a currently active serial killer known as Buffalo Bill. The interview becomes bilateral as Lecter asks Starling to tell him personal things about herself in return for his answering her questions and helping her profile Buffalo Bill. And when Lecter then takes his turn as interviewer, he displays, in pressing his questions, a knowing empathic understanding of the experiences Clarice relates to him, particularly, the terror she experienced one morning as a child living on a farm when she awoke to the sound of lambs being slaughtered.

While someone who lacks a conscience but has a developed capacity for empathy is thus imaginable in the abstract, concretely no such person is likely to exist in modern society. The reason—and this is an empirical conjecture—is that the development of the capacity for empathy in a child who, despite growing up in modern society, lacks a conscience is bound to be stunted. Hoffman describes the development of the capacity at later stages as consisting in processes by which the child comes to exercise the capacity in the course of learning to make increasingly complex judgments of fairness and justice on the basis of moral standards and norms that it has internalized. These processes occur in the context of the child's participating in and becoming integrated into the increasingly complex cooperative arrangements that characterize modern society. As children venture out from their homes and engage with others of their own age, enter and advance through school, join social organizations outside of school, get their first jobs, and participate in organized activities to which principles of mutuality and reciprocity are essential, they are called on more and more to think about and adjust to the different situations of those with whom they are interacting. They are called on more and more, that is, to understand others and their situations empathically when making judgments of fairness and justice. A child who has not acquired a conscience will have much greater difficulty in becoming integrated into these arrangements and, indeed, will never be fully integrated into them since the principles of mutuality and reciprocity essential to cooperative arrangements will never become in such a child second nature. Consequently, in the broader social contexts beyond the home out into which children typically venture, a child who has never acquired a conscience will not be making judgments of fairness and justice that enlist and enlarge his or her capacity for empathy.

Quite the contrary, the estrangement that results from failure to integrate fully into cooperative arrangements is likely to cause such a child to regress to the earlier stage of egocentricity. This, too, is an empirical conjecture. Evidence for it, however, exists in the traits that contemporary psychiatric and psychological studies of people who lack a conscience have come to identify as characteristic of this condition. Such people are generally classified as psychopaths, and the traits characteristic of their condition include, in addition to their lacking a conscience, persistent wrongdoing, absence of guilt despite knowledge of the difference between right and wrong, and egocentricity. Plainly, if Hoffman's account of guilt were correct, that is, if the liability to the emotion were rooted in the capacity for empathy, a psychopath's egocentricity would be sufficient to explain his or her pathology. It would, that is, explain the union of the traits that are characteristic of the condition. But Hoffman's account, as we saw, rests on a confusion. Hence, a psychopath's lack of empathy is not the telltale sign of the pathology's root cause. It is, instead, a trait that is associated in the psychopathic personality with other traits that serve as the pathology's markers. Its conjunction in psychopathy with these other traits, the lack of a conscience, in particular, is therefore evidence of processes that not only arrest in a child who lacks a conscience the further development of its capacity for empathy after its internalization of moral standards and norms, but also cause such a child to regress to an earlier stage of egocentricity. And the stronger the association of egocentricity with the lack of a conscience, given the independence of these traits from each other, the greater is the evidential support it provides for the existence of these processes.

The deficits that are characteristic of a psychopathic personality, an incapacity for empathy and the lack of a conscience, correspond to two distinct dimensions of human sociability. The capacity for empathy enables people to connect with one another through shared sentiments and feelings. It can thus be a source of solace to those who suffer misfortunes, for communicating to others who have suffered misfortunes one's empathic understanding of what they are going through can lessen the feeling of isolation misfortune brings and thereby make their suffering more bearable. In addition, the capacity makes possible solidarity, through greater connection, in relationships among people who regard each other as equals. The possession of a conscience, on the other hand, facilitates cooperation among people each of whom has private interests the promotion of which sometimes conflicts with cooperating with others in pursuit of common interests. At those times, the conscience of each cooperator works to maintain his or her fidelity to the mutual understanding on which the cooperation of all is based. Such fidelity makes each trustworthy in eyes of the others. It is the cement of the social relations that any sizeable human community comprises.

This second dimension of human sociability is the social dimension of guilt. The oldest problems of ethics, those embedded in the conversations between Socrates and the sophists that Plato recorded, derive from it. When Glaucon and Adiemantus, for instance, in book 2 of Plato's *Republic*, reformulate the challenge to the value of living a just life that Thrasymachus in book 1 had raised, they press Socrates to show that such a life is superior to the life of secretly practicing injustice while maintaining a reputation for being just. Because someone who so practiced injustice recognizes the importance to achieving his ends of having the reputation of being just, he clearly sees value in being trusted by others. At the same time he sees no value, given that he can maintain that reputation while practicing injustice, in being trustworthy. The challenge that Glaucon and Adiemantus, at the dawn of Western ethics, ask Socrates to meet is thus the problem of defending the supreme value to living a good human life of being trustworthy. Nearly twenty-five hundred years later, Freud, in *Civilization and Its Discontents*, resurfaced the same challenge when he declared at the beginning of the work's closing chapter that "the sense of guilt [is] the most important problem in the development of civilization."[25]

NOTES

1. Sigmund Freud, *Das Unbehagen in der Kultur*, p. 100ff. For the English translation, see *Civilization and Its Discontents* in *The Standard Edition of the Complete Psychological Works of Sigmund Freud*, v. 21, pp. 123ff. Hereafter this multivolume work will be abbreviated SE.

2. *Das Unbehagen in der Kultur*, 119.

3. *Vertigo*, directed by Alfred Hitchcock, screenplay by Alec Coppel, Samuel Taylor, and Maxwell Anderson.

4. William Shakespeare, *Henry VI, pt. 3, act V, scene vi, line 11*. Richard is responding to Henry's expression of fear but is no doubt also engaged in self-description.

5. *Shadow of a Doubt*, directed by Alfred Hitchcock, screenplay by Alma Reville, Thornton Wilder, and Sally Benson.

6. See Herbert Morris, "Guilt and Suffering" in his *On Guilt and Innocence: Essays in Legal Philosophy and Moral Psychology*, 89–110.

7. *Das Unbehagen in der Kultur*, 107.

8. Freud gave this account late in his career. See *Symptoms, Inhibitions, and Anxiety*, SE. v. 20. On his earlier account, anxiety was an effluent of repressed instinctual, specifically, erotic, energy and had no inherent intentionality. See "Freud" in my *From Psychology to Morality: Essays in Ethical Naturalism* for discussion of Freud's different accounts of anxiety.

9. On a more exact formulation of Freud's theory, the authoritative force in the human personality belongs to the part of the mind Freud called "the superego," and conscience is a function of the superego. For simplicity's sake, I treat conscience and

the superego as equivalent. See Freud, *New Introductory Lectures on Psychoanalysis*, SE, v. 22, 59–66.

10. *Civilization and its Discontents*, SE, v. 21, 127.

11. Ibid., 125.

12. *Das Unbehagen in der Kultur*, 100.

13. See *The Economic Problem of Masochism*, SE, v. 19, 166.

14. See "All Kinds of Guilt" in my *Emotions, Values and the Law* for discussion of these cases and how they fit the Raskolnikov model. In this regard, it is important to see that one's belief that one is guilty resides in one's conscience since many people who experience such guilt would rightly deny that they had done anything wrong. Plainly, understanding the mind as divided—"Part of me," the person might say, "believes that I'm guilty even though I don't believe it"—is essential to these cases fitting the Raskolnikov model. On the importance of a divided mind for understanding how someone could hold contradictory beliefs, see Donald Davidson, "Paradoxes of Irrationality," in his *Problems of Rationality*.

15. This is not to say that submitting to punishment has no such reparative function. To the contrary, one cannot make whole the relations one's wrongdoing ruptured as long as those whom one wronged or disobeyed remain angry and hostile toward one, and acceptance of punishment can serve to assuage their anger and hostility. It can serve to redeem one in their eyes. It, too, may be necessary to gain the forgiveness of those whom one wronged or to receive absolution from those who have the authority to grant it.

16. See e.g., Michael Friedman, "Toward a Reconceptualization of Guilt"; Allan Gibbard, *Wise Choices, Apt Feelings: A Theory of Normative Judgment*, 126–50; and Martin Hoffman, *Empathy and Moral Development: Implications for Caring and Justice*.

17. David Hume, *A Treatise of Human Nature*, bk. II, pt. 1, sec. xi.

18. Hoffman, 71–73.

19. Ibid., 72.

20. Ibid., 114.

21. Ibid., 115–16.

22. Ibid., 116.

23. See e.g., Melanie Klein, "A Contribution to the Psychogenesis of Manic-Depressive States" in her *Love, Guilt and Reparation: And Other Works 1921–1945*.

24. *The Silence of the Lambs*, directed by Jonathan Demme, screenplay by Ted Tally.

25. SE, v. 21, 134.

BIBLIOGRAPHY

Davidson, Donald. *Problems of Rationality*. Oxford: Oxford University Press, 2004.

Deigh, John. *Emotions, Values and the Law*. New York: Oxford University Press, 2010.

———. *From Psychology to Morality: Essays in Ethical Naturalism*. New York: Oxford University Press, 2018.

Freud, Sigmund. *Das Unbehagen in der Kultur.* Wien: Internationaler Psychoanlytischer Verlag, 1930.

———. *The Standard Edition of the Complete Psychological Works of Sigmund Freud*, James Strachey, ed. London: Hogarth Press, 1981.

Friedman, Michael. "Toward a Reconceptualization of Guilt," *Contemporary Psychoanalysis* 21 (1985): 501–47.

Gibbard, Allan. *Wise Choices, Apt Feelings: A Theory of Normative Judgment.* Cambridge, MA: Harvard University Press, 1990.

Hoffman, Martin. *Empathy and Moral Development: Implications for Caring and Justice.* Cambridge: Cambridge University Press, 2000.

Hume, David. *A Treatise of Human Nature.* 2nd ed., L. A. Selby-Bigge, ed. Oxford: Oxford University Press, 1978.

Klein, Melanie. *Love, Guilt and Reparation: And Other Works 1921–1945.* New York: Dell Publishing Co., 1975.

Morris, Herbert. *On Guilt and Innocence: Essays in Legal Philosophy and Moral Psychology.* Berkeley: University of California Press, 1976.

Shakespeare, William. *Henry VI, Part III.*

Chapter 4

Against Exclusively Retrospective Guilt

Heidy Meriste

INTRODUCTION

Guilt is usually thought of as a retrospective emotion: Someone did something terrible and is later tormented by pangs of conscience. Lady Macbeth is a good example. Early on in the play, she coldheartedly encourages her husband to kill King Duncan, but soon after the murder, she develops an alarmingly guilty conscience. Often, retrospectiveness goes as a tacit assumption that manifests itself in definitions of guilt that speak of the misdeed in the past tense.[1] Some authors, however, go further and tie guilt more explicitly with elements that seem to exclude the possibility that guilt might also be attached to present and future moral failures. One such element is the wish to turn *back* time and to *undo* the deed.[2] Such a wish implies that had the person been at his right mind, he would not have committed the wrong in the first place. The wrong took place either because he did not care about morality enough or because he failed to realize the full gravity of the wrong. As those give way to a more complete understanding and a change of heart, it is only later that the person comes to feel guilty. At least that is how the story goes. Perhaps the clearest formulation of this narrative of exclusively retrospective guilt is outlined by Gunnar Karlsson and Lennart Gustav Sjöberg:

> [G]uilt as a phenomenon has a very clear temporal unfolding. The moment of the guilt feeling occurs after that moment in which the action that is the source of the guilt feeling has been committed. [. . .] First one lives through an action in an "innocent way," but this action becomes after the reconstruction constituted as a moment of negligence.[3]

As the authors make clear, there is no guilt feeling while the act is committed. One just goes through life in "a 'mindless' and easy-going way."[4] The misdeed is described as an "act of negligence." All this leaves no room for intentionally and knowingly committing a wrong.

Perhaps not all philosophers agree with this story. But the story is widespread enough to merit attention. It runs like a red thread through autobiographical descriptions of guilt, which Karlsson and Sjöberg's study is based on. It makes good fictional stories, allowing us to track the moral development of the protagonist. And it also resonates with a long-standing tradition in phenomenology that considers guilt as the emotion that helps to break down the barrier of pride—understood in terms of living a careless, easygoing life without much moral reflection and self-scrutiny.[5]

The aim of this chapter is to expand our understanding of guilt by showing that guilt is not necessarily retrospective—it can also be present- and future-focused. More specifically, the discussion will proceed as follows. First, I will provide a definition of guilt and clarify what it is that I have in mind when I say that an emotion can be past-, present- or future-focused. Then I deal with a seeming obstacle that stands in the way of imagining present- and future-focused tokens of guilt. This obstacle lies in the fact that there would have to be a rather peculiar tension between caring about morality (which makes one susceptible to guilt in the first place) and nevertheless knowingly acting against it. However, I will go on to argue that rather than making non-retrospective guilt impossible, this tension makes it particularly interesting. The sections that follow are respectively dedicated to present- and future-focused guilt. With regard to present-focused guilt, the existence of which is somewhat less controversial than the existence of future-focused guilt, my main aim is to show that it is more widespread than one might think. I will also argue that there are certain forms of guilt, more specifically forms of omission- and disposition-guilt, that are bound to be the strongest in a present- rather than past-focused form, and the phenomenology of which is very different from that of past-focused guilt. In the case of future-focused guilt, the existence of which is perhaps somewhat more controversial, my main focus will be on further defending the claim that there are indeed cases that can correctly be described as truly future-focused. On the one hand, I will show that future-focused guilt shares the same core evaluation, action tendency, and phenomenological feel with more familiar cases of past- and present-focused guilt. On the other hand, I will also tackle reductionist attempts to show that future-focused guilt can be explained in terms of past- and present-focused guilt.

DEFINITIONS: GUILT AND TEMPORAL FOCUS

As the focus of my analysis lies in defending the *possibility* of present- and future-focused guilt, not their *fittingness* or *moral justification*, most of my inquiry does not hang on the details of how exactly we should define the contours of guilt. The most crucial thing is that my analysis applies to guilt, and emotions in general, only insofar as they are intentional phenomena, which means that they must have an object that can be described in relatively specific terms. As such, they are to be distinguished from free-floating moods that focus on nothing in particular or could be vaguely conceived as being about everything. Thus, a treatment of existential guilt that lacks an intentional object falls beyond the scope of this chapter.

With regard to the specifics, I will confine myself to giving only a rather broad outline. First, I would like to highlight that guilt presupposes and reflects *a concern for morality*. That means that if one does not care about morality, they will not be susceptible to guilt. Morality, in turn, is to be understood in a rather wide sense, so that it includes both a concern for more abstract moral rules but also a more direct concern for other people and their well-being.[6] Secondly, I take it that, in prototypical cases at least, guilt involves three key components: a special kind of *evaluation, action tendency*, and *phenomenological feel*.[7] At this point, it is important to note that the characteristic evaluation lies in viewing the intentional object as manifesting a moral failure on the subject's part. As such, guilt is a special way of being directed toward self-related immoral things like one's own actions, omissions, and dispositions.[8] The exact nature of the relevant action tendency and phenomenological feel will be illuminated later.[9]

Temporal focus is understood as an intrinsic structural feature of an emotion that I consider to be determined by whether the intentional object of the emotion, i.e., that which the emotion is about, is perceived as located in past, present, or future—and so with respect to the phenomenal "now" rather than objective time. By the phenomenal "now," I mean the point of time where the subject currently perceives herself as existing. This allows for time traveling by simulation—it is possible to imagine oneself into some situation that is taken to be located in either objective past or future, or even into some alternative reality that has no clear relation with the objective time of our own reality. But whether the imagined scenario itself is taken to belong to past or future is an extrinsic matter that does not reflect in the inner structure of the emotion itself. This becomes important when distinguishing truly future-focused guilt from cases where one merely simulates a future misdeed and comes to feel retrospective guilt within this simulation.

As a note of caution, I would like to emphasize that even though I talk about past-, present-, and future-focused episodes of guilt, I do not mean to suggest that episodes of guilt can always be neatly categorized as focused on only one temporal dimension. Insofar as the object of guilt—be it an act, omission, or something else—may extend in time, there can also be mixed forms of guilt. In fact, as it will be seen, in normal circumstances, future-focused guilt is not likely to exist in a pure form but will be combined with a present-focused aspect.

A PECULIAR TENSION

The main obstacle in the way of imagining present- and future-focused cases of guilt lies in the fact that, in those cases in particular, there is a special tension between the precondition of guilt and its characteristic evaluation. Let me explain. On the one hand, one needs to care about morality, so that they would be susceptible to guilt in the first place. On the other hand, guilt also requires one to evaluate the deed[10] in question as immoral. But if the deed is supposed to be located in the present or the future, this gives rise to a puzzle: Why would someone who cares about morality go on and knowingly commit, or plan committing, a wrong?

Insofar as people strive toward consistency, it might seem sensible to expect that a person who cares about morality will either not go through with an immoral deed, or he will rationalize it for himself and cease to view the deed as immoral. At best, such cases might leave room for rather fleeting episodes of transitional guilt that would exist only in virtue of a fragile balance that soon ends up in the dissolution of guilt. But since I want to make a strong case for the existence of present- and future-focused guilt, I will focus on more stable cases about which there is likely to be less disagreement.

Focusing on actions, there are two main types of cases that provide a more stable ground for present- and future-focused guilt: lucid cases of weakness of will, and cases where one is torn between plural values or loyalties. This twofold division is based on the degree to which the person identifies with the action and considers it as an all-in-all right thing to do. In weakness-of-will cases, one just gives in to a short-term impulse and thus acts against one's best judgment. For example, one may feel guilty while cheating on one's partner, or while breaking one's diet and indulging in an unhealthy meal.[11] Since acting on an impulse is usually not something that one plans ahead and could thus feel guilty about in advance, I will talk more about those cases under the heading of present-focused guilt. Cases of pluralism, on the other hand, are to do with more stable concerns that one does identify with, not just fleeting impulses. In those cases, one's moral concerns that give rise to guilt are outweighed by either other moral concerns (as in the case of tragic dilemmas, or more daily kind of loyalty conflicts), or nonmoral concerns (e.g., personal ambitions). In both cases, one may well think that their final course of action is all-in-all rational, but there is also a painful awareness that it comes at a moral cost. As I will be arguing, insofar as the person has already made up her mind about what she will do, those cases can give rise to guilt already in a future-focused form.

In fact, it is the very tension between caring about morality and knowingly acting against it that makes the above-mentioned cases particularly interesting. Those episodes are very different from present- and future-focused episodes of emotions that involve a positive form of self-evaluation. In the case of pride, one's evaluation is in alignment with one's actions. Thus, one can act in harmony with oneself.[12] Present- and future-focused forms of guilt, however, are disruptive: They involve a peculiar tension between what the person does or plans and how they evaluate the deed in question.

Of course, there is a sense in which exclusively retrospective guilt involves a tension as well, but the tension in present- and future-focused forms is much more pointed. In the case of retrospective guilt, one may feel that the past self who committed the wrong is, to use Gabriele Taylor's words, "alien to himself."[13] One might say that he does not realize how he could have done something like that and swear that he would never do so again. But the present self is nevertheless conceived of in a harmonious way—as univocally condemning both the deed and the past self who committed it.[14] This kind of distancing is much more difficult when one is currently committing the wrong. At the very moment of committing the wrong, it is much harder to put the blame on some alien self because there is a stronger sense in which one is that very self that is committing the deed. There is, of course, nevertheless a split, of a synchronic rather than diachronic kind. But, leaving aside pathological cases, it is highly unlikely that this synchronic split must be perceived in terms of being taken over by some "alien self." Insofar as he nevertheless commits or plans to commit the deed, he must, at least to some extent, be identifying with the motives and impulses that pull him in that direction. It is usually just retrospectively that one labels the earlier self as "alien."

To sum up, I hope to have shown in this section that while there is a tension between caring about morality and knowingly violating its demands, this does not make present- and future-focused guilt impossible. Instead, it makes it unique and interesting.

PRESENT-FOCUSED GUILT

There are various psychological reasons why people may not always feel present-focused guilt or might try to avoid it. When carried away by an impulse, the person might simply be so absorbed in the activity that he fails to take a self-reflective stance. Similarly, some crimes, e.g., a complicated jewelry theft, may require such focused attention, that if one wants to succeed, then they will be better off focusing all of their attention to the task at hand and chasing all other thoughts away. But surely it is not impossible to do something and have a self-reflective stance at the same time. People are not always fully absorbed in what they do. Their mind may wander, or they may stumble upon some external cue that reminds them of the wrongness of their action, e.g., one might notice a wedding ring on their finger while cheating on their partner. Thus, I take it that the existence of present-focused guilt requires no further argument apart from listing a variety of reasons and examples concerning why one might act against one's moral convictions, as I did in the last section. Instead, I will take it as my task to further show that cases of present-focused guilt are actually more widespread than one might think and that there are indeed some types of guilt that are bound to be the strongest only in their present-focused form—types of guilt that are unique in their phenomenology and that have been unfairly overlooked in philosophical literature.

Usually, when we think of guilt we think of guilt about certain *actions*. This is why lucid cases of weakness of will where one gives in to some temptation provide us with a good example of present-focused guilt. This includes both milder cases like giving in to an unhealthy craving,[15] and also more serious cases like cheating on one's partner. In a sense, both could be labeled as "guilty pleasures"—as sweet as those experiences may be, they can be tinged with a bitter sense of guilt. Metaphorically, it could even be said that both types of cases involve indulging in a forbidden fruit. However, insofar as those cases tend to be short in duration, they fail to provide a stable ground for more long-lasting cases of present-focused guilt. As soon as the deed is done, present-focused guilt will automatically turn into past-focused guilt. Thus, it is no wonder that most of the time we are burdened by retrospective guilt and that retrospective guilt has received much more attention than present-focused one. But once we turn our attention away from actions and focus on *omissions* and *dispositions*, both of which tend to last longer than actions, present-focused instances of guilt become much more visible.[16]

First, let us focus on omissions. Or, to be exact, my special interest will be in long-lasting omissions that are due to the weakness of will. Differently from actively doing something, omissions often just require one to be passive. This explains why they tend to last longer. After all, there is not much you have to do in order to engage in an omission. Since omissions are so easy, I see no reason to think that they are less frequent than actions. Throughout the history of philosophy, they may have received less attention from moral philosophers because actions have traditionally been associated with greater moral wrongs than omissions, but even in moral philosophy, this has started to change, and more attention is also focused on our omissions (e.g., not helping the poor and contributing to charity).[17]

Similarly to actions, omissions, too, can easily be combined with the weakness of will. It takes willpower to come out of one's comfort zone and take action. But unless the omission is combined with some substitute activity and special pleasure, it tends to lack the "guilty pleasure" aspect that succumbing to some fleeting impulse so often might have.

What is interesting about present-focused omission-guilt is that it has a unique phenomenology that contrasts with that of retrospective guilt. Conceptions of guilt that are mainly focused on retrospective instances tend to describe guilt as involving a dramatic sense of irreversibility. For example, Karlsson and Sjöberg say:

> The reconstruction [of past act or omission as wrong], bringing us to the *moment of guilt*, opens up a deeper existential dimension, based upon an understanding of the finite and irrevocable character of life. This existential dimension catches the burden of responsibility, time and guilt. What one has done cannot be undone; an action has been performed in a finite existence.[18]

The authors emphasize the "irrevocable character of life" and point out that one cannot undo what has already been done. I do not wish to deny that present-focused instances of guilt can sometimes make us think about the finite character of existence. When procrastinating, one may well realize that while slacking off and doing nothing particularly productive, they are wasting valuable time—time that they will not be able to get back. But there need not be any dramatic sense of irreversibility in present-focused instances of omission guilt because, differently from the past, which remains unalterable, one has more power over the present. People can rid themselves of present-focused guilt by simply pulling themselves together and doing the thing that they have been omitting. Instead of the dramatic sense of irreversibility, present-focused tokens of omission guilt can be characterized by a kind of nagging awareness that one is in the wrong as long as one does not do something about the omission. This kind of nagging awareness might not always be very pointed, but it can nevertheless be there in the background and, after every now and then, remind itself to the subject. While this kind of guilt might not be the best material for tragic novels, this is the more everyday experience of guilt, which is likely to be familiar to many people.

Secondly, let us focus on disposition guilt. By disposition guilt I mean the guilt that one feels about their character traits. This should not be confused with the disposition to feel guilty (i.e., guilt-proneness), which is a matter of having a tendency to feel guilt for all kinds of things. True disposition guilt has not received much attention. Normally, the intentional object of guilt is supposed to be a deed or an omission, whereas matters of character have been supposed to lie in the sphere of shame. But this cannot be right in all cases. As pointed out by Patricia Greenspan, one might feel "guilt about not being very bright or ambitious—not having what it takes to succeed in the way that one's parents may have had in mind."[19] While this is an instance of feeling guilty about a character trait that is only subjectively perceived as immoral, I think it is also possible to feel guilt for more objectively immoral character traits. For example, one might feel guilty of not being empathic and sensitive enough to other people's needs, especially in the context of romantic relationships. Of course, such guilt may be triggered by a particular instance where one is insensitive to the loved one's needs, but often the problem arises not so much because of one particular instance, which, taken in isolation, may well be excusable, but because of the underlying tendency to overlook other people's needs. So, when one feels guilty, their guilt can track this general insensitivity. All these cases of character-focused guilt are present-focused insofar as they are directed at one's current character flaws. And all these cases are cases of guilt because they are focused on the character flaws insofar as through having those flaws one perceives oneself as letting another person down. Especially in the context of special relationships like familial and romantic ones, where we are taken to owe more to our loved ones than for mere strangers, it is perfectly conceivable that one might feel guilty for one's character flaws. This is not to deny that one might feel shame as well. While it is beyond the scope of the current chapter to explain how guilt differs from shame, the least that can be said is that the idea that guilt is focused on actions and shame on character is too simplistic to make sense of disposition guilt.

Last but not least, a few words about the special relationship that the above-mentioned cases of omission- and disposition-guilt have with present-focused guilt. While I do not think that cases of action guilt have a privileged relationship with present-focused guilt (as said, as soon as the deed is done, present-focused guilt will automatically turn into past-focused guilt), I do think that omission- and disposition-guilt are bound to be the strongest in the present-focused form. Given the nature of omissions and dispositions as something more automatic and enduring than actions, it usually takes conscious will and effort to get over them. Thus, by the time they cease to exist, the person must have done something to remedy the problem and guilt is unlikely to be as intense as before. (Though one may still, of course, continue to feel guilty that it took her so long to change the situation.) In case of actions, however, the matter is different. The fact that an action—take theft, for instance—is over and done with makes the situation in no way better. Once the action is completed, there is no inherent compensation involved in ceasing to do the thing.

Ironically, while the special tie with the present is something that makes omission- and disposition guilt unique and interesting, it might well be one of the reasons they have not received that much attention. The fact that they are likely to fade after the omission or disposition has been left behind, combined with the fact that their enduring nature makes them lack the pointed drama that is characteristic of immoral actions, may well render them more invisible.

All in all, I hope to have shown that present-focused guilt is more common than one might initially think and that it would be a mistake to overlook this important form of guilt. Omissions and dispositions are just as important as acts, and focusing on the special kind of guilt that can be attached to them can expand our understanding of the phenomenology of guilt. It helps us see that guilt need not always involve a tragic sense of irreversibility but can also manifest itself in a more constant kind of nagging awareness that one is in the wrong as long as they do not do anything about the matter.

FUTURE-FOCUSED GUILT

While present- and future-focused cases stand apart from past-focused instances of guilt insofar as they necessarily require a knowing tension between caring about morality and knowingly acting against it, there is still some continuity between past-focused guilt and present-focused guilt. Both are reactions to states of affairs that have become real.[20] For this reason, future-focused guilt might be somewhat harder to imagine than present-focused guilt. After all, nothing has happened yet. Unless deluded or self-deceived, a person cannot seriously believe that they *are* already guilty (at least not guilty of the imagined future misdeed). So how could they *feel* guilt if they do not believe that they *are* guilty? The current section is aimed at clearing all such doubts. I want to show that future-focused instances of guilt do indeed exist and are correctly described as future-focused. I begin with remarks about the temporal orientation of emotions in general. Then, I will show that there is nothing in the evaluation, action tendencies, and phenomenology of guilt that would prevent it from being directed toward the future. Last, I will also tackle reductionist strategies to explain future-focused episodes of guilt away as more familiar forms of past- and present-focused guilt.

To begin with, let us clear some ground about the temporal orientation of emotions in general. More specifically, I want to highlight that it is not a matter of some higher necessity that emotion types must have a restricted temporal orientation. This might not seem obvious, as there is a long tradition of differentiating between the so-called backward- and forward-looking emotion types.[21] Backward-looking emotions like joy and sadness have been considered to be directed at past and present objects that have become real, while forward-looking emotions like hope and fear have been considered to be focused on potential future states of affairs.[22] But, as it has been well shown by Robert M. Gordon, the criterion that differentiates between the emotion types that are meant to be captured by those categories seems to be better described in terms of their relationship with perceived certainty rather than tense. According to him, traditionally backward-looking emotions like joy and sadness are reactions to states of affairs that one takes as certain, and traditionally forward-looking emotions like hope and fear are oriented toward things that we are uncertain about.[23] What supports this idea is that we can imagine a number of counterexamples that fulfill the requirement of perceived certainty/uncertainty but do not fulfill the requirement of tense. On the one hand, we can imagine cases where the so-called forward-looking emotions are focused on the past. In a situation where one has been in the dark about when a certain train arrived, it is intelligible that one might be afraid or hopeful that the train arrived late.[24] Similarly, one might hope that they passed an exam yesterday, especially given that the professor has already determined the result but one is not yet aware of it.[25] On the other hand, and more importantly for the current context, we can imagine cases where the so-called backward-looking emotions are focused on the future. A conductor who knows in advance that the train will arrive late may feel joy or sadness because this might relate to avoiding congestion at the terminal.[26] Moreover, it has also been suggested that a mother can already be sad and grieve over a future loss of her son when he is sentenced to death,[27] and that one might regret soon having to notify a mother about the death of her son.[28] What unites all those cases is that one is convinced of the occurrence of the future state of affairs.

I think that Gordonian cases have a great intuitive appeal. His theory is also attractive in the sense that while accommodating more cases, it helps us see why the categorization in terms of temporal orientation might have arisen in the first place—because we are more uncertain about the future and we tend to know much more about the past and the present. But even if one is not immediately convinced by all the above-mentioned examples (e.g., those of regret and grief), the cases of joy and sadness are sufficient to erode the general claim that all emotions are neatly tied to only some temporal dimensions and not the others. It is a common thing that people are sad about future states of affairs. They might be sad that they will not be able to make it to some important future event, or that their favorite TV series will end with the ongoing season, or that they will have to go to work on Monday again, and so on.[29] Furthermore, the comparison with sadness is especially relevant for the consideration of guilt, because if there is some truth to the division that is supposed to be captured by the categories of backward- and forward-looking emotions, then guilt would surely belong in the same category as sadness rather than fear. After all, when feeling guilt, one is not hesitant about the occurrence of the deed—like one would have to be in case of hope or fear. My challenge to those who are skeptical about the possibility of future-focused guilt (or those of grief and regret as well, if they wish) is thus the following: What is it that makes guilt so different from sadness, so that one can be future-focused and the other cannot?

As there are no general reasons that would require all emotion types to be temporally restricted, it seems that if there are indeed any reasons why some emotion types are so, they would have to lie in the particular shape of the emotion type in question.[30] In most part, I will talk about the shape of guilt in terms of its distinctive evaluation. Later, however, I will also turn to its action tendencies and phenomenological feel.

Compared to sadness, guilt involves a more narrow evaluation. While sadness involves a general kind of negative evaluation, guilt involves a more specific, moral kind of negative evaluation that can only be extended to our own moral failures. Does that somehow prevent guilt from being directed at future states of affairs? The short answer is "no." Inspired by Gordonian cases, what seems crucial is the fact that one believes in the occurrence of the future state of affairs that would constitute the intentional object of guilt. And there is no reason why one could not have such a belief. As already shown earlier, in cases of pluralism, one may well know in advance that they will sacrifice something of moral value.[31] Thus, it is also possible to feel future-focused guilt. Tragic dilemmas, where any course of action is taken to come at a grave moral cost, provide us with especially intense episodes of future-focused guilt. Imagine a fictionalized version of Abraham, who has to either sacrifice his son Isaac or disobey God, who demands this sacrifice.[32] Insofar as he has made up his mind about going through with the sacrifice (perhaps already the night before), he might well feel future-focused guilt because he sincerely believes that he will lay a knife on his son. In fact, even if trust in God should have assured him that the sacrifice was for the best, it seems likely enough that one of the reasons why the situation was so hard was precisely the fact that there were also some future-focused guilt feelings for betraying his son that were hard to suppress.

Of course, some readers might be skeptical about whether Abraham, or really any of the people confronted with a tragic dilemma where they are forced to choose between one of the two evils through no fault of their own, *should* indeed feel guilt. This is a debatable theoretical claim the discussion of which falls beyond the scope of the current chapter. What I am currently concerned with is simply whether people *can* and *do* feel such guilt. As such, I am not making a claim about the appropriateness of future-focused guilt but only about its possibility. What matters for the possibility of such guilt is not whether there is any moral wrong from an objective normative standpoint (though there may well be), but merely whether the person subjectively believes that there is a moral wrong. And there are plenty of people, moral philosophers included, who do believe so.[33] However, for those whose personal moral beliefs make it hard to empathize with people involved in tragic dilemmas, I would suggest thinking of cases that involve a conflict between moral and non-moral values. Here are a few examples where morality could be construed as competing with selfish concerns. For instance, one can feel guilty for soon ending a relationship, knowing that this will cause great pain to one's partner, who has done nothing wrong. Or imagine a fictionalized version of Gauguin, who has made up his mind about leaving his family and moving to Tahiti in order to become a great artist.[34]

Admittedly, cases of future-focused guilt are less common than cases of retrospective guilt. They are also less common than future-focused forms of sadness. This might explain why we are not used to talking about future-focused guilt but the relative rarity is not a good enough reason to deny that future-focused guilt is a real phenomenon. Another reason the talk about future-focused guilt may sound weird is that "guilt" can stand for two different things—the objective state of *being* guilty and the subjective *emotion* of guilt. Being objectively guilty means that the person is morally at fault, and, as such, it does require that a wrongdoing has taken place. But it is important to note that guilt as an emotion does not require that one believe that one *is already* objectively guilty—just like sadness does not require that one believe that something sad *has already* happened. It only requires that one believes in the occurrence of some misdeed that they were/are/will be guilty of. What is important is the evaluation of the believed deed as immoral—as something for which the person would bear objective guilt.

So far, I have dispelled doubts about whether the specific evaluation at the heart of guilt might prevent it from being directed toward future states of affairs. But one might wonder whether the allegedly future-focused cases of guilt are also sufficiently similar to retrospective cases with respect to the other two central elements of emotions—their action tendency and phenomenological feel. Concerning the action tendency, it may seem nonsensical to talk about *compensating* for a wrong before it has been committed, or about *restoring* a relationship before it has been damaged. Yet, once we frame the action tendency in more general terms—as a motivation to strive toward a certain moral balance and to maintain good relationships—then it appears that it can make sense to take steps toward those goals before the misdeed. For example, even though Gauguin would still go on and abandon his family because his concern for his family is not the one that triumphs in his overall motivational framework, he could nevertheless leave some money to them in order to ease his conscience. And Abraham may take extra steps before the sacrifice to be as good and kind to his son as possible. Moreover, it should not be forgotten that ultimately we are just talking about an action *tendency*, so even if Abraham was to be separated from his son before the sacrifice and there would be nothing that he could *actually* do, the tendency would still be there.

Still, what about the feeling component and its distinctive phenomenology? Is it not bound to differ depending on whether emotion is felt before or after the misdeed? While I do agree that there is a difference, I think it boils down to variations in intensity and inessential details. To begin with, it is worth noting that the exact phenomenology of guilt is bound to differ from person to person and time to time anyway. The question is whether the difference between past- and future-focused guilt is big enough to warrant the conclusion that we are facing different emotion types. For instance, there is also a difference in pre- and post-fact sadness, yet we still label both as instances of sadness. Of course, it is no wonder that once we have actually done something, we are likely to represent it more vividly, but this has an impact only on the intensity of the feeling, not on its basic shape. The basic shape of the feeling is closely tied to the evaluative component and action tendency. The evaluation at the heart of guilt is mirrored in the particular way that one is pained by being involved in a moral wrong, with a feeling of tension arising from the fact that one is at odds with one's conscience. And the action tendency is mirrored in the felt readiness to do something about the matter so as to relieve the tension. Given that past- and future-focused guilt share the same basic evaluation and action tendency, there is no reason to expect a radical divergence at the phenomenological level. At least, the burden is on my opponent to argue that there are such reasons.

In fact, while earlier I showed that some *present*-focused forms of guilt can have a very different phenomenology compared to classic cases of past-focused guilt, it seems that *future*-focused guilt is actually rather similar to past-focused guilt. Since both are characteristically focused on actions, they are both more pointed than those forms of present-focused guilt that we might feel for long-lasting moral failures like omissions, which tend to elicit a more diluted form of guilt.

Of course, there are details that are missing in case of future-focused guilt. For instance, there is no tragic sense of the irreversibility of lived time. Yet, once we take a closer look, it becomes evident that the added sense of tragedy can be accounted by other means. It can also derive from being trapped in circumstances that do not allow us to uphold all our loyalties and to translate all our values into action. But regardless of whether we are talking about the irreversibility of time or the inevitability of the circumstances, we are dealing with something that cannot be changed. This highlights the fact that guilt is an emotion of perceived certainty.

In addition to helping to put the tragic aspect into perspective, there is also one other aspect of guilt that comparison with future-focused guilt helps to clarify in more general terms. Before giving it a label, let me first explain how this aspect is supposed to manifest itself in the case of past-focused guilt. When talking about guilt as an essentially retrospective emotion, Steinbock says that guilt would be possible even if we imagined an abnormal experience of time where there would be no sense of future, adding that "an overwhelming sense of guilt might itself close down the future."[35] While Steinbock denies that guilt could take place in the opposite case when all past were lost, I hope that my defense of future-focused guilt helps us see that this need not be the case. For Abraham, all his existence might be overshadowed by the sacrifice that he believes waits ahead. There is a sense in which the past might well cease to exist for him because he only lives toward the horrible event of laying a knife on his most beloved son. The more general feature that such all-absorbing past- and future-focused episodes seem to highlight is the gravitating force of the intentional object. To some extent, this is a feature of all emotions, but there is also something special about negative emotions. It tends to be easier to get trapped in them. They can absorb all our attention and not let us go—at least unless we do something about the state of affairs at which they are directed. Positive emotions, however, can have a freeing potential. They can alert us that everything is good, and let us move on with our lives and direct our attention elsewhere.

So, what concerns phenomenological characterizations of guilt that involve a reference to time-specific elements like painful awareness of the irreversibility of lived time or guilt's potential to close down the future, then these should be considered as inessential details that reflect only one possible way how some more general feature may manifest itself. While interesting on their own, they should not make us blind to other, equally interesting, forms that guilt might take.

Still, there have been doubts about whether allegedly future-focused cases are indeed correctly described as truly future-focused. It might seem tempting to explain them away as special cases of past- or present-focused guilt. While I think that the very idea of opting for this kind of strategy is somewhat question-begging if one cannot first point out a more general reason why guilt could not be future-focused, I will nevertheless take a closer look at two types of reductionist challenges. The first reduces future-focused guilt to what I call simulation guilt, and the second aims to re-describe the intentional object as something that is located in the present—be it in the form of one's current character or just a mere intention.

According to the first strategy, the seemingly future-focused episodes of guilt are cases of simulation guilt—we just simulate the future scenario in our mind and come to feel past- or present-focused guilt within this imagined scenario. Thus, if Abraham feels guilt for the future sacrifice, this would be so because he imagines that the sacrifice had already taken place. But simulation seems to be neither necessary not sufficient. First, while I do not want to deny that, in many cases, simulation can play an important role in triggering future-focused guilt, it could be argued that it is not necessary because the painfulness of the event may well keep the person from visualizing it too vividly, or indeed from imagining it at all. It might simply be too painful for Abraham to engage in this kind of simulation. But even if this was not the case, simulation alone could hardly be sufficient to account for the intensity and persistence of Abraham's guilt. Simulation guilt could be felt even if one had no intentions of actually doing something. Abraham, however, is not just conducting a thought experiment; he is involved in a real-life situation where he sincerely believes that he will end up sacrificing his son. This is why he is weighed down by the burden of guilt even when he is not currently simulating the future scenario.

The second strategy consists in saying that seemingly future-focused episodes of guilt are actually disguised cases of present-focused guilt—what one is actually feeling guilty about is not the future action but something that already exists in the present. This line of thought has been pursued by Anthony J. Steinbock, who insists that guilt can only be felt about accomplishments that have already taken place.[36] More specifically, he argues that what is crucial is that the thought about the future event be aligned with whom I experience myself "to be": "I am this person who cheats or who will steal (without ever having done such and such before). I experience it as possible for me."[37] This sounds like an instance of present-focused character guilt, the possibility of which was defended in the previous section. However, it might be doubted whether the person must necessarily view himself as having a corrupt character. Abraham, who is involved in a tragic dilemma, does not seem to be suffering from any serious character flaw.[38] But Steinbock's strategy would work equally well if we substituted character with intention. Abraham might think that the very intention to sacrifice his son already implies that in his mind he has betrayed him. So, even though nothing has happened on the physical plane, there is nevertheless a relational harm at the attitudinal level.[39]

Regardless of whether we reduce the matter to character or intention, it is not my wish to deny that one could feel guilt about those as well. All I want to show is that there must be more at stake. Unfortunately, this is not that easy to do because a strong intention to commit a future deed (a precondition of present-focused guilt) and the belief that one will commit the future deed (a precondition of future-focused guilt) seem to go hand in hand.[40] If one intends to do something, he believes that he will do so. Otherwise, he simply intends to try (and believes that he will try). Perhaps if someone was told by a fortune-teller that he will commit a heinous crime, he might already feel guilty about it even though there is no intention present yet (given that he believes the fortune-teller, of course). But since this is such a rare and exotic case, I suspect that people might have very different intuitions about it, and thought experiments of the sort would not help us settle the matter.

Thus, we have to disentangle future-focused guilt and intention guilt in some other way. The best way to do so is by appealing to a retrospective case where the intention did not result in an actual deed. Only then can we be sure that we have isolated a pure form of intention guilt, that could in no way be mixed with action guilt. So, let us imagine a scenario where eventually Abraham receives a message from God that he does not have to sacrifice his son after all, and the sacrifice does not go through (as in the original story). In this scenario, he might still feel guilty that he intended to sacrifice his son. Yet, at least assuming that Abraham acknowledged the possibility of moral luck,[41] this kind of pure intention guilt pales in comparison with the intense sense of guilt that Abraham experiences before the sacrifice. So, one for sure, mere intention guilt cannot be sufficient to account for Abraham's heavy conscience. Moreover, based on the intensity, his guilt feelings are much closer to the scenario where he has indeed sacrificed the son. So, the best explanation is that in addition to feeling guilt about the mere intention, he is already feeling guilt about the believed sacrifice as well.

One might try to block this line of thought by saying that past-focused intention guilt is not an apt ground to make conclusions about the intensity of present-focused guilt. First, it might be objected that past-focused intention guilt is bound to be smaller because one has already given up the intention, and this somehow compensates the matters. In many cases, this would be a good ground for feeling less guilt because it would indicate a change of heart. But it is important to note that in this particular case, there is no change of heart on Abraham's part. Would the occasion arise where he had to sacrifice the boy again, he would be willing to do so.

Secondly, one might try to appeal to the fact that, all other things considered equal, emotions are bound to be the strongest when their intentional object is immediately present, and to fade as the state of affairs comes to pass. I have no intentions of disputing that claim. But it should be noted that this is a matter of a more gradual shift. Yet, the shift from the guilt feelings that Abraham feels before the believed sacrifice to the mere intention guilt that he might feel afterward is more abrupt. At one moment he is burdened by an unbearably heavy conscience, and soon after, all that is left is mere retrospective intention guilt.

As we are talking about small distances in time, there is no reason to expect a big difference between the intensity of present- and past-focused intention guilt. If something is immoral, then it is equally immoral regardless of whether it belongs to the past or the present. And given that one realizes its immorality and cares about the matter, their guilt feelings should be similarly intense in both cases. Let us think about the guilt that one might feel for something other than the mental act of intention—for instance, for the physical act of theft. I doubt that anyone would want to say that a scrupulous thief would automatically feel less guilt just because the theft is over and they are currently not committing it anymore.[42] But this is exactly the type of claim that one would make when they appealed to the idea that present intention is likely to elicit more guilt than past intention. If it does indeed seem to elicit more guilt, then this is precisely because one feels guilt not just about the present intention but also about the future deed that he is intending.

On top of that, it could also be argued that locating the intentional object of Abraham's guilt feelings in the present intention is a suspicious theoretical move that misrepresents the phenomenology of the case. Abraham's attention is not so much directed toward his own mental state of intending to sacrifice his son, it is more directly focused on the believed sacrifice itself. In other words, his guilt is not characterized by the thought, "Oh no, what an awful intention I have!" It is characterized by the thought, "Oh no, what an awful thing I am going to do!"

For all the above-mentioned reasons, the reductionist strategy will ultimately fail. At best, it shows that there must be something already present in the person that implicates them in the future event—be it in the form of character or intentions. But this is not a sufficient reason to exclude a truly future-focused element—especially given that without this added element it is hard to make sense of the intensity of one's guilt feelings before the misdeed.[43]

Given my positive defense and the refutation of reductionist challenges, I take myself to have introduced a type of guilt that has gone unnoticed in philosophical reflection. Last but not least, I would also like to add that it is important to acknowledge the possibility of future-focused guilt because it reveals an important blind spot in our current conceptual distinctions. Namely, there is a tendency to differentiate between retrospective and anticipatory guilt.[44] But when people talk about anticipatory guilt, what they usually have in mind is just what I have called simulation guilt. Simulation guilt, however, is only extrinsically connected to the future in that we simply happen to locate the simulated scenario in the future. We could also locate it in the present of some alternative reality, but the temporal location would not change the content of the simulation and the fact that within the simulation we nevertheless come to feel retrospective guilt. Retrospective guilt, however, is not labeled as retrospective by an extrinsic criterion. We do not call it retrospective because we imagine ourselves into the past and then, while re-experiencing this past as present, come to feel guilt. We call it retrospective because the inner structure of the emotion token itself is focused on the past, i.e., the intentional object of the emotion is perceived as belonging to the past with respect to the phenomenal "now." Thus, the distinction ends up being rather misleading because the criterion based on which the emotion is labelled as retrospective or anticipatory shifts from internal to external. My suggestion is that we would be better off contrasting between past-, present-, and future-focused guilt, and should consider simulation-guilt as belonging to a somewhat different category.

CONCLUSION

The aim of this chapter was to challenge the idea that guilt is an exclusively retrospective emotion and to expand our understanding of guilt by defending the existence of present- and future-focused episodes of guilt, and illuminating their unique phenomenology.

As I have shown, the emotional episodes involving these kinds of guilt are unique in that they must involve a peculiar kind of tension between caring about and nevertheless acting, or intending to act, against it. While this tension does not render present- and future-focused guilt impossible, it often creates a fragile balance that may easily dissolve into rationalizing the action or giving it up. Yet, as I have argued, there are circumstances like weakness of will and cases of value pluralism that allow us to imagine present- and future-focused guilt in more stable forms as well.

My main point about present-focused guilt, the existence of which is perhaps somewhat less controversial than the existence of future-focused guilt, was that it has been unfairly overlooked in philosophical literature and that there are indeed some special forms of guilt among omission- and disposition-guilt that are bound to be the strongest only in the present-focused form. In particular, guilt for long-lasting omissions that are due to the weakness of will is unique in that its phenomenology can be very different from standard cases of retrospective guilt. It need not involve any tragic sense of irreversibility but may instead manifest itself in a more constant kind of nagging awareness that one is in the wrong unless he does something about the situation.

My main point about future-focused guilt was that it is perfectly conceivable in special circumstances like tragic dilemmas and other cases of value pluralism where one is torn by different competing values and loyalties and sincerely believes that he will betray one of them. Since future-focused guilt shares the same core evaluation, action tendency and characteristic feel with more familiar cases of past- and present-focused guilt, there is no good reason to deny it the status of true guilt. And reductionist attempts to write it off as something else fail to do justice to the intensity and persistence of the emotion. From a phenomenological aspect, it is also interesting to note that differently from more diluted forms of present-focused guilt, future-focused guilt is rather similar to classic instances of retrospective guilt. It shares the same pointed character and the potential to absorb one's attention to the extent that it may close down all other temporal dimensions. Yet it also helps us see that the added sense of tragedy that is usually accounted by the irreversibility of lived time may also be due to being trapped in unfavorable circumstances, from which there is no good way out. But whether one's caught in the web of time or circumstances does not make a substantial difference. At bottom, both options highlight that the misdeed is perceived as certain. And this is so regardless of whether it belongs to the past, the present, or the future.

NOTES

1. Here are some examples: "[G]uilt is concerned with a deed which has violated certain norms" (Ben-Ze'ev 2001: 498); "[T]he core relational theme for guilt is something like: someone I am concerned about has been harmed and I have responsibility for that in virtue of what I have done or failed to do" (Prinz & Nichols 2010: 134); "The person feeling guilt believes that she has done something forbidden and that in doing what is forbidden she has disfigured and so harmed herself" (Taylor 1985: 103).

2. For example, Martin Buber characterizes guilt as accompanied by an existential insight into "the irreversibility of lived time" (Buber 1957: 116). Similarly, Karlsson and Sjöberg speak of guilt in relation to "the finite and irrevocable character of life" (Karlsson & Sjöberg 343).

3. Karlsson & Sjöberg 2009: 339.

4. Karlssön & Sjöberg 2009: 340.

5. See Scheler 1987; Steinbock 2014. See also Camus's novel *The Fall*.

6. While this preference might have an influence on whether we conceive certain guilt episodes as fitting, it will not influence my argument concerning the possibility of present- and future-focused guilt.

7. As such, I will cover the three main elements of emotions that figure in most emotion theories. See, for instance, Scarantino & de Sousa 2018, where they differentiate between three corresponding categories of emotion theories.

8. See more about how guilt might be attached to dispositions from the section "Present-Focused Guilt."

9. See the section "Future-Focused Guilt."

10. As already said in the section "Definitions: Guilt and Temporal Focus," I allow the possibility that guilt may be focused on omissions and dispositions as well. It is only for convenience's sake that I sometimes keep on talking about deeds only.

11. Insofar as I defined guilt in terms of morality, it may seem inconsistent to refer to seemingly non-moral cases like guilt for breaking a diet. But there is no inconsistency here. Even if one does not think that there is a general moral duty to eat healthy, those cases can be viewed as instances of breaking a tacit or explicit promise to oneself. Through promises, all kinds of non-moral failures can become morally relevant because they involve letting oneself, or other people, down. As such, I oppose Velleman (2003).

12. Of course, there is also a more general kind of tension between being absorbed in some activity and taking a self-reflective stance at the same time. In that sense, even pride can be somewhat disruptive. Yet the tension is of different kind and much greater in case of emotions that involve negative self-evaluation.

13. Taylor 1985: 135.

14. These comments are not meant as general claims about all cases of retrospective guilt but only about those particularly common cases where one either did not realize the full gravity of the wrong before or simply did not care as much as they care now.

15. While some think that breaking a diet is an instance of nonmoral guilt, it could be argued that it involves letting oneself down and is thus akin to breaking a promise to oneself. Many things that are nonmoral matters may become moral through promises.

16. In addition, it could also be argued that one can feel present-focused guilt for more general states like that of being alive, as in case of survivor guilt, but since this is a controversial topic on its own and has already received a lot of attention, it will have to stay beyond the scope of the current chapter.

17. There is a substantial debate on killing and letting die. For example, see Singer 1972.

18. Karlsson & Sjöberg 2009: 343.

19. Greenspan 1995: 160.

20. On the reality aspect, see Graver 2008: 55.

21. More specifically, the distinction between backward- and forward-looking emotions is part of a long-standing tradition that differentiates between four principal emotions, which could roughly be labeled as joy, sadness, hope, and fear, and holds that all other emotions are subspecies of these four. While this classification is perhaps not so common in contemporary emotion research, it can be traced back to Ancient Greek and Roman philosophy, especially the Stoics, and it continued to be popular during medieval times and Renaissance (Fieser 1992).

22. See Gordon 1987: 25. The reality aspect, as already mentioned, is taken from Graver 2008: 55.

23. See Gordon 1987: 25–27. To be exact, Gordon requires something stronger than perceived certainty. He also insists that one must actually *know* that something will be the case, i.e., they must *get the facts right*. While this might be relevant to how we sometimes construct more complex sentences like "Romeo was sad that Julia is dead," this has little relevance from the viewpoint of emotion theory, because from the subjective point of view (which emotions essentially reflect), Romeo is nevertheless sad about Julia's death. (For a similar point and further references, see Salmela 2014: 109n5.)

24. Gordon 1987: 26.

25. Schumacher 2003: 69.

26. Gordon 1987: 25–26.

27. Lyons 1985: 89.

28. Landman 1993: 52.

29. Perhaps one might try to say that it is actually just the present belief in the future event that our attention is directed to, and that those examples should thus be considered as present-focused. But this would be to confuse the intentional object of an emotion with its cause. While a belief may indeed trigger the emotion, a person who is sad about the fact that she has to go to work on Monday is not just sad about having a certain belief. If that was the case, she should have to welcome the prospect of having her beliefs changed by some advanced piece of technology that would be

capable of such thing. But she does not just wish that she would have different beliefs; what she really wishes is that actually, too, she would not have to go to work so soon. She is concerned about the content of the beliefs, not the mere fact of having the beliefs.

30. I take the notion of *shape* from D'Arms and Jacobson 2000.

31. See the section "A Peculiar Tension."

32. There are also other similar cases related sacrificing one's child. For instance, see Nussbaum's discussion of Agamemnon and Iphigenia (2001: 32ff).

33. See Tessman 2017; Hursthouse 1999; Nussbaum 2001.

34. For the sake of the argument, let us assume that he does not take it as his moral duty to develop his talents and become a good artist.

35. Steinbock 2014: 105.

36. Steinbock 2014: 105. He restates this claim in several different ways but unfortunately I was not able to detect that he would have given any further argument to why this must be the case.

37. Steinbock 2014: 104.

38. At least his involvement in this particular dilemma does not suggest one. Whether he might have had any character flaws in general is not under question here.

39. See Smith 2011 on guilty thoughts and relational harm.

40. At least when we talk about intention in a strong sense, which is the sense that allows us to state the reductionist argument in its strongest form.

41. There would be no difference in the intensity of his guilt feelings if he believed that only our mental states are of moral value, and the fact that they fail to translate into action because of some external factors (like God calling the sacrifice off) has no moral significance whatsoever. But there is no reason why we should attribute such views to him. For many people, it would indeed make a huge moral difference whether the boy lives or dies (see Nagel 1979). So, let us assume for the sake of the argument that it does make a moral difference to him as well.

42. Of course, as time passes, all emotions may eventually fade. But I am not talking about so long distances here. The case that is ultimately in question is Abraham's first scenario where the sacrifice is called off, and Abraham may still continue to feel guilt about having intended to go through with it.

43. Of course, a true reductionist might just deny my assumption that the guilt that Abraham feels before the believed sacrifice is bigger than the intention-guilt that he would feel after the sacrifice was called off. They might try to say that the intensity of the emotional episode is accounted by other negative emotions like the sadness that Abraham feels about the believed death of his son. This would take us to a point where an intuition goes against an intuition. I have expected that most people would share my intuition about the intensity of Abraham's guilt before the sacrifice. But for those who do not I would like to emphasize that since future-focused guilt is always bound to be accompanied by something immoral that is already present, reductionism is likely take the form of an irrefutable dogma. Whatever one said, the reductionist could still keep on insisting that ultimately it must all come down to past- or present-focused guilt. Stating irrefutable dogmas has little argumentative merit, though. So, rather than merely insisting that future-focused guilt is reducible to something else, the reductionist would do better to motivate his insistence by stating a clear argument

to why it is that we should exclude the possibility of future-focused guilt. By appealing to the evaluation, action tendency, and phenomenological feel, I have already stated several reasons to prove the contrary. Now, the burden of proof is on my opponent to show me wrong.

44. Most notably, this distinction has been employed by Patricia Greenspan, who gives anticipatory guilt an important role in moral development. She argues that the motivational force of the moral "ought" rests in part on the tendency to generate this kind of guilt (Greenspan 1995: 67). She does not give a very specific outline of the inner structure of anticipatory guilt but based on the function she gives to it, it seems evident that she must be talking about simulation guilt. Simulating potential future scenarios can easily make us feel guilt and revise our actions. But those more stable forms of truly future-focused guilt that I have been talking about are not likely to prompt a change because they require that the agent is already pretty firmly settled on committing the wrong.

REFERENCES

Ben-Ze'ev, A. 2001. *The subtlety of emotions*. MIT Press.
Buber, M. 1957. Guilt and guilt feelings. *Psychiatry, 20*(2), 114.
d'Arms, J., & Jacobson, D. 2000. The moralistic fallacy: On the "appropriateness" of emotions. *Philosophy and Phenomenological Research, 61*(1), 65–90.
Dill, B, & Darwall, S. 2014. Moral psychology as accountability. In: D'Arms, J. & Jacobsen, D. (eds), *Moral psychology and human agency*. Oxford University Press.
Fieser, J. 1992. Hume's classification of the passions and its precursors. *Hume Studies 18*(1): 1–17.
Gordon, R. M. 1987. *The structure of emotions: Investigations in cognitive philosophy*. Cambridge University Press.
Graver, M. R. 2008. *Stoicism and emotion*. University of Chicago Press.
Greenspan, P. S. 1995. *Practical guilt: Moral dilemmas, emotions, and social norms*. Oxford University Press.
Hursthouse, R. 1999. *On virtue ethics*. Oxford University Press.
Karlsson, G., and Sjöberg, L. G. 2009. The experiences of guilt and shame: A phenomenological-psychological study. *Human Studies 32*(3): 335.
Landman, J. 1993. *Regret: The persistence of the possible*. Oxford University Press.
Lyons, W. 1985. *Emotion*. Cambridge University Press.
Morris, H. 1987. Nonmoral guilt. In: Shoeman, F. (ed), *Responsibility, character, and the emotions* (220–49). Cambridge University Press.
Nagel, T. 1979. Moral luck. In: *Mortal questions*. Cambridge University Press, 24–38.
Nussbaum, M. C. 2001. *The fragility of goodness: Luck and ethics in Greek tragedy and philosophy*. Cambridge University Press.
Prinz, J., and Shaun Nichols. 2010. Moral emotions. In: *The moral psychology handbook*. Oxford University Press.
Salmela, M. 2014. *True emotions* (Vol. 9). John Benjamins Publishing Company.

Scarantino, Andrea and de Sousa, Ronald. Emotion. *The Stanford encyclopedia of philosophy* (Winter 2018 Edition), Edward N. Zalta (ed.), https://plato.stanford.edu/archives/win2018/entries/emotion/.

Scheler, M. 1987. Repentance and rebirth. In: *Person and self-value* (pp. 87-124). Springer, Dordrecht.

Schumacher, B. N. 2003. A philosophy of hope: Josef Pieper and the contemporary debate on hope. Fordham University Press.

Singer, P. 1972. Famine, affluence, and morality. Philosophy & Public Affairs, 229–43.

Smith, A. 2011. Guilty thoughts. In: Bagnoli, C. (ed), *Morality and the emotions.* (pp. 235–56). Oxford University Press.

Steinbock, A. J. 2014. *Moral emotions: Reclaiming the evidence of the heart.* Northwestern University Press.

Taylor, G. 1985. *Pride, shame, and guilt: Emotions of self-assessment.* Clarendon Press.

Tessman, L. 2017. *When doing the right thing is impossible.* Oxford University Press.

Velleman, J. D. 2003. Don't worry, feel guilty. *Royal Institute of Philosophy Supplements, 52,* 235–48.

Chapter 5

Anticipatory Guilt

Alison Duncan Kerr

Sometimes we feel an emotion about an event that is happening right now—I feel fear when I encounter a mountain lion while I am hiking. Sometimes we feel an emotion about an event that happened in the past—I feel embarrassed when I think back to the time I asked a new colleague an awkward question at a dinner party. At other times, we feel an emotion when we *anticipate* how we might feel in response to a possible event in the future—I feel guilt when I consider whether I should fib to my parents. Most emotion research considers present-time emotions (e.g., my fear example), some focus on retrospective emotions (e.g., my embarrassment example), but few consider future emotions (e.g., my guilt example). This distinction between present-time, retrospective, and anticipatory emotions is about the *object* of the emotion (i.e., what the emotion is about)—not *when* the emotion is felt. Guilt, in particular, is most often considered retrospectively—more often than not, we think about instances of guilt concerning something from the past.[1] Because backward-looking guilt typically receives more attention, examining it as a case for forward-looking emotions could shed new light on guilt. There are more unexplored issues to investigate.

In §1 through §3, I discuss the nature of guilt and present different ways to understand guilt. In §4 I focus on traditional ways to assess emotions in general, and guilt in particular, along various dimensions. In §5, I present a worry for how to make sense of anticipatory guilt according to the traditional assessments, and motivate another problem about anticipatory guilt—namely empirical findings that we systematically *overestimate* how much guilt we would feel in a given situation. Finally, in §6, I argue that despite the empirical results on overestimation, anticipatory guilt is not irrational.

FORWARD AND BACKWARD GUILT

My twelve-year-old Portuguese Water Dog, Xeno, has had severe arthritis for some time now. The veterinarian has tried various methods to help Xeno, but unfortunately, at this point, it has been getting worse. He seems to be in severe pain. Xeno can barely get down the back steps to do his business in the back garden, and so his accidents in the house are getting to be more frequent. The pain medications no longer seem to be improving his quality of life. And Xeno no longer goes upstairs to play with the children in their bedrooms, which used to be a favourite pastime of his. After a conversation with Xeno's veterinarian, I consider having Xeno euthanized (a veterinarian injects him with a fatal cocktail intended to end his life). Suddenly, in light of imagining the scenario where I decide to have Xeno euthanized, I am overwhelmed by the feeling of guilt. (It is not merely *imagining* the possibility of putting Xeno down that is worthy of guilt—I think that it is reasonable to consider this option. So, I do not feel guilt about *considering* the option of putting Xeno down.) I am imagining how I will feel *after* I put Xeno down. As I deliberate about making this decision, I feel a bout of *anticipatory* guilt.

Consider another example. This one is a classic and extensively discussed example, with written concerning arguments that would take us far astray from the topic at hand, from Donald Davidson about a climber:

> A climber might want to rid himself of the weight and danger of holding another man on a rope, and he might know that by loosening his hold on the rope he could rid himself of the weight and danger. This belief and want might so unnerve him as to cause him to loosen his hold, and yet it might be the case that he never *chose* to loosen his hold, for there will remain the *two* questions *how* the belief and the want caused the second want, and *how* wanting to loosen his hold caused him to loosen his hold.[2]

There are several different ways in which to imagine what is happening with this climber with respect to his emotional response to this situation. It seems that the climber might deliberate about what would happen if he were to loosen his hold on the rope (he would rid himself of the weight and danger of holding on to the other man). In this interpretation, the climber feels anticipatory guilt.

In order to be clear about anticipatory guilt, we need to distinguish it from meta-emotions, fiction-emotions, and the anticipation of an emotion. Some of the literature on these terms is confusing.

First, an *occurrent emotion*, in this literature is sometimes referred to as an immediate emotion[3]; it is one that is experienced or felt at the time in question.

This is just a standard felt emotion in the way we commonly use emotion terms. For example, I feel fear when I see a mountain lion charging me.

Next, there are meta-emotions, which are occurrent emotions about an emotion—the object can be about a past, present, or future emotion. Imagine that I feel fear about giving an important talk in front of the principal of the university. I know when I feel fear about giving a talk, I tend to stumble through my talk. When I notice that I feel this bout of fear, I suddenly feel angry about my fear—this is a *meta-emotion*. Similarly, I might be angry that I feel disgusted at the sight of blood (because I had hoped to be a doctor). Or, I might be sad that I feel jealous (because I thought I was more secure in my relationship). A meta-emotion is an emotion whose object is another emotion.

Emotions may be felt toward real or fictional objects. When reading of Romeo drinking the poison, I feel sad. My sadness makes sense, despite the fact that the object of my sadness is not real—Romeo's death is tragic and Shakespeare's writing is compelling. While one might argue that my sadness does not make sense because Romeo is merely a fictional character, my sadness is different from other possible emotional responses. Indeed, other emotions might not make sense toward this fictional case; e.g., it would be unreasonable for me to feel guilt. Similarly, shame or envy would not make sense in light of Romeo's death as the object of my occurrent felt emotion. This topic, *fiction-emotions*, arises again below.[4]

At times, we also merely think about emotions without actually feeling them. While sitting by a campfire in the Teton Mountains, I think about how I would feel if I were to encounter a female moose and her calf where the moose fiercely charged me. I reason that fear would be the obvious and appropriate response in that scenario. Imagine that, while sitting by the fire, I do *not* experience or feel this fear as I am imagining the scenario. It merely is a thought that passes through my head: *If a moose charged me, I would feel fear.* This is called an "*anticipated emotion*," and it is *not* an occurrent emotion. Anticipated emotions are discussed in relation to decision-making[5]; they are emotions that one expects (or forecasts) to be felt if a future event occurs.[6]

Examples of anticipated emotions occur when one makes a decision *in order to* feel an emotion. Perhaps I am currently feeling sad, but I want to no longer feel sad and instead, I want to feel amused. I might decide to watch a comedy in order to feel amused. Other cases are harder to imagine, like wanting to feel guilty. Nonetheless, I might imagine that I will feel guilty if I steal my friend's last piece of carefully saved chocolate from her trip to Belgium. It is more plausible that I desire the chocolate and suffer the consequences of feeling guilty than it is that I desire the guilt and suffer the consequences of consuming the chocolate. When I decide to watch a comedy in order to feel amused or in order to avoid feeling sad, this is a case of expected (or anticipated) amusement.[7] Sometimes our decision-making involves the consideration of an anticipated emotion (among many other considerations); other times, the anticipated emotion is of central concern for the decision.[8]

THE NATURE OF GUILT

Guilt is an emotion that has negative valence—it does not feel good to feel guilt; it is unpleasant.[9] In addition, guilt is often thought of as an emotion that concerns the violation of social norms.[10] One feels guilty when one's actions violate a socially designed rule or standard.[11] In addition, the feeling of guilt generally implies a sense of responsibility for some wrongdoing.

Guilt, like other emotions, is associated with action tendencies.[12] When one feels guilt, one has the tendency to be motivated to perform reparative acts.[13] However, studies suggest that there is not a reliable external display of guilt.[14] In general, an agent feels guilt when she realizes that she has done wrong and that she is responsible for that which she has done wrong. For our purposes here, we do not need to go into more detail about the nature of guilt.

CATEGORIZING EMOTIONS

The standard distinction in the literature is between *anticipatory* emotions and *anticipated* emotions.[15] When Maria Miceli and Cristiano Castelfranchi present their extensive account on this distinction, they identify a third possibility as well—two of which they claim are the traditional distinctions (anticipatory and anticipated), and the third is the more novel contribution (anticipated and felt). An anticipatory emotion is "always currently experienced, phenomenologically real affective responses to possible future events that have positive or negative implications for the self."[16] So, an *anticipatory emotion* is one that is occurrent, or genuinely felt, and whose object is some possible future event. In contrast, anticipated emotions, according to Miceli and Castelfranchi, are "mere cognitions about future emotions."[17] So, anticipated emotions contrast with anticipatory emotions in that they are not occurrent emotions. However, Miceli and Castelfranchi and Baumgartner et al. argue that there is the additional relevant possibility of anticipated and felt:

> This joy about a future event is called "Vorfruede" in German and "voorpret" in Dutch (literally pre-joy), and it may be translated as pleasant anticipation. Although this emotion shares some similarities with anticipatory emotions because it is a phenomenologically "real" affective reaction that is experienced in the present, not an affective forecast of some hypothetical future scenario, we would not classify it as an anticipatory emotion in our terminology (at least not as an unambiguous example of anticipatory emotions).[18]

The idea is that one contemplates the future, thinks one will feel a particular emotion in that future scenario, e.g., joy, and one then feels that joy as well (despite the future event not having happened yet).

The terms *anticipatory*, *anticipated*, *anticipate*, *anticipating*, and *anticipation*, and how these can apply to emotions (felt or not), beliefs, and actions, is entirely confusing. Instead of *anticipatory*, I prefer *simulated* because these emotions need not be compelled by an anticipation at all. One could instead just imagine a possible emotion and feel it, but not have any anticipation that this emotion is likely. Similarly, instead of *anticipated*, I prefer *expected*.

Rather than the three categories, suggested by Miceli and Castelfranchi and Baumgartner et al., it is helpful to be able to distinguish between four related possibilities. This is where my suggested change from *anticipatory* to *simulated* and *anticipated* to *expected* helps as well.

1. *Simulated Emotion*: a person P at time t_1 in deliberation contemplates doing action A at a later time t_2 and P *feels* emotion E_1 at t_1 as if P is doing A.[19]

   Emotion E_1 in this definition of a *simulated emotion* is how an anticipatory emotion is understood—it is presently felt—it is an occurrent emotion. A simulated emotion can occur when one is imagining any scenario and feels the emotion that one would feel if that scenario were to obtain. In contrast, an expected emotion need not be occurrent or felt.

2. *Expected Emotion*: a person P at time t_1 in deliberation contemplates doing action A at a later time t_2 and P *thinks* that she will feel emotion E_1 at t_2; emotion E_1 in this scenario is an anticipated emotion—it is not felt, rather it is just thought about.

   When one deliberates about a future scenario, one might produce an expectation (about an emotion) that one would feel in that future scenario. An expected emotion is similar to what theorists call "anticipated emotion."

3. *Expected-and-Felt Emotion*: a person P at time t_1 in deliberation contemplates doing action A at a later time t_2 and P *thinks* that she will feel emotion E_1 at t_2, and then as a result of thinking about these things, P feels E_1 at t_1; emotion E_1 in this scenario is an anticipated and felt emotion—it is felt, but as a consequence of the thought.

   Moreover, expected-and-felt emotions can be understood in two different manners. First, when one deliberates about a future scenario, and one thinks of an emotion one expects that one will feel; then, if one also feels that expected emotion, it is when

3a. the expected emotion matches the felt emotion.

   Consider the following example above: While rubbing my pregnant belly, I think about how I will feel when I first hold my twin girls (expected joy); as I deliberate, I start to feel some of this joy. This contrasts with a different sort of expected emotion. Instead, imagine one deliberates about a future scenario, and one thinks of an emotion one expects that one will feel; then, if one feels a different emotion about that expected emotion, it is when

3b. the expected emotion does not match the felt emotion.

Imagine, again, that I am rubbing my pregnant belly, and I think about how I will feel when I first hold my twin girls (expected joy). As I deliberate about this expected joy, I start to feel overwhelmed with fear (perhaps that I will not get to feel that joy). In what follows, I will be using only *simulated* and *expected* to refer to these emotions.

EMOTION ASSESSMENTS

There are several different standards according to which we can assess the appropriateness of guilt. Even if the terminology differs, emotion theorists commonly assess emotions along three dimensions: fit, warrant, and benefit. I call this collection of assessments the *traditional assessments*.

To begin with, consider *fit*: An agent's emotion is *fitting* in a certain situation if and only if the emotion corresponds to the relevant features of the agent's situation. A fitting emotion is often seen as roughly analogous to a true belief—the emotion has gotten the situation right.[20] For example, when one feels fear, one's fear is fitting if one is in genuine danger. An agent's emotion can fail to be fitting with respect to the *type* of emotion (e.g., an agent feels fear, but the agent is not actually in danger).

An agent's emotion can also fail to be fitting with respect to magnitude.[21] This sort of failure is concerned with the strength or intensity of the emotion. If I feel deeply intense fear (the strength appropriate for being face to face with a hungry wild lion) in response to walking barefoot on a wooden floor prone to giving splinters, my fear would be unfitting with respect to magnitude but would be fitting with respect to type. For example, I am in genuine danger of getting a painful splinter in my foot, but such intense fear does not fit my situation. When I see a snake in my garden in Scotland, a little fear is fitting, but intense fear is not. Similarly, imagine that I lie to a friend about how much money I earn. It was a little lie with the (paternalistic) intention to protect my friend's feelings, but we are normally very honest with one another. Even though there are no real negative consequences of this lie, I still feel guilty that I lied to her—in this case, my guilt is fitting. Now, instead imagine that I feel severe guilt over this little lie told in the passing, despite it having no significant consequences for my life, my friend's life, or our friendship. In this case, while my guilt is fitting with respect to type, it is not fitting with respect to magnitude—a little guilt is fitting, but a severe bout of guilt is not.

Also, note that just because an emotion is fitting, it does not follow that one *ought to* feel the emotion. In the case of guilt, an agent's bout of guilt is fitting if and only if the agent knowingly violates a normative standard such that the agent's actions go against the standard. There are plenty of situations where, all things considered, it would be irrational or nonsensical to feel an emotion even though it is fitting. For example, when one does not know that one is in danger, then it does not make sense to feel fear. Similarly, I might wrong a friend such that it would be fitting to feel guilt; however, if I do not know that I wronged my friend, then it would not make sense for me to feel guilty.[22]

Next, consider warrant: An agent's emotion is *warranted* in a certain situation if and only if the agent has evidence for the fittingness of the emotion. If I feel fear when I turn a corner on a path and see a mountain lion, then my fear is fitting because I am in genuine danger. Instead, imagine that this is a mountain lion taxidermy (one so expertly done that it appears very much alive!), though I do not realize it. In this case, my fear is not fitting (I am not in genuine danger), but it is warranted (from my perspective, I do have good reason to feel fear in this situation). When I intentionally stomp on my friend's foot (and I know that my friend does not deserve any harm) and see her cringe in pain, I have good reason to feel guilt; I have good evidence that I am responsible for my friend's suffering. My guilt is thus warranted. If my friend tricks me into thinking that I successfully stomped on her foot, despite the fact that I neither stomped on her foot nor hurt her, then my guilt would be warranted as well, but it would be unfitting.

According to the third traditional assessment, an agent's emotion is *beneficial* in a certain situation if and only if the emotion contributes to the agent's well-being.[23] Imagine that my guilt concerning my stomping on and hurting my friend's foot causes me immediately after to dote on my friend to make sure that she is okay. My friend recognizes my obvious guilt and my attempts at reparation, and this actually causes our friendship to develop and strengthen. In this scenario, then, in addition to being both fitting and warranted, my fear is beneficial.

Now we are in a position to reconsider an issue about the nature of guilt: whether responsibility really is a necessary condition for feeling guilt. Those theorists who say responsibility is necessary worry about how to account for those who suffer from survivor's guilt or for innocent victims of assault who feel guilty. Some claim that these bouts of guilt are a distinct emotion type—a more "primitive" form of guilt.[24] One worry about this view is that these bouts of guilt tend to be felt by adults who also have non-primitive bouts of guilt—so what would make some bouts primitive while others are not, all within the same mature agent? An explanation of this has not been supplied and is hardly obvious.

Consider that the *Diagnostic and Statistical Manual of Mental Disorders* now considers survivor's guilt to be a symptom of post-traumatic stress disorder (PTSD). Many of the soldiers who participated in war, the people who survived the Holocaust, and people who successfully fought off cancer, have felt guilty that they survived when those they knew and loved did not. These bouts of guilt are understandable to some extent—these people went through experiences that were deeply frightening, exhausting, and devastating. Nonetheless, they did nothing wrong by surviving these harrowing experiences. In other words, their guilt is *not fitting*.

For example, consider Italian chemist, Primo Levi, a Holocaust survivor who published a memoir about his time in Auschwitz.[25] Levi, like many others who feel and discuss survivor's guilt, acknowledges that he has nothing to feel guilty about (with respect to his survival). However, even an awareness of one's innocence does not always rid oneself of the survivor's guilt. People who have PTSD often need medication or therapy to help overcome it. Instead of a "primitive" form of guilt, survivor's guilt or the guilt that one feels as an innocent victim, is an unfitting (but perhaps understandable for other reasons) bout of guilt.

One does not have to feel all the possible emotions that it would be fitting for one to feel (e.g., one has heard a joke too many times and so no longer finds it funny, despite the fact that it is still objectively funny). Sometimes we feel emotions that are neither fitting, nor warranted, nor beneficial, yet it is still understandable that we feel them. In other words, while the emotion is not justified in any way, we can still understand why one felt this way. It is more reasonable to hold that survivor's guilt is just like any other type of guilt, except that it happens to be both unfitting and unwarranted. Accordingly, I do *not* assume that responsibility is a necessary condition for feeling guilt, although it is necessary for guilt to be fitting.

ASSESSMENTS OF SIMULATED GUILT

The traditional assessments (fit, warrant, benefit) are popular and powerful tools for investigating standard bouts of occurrent emotions. However, it is less clear how well they work in less familiar cases. How ought we assess simulated emotions, meta-emotions, and fiction-emotions?

With meta-emotions, the assessments may be understood fairly straightforwardly—the object of the emotion is just slightly different. Imagine that I feel sad that I feel jealous (because I thought I was more secure in my relationship). My jealousy is the object of my sadness. My jealousy is indicative of my insecurity in my relationship, so my sadness is fitting and warranted.

With fiction-emotions, it is more complex. If I feel fear while watching a horror film (e.g., at Hannibal's escape in *Silence of the Lambs*), it might seem that my fear is unfitting because I am not in genuine danger—but my fear is still getting *something* right about the fictional situation. Recall my sadness as I read of Romeo's death seems fitting (Romeo's death is tragic) and warranted (Shakespeare's writing is compelling and helps me to understand the tragedy of Romeo's situation). If instead I felt pride at Romeo's death, that would be unfitting. With regard to fiction-emotions, concerns about magnitude will be particularly relevant. While a death like Romeo's might be worthy of extreme sadness for Juliet or for Romeo's family, it will not be fitting for me to feel such an extreme bout of sadness. We do not need to decide this matter here.[26]

Now consider simulated guilt. There are two situations concerning guilt of a possible future event that are easily confused. On one hand, I might feel guilt as I contemplate making a particular choice and I realize that if I were to make that choice, I would also likely feel guilty about that future time. Simulated guilt usually occurs when (i) a person imagines some situation in which it would be appropriate to feel guilt, and (ii) the person presently feels guilt while imaging the situation. On the other hand, I might contemplate making a particular choice and I feel guilty *just because I am contemplating the choice*. In the former situation, I am feeling guilt and the object of my guilt is the simulated situation. In the latter situation, the object of my guilt is the mere fact that I am contemplating the choice in my decision-making. The former is simulated guilt. The latter is guilt about that fact that I am deliberating about a certain option.

How do we assess simulated guilt? The fittingness conditions for a simulated emotion cannot be the same for the fittingness conditions for a standard occurrent emotion. If it were, then simulated guilt would always be unfitting because the thing for which one would be feeling guilty has not yet occurred. Recall the example with Xeno, my dog. As I deliberate about whether I will bring him to be euthanized, I imagine how I will feel if I were to make that choice, and then I am overwhelmed with simulated guilt. Recall that I do not feel guilty about this deliberation—I think that it is reasonable merely to consider this option. Rather, I feel simulated guilt as I imagine a scenario where I chose to have Xeno euthanized. I have not carried out any actions, so I am not responsible for causing any harm or violating social norms. Thus, if we were to assess my guilt as a standard occurrent emotion, then my guilt would count as unfitting. Nonetheless, I am feeling genuine guilt, but it is not about anything I have done. While thinking about what to do, I feel right now what I *would feel* in the imagined scenario.

Consider this way of thinking about fit: an agent's SIMULATED emotion is *fitting* in a certain situation if the SIMULATED emotion corresponds to the relevant features of the agent's IMAGINED situation. I am thinking about my friend who has a very small income and is insecure about it. She knows that I was trying to get a raise. When I see her tonight, I know she will ask if I got the raise. I wonder, will she ask me what my new salary is? I feel uncomfortable telling her how large my new salary is, so I consider whether I might not tell her the truth if she were to ask me. As I am imagining the scenario where I do not tell her the truth, I feel a twinge of simulated guilt. In general, it is wrong to lie to a friend. Imagine that I lie to my friend about my salary and felt guilty about it—my guilt would be fitting. So, in this case, my simulated guilt does correspond to the relevant features of my imagined situation. Thus, my simulated guilt, in this situation, is fitting. If instead I feel simulated *fear* in this situation, then my simulated fear in this situation would be unfitting—it would not correspond to the relevant features of my imagined situation.

There is a further complication in trying to understand fittingness cases for simulated guilt. Just as assessments of fit are concerned with the magnitude of the emotion, assessments of simulated emotions for fit will also be sensitive to fit with respect to magnitude. If I feel an extremely strong and overwhelming bout of simulated guilt in this scenario, then it seems that my simulated guilt would be unfitting due to magnitude—it would only make sense to feel a little simulated guilt in response to my potentially lying to my friend about my salary—this is not a significant lie and my intentions are good-natured (I am worried about hurting my friend's feelings).

Should we think about the fittingness conditions for simulated emotions as answerable to: (i) how I *would in fact* feel if the imagined scenario were to obtain, or (ii) how I *should* feel if the imagined scenario were to obtain? In short, is a simulated emotion targeting me or my situation? It seems to me that emotions are fundamentally oriented toward situations and so we should think of the assessments of simulated emotions as answerable to the imagined situation, not the emotion I turned out to actually feel.

TOO MUCH GUILT?

Studies suggest that we overestimate the impact our emotions when we make predictions (either simulated emotions or expected emotions) about our future emotions. This occurs with emotions having both positive and negative valance. For example, professors overestimate the strength of happiness and how long the happiness will last in response to a positive tenure decision,[27] both men and women mis-predict how upset they would be after a breakup with a romantic partner,[28] and people overestimate how happy they will be after their favorite sports team wins a crucial game.[29]

One might wonder if these results entail that simulated emotions are mostly unfitting. One might hold that since the simulated emotion is felt much stronger than the emotion I feel in the actual scenario, it is unfitting in terms of magnitude. This view does not need to say that simulated emotions are necessarily unfitting. Rather, it entails that, empirically, they mostly are unfitting. Let us call a simulated emotion's *counterpart* the emotion that the agent would feel in the actual scenario (i.e., at t_2). The concern is that if the emotion being simulated were felt at t_2, then it would be unfitting due to magnitude. And, so, then, perhaps the simulated emotion is best understood as also unfitting due to magnitude.[30]

Consider a single token of simulated guilt: my simulated guilt concerning my dog Xeno. When I deliberate about what I ought to do, and I imagine how I would feel having made the decision to euthanize Xeno, I am overwhelmed with simulated guilt. While we cannot actually put a number on the strength of magnitude of an emotion, for argument's sake, let us imagine that in this scenario I feel guilt at magnitude #4 (out of 10). After having had the veterinarian euthanize Xeno, I feel guilt at magnitude #2 (out of 10). After Xeno has been euthanized, a little bit of guilt is fitting for me to feel—perhaps if I did not work so hard, I would have walked him a bit more when he was younger to keep in better shape and stave off the arthritis a bit. In general, I did take excellent care of Xeno, but I could have done better. So, it would be unfitting for me to feel guilt (after I have had Xeno euthanized) at magnitude #7, but a magnitude #2 is fitting.

For this situation, let us use "guilt^S" for simulated guilt during deliberation, and "guilt^A" for the guilt felt after Xeno has been euthanized. How do we assess the guilt^S? One option is to assess it according to the standards of fit for guilt^A. My guilt^A felt at a magnitude of #2 (our euthanizing Xeno) is fitting. But, let us imagine that if it was felt over a #4, then it would no longer be fitting. Then, my guilt^S that is felt at magnitude #7 would be unfitting. And we know this tends to be the relationship between a simulated emotion and its counterpart emotion—where the simulated emotion is much stronger in magnitude than is the counterpart emotion that occurs in the actual situation.

The result of this way of thinking about fit, then, would be that the vast majority of simulated emotions are unfitting. One kind of objection to such a view stems from charity considerations—it would be strange if the vast majority of our simulated emotions are unfitting. Donald Davidson argued something similar about the truth of beliefs—any theories about truth and beliefs ought to be charitable enough to not have an outcome that the vast majority of everyone's beliefs are false.[31] It seems likewise that any theory about the fittingness conditions for simulated emotions should not result in the vast majority of everyone's simulated emotion being unfitting.

One way to avoid saying that nearly all simulated emotions are unfitting in terms of their magnitude, is to posit that simulated emotions are understood as having a *magnitude factor*. That is, one adjusts one's assessment of the magnitude of the emotion by a certain amount, depending on the emotion and situation. Some simulated emotions could still be unfitting, of course. In our example above, one might multiply the magnitude of guilt^S by .5 to get a better estimate of guilt^A.

One might argue that this magnitude factor view seems ad hoc. It does not seem ad hoc if we understand why the systematic overestimation occurs. One good explanation is that, as empirical evidence suggestions, simulated emotions promote beneficial behavior and impede harmful behavior. If simulated positive valanced emotions promote beneficial behavior and simulated negative valanced emotions impede harmful behavior, then there would be evolutionary pressure to overestimate the magnitude of all emotions in simulations. According to empirical studies, having these simulated emotions, felt at stronger magnitudes, is really important for successful deliberation. It is when we look at patterns of emotion tokens, not just the single emotion tokens, that we can really appreciate the benefits of simulated emotions.

One outcome of this investigation is the similarity between simulated emotions and fiction-emotions. There are certain emotions that are appropriate in light of the *fictional* context, and others that are inappropriate in light of the *fictional* context. Perhaps practicing emotional responses in fictional contexts helps to align our emotions in real-world contexts. Similarly, it seems that simulated emotions could help to align our emotions in real-world contexts as well. When one feels simulated guilt about a future event, it helps to understand whether that guilt would be fitting in that future scenario. Yet, there still is a range of appropriateness. Just as a fiction-emotion could be felt too strongly (e.g., the magnitude of fear felt toward Hannibal's escape in *The Silence of the Lambs* would likely be unfitting if felt at the same magnitude toward the nihilists in *The Big Lebowski*), a simulated emotion could still be felt too strongly. Perhaps, then, while my guilt^S felt at a magnitude #4 is fitting (given that only magnitude #2 for guilt^A is fitting), my guilt^S felt at a #9 would clearly be unfitting (even given the magnitude factor constraint).

CONCLUSION

This chapter has been a detailed investigation into the fittingness conditions for what has been called "anticipatory" guilt. I suggest that, due to the confusion in the literature between the various related terms, "simulated" is a more appropriate term. I also discussed some potential problems for the natural views on fittingness conditions for simulated guilt, and some potential routes to resolve them.

NOTES

1. See Meriste (chapter 4 in this book) for a similar interpretation of the focus being on *retrospective* guilt.
2. Davidson, 1973, 79.
3. Rick and Loewenstein (2008), Baumgartner, Pieters, and Bagozzi (2008).
4. Note that I am using "fiction-emotion" rather than "fictional-emotion." The latter might be an emotion that is purely fictional—not one that a human would ever actually feel. For example, "bluablua" is a fictional emotion: It is associated with the topsy-turvy, heart-racing, sweat-inducing, positive valance sentiment one has when one sees a very plain stone while on a walk. For discussions on emotional responses to fiction, see: Feagin (1988), Neill (1993), Brock (2007), Young (2010), and Cova and Teroni (2016).
5. Scherer (2003).
6. Some refer to these as anticipated (rather than anticipatory) emotions. See Baumgartner, Pieters, Bagozzi (2008).
7. It is often thought that motivation to avoid feeling an emotion rather than motivation to avoid making a wrong choice might be detrimental to decision-making (Miceli & Castelfranchi 2015: 194).
8. Some theorists refer both to anticipatory emotions and to anticipated emotions as affective reactions. However, the latter is not an *affective* reaction. Indeed, it is not even an *emotion* at all. It is merely a *thought* (or belief) *about* an emotion one expects to have. Certainly, many decisions are made concerning mere thoughts about what one's emotional response might be in a situation. Baumgartner, Pieters, Bagozzi (2008).
9. Some theorists argue that guilt is a moral emotion—for the necessary connection between morality and guilt, e.g., Miceli and Castelfranchi (2015). Others, using anecdotal evidence, suggest otherwise: "To mention one example, as far as I can tell, I am not susceptible to nontrivial guilt feelings, yet I have moral principles and seem (at least to myself) to be a relatively moral person" (Harman 2009: 7). However, we might explain Harman's comment if we consider that some early childhood development theorists suggest that the ability to experience guilt might be dependent upon crucial cognitive benchmarks, e.g., Kochanska et al. (2002); and Laguttuta and Thompson (2007).
10. Godek and LaBarge (2006); Baumeister et al. (1994); Miceli and Castelfranchi (1998, 2015).
11. Godek and LaBarge (2006).
12. Fridja (2007).
13. Deem and Ramsey (2016); Brady (2013: 20).
14. Kochanska and Aksan (2006); Ferguson et al. (2007).

15. Miceli and Castelfranchi (2015).
16. Baumgartner et al. (2008: 686).
17. Miceli and Castelfranchi (2015: 190, 197); Fridja (2004); Loewenstein and Lerner (2003); Rick and Loewenstein (2008).
18. Baumgartner et al. (2008: 695). Miceli and Castelfranchi also discuss these exact terms (2015: 197).
19. A simulated emotion is still one feels for which the object is a possible future object. This differs from the sort of scenario where an agent seeks to have a particular emotional response—e.g., an agent puts on a comedy because she wants to feel amused.
20. D'Arms and Jacobson (2000: 68).
21. D'Arms and Jacobson (2000: 73) discuss this distinction, but rather than "magnitude" and "type" they use "size" and "shape."
22. Harman (2009) emphasizes for several reasons that even if guilt is fitting and even warranted in a certain situation, that still does not entail that one ought to feel it.
23. In D'Arms & Kerr (2008), we use "prudential" and gloss it as concerned with the self-interested advisability of the emotion; this use of "prudential" is analogous to my use of "beneficial" here and throughout this chapter. For assessments similar to this use of "beneficial," Greenspan (1988) uses "adaptive," Gibbard (1990) uses both "advantageous" and "pragmatic," and Jones (2003) uses "strategically wise."
24. Miceli & Castelfranchi (2015: 94 fn 17).
25. Levi (1947).
26. Gendler and Kovakovich (2006).
27. Gilbert et al. (1998).
28. Eastwick et al. (2008).
29. Wilson et al. (2000).
30. It might be the simulated emotions vary from their counterparts in terms of magnitude, but they both fall within the range of fit. Perhaps this is the case. However, if it is the case, then we no longer must respond to the concern that simulated emotions are nearly always unfitting. My discussion focuses on the problematic outcome.
31. Davidson (1982: 99–100).

REFERENCES

Baumgartner, H., Pieters, R., and Bagozzi, R. P. (2008) "Future-Oriented Emotions: Conceptualization and Behavioral Effects," *European Journal of Social Psychology* 38: 685–96.

Baumeister, R.F., Stillwell, A.M., Heatherthon, T.F. (1994) "Guilt: An Interpersonal Approach," *Psychological Bulletin* 115: 243–67.

Brady, Michael. (2013) *Emotional Insight: The Epistemic Role of Emotional Experience*. Oxford: Oxford University Press.

Brock, Stuart. (2007) "Fiction, Feelings, and Emotions," *Philosophical Studies* 132: 211–42.

Cova, Florian and Teroni, Fabrice. (2016) "Is the Paradox of Fiction Soluble in Psychology?" *Philosophical Psychology* 29.6: 930–42.

D'Arms, Justin and Jacobson, Daniel. (2000) "The Moralistic Fallacy: On the 'Appropriateness' of Emotions," *Philosophy and Phenomenological Research* 61.1: 65–90.
D'Arms, Justin and Kerr, Alison Duncan. (2008) "Envy in the Philosophical Tradition," in *Envy: Theory and Research*. Oxford: Oxford University Press: 39–59.
Davidson, Donald. (1973) "Freedom to Act," in (1980) *Essays on Actions and Events*. Oxford: Clarendon Press.
———. (1982) "Rational Animals," *Dialectica* 36.2: 317–27.
Deem, Michael J. and Ramsey, Grant. (2016) "Guilt by Association?" *Philosophical Psychology* 29.4: 570–85.
Eastwick, P.W., Finkel, E.J., Krishnamurti, T., Loewenstein, G. (2008) "Mispredicting Distress Following Romantic Breakup: Revealing the Time Course of the Affective Forecasting Error," *Journal of Experimental Social Psychology* 44: 800–7.
Feagin, Susan L. (1988) "Imagining Emotions and Appreciating Fiction," *Canadian Journal of Philosophy* 18.3: 485–500.
Ferguson, T. J., Brugman, D., White, J., and Eyre, H. L. (2007) "Shame and Guilt as Morally Warranted Experiences," in *The Self-Conscious Emotions: Theory and Research*. J. L. Tracy, R. W. Robins, and J. P. Tagney, Eds. New York: Guilford.
Frijda, Nico H. (2004) "Emotion and Action," in *Feelings and Emotions: The Amsterdam Symposium*. A.S.R. Manstead, N. H. Frijda, and A.H. Fischer, Eds. Cambridge: Cambridge University Press: 158–73.
———. (2007) *The Laws of Emotions*. London: Lawrence Erlbaum Assoc.
Gendler, Tamar Szabo and Kovakovich, Karson. (2006) "Genuine Rational Fictional Emotions," in *Contemporary Debates in Aesthetics and Philosophy of Art*. M. Kieran, Ed. Oxford: Blackwell Press.
Gibbard, A. (1990) *Wise Choices, Apt Feelings: A Theory of Normative Judgment*. Cambridge, MA: Harvard University Press.
Gilbert, D.T., Pinel, E.C., Wilson, T.D., Blumberg, S.J., Wheatley, T.P. (1998) "Immune Neglect: A Source of Durability Bias in Affective Forecasting," *Journal of Personality and Social Psychology* 75.3: 617–38.
Godek, J. and LaBarge, M.C. (2006) "Mothers, Food, Love and Career—The Four Major Guilt Groups? The Differential Effects of Guilt Appeals," *Advances in Consumer Research* 33.1: 511.
Greenspan, P.S. (1988) *Emotions and Reasons*. New York: Routledge.
Harman, Gilbert. (2009) "Guilt-Free Morality," *Oxford Studies in Metaethics* 4: 203–14.
Jones, Karen. (2003) "Emotional Rationality as Practical Rationality," in *Setting the Moral Compass: Essays by Women Philosophers*. C. Calhoun, Ed. Oxford: Oxford University Press, 333–52.
Kochanska, G. and Aksan, N. (2006) "Children's Conscience and Self-Regulation," *Journal of Personality* 74: 1587–618.
Kochanska, G., Gross, J. N., Lin, M., and Nichols, K. E. (2002) "Guilt in Young Children: Development, Determinants, and Relations with a Broader System of Standards," *Child Development* 73: 461–82.

Lagattuta, K. H. and Thompson, R. A. (2007) "The Development of Self-Conscious Emotions: Cognitive Processes and Social Influences," in *The Self-Conscious Emotions: Theory and Research*. J. L. Tracy, R. W. Robins, and J. P. Tagney, Eds. New York: Guilford.

Levi, Primo. (1947) *If This Is a Man—The Truce*. London: Penguin Books.

Loewenstein, G. and Lerner, J.S. (2003) "The Role of Affect in Decision Making," in *Handbook of Affective Science*. R. Davidson, H. Goldsmith, and K. Scherer, Eds. Oxford: Oxford University Press: 619–42.

Meriste, Heidy. (2019) "Beyond Retrospective Guilt," in *The Moral Psychology of Guilt*. C.J. Maley and B. Cokelet, Eds. London: Rowman & Littlefield International.

Miceli, Maria and Castelfranchi, Cristiano. (2015) *Expectancy and Emotion*. Oxford: Oxford University Press.

Miceli, Maria and Castelfranchi, Cristiano. (1998) "How to Silence One's Conscience: Cognitive Defences Against the Feeling of Guilt," *Journal for the Theory of Social Behaviour* 28.3: 287–318.

Neill, Alex. (1993) "Fiction and the Emotions," *American Philosophical Quarterly* 30.1: 1–12.

Rick, S. and Loewenstein, G. (2008) "Intangibility in Intertemporal Choice," *Philosophical Transactions of the Royal Society B*: Biological Sciences 363: 3813–24.

Scherer, K. R. (2003) "Vocal Communication of Emotion: A Review of Research Paradigms," *Speech Communication* 40: 227–56.

Young, Garry. (2010) "Virtually Real Emotions and the Paradox of Fiction: Implications for the Use of Virtual Environments in Psychological Research," *Philosophical Psychology* 23.1: 1–21.

Wilson, T.D., Wheatley, T.P., Meyers, J.M., Gilbert, D.T., and Axsom, D. (2000) "Focalism: A Source of Durability Bias in Affective Forecasting," *Journal of Personality and Social Psychology* 78: 821–36.

Wilson, T.D., and Gilbert, D.T. (2005) "Affective Forecasting: Knowing What to Want," *Current Directions in Psychological Science* 14: 131–4.

Section 2

UNDERSTANDING GUILT AND ITS FUNCTIONS

Chapter 6

The Evolution of Guilt and Its Non-Instrumental Enactments

Blaine J. Fowers

Many scholars recognize a suite of emotions that have been termed "secondary emotions," "self-conscious emotions," or "moral emotions." These emotions are termed "self-conscious" because they include self-evaluation (Lewis 2018; Tracy, Shariff, and Cheng 2010). Self-conscious emotions stand in contrast to "basic" emotions such as anger, fear, disgust, sadness, and happiness. There is more evidence for and scholarly consensus about basic emotions than about self-conscious emotions. Basic emotions have a clearer biological basis, are recognized through virtually universal facial expressions, and emerge earlier in development because they do not require self-referencing (a development that ordinarily occurs in the third year of life).

Nevertheless, evidence is accumulating for the universality of self-conscious emotions (Tangney, Stuewig, and Mashek 2007; Tracy and Robins 2004), but there remains some dispute about whether what are called self-conscious emotions are truly emotions (e.g., Ekman 1994; Smith, Webster, Parrott, and Eyre 2002). These emotions include pride, guilt, shame, and awe. Wolf, Cohen, Panter, and Insko (2010) stated that "shame proneness and guilt proneness are traits that reflect individual differences in cognitive, affective, and behavioral responses to personal transgressions" (338). This chapter focuses on the role of guilt as an evolved moral emotion and guilt-proneness as a positive moral trait. In this chapter, I discuss guilt as an ordinary emotion evoked by the recognition that specific actions have created a breach or tension in a valued relationship or group membership. I also discuss guilt-proneness as emerging as an individual difference variable that predicts the avoidance of immoral behavior. I do not address generalized guilt, which is the experience of a vague and pervasive feeling that one is at fault without any specific transgression. For a more detailed discussion of problematic forms of guilt, see Maibom (this volume).

In individual development, the moral emotion of guilt emerges as early as two years of age, when children begin to evaluate their own actions according to standards of conduct they have learned (Kochanska, Gross, Lin, and Nichols 2002). As children develop the capacities for recognizing others' evaluations of them, for self-referencing, and for self-evaluation, they become capable of guilt or shame following a failure or transgression. Typically, when a child meets or exceeds expectations (especially difficult expectations), he or she experiences pride. Similarly, when a child fails to meet expectations (especially easy ones), he or she experiences guilt or shame. A central feature of guilt is that the individual believes that he or she is responsible for the transgression.

Modern psychological research on guilt was inaugurated by Lewis's (1971) distinction between guilt and shame. When poor performance is attributed to stable global aspects of the self, it tends to elicit shame, whereas attributions to unstable, specific instances (one's behavior) tend to elicit guilt. Thus, the emotion of guilt is generally seen as the expression of a failure at the level of behavior, whereas shame is understood as the expression of a failure at the level of the person. Contemporary variants of Lewis's approach to shame and guilt have retained and explored this distinction (Cohen, Panter, and Turan 2012; Tangney et al. 2007).

Lewis (2018) describes a model of four self-evaluative emotions that result from an internal attribution of responsibility. Lewis focuses on whether the individual believes that he or she succeeded or failed in fulfilling social norms and on whether that success or failure is attributable to a global or specific source within the individual. When one succeeds in meeting a social standard, a positive emotion (pride or hubris[1]) is elicited, and when one fails, a negative emotion (guilt or shame) is elicited. When the source of the success or failure is specific (i.e., a behavior), pride or guilt is experienced. When the source is global (i.e., the whole person), then hubris or shame is evoked. Thus, guilt is the emotion that results from a failure to meet a social standard in one's behavior. The emotion of shame emerges when one perceives a failure in meeting a social expectation that is due to a defect in one as a person. In contrast, pride and hubris emerge when an individual meets a social norm, with pride being associated with behavior and hubris with interpreting the success as an expression of who one is as a person.

Emotions are termed moral because they involve a self-evaluation regarding whether one has met a standard, rule, or goal (Lewis 2018). Culture is central to the self-conscious emotions because cultural norms (i.e., standards, rules, and goals) specify when pride, shame, or guilt are appropriate. As Tracy and Robins (2004) summarize, "society tells us what kind of person we should be; we internalize these beliefs in the form of actual and ideal self-representations; and self-conscious emotions motivate behavioral action toward the goals embodied in these self-representations" (107).

Although guilt has been frequently discussed in terms of the violation of abstract moral imperatives, Baumeister and Leary (1995) made the point that guilt most often appears in empirical studies in close interpersonal relationships. They interpret this evidence to mean that "episodes of guilt can thus be understood as responses to disturbances or threats to interpersonal attachments" (507). Guilt is an aversive emotion that incentivizes the individual to rectify the mistake or transgression that has created tension or a breach in a relationship (Tangney and Dearing 2002). Because guilt is focused on behavior, guilt can often be resolved through an apology, corrective actions, and reconciliation. Therefore, guilt can be seen as a motivator of relationship repair when one has acted against or failed to act in accordance with relational expectations.

Cohen and her colleagues (Cohen et al. 2012; Cohen, Wolf, Panter, and Insko 2011) have explored a trait-focused aspect of guilt that they term guilt-proneness. They suggest that guilt-proneness is likely to reduce immoral behavior because a guilt-prone individual is inclined to avoid committing a transgression and thereby circumvent the anticipated negative emotion of guilt. Guilt-proneness means that the social standards that guide behavior have been internalized, an important point to which I return later. This internalization of standards means that guilt-prone individuals require less public surveillance to prevent moral transgressions and that they are unlikely to commit misdeeds even if the misdeeds are difficult for others to detect. See McGee and Giner-Sorolla (this volume) for a complementary account of the internalization process for guilt.

Reviews of the literature on guilt and shame suggest that guilt- and shame-proneness can be reliably differentiated empirically (Wolf et al. 2010) and that guilt is generally more closely related to moral behavior than is shame (Tangney et al. 2007). An fMRI study suggests that neural activations differ for pride, guilt, and basic emotions (Gilead, Katzir, Eyal, and Liberman 2016). Recent studies also confirm that guilt-prone individuals are less likely to exploit legal loopholes, engage in unethical business decisions, negotiate unethically, or lie for monetary gain (Cohen et al. 2011).

GUILT AS AN ADAPTATION

As a moral emotion that helps to keep important relationships intact, guilt has attracted significant attention from evolutionary scientists. The standard conception of guilt is that it motivates the individual to scan his or her behavior to identify transgressions that could threaten important relationships and to make amends for the transgression to repair the relationship. A transgression is the violation of a norm, expectation, or standard that could threaten a close relationship or an important group membership. Guilt-proneness is a stable tendency to avoid actions that induce the negative emotion of guilt. Guilt and guilt-proneness attract the attention of evolutionary thinkers because close relationships and group memberships are key contributors to reproductive success, and their maintenance is therefore imperative on an evolutionary account.

An evolutionary account of guilt begins with the idea that the capacity to feel guilt has been naturally selected. Selection occurs when naturally occurring genetic mutations somehow increase the organism's reproductive success. Examples include binocular vision, which enhances sight and distance recognition; cooperation, which increases resources through mutuality; and pathogen avoidance, which helps to maintain health. The term *fitness* refers to reproductive success. In the course of thousands of generations, organisms with a fitness-enhancing trait will proliferate through a population until all or most of the individuals in the population have this trait.

Every species confronts long-standing challenges or problems for its reproductive success. Traits are selected because they give organisms a leg up on such an enduring problem. Because adaptations to the design of the species solve these long-standing problems, these problems are known as adaptive problems. Adaptive problems threaten survival (finding food, maintaining safety) and reproduction (mate selection, provisioning offspring). An adaptive problem must be long-standing for there to be enough time for an adaptive trait to be selected. There are several theories about the evolution of bipedalism in humans, for example, but all are related to fitness advantages. Our ancestors might have acquired bipedal locomotion because standing upright provides a larger visual field, because it frees one's hands for tool use or carrying, or because it is possible to move more economically over greater distances. These explanations are not necessarily mutually exclusive. The point is that the explanations can individually or collectively explain this adaptation as a solution to long-standing problems of finding food, avoiding threats, and navigating terrain. When a trait solves one or more adaptive problems, it is an adaptation.

The capacity to recognize one's own and others' wrongdoing, rule violation, or substandard performance is necessary because humans are intensely social beings. Humans depend greatly on one another for daily maintenance and survival, which means that an individual's action or inaction can strongly affect one's own welfare, but also others' fitness. Monitoring one's own and others' potentially harmful actions is therefore very important for fitness. Errors and transgressions occur with some frequency. Therefore, guilt, the emotion that leads to the recognition and resolution of transgressions, is adaptive because guilt makes it possible to maintain harmonious relationships, role fulfillment, cooperation, and group solidarity for error-prone humans.

ADAPTIVE PREREQUISITES TO GUILT

If we take the capacity to experience and be moved by the emotion of guilt to be an adaptation, we must assume several prior adaptations. Guilt appears to be designed to facilitate well-functioning relationships, from dyads to large groups. For guilt to be important, these relationships and group memberships must be essential, and evolutionary scientists have consensus on the centrality of relationships and group membership for human fitness (Fowers 2015; Tomasello 2014).

These ongoing relationships are also governed by social norms, and norms have been amply documented as adaptations (Henrich and Henrich 2007). Violating norm expectations is a key circumstance that elicits guilt (Lewis 2018). It is widely understood that norms must be enforced, which means that individuals are held accountable by others for their actions (Fowers 2015; Tracy and Robins 2004). Guilt is the emotional response that indicates that the transgressing individual accepts that accountability and is responsive to it (Kochanska et al. 2002). This accountability includes the possibility of exclusion or other serious punishments for norm violations (Fowers 2017). To be accountable to members of one's group, individuals must be seen as relatively separate and responsible for their behavior, and these conditions create the necessity for individuals to have an identity (Fowers 2015). Social accountability must be monitored by the individual to avoid committing transgressions or to recognize that one is responsible for a relationship problem. This self-monitoring is facilitated by the capacities to self-evaluate (Tracey et al. 2010) and to understand the intentions and experiences that other people have (Tomasello, Carpenter, Call, Behne, and Moll 2005). The well-documented trait of guilt-proneness indicates that some individuals are more inclined to guilt feelings and therefore are less likely to commit transgressions. Guilt-proneness clarifies that anticipatory guilt is powerful in the avoidance of moral transgressions (Cohen et al. 2011; Cohen et al. 2012). Of course, guilt-proneness can lead to experiencing excessive or overly frequent guilt for small or nonexistent transgressions, which can be problematic. The emphasis in this chapter is on functional guilt-proneness, however.

Another very basic capacity of emotional systems is to motivate behavior, which in this case means that, in response to norm violation, there must be an emotional experience that will motivate relationship repair and communicate willingness to comply with norm expectations. Guilt is the emotional experience that motivates relationship repair (Tracy and Robins 2004). Finally, humans must be able to recognize when amends have been made and to forgive someone for a transgression (McCullough 2008). The combination of guilt that leads to a transgressor's efforts to make amends and forgiveness, which is the acceptance of those efforts and amends-making, can lead to relationship repair, and even, in some cases, to relationship strengthening.

I have sketched a complex system of adaptations that constitute the context within which the emotional experience of guilt appears to function. In this account, guilt is a motivator for the essential human function of maintaining smoothly operating relationships and groups. Social cues that elicit guilt include verbal or nonverbal expressions of hurt or anger, social distancing, and criticism. Ideally, guilt emerges prior to or early in the violation of valued others' expectations so that an individual can communicate a willingness to abide by those expectations and alter his or her behavior to avert serious relationship damage. Expressions (verbal or nonverbal) of guilt indicate an acceptance of accountability to others and are an important aspect of amends-making when one has transgressed a norm.

Although there is some consensus among evolutionary thinkers about the general outlines of this evolutionary account, and the available evidence generally favors this understanding, it is far from incontrovertible. Even if we accept the view I have presented, however, there is a very significant conceptual problem. The story of guilt is generally told with the understanding that it is simply a mechanism for avoiding social punishment and relationship ruptures that can threaten an individual's fitness. To the extent that that is taken as a full account of the function of guilt, it raises three key questions about the idea of guilt as a *moral* emotion.

First, guilt and amends-making are generally seen as the means by which one can avoid negative relationship consequences. This is typically discussed by evolutionary scientists in terms of a means-end relationship. If guilt is simply a means to a desired outcome, it could be replaced by some other means that might be more effective or less costly. Simply assuming a means-end relationship between guilt and relationship harmony is too quick, however. It is important to consider whether there is a constituent-end relationship wherein guilt may be inherently tied to relationship harmony, such that guilt cannot be easily separated from what it means to be part of a relationship or group. In the next section, I explore how the concept of identity clarifies that constituent-end relation.

Second, if guilt is simply designed to help us avoid negative consequences that might be imposed by others, what makes the experience and expression of guilt praiseworthy in any way? Guilt may be entirely selfishly motivated insofar as it serves to reduce negative consequences for the actor. Indeed, there is a long tradition in evolutionary science, from Huxley and Spencer to Williams and Dawkins, that sees human behavior as fundamentally self-interested and competitively motivated. Moreover, many evolutionary scientists see morality as a matter of self-sacrifice (Krebs 2011), leading to a view of normal behavior as self-interested and moral behavior as an exception to normal behavior that requires self-sacrifice. In discussing Aldous Huxley's legacy in evolutionary thought, Williams (1988) voiced the common view that the "modern concept of natural selection . . . can be honestly described as a process for maximizing short-sighted selfishness" (385).

The insistence that self-interest is at the bottom of all motives, including the motivational efficacy of guilt, is a manifestation of individualism, the view that the individual is the fundamental unit of social reality for humans. Individualism dismisses human groups as mere collections of individuals that have no primary reality. Foremost among the blind spots of individualism for this discussion is that this viewpoint fails to see that when individuals identify with groups, it transforms their cognition, affect, and behavior. As I explain in the next section, activating one's identity as a group member can be as powerful a motive as self-interest, which means that group identification is extremely important for evolutionary explanations of human behavior.

Third, psychologists frequently portray psychological phenomena such as guilt as mechanisms that have causal antecedents. Such accounts portray guilt and other human experiences as resulting from causal forces that are largely beyond the individual's awareness and choice. They suggest that guilt is an automatic, knee-jerk reflex that is mechanistic rather than involving human agency in the selection and endorsement of standards, ideals, or goals. In contrast, agentic theorists think that the violation of expectations is the origin of guilt. If that is true, then the causal account seems to rule out or at least minimize agency and therefore responsibility for the emotion of guilt. Yet the perception of responsibility for a transgression and the impetus to personally make amends for it is central to the emotion of guilt, as we have already seen. It seems that the evolutionary account must either abandon its portrayal of guilt as a moral emotion or find a richer understanding that can clarify the basis for seeing guilt as a moral emotion. In the remainder of this chapter, I outline an account that clarifies the moral role that guilt plays.

A CONSTITUENT-END ACCOUNT OF GUILT

The core problem with the standard evolutionary account of guilt is that it is portrayed in a simple means-end fashion: Guilt is the means to avoid negative social sanctions. One could also avoid those sanctions by successfully hiding one's transgressions or by convincing others that one did not actually commit a transgression. In addition, one could avoid negative consequences through dominance displays that cow others if one has the status to use them or, if one has relatively low status, submission displays might allay others' inclinations to punish. In Boehm's (2012) view, submissive displays have been "providing individual fitness benefits for at least 8 million years" (106).

The point is that there are multiple ways to avoid social punishments for transgressions, and if one's only goal is that avoidance, then an intelligent actor will pick the method most likely to succeed in each circumstance. The availability and relative interchangeability of means to reach a given end are key features of an instrumental form of activity (Fowers 2010). The relative interchangeability of the means indicates that there is no inherent connection between the means and the end. That is, means are selected on the basis of criteria that are independent of the end, such as the efficacy, efficiency, cost, or risks of the means. The instrumental approach also construes the outcome as the primary value, placing it much higher in importance than the way the end is achieved.

A constituent-end form of activity provides a contrast to a means-end approach. Constituent-end activities are those in which the means and the end cannot be separated because the means help to constitute the end. A simple example of a constituent-end activity is going for a walk when there is no specific destination or outcome of the walk. The aim is to walk, and a walk is constituted by the activity of walking. Of course, one could say that the "true" aim of going for a walk is the pleasure it provides, and it is true that those who take walks typically enjoy them. From a constituent-end perspective, however, the pleasure is not a separate and distinct outcome of walking, something that occurs as a consequence of walking. Rather, the pleasure emerges in the walking. It supervenes on the walking, but it cannot be separated from the activity. It also seems clear that walking-pleasure is not the same as ice-cream-eating-pleasure or drug-induced-euphoria-pleasure. Each pleasure has a different cast specifically related to the kind of activity with which it is associated.

Relational life for humans certainly has some instrumental aspects. There are relationships that are reasonably approached in a means-end manner, including those that are characterized primarily by economic exchange. Means-ends interactions are entirely appropriate, even in close relationships when the completion of a task or a specific outcome is desirable. A problem arises if means-ends activity is seen as the only conceivable form of human action. An exclusively instrumental portrayal of human activity is called instrumentalism (Fowers 2010), and this viewpoint can only portray actions in means-end terms.

The shortcoming of instrumentalism is that it interprets actions that have meaning and value in themselves (e.g., spending time with friends or canoeing) as means that are secondary to some separable outcome (e.g., social support or a destination). If activities have inherent value for agents but observers or theorists construe them as mere means to an end, this amounts to a significant distortion of the agent's self-understanding, which would require a strong justification. The plausibility or fundamental character of instrumentalist interpretations are generally assumed and therefore seldom accompanied with sufficient justification for overriding agents' claims of inherent value.

GUILT AS A CONSTITUTIVE MORAL EMOTION

With the distinction between instrumental and constitutive actions in hand, I can now discuss how the emotion of guilt can be constitutive for individuals. This more complex understanding begins with the recognition that close relationships and important group memberships are not simply resources to be managed, and standards are more than externally imposed rules. Relationships and standards are constituents of the agent's identity, and transgressions undermine the agent's identity as such-and-such a kind of person or such-and-such a type of relationship partner. Indeed, Tracy and Robbins (2004) suggested that the relevance of the perception that one's identity is at issue is a necessary element of all self-conscious emotions.

To see this possibility, it is helpful to return to the basic function of guilt for maintaining one's good standing within a group. Of course, it is possible to see group membership as an outcome that is a separable consequence of developing relationships with group members, following group norms, and participating in group activities. On this view, one ticks the boxes of group membership, and the consequence is that one belongs. This is a rather superficial and unhelpful construal of group membership, however, because it misses a central feature of belonging, which is that the individual not only *acts* as a group member but also *identifies* as a group member. The individual's identification as a group member is generally synchronized with the degree to which the other members of the group recognize him or her as belonging. That is, others also identify the individual with the group.

Identity is generally seen as a process that is internal to individuals, but this common assumption does not square well with Brewer's (2007) theory of extended identity and related research. Many years ago, Brewer (1991) questioned psychological and philosophical views of the individual as the fundamental unit of social reality and of group membership as little more than affiliations or alliances that serve individuals' interest. In contrast, she claimed that collective identity is often prepotent because group membership is so important. If she is right, group identity should show up in affect, cognition, and behavior. In several ingenious studies, investigators have found that when participants are primed to think of themselves as group members (even of relatively trivial groups), they actively promote the group's interest over their individual interest (e.g., De Cremer and van Dijk 2002; Filippin and Guala 2017; Goode, Keefer, Branscombe, and Molina 2017; van Vugt and

Hart 2004). These results suggest that identification with a group is rather easily achieved and reliably induces a tendency to benefit the group even when that is individually costly.

Brewer (2007) suggested that individuals have both an identity as an individual distinct from other group members and a group identity. At times the individual identity is paramount, and the person understandably pursues his or her self-interest. At other times, one's group identity is activated, and one tends to act in ways that benefit the group. Cialdini et al. (1997) discussed the power of activating group and relationship identification in this way: "As the self and other increasingly merge, helping the other increasingly helps the self . . . when the distinction between self and other is undermined, the traditional dichotomy between selfishness and selflessness loses its meaning" (490). That is, one wants to act in favor of the group because one identifies with the group.

Among children, the process of identifying with their familial, ethnic, or religious group is a virtually automatic developmental process (Kochanska et al. 2002). The internalization of norms and practices occurs as soon as the child is capable of it and high-fidelity imitation is a key aspect of how infants and children learn how to participate smoothly in social interactions (Hurley and Chater 2005). Indeed, the emotion of guilt develops in the third year of life as the child begins to recognize incidents in which he or she has failed to live up to social expectations. Unless this process is disrupted, the child is inducted into the group and remains a member even through questioning and perhaps struggling to some degree with that identification. Group identification can, of course, go awry when individuals have difficulty complying with norms and are excluded from the group. Yet social exclusion is a potentially catastrophic detriment to an individual's psychological and physical well-being (e.g., Cacioppo and Patrick 2008; Holt-Lunstadt, Smith, and Layton 2010).

The emotion of guilt is a key detector of potential social exclusion when one has run afoul of social expectations. As noted, it motivates the individual to bring his or her behavior back into norm compliance. But if both individual and group identity are elements that help to constitute the individual as the person that he or she is, then this norm compliance dynamic is more than a means to avoid a painful punishment. In this case, norm compliance helps to constitute the person as a group member, which means that norm violations are as much a breach of the person's identity as they are a failure to observe social custom. Therefore, feeling guilt about a norm violation is as much a reminder about fidelity to one's identity as a group member as it is a reminder to avoid social punishment. This is because following norms helps to constitute the individual as a group member. The individual's identification with the group has benefits, but it also has value in its own right.

Sripada and Stich (2007) also argued that culture and norms transcend an instrumentalist construal. They suggested that people often pursue social norms as "ultimate ends," meaning that the ends are seen as inherently worthwhile aims, rather than being just a means to a separable end. From this perspective, guilt motivates identity repair, but I am suggesting that this is often a constituent-end relation rather than a means-end relation. One way to see this is to recognize that guilt is experienced at least as often as a violation of *how* one should act (e.g., as kind or loving) as it is for simple rule-breaking (e.g., stealing). Repairing how one acts is a constituent-end activity because the only way to achieve the goal of changing how one acts is through acting in the preferred manner.

COULD CONSTITUTIVE NORM FOLLOWING AND GUILT HAVE EVOLVED?

Some readers may find the account of a constitutive form of guilt I have just outlined to be interesting, but implausible because they believe that it could not have evolved due to the common view that evolution only favors features that work to improve individual fitness. It is easier to see the inherent power of norms and guilt if one recognizes group selection. Put simply, group selection is the view that natural selection operates by favoring features that enhance group fitness as well as features that favor individual fitness. That is, under group selection, a genetic variation in individuals within a population can be selected if the variation adds to the reproductive success of the group. One argument for group selection is straightforward: When a variation benefits the group, it will lead to more reproduction by group members, and the group will "seed" other groups with some of those offspring, thereby spreading the variation. It is also possible that more successful groups will simply outcompete less well-adapted groups. Some theorists believe that group selection is the basis for the natural selection of cooperation among humans, for example. Yet I believe that it is possible to argue for even the more difficult case of the individual selection of a constitutive form of guilt. A successful argument for individual selection is also sufficient for a group selection model because the latter always includes the former.

The key to the evolution of a constitutive form of guilt is to return to the profound sociality of humans. Our species has a long history of reproductive success only within a group context (Fowers 2015; Tomasello 2014). One requirement for this is mutual protection, and humans who live and reproduce in groups are rarely preyed upon by other animals. As amazing as it seems, the primary (but not the only) selection pressures on humans have been other humans (Heatherton 2010). One ongoing threat has been competition or aggression from other human groups, and the most successful response has been to remain well-ensconced in one's own group. The second threat is potential expulsion from one's own group, which can occur if an individual violates important expectations either egregiously or repetitively (Williams 2007). Clearly, the emotion of guilt can serve to alert one to the second threat of norm violations and motivate any relationship repair that is necessary. This much can be accommodated by a means-end account of guilt based on self-interest.

As already noted, a constituent-end account views guilt as much as a reaction to a lack of fidelity with one's identity and commitment to the group as it views guilt as a punishment-avoidance mechanism. Such a fidelity-oriented cuing of guilt could arise if there were selection pressures that made it advantageous to identify with and internalize the social norms to which one must comply as a group member. Surveillance of norm compliance is ubiquitous for humans (Henrich and Henrich 2007), and it is further strengthened by gossip among group members regarding others' norm compliance (Boehm 2012). Therefore, one's reputation—for noncompliance, spotty compliance, or full compliance—is an important factor in how one is viewed by other group members.

I suggest that when group members observe one another, they attend to the degree of commitment that each individual demonstrates to the standards and practices of the group. As group members evaluate this commitment, they will notice that some group members comply with group norms only when others are observing or only to the extent necessary to avoid punishment. This is paradigmatically instrumental compliance. Yet other group members may comply with group norms automatically and with conviction because they have internalized those expectations. That is, these individuals have made the norms part of their identity.

When group members are choosing preferentially among their fellows for cooperation partners, allies, or collaborators in mutual defense, the individuals who have demonstrated stronger commitment to the cohesion and strength of the group are more likely be chosen. If this is accurate, then internalizing group norms and making them part of one's identity would lead not only to relatively effortless compliance (a benefit in itself), but also to being identified by others as a very worthwhile group member, one who is likely to receive preferential treatment. Preferential treatment in matters such as cooperation or alliances contributes to reproductive fitness. This means that making norm compliance a matter of identification and automaticity would garner significant fitness benefits, rendering it a very adaptive capacity.

One line of theory and research that lends credence to this analysis is social categorization theory (Hogg 2004), especially research focused on what is called prototypicality. As Hogg noted, "social categorization . . . produces ingroup identification, a sense of belonging, self-definition in group terms, and ingroup loyalty and favoritism" (209). Loyalty and favoritism are two forms of benefits accorded to ingroup members generally, but these benefits are even more pronounced when one is seen as a prototypical group member. Hogg argues that when individuals are categorized as ingroup or outgroup members, this judgment is based primarily on a set of features that identify a group prototype (e.g., attire, mannerisms, accent, etc.). This means that any individual will be perceived as more or less prototypical for the relevant group. Hogg describes a research program that documents that "some people are more prototypical than others . . . [and] such people are consensually liked, which furnishes them with the capacity to actively gain compliance with their requests. . . . Consensual attractiveness also confirms differential popularity and public endorsement" imbuing the individual "with prestige and status, and instantiates an intragroup status differential" (215–216). These results are also compatible with theory and research from the social identity perspective (Tajfel 1981). Such prototypical leadership and centrality are not simply an exercise of unilateral power. Rather, these individuals are "intrinsically persuasive because they embody the norms of the group" (Hogg 2004, 217).

Social status is related to multiple fitness benefits across many animal species (Sapolski 2004), and status is signaled with many behaviors such as eye contact and posture (Cummins 2012). Socioeconomic status is the most widely recognized form of status in humans, and it is a very strong and well-established negative predictor of morbidity and mortality (e.g., Evans, Wolfe, and Adler 2012; Marmot 2011). Therefore, the internalization of norm expectations is linked to group prototypicality, which confers likeability and status on the individual, directly affecting longevity and reproductive fitness.

The strong selection pressure favoring prototypicality clarifies how an individual who readily and automatically meets social expectations as a matter of fidelity to his or her identity will have enhanced reproductive success compared to halfhearted compliers or merely punishment-avoiding individuals. Those who are assessing the degree to which they can depend on an individual's commitment to cooperative, norm-following, or alliance-related behavior would readily perceive whether an individual is fully committed to these activities, in contrast to someone who only participates in these activities on a contingent basis. It would be relatively easy to detect who can be depended upon to cooperate, follow customs, or maintain alliances as a matter of course. Those individuals would be more reliable and therefore better interaction partners, all other things being equal. This will lead to more consistent mutually benefiting activity, which will, in turn, increase fitness. Cooperation, group belonging, and stable alliances are among the most powerful selection factors in the human lineage (Fowers 2015).

The pathway through which individuals come to be fully committed to the group or a relationship is through coming to identify with the group or other person. As an individual internalizes group norms, which includes many social expectations specific to each group, he or she comes to identify with the group through the mutual expectations those norms entail, through enacting the required behavior, through a process of habituation, which ultimately leads to the norm compliance becoming automatic and habitual. By identifying with the group, the individual comes to be spontaneously motivated to act as a group member. In addition to the specific norm expectations of a given group, cooperation and alliance formation are generally important activities in human groups. These activities also have norm expectations with which the individual can identify and internalize. Doing so would make the individual a very reliable cooperator or alliance partner.

There are two additional features of this identity-fidelity formulation of guilt experience. The first is that the trait of guilt-proneness can contribute to acting consistently with social expectations because this trait preempts behavior that would be guilt-inducing (Cohen et al. 2012). The second is that individuals are responsible for the degree to which they conform to social expectations or act primarily in self-interested ways that might disadvantage others. There is room for choice in how much one identifies with a relationship partner or a group. Greater commitment to these relationships will lead to a stronger identity and more thorough norm-following behavior. Although automaticity is frequently discussed as a noncognitive form of activity, it is well-known that individuals can make actions automatic through explicit commitment to those actions and active choices in making the actions habitual (Bargh 1994). Automatic norm-following can therefore be developed as a cultivated habit.

The emphasis on identity clarifies that the reason for acting in accordance with social expectations is a desire to maintain fidelity with the norms of the group with which one identifies. This identity-fidelity formulation clarifies that having a well-established place within the group need not involve aggression or dominance, although it could. Humans evolved primarily by successfully reproducing in hunter-gatherer groups, and all the adaptations discussed in this chapter emerged prior to the advent of agriculture and sedentary communities. Egalitarian social arrangements predominate in hunter-gatherer societies because these groups do not allow anyone to control anyone else in the group (Boehm 2012). When an individual tries to take control, the group as a whole sanctions this activity. Therefore, prototypicality in hunter-gatherer groups involved an egalitarian stance rather than a stance of dominance. With the advent of surplus goods and status based on the accumulated wealth that agriculture and sedentary life made possible, hierarchical social arrangements gained ground. Human social groups can now be arranged either in an egalitarian or hierarchical fashion, with many social groupings including both forms of arrangements and the tensions that engenders. It is important to note, however, that identification with the group occurs in both egalitarian and hierarchically arranged social groups.

CONCLUSION

In this chapter, I argued that guilt is a moral emotion because it motivates relationship repair following a relational transgression. Guilt evolved to assist individuals to maintain good relationships with the people with whom they have mutual dependencies, but also sometimes differing interests or experiences. Guilt-proneness appears to function as a preemptive trait that leads individuals to avoid transgressions in advance. Guilt is an important emotion because relationship maintenance has been a powerful selection factor for humans. The experience and effectiveness of guilt as a motivator is predicated on many human adaptations that enriched our sociality, particularly on the presence and enforcement of social norms and expectations.

Although guilt and other adaptations are generally viewed within an instrumental framework that portrays these adaptations as relatively arbitrary means to the end of reproductive fitness, I argued that a constituent-end interpretation of this evolution better illuminates the richness and power of the function of guilt. From a constituent-end perspective, the experience of guilt is as much a manifestation of a breach of one's identity and internalized standards as it is a matter of avoiding aversive relationship consequences. The internalization of social expectations is a key aspect of normal child development, and individuals identify strongly with their primary groups, setting the stage for guilt as a signal that the person needs to reestablish fidelity to one's accepted identity and to internalized standards.

This constituent-end interpretation of guilt is novel and therefore controversial. I presented evidence for it, but it has not been directly tested empirically. Such assessments seem warranted given the additional conceptual clarity and nuance that this perspective offers. The constituent-end interpretation of guilt can also be generalized to account for many aspects of the evolution of morality. I have explored specific cases of constituent-end explanations for human ethical-mindedness elsewhere (Fowers 2015), but a general account of human moral commitments in constitutive terms is needed to resolve the inherent self-contradiction of conceptions of morality that are based entirely on self-interested, instrumental action.

NOTE

1. Hubris is seen as a positive emotion by Lewis because it is associated with accomplishment and a positive perception of the self.

REFERENCES

Bargh, John. A. 1994. "The Four Horsemen of Automaticity: Awareness, Intention, Efficiency, and Control in Social Cognition." In *Handbook of Social Cognition: Basic Processes; Applications, Vols. 1–2, 2nd ed.*, edited by Robert S. Wyer and Thomas K. Srull, 1–40. London, Psychology Press.

Baumeister, Roy F., and Leary, Mark. R. 1995. "The Need to Belong: Desire for Interpersonal Attachments as a Fundamental Human Motivation." *Psychological Bulletin, 117:* 497–529.

Boehm, Christopher. 2012. *Moral Origins: The Evolution of Virtue, Altruism, and Shame.* New York, Basic.

Brewer, Marilyn B. 1991. "The Social Self: On Being the Same and Different at the Same Time." *Personality and Social Psychology Bulletin, 17:* 475–82.

Brewer, Marilyn B. 2007. "The Importance of Being *We*: Human Nature and Intergroup Relations." *American Psychologist, 62*(8): 728–38.

Cacioppo, John T., and Patrick, William. (2008). *Loneliness: Human Nature and the Need for Social Connection.* New York, W. W. Norton.

Cialdini, Robert B., Brown, Stephanie L., Lewis, Brian P., Luce, Carol, and Neuberg, Steven L. 1997. "Reinterpreting the Empathy-Altruism Relationship: When One into One Equals Oneness." *Journal of Personality and Social Psychology, 73:* 481–94.

Cohen, Taya R., Panter, A. T., and Turan, Nazli. 2012. "Guilt Proneness and Moral Character." *Current Directions in Psychological Science, 21*(5): 355–59.

Cohen, Taya R., Wolf, Scott. T., Panter, A. T., and Insko, Chester A. 2011. "Introducing the GASP Scale: A New Measure of Guilt and Shame Proneness." *Journal of Personality and Social Psychology, 100*(5): 947–66.

Cummins, Denise D. 2012. "Dominance, Status, and Social Hierarchies. In *The Oxford Handbook of Evolutionary Perspectives on Violence, Homicide, and War*, edited by Todd K. Shakelford and Viviana A. Weekes-Shakelford, 676–97. Oxford, Oxford University Press.

De Cremer, David, and Van Dijk, Eric. 2002. "Reactions to Group Success and Failure as a Function of Identification Level: A Test of the Goal-Transformation Hypothesis in Social Dilemmas." *Journal of Experimental Social Psychology, 38:* 435–42.

Eisenberg, Nancy. 2002. "Empathy-Related Emotional Responses, Altruism, and their Socialization." In *Visions of Compassion: Western Scientists and Tibetan Buddhists Examine Human Nature*, edited by Richard J. Davidson and Anne Harrington, 131–64. Oxford, Oxford University Press.

Ekman, Paul. 1994. "All Emotions Are Basic." In *The Nature of Emotion: Fundamental Questions*, edited by Paul. Ekman and Richard J. Davidson, 15–19. New York, Oxford University Press.

Evans, William., Wolfe, Barbara, and Adler, Nancy. 2012. "The SES and Health Gradient: A Brief Review of the Literature." In *Biological Consequences of Socioeconomic Inequalities*, edited by Barbara Wolfe, William Evans, and Teresa E. Seeman, 1–37, New York, Russell Sage Foundation.

Filippin, Antonio, and Guala, Francesco. 2017. "Group Identity as a Social Heuristic: An Experiment with Reaction Times." *Journal of Neuroscience, Psychology, and Economics, 10*(4): 153–66.

Fowers, Blaine J. 2010. "Instrumentalism and Psychology: Beyond Using and Being Used." *Theory & Psychology, 20:* 1–23.

Fowers, Blaine J. 2015. *The Evolution of Ethics: Human Sociality and the Emergence of Ethical Mindedness.* London, Palgrave/McMillan.

Fowers, Blaine J. 2017. "The Deep Psychology of Eudaimonia and Virtue: Belonging, Loyalty, and the Anterior Cingulate Cortex." In *Varieties of Virtue*, edited by David Carr, James Arthur, and Kristján Kristjánsson, 199–216. London, Palgrave/MacMillan.

Gilead, Michael, Katzir, Mayaan, Eyal, Tal, and Liberman, Nira. 2016. "Neural Correlates of Processing 'Self-Conscious' vs 'Basic' Emotions. *Neuropsychologia, 81*: 207–18.

Goode, Chris, Keefer, Lucas A., Branscombe, Nyla R., and Molina, Ludwin E. 2017. "Group Identity as a Source of Threat and Means of Compensation: Establishing Personal Control through Group Identification and Ideology." *European Journal of Social Psychology, 47*(3): 259–72.

Heatherton, Todd F. 2010. "Building a Social Brain." In *Cognitive Neuroscience of Mind: A Tribute to Michael S. Gazzaniga*, edited by P. A. Lorenz-Reuter, K. Baynes, and G. R. Mangun, 173–88. Cambridge, MIT Press.

Henrich, Natalie, and Henrich, Joseph. 2007. *Why Humans Cooperate: A Cultural and Evolutionary Explanation.* Oxford, Oxford University Press.

Hogg, Michael A. 2004. "Social Categorization, Depersonalization, and Group Behavior." In *Self and Social Identity*, edited by Marilyn B. Brewer and Miles Hewstone, 203–31. Malden, Blackwell.

Holt-Lunstad, Joan, Smith, Timothy B., and Layton, J. Bradley. 2010. "Social Relationships and Mortality Risk: A Meta-Analytic Review." *PLOS Medicine, 7*: 1–20.

Hurley, Susan, and Chater, Nick. 2005. "Introduction: The Importance of Imitation." In *Perspectives on Imitation: From Neuroscience to Social Science, Vol. 1*, edited by Susan Hurley and Nick Chater, 1–52. Cambridge, MIT Press.

Kochanska, Grazyna, Gross, Jami N., Lin, Mei-Hua, Nichols, Kate E. 2002. "Guilt in Young Children: Development, Determinants, and Relations with a Broader System of Standards." *Child Development, 73*: 461–82.

Krebs, Daniel, L. 2011. *The Origins of Morality.* Oxford, Oxford University Press.

Lewis, Helen B. 1971. *Shame and Guilt in Neurosis.* New York, International Universities Press.

Lewis, Michael. 2018. "Self-Conscious Emotions: Embarrassment, Pride, Shame, Guilt, and Hubris." In *Handbook of Emotions* (4th ed.), edited by Feldman Barrett, Lisa, and Lewis, Micheal, 792–814, New York, Guilford.

Marmot, Michael. 2011. "Health in an Unequal World." *The Lancet, 368*: 2081–94.

McCullough, Michael E. 2008. *Beyond Revenge: The Evolution of the Forgiveness Instinct.* San Francisco, Jossey-Bass.

Sapolsky, Robert. M. 2004. "Social Status and Health in Humans and Other Animals." *Annual Review of Anthropology, 33*: 393–418.

Smith, Richard H., Webster, J. Matthew, Parrott, W. Gerrod, and Eyre, Heidi L. 2002. "The Role of Public Exposure in Moral and Nonmoral Shame and Guilt." *Journal of Personality and Social Psychology, 83*: 138–59.

Sripada, Chandra S. and Stich, Stephen. 2007. "A Framework for the Psychology of Norms." In *The Innate Mind, Vol. 2: Culture and Cognition*, edited by Peter Carruthers, Stephen Laurence, and Stephen Stich, 280–301. Oxford, Oxford University Press.

Tajfel, Henri. 1981. *Human Groups and Social Categories*. Cambridge, Cambridge University Press.

Tangney, June P., and Dearing, Ronda L. 2002. *Shame and Guilt*. New York, Guilford.

Tangney, June P., Stuewig, Jeff, and Mashek, Debra J. 2007. "Moral Emotions and Moral Behavior." *Annual Review of Psychology, 58*: 345–72.

Tomasello, Michael. 2014. "The Ultra-Social Animal." *European Journal of Social Psychology, 44*: 187–94.

Tomasello, Michael, Carpenter, Malinda, Call, Josep, Behne, Tanya, and Moll, Henrike. 2005. "Understanding and Sharing Intentions: The Origins of Cultural Cognition." *Behavioral and Brain Sciences, 28*: 675–735.

Tracy, Jessica L., and Robins, Richard W. 2004. "Putting the Self into Self-Conscious Emotions: A Theoretical Model." *Psychological Inquiry, 15*: 103–25.

Tracy, Jessica L., Shariff, Azim F., and Cheng, Joey T. 2010. "A Naturalist's View of Pride." *Emotion Review, 2*: 163–77.

van Vugt, Mark, and Hart, Claire M. 2004. "Social Identity as Social Glue: The Origins of Group Loyalty." *The Journal of Personality and Social Psychology, 86*(4): 585–98.

Williams, George C. 1988. "Huxley's Evolution and Ethics in Sociobiological Perspective." *Zygon, 23*: 383–407.

Williams, Kipling D. 2007. "Ostracism." *Annual Review of Psychology, 58*: 425–52.

Wolf, Scott T., Cohen, Taya R., Panter, A. T., and Insko, Chester A. 2010. "Shame Proneness and Guilt Proneness: Toward the Further Understanding of Reactions to Public and Private Transgressions." *Self and Identity, 9*(4): 337–62.

Chapter 7

Improving Our Understanding of Guilt by Focusing on Its (Inter)Personal Consequences

Ilona E. De Hooge

During the past decades, scholars have focused on the emotion of guilt and deliberated on the function of this negative emotion. Diverging answers on the question why we experience this emotion have been generated over time. For example, in the sixties and seventies of the past century, scholars such as Lewis (1971) viewed guilt as a self-conscious emotion that arises after a personal transgression. Guilt was understood as a negative emotion that is elicited by negative appraisals of personal conduct, where one's self is affirmed to manage the emotion (Bendix 1992; Lewis 1993; Piers & Singer 1953; Steele 1988). The function of guilt was perceived as protecting and restoring one's self-integrity after having conducted a transgression (Freud 1917/1957, 1923/1961). In the nineties, theorizing on guilt shifted more toward the idea that guilt can be seen as a social emotion that arises after appraisals of others' evaluations of the self (e.g., Barrett 1995; Kugler & Jones 1992). Here, guilt is a negative emotion that signals that one's status as a group member may be threatened due to a transgression, and the function of guilt is avoiding social exclusion by showing others the positive aspects of oneself. Later, scholars developed the idea that guilt is mostly a moral emotion that results from appraisals of having violated other people's concerns (e.g., Baumeister, Stillwell, & Heatherton 1994; Haidt 2003). In this case, guilt signals that one's relationships have been threatened or damaged due to an interpersonal transgression. The function of guilt is then to manage one's social relationships by affirming the threatened relationships, and to enforce communal norms of mutual concern and nurturance by evoking feelings of caring and commitment (Izard 1991; Leith & Baumeister 1998).

These diverging views on the function of guilt have not provided a conclusive answer to the question of why we experience guilt. Although it might be impossible to develop such a conclusive answer, one interesting approach to advance our understanding of the function of guilt is to take a look at guilt's consequences. A stream of research has recently empirically examined the effects that guilt can have on decision-making and on behaviors such as gift-giving or cooperating in social dilemmas (De Hooge 2014; Ketelaar & Au 2003), self-improvement behaviors (Allard & White 2015), and behaviors at the expense of others (De Hooge, Nelissen, Breugelmans, & Zeelenberg 2011). By presuming that these behaviors can be understood as an expression of, or the result from, the function of guilt, developing an integrative overview of guilt's consequences can be a fruitful approach to better understand the function of guilt. This chapter provides such an overview of the recent empirical findings concerning the interpersonal consequences of guilt, and integrates these findings into one perspective on the function of this interesting emotion.

DEFINING GUILT

Early literature on guilt defined it as a negative feeling resulting from intrapsychic, moral conflicts. Freud, for instance, perceived guilt feelings to result from a conflict between the superego and the id. The superego reflects an adaptation of the human organism to civilization, whereas the id reflects people's basic, instinctual drives (Freud 1930/1961). Guilt would then be a moral sense ensuing from conflicts when living with other people (Freud 1909/1955, 1917/1957, 1923/1961), or a self-mediated punishment for violating internal standards of moral behavior (Mosher 1968). Based on this view, guilt would mostly result in destructive *intrapersonal* responses such as self-punishment, negative perfectionism, and self-hate (Fedewa, Burns, & Gomez 2005; Kugler & Jones 1992; Lindsay-Hartz, De Rivera, & Mascolo 1995; Nelissen & Zeelenberg 2009), and could underlie psychological issues such as melancholia, depression, obsessional neuroses, psychosis, and masochism (Fedewa et al. 2005; Freud 1909/1955, 1917/1957, 1923/1961; Harder, Cutler, & Rockart 1992).

In later years, the focus of guilt theories shifted more toward guilt's *interpersonal* side, perceiving guilt as a negative emotion resulting from actions of individual volition (Weiner 1985), or more specifically from moral transgressions in which people appraise the situation as having violated an important norm and thereby having hurt, intentionally or unintentionally, another person ("the victim"; Fessler & Haley 2003; Izard 1977; Ortony, Clore, & Collins 1988; Tangney 1991; Tangney & Dearing 2002; Tracy & Robins 2006; Zeelenberg & Breugelmans 2008). Guilt is a form of distress that occurs when one gets more out of an interpersonal relationship than others do (Adams 1963; Nelissen 2014; Walster, Berscheid, & Walster 1970).

It emerges along with a sense of self and relates to a sense of responsibility regarding societal rules for interpersonal behavior (Izard 1977), further characterized by a high degree of self-agency (Frijda, Kuipers, & Ter Schure 1989) and control (Wicker, Payne, & Morgan 1983). Following the transgression, people experience feelings of tension, remorse, distress over another person's well-being, and a sense of personal responsibility (Berndsen & Manstead 2007; Ferguson, Stegge, & Damhuis 1991; Lewis 1971; Tangney, Stuewig, & Mashek 2007). Guilt is thought to generate a preoccupation with the transgression itself (i.e., what was done) (Ferguson et al. 1991; Lewis 1971; Tangney 1999) and/or with the victim thereof (i.e., who was harmed) (Baumeister et al. 1994; Izard 1991; Lewis 1987; Tangney 1999). As most research on the interpersonal consequences of guilt have used this last characterization to study the consequences of the emotion and to distinguish it for example from shame and regret (De Hooge, Zeelenberg, & Breugelmans 2007; Gausel, Leach, Vignoles, & Brown 2012; Sanftner, Barlow, Marschall, & Tangney 1995; Tangney, Wagner, Fletcher, & Gramzow 1992; Zeelenberg & Breugelmans 2008), this definition of guilt will also be used in the present chapter. Thus, guilt is taken to be an emotion that focuses on transgressions against others, sometimes resulting in accompanying thoughts about that transgression or about the person who was harmed by that transgression.

GUILT'S INTERPERSONAL CONSEQUENCES

The emotion of guilt can be empirically related to an extensive variety of interpersonal consequences, which sometimes even seem contradictory. For example, guilt has been found to motivate both pro-social behavior toward others (Coulter & Pinto 1995; De Hooge et al. 2007; Ketelaar & Au 2003) and self-punishment (Nelissen 2012; Nelissen & Zeelenberg 2009), or to motivate helping of others (Cunningham, Steinberg, & Grev 1980) and behavior at the disadvantage of others (De Hooge et al. 2011). It is therefore a challenge to integrate all existing findings on the consequences of guilt into one, coherent picture.

When taking a close look at the consequences of guilt, it seems that they can be categorized on the basis of multiple dimensions: the study method, the valence of the consequence, and focus of the consequence. A rough distinction can be made between two types of study methods. First, there are studies that examine the phenomenology of guilt by focusing on people's previous guilt experiences and their self-reported related thoughts, feelings, appraisals, and action tendencies (e.g., Frijda et al. 1989; Tangney, Miller, Flicker, & Barlow 1996; Wicker et al. 1983). Usually, the goal of these studies is to differentiate specific emotions, of which guilt is one examined emotion. These studies have provided a wealth of information about the cognitions, appraisals, and feelings of the emotion and about the motivators that guilt can entail. A second type of study is more oriented toward the consequences of guilt. The goal of these behavioral studies is to demonstrate how specific emotions, such as guilt, can differentially affect behaviors (e.g., De Hooge 2014; Iyer, Schmader, & Lickel 2007; Nelissen, Dijker, & De Vries 2007). In these studies, guilt feelings are frequently induced, and the participant's subsequent behavior of interest is observed or measured. These studies have provided new, interesting insights into the effects of guilt in specific situations that have not been discovered with the self-report phenomenological studies.

A second way to categorize the consequences of guilt can be based on the valence of the consequences. Guilt has been found to generate positive behaviors, such as forgiveness (McCullough, Worthington, & Rachal 1997; Strelan 2007), helping (Cunningham et al. 1980), and donating to charity (Basil, Ridgway, & Basil 2006; Coulter & Pinto 1995; Xu, Bègue, & Bushman 2012), but also negative behaviors such as self-punishment (Nelissen & Zeelenberg 2009) or acting to the disadvantage of others (Cryder, Springer, & Morewedge 2012; De Hooge et al. 2011). Whether these behaviors should be categorized as positively or negatively valenced depends upon the perspective. For example, self-punishment can be categorized as bearing a negative consequence for the transgressor, but it does not have to be positive or negative for victims of the transgression or for onlookers. The behavior might even be seen as a positive result for victims when self-punishment is interpreted as a sign of remorse from the transgressor (Nelissen 2012). Similarly, altruism or pro-social behavior might be interpreted as a positive consequence from an interpersonal or relationship point of view, but from an economic viewpoint that focuses on an individual's resources, altruism bears a negative result for the transgressor (Dawes 1980). To simplify this discussion, I categorize the consequence as positive or negative from the vantage of whom the behavior is directed toward. This relates to the third categorization of guilt: the focus of the consequence.

Behaviors can be targeted at different recipients: A behavior might, for example, be focused on the actor (e.g., I want to reward myself), on one other person (e.g., I want to give a gift to my spouse), on a small group of people (e.g., I want to take my family on a trip as a treat), or on a large group of people that are not necessary acquainted with the actor (e.g., I want to give money to a charity). Similarly, guilt-driven behaviors can be focused on the transgressor (e.g., self-punishment; Bastian, Jetten, & Fasoli 2011), or on the victim(s) of the transgression (e.g., cooperation or compliance with the victim, compensation of the victim; Ketelaar & Au 2003; Konoske, Staple, & Graf 1979; Yu, Hu, Hu, & Zhou 2013). Guilt-driven behaviors can also be focused on another individual who is not the victim of the transgression, but who might be aware of the guilt-causing event (e.g., cooperation with,

Table 7.1 (Inter)Personal Consequences of Guilt

Type of Consequence	Consequence	References
Phenomenological Findings (Self-reported tendencies)	Forgiveness	(McCullough et al. 1997; Strelan 2007)
	Heightened sense of responsibility	(Breugelmans & Poortinga 2006; Izard 1977)
	Tendency to apologize	(Schmader & Lickel 2006; Zeelenberg & Breugelmans 2008)
	Desire to be forgiven	(Roseman et al. 1994; Zeelenberg & Breugelmans 2008)
	Tendency to make amends, to make up, set things right	(Breugelmans & Poortinga 2006; Fontaine et al. 2006; Lindsay-Hartz 1984; Tangney et al. 1996)
	Desire to undo transgression	(Zeelenberg & Breugelmans 2008)
Behavioral Findings Positive other-focused consequences	Altruism (toward one other)	(Darlington & Macker 1966; Regan 1971; Regan et al. 1972)
	Charity donations (others in general)	(Basil et al. 2006; Coulter & Pinto 1995; Xu et al. 2012)
	Compensatory behavior (toward victim)	(Iyer et al. 2003; Iyer et al. 2007; Leach et al. 2006; Yu et al. 2013)
	Compliance	(Freedman 1970; Freedman et al. 1967; Konoske et al. 1979)
	Cooperation (with one other)	(De Hooge et al. 2007; Ketelaar & Au 2003; Nelissen et al. 2007)
	Gift-giving (to victim)	(De Hooge 2014, 2017)
	Helping	(Cunningham et al. 1980)
Negative other-focused consequences	Avoidance of others	(De Hooge et al. 2018; 2019)
	Reduced guilt feelings without action of oneself	(De Hooge 2012; Schmitt et al. 2008)
	Reparative behavior at expense of others	(Cryder et al. 2012; De Hooge et al. 2011)
Self-focused consequences	Physical cleansing	(Zhong & Liljenquist 2006)
	Purchase of self-improvement products	(Allard & White 2015)
	Self-punishment	(Bastian et al. 2011; Nelissen 2012; Nelissen & Zeelenberg 2009)

Note. This table does not provide, nor is it intended to provide, an all-inclusive overview of existing research on guilt.

helping of, or altruism toward a person unrelated to the guilt-causing event; Cunningham et al. 1980; De Hooge et al. 2007; Nelissen et al. 2007; Regan 1971; Regan, Williams, & Sparling 1972). Finally, the behavior can be focused on a group of people (others in general) who are not the victims of the transgression (e.g., donation to a good cause; Darlington & Macker 1966). Using the valence and focus of the consequence to categorize the relevant empirical findings on guilt generates an interesting overview for improving our understanding of the function of guilt (see Table 7.1).

FINDINGS OF PHENOMENOLOGICAL STUDIES ON GUILT

Guilt has frequently been studied by asking people to remember their previous guilt experiences and to report their accompanying cognitions, feelings, appraisals, and behavioral tendencies, either as open answers or on self-report rating scales. In these phenomenology-focused studies, guilt has been related to a heightened sense of personal responsibility, compliance, and forgiveness (Breugelmans & Poortinga 2006; Freedman, Wallington, & Bless 1967; Izard 1977; McCullough et al. 1997; Strelan 2007; Tangney et al. 1992). People experiencing guilt reported wanting to "undo what had happened" (Zeelenberg & Breugelmans 2008) and feeling angry with themselves (Ellsworth & Tong 2006; Zeelenberg & Breugelmans 2008).

Moreover, the emotion has been linked to reparative intentions (Schmader & Lickel 2006; Tangney 1993). People have reported stronger desires to make amends after having described a guilt experience compared to shame or embarrassment experiences (Tangney et al. 1996). In other studies, people reported desires to apologize (Schmader & Lickel 2006; Zeelenberg & Breugelmans 2008), to be forgiven (Roseman, Wiest, & Swartz 1994; Zeelenberg & Breugelmans 2008), to "set things right" (Lindsay-Hartz et al. 1995), or "to do something to make it better" (Schmader & Lickel 2006) following their guilt experiences. These behavioral tendencies have been replicated across a wide array of cultures with similar study methods (Breugelmans & Poortinga 2006; Fontaine et al. 2006), and they have been categorized by most scholars as positive behavioral tendencies.

It is difficult to categorize these self-reported behavioral tendencies on the basis of the focus of the consequence. In most, if not all, of these studies the focus of the behavioral tendency has not been taken into account: the items are formulated in a general way (e.g., "I want to apologize"; "I want to make amends"), without specifying whether such actions would focus on the transgressor (e.g., self-forgiveness), on the victim of one's transgression (e.g., "I want to apologize to the person I've hurt"), or on non-victims (e.g., "I want to apologize to everybody who knows about the transgression"). Consequently, this line of research has spurred the idea that guilt is a negative emotion with positive, interpersonal consequences for everyone in the surrounding of the transgressor.

FINDINGS OF BEHAVIORAL STUDIES ON GUILT

Behavioral studies on guilt attempt to induce guilt in participants and measure their subsequent behaviors. Guilt has frequently been induced in hypothetical situations in which people have to imagine themselves being in a guilt situation (e.g., Berndsen & Manstead 2007; Cryder et al. 2012; Soscia 2007), or in surveys in which people are asked to remember personal experiences in which they have experienced guilt feelings (e.g., De Hooge 2014; De Hooge et al. 2007; Ketelaar & Au 2003; Nelissen et al. 2007). Some studies have used lab inductions of guilt to generate in situ guilt feelings in a socialy constructed situation (Carlsmith & Gross 1969; Darlington & Macker 1966; De Hooge 2012; De Hooge et al. 2011). In our lab inductions of guilt, for instance, we manipulated feedback on performance in games such that participants earned lottery tickets based on their own performance and the performance of another participant. When participants subsequently played games to earn lottery tickets for the fellow participant, the feedback announced that the fellow participant did not earn lottery tickets due to bad performance of the participant (De Hooge 2012; De Hooge et al. 2011). Other examples of in situ guilt inductions are making participants believe that they gave electric shocks to another participant in a study (Carlsmith & Gross 1969) or that they harmed the performance of a fellow student on an important exam (Darlington & Macker 1966). The guilt induction in behavioral studies is then followed by a distinct decision situation in which researchers measure or observe the behaviors. These studies have revealed different types of consequences.

Positive Other-Focused Consequences

In behavioral studies the focus of the consequence is almost always specified. This makes it possible to examine whether guilt motivates positive or negative behaviors toward the victim of the transgression, toward individuals other than the victim, or toward others in general. A first group of behavioral studies has focused on behaviors targeted at the victim of the transgression. For example, after participants made unfair offers in the first rounds of a social dilemma game, they have been found to act more pro-socially in subsequent rounds of the social dilemma game compared to participants who did not make unfair offers in the first rounds (Ketelaar & Au 2003). Participants believing that they gave electric shocks to another participant showed a higher tendency to give in to requests that were unrelated to the shock situation when those requests were made by the participant allegedly receiving the shocks (Carlsmith & Gross 1969). Similar findings have been found for compliance to requests of the victim (Konoske et al. 1979) and for compensatory behaviors aimed at the victims (Iyer, Leach, & Crosby 2003; Iyer et al. 2007; Leach, Iyer, & Pedersen 2006; Yu et al. 2013). These findings reveal that guilt feelings can generate positive behaviors toward the victim of the transgression.

Guilt has also been found to motivate positive behaviors toward individuals other than the victim. For instance, after having described previous guilt experiences, participants played social dilemma games in which they divided money between themselves and another individual (e.g., De Hooge et al. 2007; Nelissen et al. 2007; Nelissen, Leliveld, Van Dijk, & Zeelenberg 2011), or they indicated their intentions to cooperate with others on an everyday cooperation measure (De Hooge et al. 2007). These studies showed guilt to motivate pro-social behavior toward those individuals compared to emotions such as shame or fear. Also, after believing that they harmed the performance of a fellow student on an exam, people have been found to agree with a request for blood donation from an unknown other person (Darlington & Macker 1966). Similarly, guilt has been shown to motivate altruism (Regan, 1971; Regan et al. 1972) and helping (Cunningham et al. 1980) toward individuals who were not the victim of the transgression.

One set of studies has examined whether guilt generates positive behaviors toward others in general who are not aware of the transgression. For example, studies in consumer research have researched whether guilt appeals in advertisements can motivate people to donate money to good causes (e.g., Basil et al. 2006; Bozinoff & Ghingold 1983; Coulter & Pinto 1995; Hibbert, Smith, Davies, & Ireland 2007). Yet it is unclear whether these studies demonstrate the consequences of guilt experienced due to the transgression that the advertisement is appealing to, or whether these studies demonstrate the influences of anticipated guilt that may arise when the individual does not donate to the good cause. It is also unclear whether these studies focus on others in general who are not aware of the transgression, or whether these studies focus on victims of a group-based harm that the individual (together with his/her social group) has caused somewhere in the past. More direct indications that guilt could motivate positive behaviors toward others come from studies that experimentally induced guilt and measured transgressors' donations to charities following a donation request that is unrelated to the guilt induction (Xu et al. 2012). These findings seemingly support the idea generated by the phenomenological studies that guilt motivates positive behaviors toward everybody in the transgressor's surroundings.

Negative Other-Focused Consequences

After such a long list of positive interpersonal behaviors following from guilt, one may wonder whether guilt could generate any negative other-focused behavior. I am not aware of any behavioral study showing guilt to motivate behaviors that further hurt or damage the victim of the guilt-generating transgression. There is some research that focuses on guilt feelings after a different individual has repaired the damage caused by the transgressor. The idea is that if guilt is a social or moral emotion motivating actions to show the positive sides of oneself to others or to repair social relationships, then the transgressor's guilt feelings and positive other-focused behaviors should not be affected by reparative actions by another individual (De Hooge 2012). Multiple experiments were run in which a guilt induction (e.g., you borrowed the valuable bicycle of a friend, but the bicycle gets stolen because you forgot to lock it) was followed by the introduction of a third individual. The third individual repaired the damage for the victim (e.g., a second friend comes along and offers a spare bike to the friend that he can keep). After this encounter, transgressors reported decreased guilt feelings, decreased self-reported reparative tendencies, and decreased pro-social behaviors compared to transgressors in a guilt situation where no reparation by a third individual had taken place. These findings speak *against* the view of guilt as a social emotion focused on making a positive impression on others in one's surroundings: If guilt would have such a function, then the presence of a third individual should have increased rather than decreased guilt feelings and positive interpersonal behaviors. Yet, the guilt feelings, reparative tendencies, and pro-social behavior did not completely disappear, supporting the view of guilt being a moral emotion that is focused on repairing social relationships. One addition should, however, be made: The findings reveal that transgressors are more focused on the necessary reparative actions or on efficient ways in which such reparative actions can be achieved, rather than on the emotional end-state or the well-being of victims. This addition is also supported by a study on collective guilt showing that transgressors' guilt feelings are reduced when repair of the damage for victims is too difficult to achieve (Schmitt, Miller, Branscombe, & Brehm 2008).

The idea that guilt is focused on repairing social relationships in efficient ways also converges with research showing that transgressors tend to repair the damage at the expense of others rather than at the expense of oneself (De Hooge et al. 2011). All behavioral studies showing positive other-focused consequences of guilt used measures where only the transgressor and one other person (e.g., the victim) were present. Consequently, in these studies it is only possible to act positively toward another individual at the expense of the transgressor's own resources (e.g., time, money, energy). Yet, when including a third individual, it is possible to act positively toward the victim at the expense of resources that would otherwise have been spent on that third individual. For example, De Hooge et al. (2011) showed that after having hurt a friend, transgressors spent more money on a birthday gift for the friend compared to a control situation. This behavior replicates the reparative behaviors toward victims that we have seen previously. Interestingly, the expensive birthday gift was paid for by reducing the amount of money spent on the birthday gift of another friend and *not* by reducing the amount of money kept for oneself. Similarly, transgressors cancelled appointments with other individuals instead of time planned for oneself when spending more time on victims of one's transgressions. This does not necessarily mean that transgressors intentionally harm third individuals: Transgressors might be temporarily unaware of the well-being of those individuals. Indeed, other studies have shown that guilt can lead to a temporary decrease in attention to the well-being of others (Cryder et al. 2012). These findings imply that guilt is not a social emotion that focuses on making a positive impression on others in one's surroundings, nor a moral emotion that focuses on maintaining one's social relationships in general. Instead, guilt seems to be an efficiently arranged moral emotion that only focuses on repairing the hurt relationship with the victim of the transgression.

Self-Focused Consequences

There is also some research examining what behaviors guilt motivates when transgressors are not in contact with others or when the caused harm is irreversible. It appears that transgressors can punish themselves by, for example, denying oneself pleasurable activities (Nelissen & Zeelenberg 2009), reducing one's rewards (Nelissen & Zeelenberg 2009), or physically hurting oneself (Bastian et al. 2011; Nelissen 2012) when they are unable to repair the hurt caused. Some studies suggest that guilt feelings can be reduced by physically cleansing oneself (Zhong & Liljenquist 2006). Finally, guilt feelings can generate the selection of products aimed at self-improvement, such as products that temporarily improve mental capacity (Allard & White 2015). Together, these findings show that guilt feelings can have direct negative or positive consequences for the transgressor herself.

AN INTEGRATIVE VIEW ON GUILT'S FUNCTION

Summarizing the (inter)personal consequences of guilt, it is clear that this negative emotion generates positive, reparative behaviors toward the victim of the transgression. Phenomenological studies show that guilt motivates behavioral tendencies to repair or make amends; behavioral studies show that guilt motivates positive behaviors such as cooperation, helping, gift giving, and altruism toward the victim; and no study to date has shown guilt to motivate negative behaviors toward the victim. This is in line with the view of guilt as a moral emotion, as long as this view formulates the function of guilt as preserving and strengthening the *hurt* relationship (Baumeister et al. 1994; Baumeister, Stillwell, & Heatherton 1995; Tangney 1995). But there are contradictory findings concerning transgressors' behaviors toward non-victims: Whereas some behavioral studies demonstrate positive behaviors toward other individuals, other behavioral studies demonstrate negative behaviors toward those others. This makes it unlikely that guilt motivates maintenance of social relationships in general.

At the same time, one may wonder how such contradictory findings can be explained. I propose that the findings have arisen due to the social contexts that studies have used. As the central concern of guilt is the damaged social relationship with the victim (Lewis 1971), ensuing behaviors are first and foremost aimed at restoring this relationship (Baumeister et al. 1994). Only when transgressors are unable to restore the relationship, for example because an experimenter forces transgressors to interact with other individuals, transgressors will search for different ways in which they can relieve their guilt. Guilt alleviation could, for instance, occur with positive behaviors toward other individuals (De Hooge et al. 2007), self-punishment (Nelissen & Zeelenberg 2009), or self-improvement (Allard & White 2015). This means that when transgressors can *choose* which social situation they would like to enter, be it in behavioral studies or in daily life, they prefer to approach the victim to restore the relationship. Moreover, transgressors prefer to socially avoid other individuals: Interacting with such others only diverts one's efforts and attention from the hurt relationship. By offering participants the possibility to select the social situation that they want to enter following a guilt induction, our most recent studies indeed reveal that guilt motivates *social approach* of victims, but *social avoidance* of other individuals (De Hooge, Breugelmans, Wagemans, & Zeelenberg 2019; De Hooge, Wagemans, Breugelmans, & Zeelenberg 2018). Thus, the function of guilt is to preserve and repair the hurt relationship, and to temporarily reduce distraction from this task by socially avoiding others.

The perspective that guilt motivates behaviors to maintain and repair the hurt relationship sounds very positive. However, the review also demonstrates that transgressors aim to repair the hurt relationship in ways that are efficient for themselves. When transgressors can repair the relationship at the expense of others rather than at the expense of themselves, they will do so (De Hooge et al. 2011). When the repair has already been done by another individual or when the repair seems impossible, guilt feelings are alleviated and transgressors hardly undertake further actions (De Hooge 2012; Schmitt et al. 2008). In sum, guilt might then function to maintain and preserve hurt relationships, but it does so in the most efficient ways possible. There thus seems to be a self-focused touch even to this moral, other-focused emotion.

REFERENCES

Adams, J. S. (1963). Towards an understanding of inequity. *The Journal of Abnormal and Social Psychology, 67*, 422–36.

Allard, T., & White, K. (2015). Cross-domain effects of guilt on desire for self-improvement products. *Journal of Consumer Research, 42*, 401–19.

Barrett, K. C. (1995). A functionalist approach to shame and guilt. In J. P. Tangney & K. W. Fischer (Eds.), *Self-conscious emotions: The psychology of shame, guilt, embarrassment, and pride* (25–63). New York: The Guilford Press.

Basil, D. Z., Ridgway, N. M., & Basil, M. D. (2006). Guilt appeals: The mediating effect of responsibility. *Psychology & Marketing, 23*, 1035–54.

Bastian, B., Jetten, J., & Fasoli, F. (2011). Cleansing the soul by hurting the flesh: The guilt-reducing effect of pain. *Psychological Science, 22*, 334–35.

Baumeister, R. F., Stillwell, A. M., & Heatherton, T. F. (1994). Guilt: An interpersonal approach. *Psychological Bulletin, 115*, 243–67.

Baumeister, R. F., Stillwell, A. M., & Heatherton, T. F. (1995). Interpersonal aspects of guilt: Evidence from narrative studies. In J. P. Tangney & K. W. Fischer (Eds.), *Self-conscious emotions: The psychology of shame, guilt, embarrassment, and pride* (255–73). New York: The Guilford Press.

Bendix, R. (1992). Diverging paths in the scientific search for authenticity. *Journal of Folklore Research*, 103–32.

Berndsen, M., & Manstead, A. S. R. (2007). On the relationship between responsibility and guilt: Antecedent appraisal or elaborated appraisal? *European Journal of Social Psychology, 37*, 774–92.

Bozinoff, L., & Ghingold, M. (1983). Evaluating guilt arousing marketing communications. *Journal of Business Research, 11*, 243–55.

Breugelmans, S. M., & Poortinga, Y. H. (2006). Emotion without a word: Shame and guilt with Rarámuri Indians and rural Javanese. *Journal of Personality and Social Psychology, 91*, 1111–22.

Carlsmith, J. M., & Gross, A. E. (1969). Some effects of guilt on compliance. *Journal of Personality and Social Psychology, 11*, 232–39.

Coulter, R. H., & Pinto, M. B. (1995). Guilt appeals in advertising: What are their effects? *Journal of Applied Psychology, 80*, 697–05.

Cryder, C., Springer, S., & Morewedge, C. K. (2012). Guilty feelings, targeted actions. *Personality and Social Psychology Bulletin, 38*, 607–18.

Cunningham, M. R., Steinberg, J., & Grev, R. (1980). Wanting to and having to help: Separate motivations for positive mood and guilt-induced helping. *Journal of Personality and Social Psychology, 38*, 181–92.

Darlington, R. B., & Macker, C. E. (1966). Displacement of guilt-produced altruistic behavior. *Journal of Personality and Social Psychology, 4*, 442–43.

Dawes, R. M. (1980). Social dilemmas. *Annual Review of Psychology, 31*, 169–93.

De Hooge, I. E. (2012). The exemplary social emotion guilt: Not so relationship-oriented when another person repairs for you. *Cognition and Emotion, 26*, 1189–207.

De Hooge, I. E. (2014). Predicting consumer behavior with two emotion appraisal dimensions: Emotion valence and agency in gift giving. *International Journal of Research in Marketing, 31*, 380–94.

De Hooge, I. E. (2017). Combining emotion appraisal dimensions and individual differences to understand emotion effects on gift giving. *Journal of Behavioral Decision Making, 30*, 256–69.

De Hooge, I. E., Breugelmans, S. M., Wagemans, F. M. A., & Zeelenberg, M. (2019). Guilt and social avoidance. Manuscript submitted for publication.

De Hooge, I. E., Nelissen, R., Breugelmans, S. M., & Zeelenberg, M. (2011). What is moral about guilt? Acting "prosocially" at the disadvantage of others. *Journal of Personality and Social Psychology, 100*, 462–73.

De Hooge, I. E., Wagemans, F. M. A., Breugelmans, S. M., & Zeelenberg, M. (2018). The social side of shame: Approach versus withdrawal. *Cognition & Emotion, 32*, 1671–77.

De Hooge, I. E., Zeelenberg, M., & Breugelmans, S. M. (2007). Moral sentiments and cooperation: Differential influences of shame and guilt. *Cognition and Emotion, 21*, 1025–42.

Ellsworth, P. C., & Tong, E. M. W. (2006). What does it mean to be angry at yourself? Categories, appraisals, and the problem of language. *Emotion, 6*, 572–86.

Fedewa, B. A., Burns, L. R., & Gomez, A. A. (2005). Positive and negative perfectionism and the shame/guilt distinction: Adaptive and maladaptive characteristics. *Personality and Individual Differences, 38*, 1609–19.

Ferguson, T. J., Stegge, H., & Damhuis, I. (1991). Children's understanding of guilt and shame. *Child Development, 62*, 827–39.

Fessler, D. M. T., & Haley, K. J. (2003). The strategy of affect: Emotions in human cooperation. In P. Hammerstein (Ed.), *The genetic and cultural evolution of cooperation* (7–36). Cambridge, MA: MIT Press.

Fontaine, J. R. J., Luyten, P., De Boeck, P., Corveleyn, J., Fernandez, M., Herrera, D., ... Egyetem, A. (2006). Untying the gordian knot of guilt and shame: The structure of guilt and shame reactions based on situation and person variation in Belgium, Hungary, and Peru. *Journal of Cross-Cultural Psychology, 37*, 273–92.

Freedman, J. L. (1970). Transgression, compliance, and guilt. In J. Macauley & L. Berkowitz (Eds.), *Altruism and helping behavior: Social psychological studies of some antecedents and consequences.* (155–61). New York: Academic Press.

Freedman, J. L., Wallington, S. A., & Bless, E. (1967). Compliance without pressure: The effects of guilt. *Journal of Personality and Social Psychology, 7*, 117–24.

Freud, S. (1909/1955). Notes upon a case of obsessional neurosis. In J. Strachey (Ed.), *The standard edition of the complete psychological works of Sigmund Freud* (Vol. 10, 151–318). London: Hogarth Press.

Freud, S. (1917/1957). Mourning and melancholia. In J. Strachey (Ed.), *The standard edition of the complete psychological works of Sigmund Freud* (Vol. 14, 237–60). London: Hogarth Press.

Freud, S. (1923/1961). The ego and the id. In J. Strachey (Ed.), *Standard edition of the complete psychological works of Sigmund Freud* (Vol. 19, 3–66). London: Hogarth Press.

Freud, S. (1930/1961). Civilization and its discontents. In J. Strachey (Ed.), *The standard edition of the complete psychological works of Sigmund Freud* (Vol. 21, 59–145). London: Hogarth Press.

Frijda, N. H., Kuipers, P., & Ter Schure, E. (1989). Relations among emotion, appraisal, and emotional action readiness. *Journal of Personality and Social Psychology, 57*, 212–28.

Gausel, N., Leach, C. W., Vignoles, V. L., & Brown, R. (2012). Defend or repair? Explaining responses to in-group moral failure by disentangling feelings of shame, rejection, and inferiority. *Journal of Personality and Social Psychology, 102*, 941–60.

Haidt, J. (2003). The moral emotions. In R. J. Davidson, K. R. Scherer & H. H. Goldsmith (Eds.), *Handbook of affective sciences* (852–70). Oxford: Oxford University Press.

Harder, D. W., Cutler, L., & Rockart, L. (1992). Assessment of shame and guilt and their relationships to psychopathology. *Journal of Personality Assessment, 59*, 584–604.

Hibbert, S., Smith, A., Davies, A., & Ireland, F. (2007). Guilt appeals: Persuasion knowledge and charitable giving. *Psychology and Marketing, 24*, 723–42.

Iyer, A., Leach, C. W., & Crosby, F. J. (2003). White guilt and racial compensation: The benefits and limits of self-focus. *Personality and Social Psychology Bulletin, 29*, 117–29.

Iyer, A., Schmader, T., & Lickel, B. (2007). Why individuals protest the perceived transgression of their country: The role of anger, shame, and guilt. *Personality and Social Psychology Bulletin, 33*, 572–87.

Izard, C. E. (1977). *Human emotions*. New York: Plenum Press.

Izard, C. E. (1991). *The psychology of emotions*. New York: Plenum Press.

Ketelaar, T., & Au, W. T. (2003). The effects of guilt on the behaviour of uncooperative individuals in repeated social bargaining games: An affect-as-information interpretation of the role of emotion in social interaction. *Cognition and Emotion, 17*, 429–53.

Konoske, P., Staple, S., & Graf, R. G. (1979). Compliant reactions to guilt: Self-esteem or self-punishment. *Journal of Social Psychology, 108*, 207–11.

Kugler, K., & Jones, W. H. (1992). On conceptualizing and assessing guilt. *Journal of Personality and Social Psychology, 62*, 318–27.

Leach, C. W., Iyer, A., & Pedersen, A. (2006). Anger and guilt about ingroup advantage explain the willingness for political action. *Personality and Social Psychology Bulletin, 32*, 1232–45.

Leith, K. P., & Baumeister, R. F. (1998). Empathy, shame, guilt, and narratives of interpersonal conflicts: Guilt-prone people are better at perspective taking. *Journal of Personality, 66*, 1–38.

Lewis, H. B. (1971). *Shame and guilt in neurosis*. New York: International Universities Press.

Lewis, H. B. (1987). Shame and the narcissistic personality. In D. L. Nathanson (Ed.), *The many faces of shame* (93–124). New York: The Guilford Press.

Lewis, M. (1993). Self-conscious emotions: Embarassment, pride, shame, and guilt. In M. L. Lewis & J. M. Haviland (Eds.), *Handbook of emotions* (563–73). New York: The Guilford Press.

Lindsay-Hartz, J. (1984). Contrasting experiences of shame and guilt. *American Behavioral Scientist, 27*, 689–704.

Lindsay-Hartz, J., De Rivera, J., & Mascolo, M. F. (1995). Differentiating guilt and shame and their effects on motivation. In J. P. Tangney & A. H. Fischer (Eds.), *Self-conscious emotions: The psychology of shame, guilt, embarrassment, and pride* (274–300). New York: The Guilford Press.

McCullough, M. E., Worthington, E. L. J., & Rachal, K. C. (1997). Interpersonal forgiving in close relationships. *Journal of Personality and Social Psychology, 73*, 321–36.

Mosher, D. L. (1968). Measurement of guilt in females by self-report inventories. *Journal of Consulting and Clinical Psychology, 32*, 690–95.

Nelissen, R. M. A. (2012). Guilt-induced self-punishment as a sign of remorse. *Social Psychological and Personality Science, 3*(2), 139–44.

Nelissen, R. M. A. (2014). Relational utility as a moderator of guilt in social interactions. *Journal of Personality and Social Psychology, 106*, 257–71.

Nelissen, R. M. A., Dijker, A. J., & De Vries, N. K. (2007). How to turn a hawk into a dove and vice versa: Interactions between emotions and goals in a give-some dilemma game. *Journal of Experimental Social Psychology, 43*, 280–86.

Nelissen, R. M. A., Leliveld, M. C., Van Dijk, E., & Zeelenberg, M. (2011). Fear and guilt in proposers: Using emotions to explain offers in ultimatum bargaining. *European Journal of Social Psychology, 41*, 78–85.

Nelissen, R. M. A., & Zeelenberg, M. (2009). When guilt evokes self-punishment: Evidence for the existence of a Dobby-effect. *Emotion, 9*, 118–22.

Ortony, A., Clore, G. L., & Collins, A. (1988). *The cognitive structure of emotions*. New York: Cambridge University Press.

Piers, G., & Singer, M. B. (1953). *Shame and guilt*. Springfield: Thomas.

Regan, J. W. (1971). Guilt, perceived injustice, and altruistic behavior. *Journal of Personality and Social Psychology, 18*, 124–32.

Regan, J. W., Williams, M., & Sparling, S. (1972). Voluntary expiation of guilt: A field experiment. *Journal of Personality and Social Psychology, 24*, 42–45.

Roseman, I. J., Wiest, C., & Swartz, T. S. (1994). Phenomenology, behaviors, and goals differentiate discrete emotions. *Journal of Personality and Social Psychology, 67*, 206–21.

Sanftner, J. L., Barlow, D. H., Marschall, D. E., & Tangney, J. P. (1995). The relation of shame and guilt to eating disorder symptomatology. *Journal of Social and Clinical Psychology, 14*, 315–24.

Schmader, T., & Lickel, B. (2006). The approach and avoidance function of guilt and shame emotions: Comparing reactions to self-caused and other-caused wrongdoing. *Motivation and Emotion, 30*, 43–56.

Schmitt, M. T., Miller, D. A., Branscombe, N. R., & Brehm, J. W. (2008). The difficulty of making reparations affects the intensity of collective guilt. *Group processes & Intergroup Relations, 11*, 267–79.

Soscia, I. (2007). Gratitude, delight, or guilt: The role of consumers' emotions in predicting postconsumption behaviors. *Psychology & Marketing, 24*, 871–94.

Steele, C. M. (1988). The psychology of self-affirmation: Sustaining the integrity of the self. In L. Berkowitz (Ed.), *Advances in experimental social psychology* (Vol. 21, pp. 261–302). New York: Academic Press.

Strelan, P. (2007). Who forgives others, themselves, and situations? The roles of narcissism, guilt, self-esteem, and adreeableness. *Personality and Individual Differences, 42*, 259–69.

Tangney, J. P. (1991). Moral affect: The good, the bad, and the ugly. *Journal of Personality and Social Psychology, 61*, 598–607.

Tangney, J. P. (1993). Shame and guilt. In C. G. Costello (Ed.), *Symptoms of depression* (161–80). New York: Wiley.

Tangney, J. P. (1995). Shame and guilt in interpersonal relationships. In J. P. Tangney & A. H. Fischer (Eds.), *Self-conscious emotions. The psychology of shame, guilt, embarrassment, and pride* (114–39). New York: The Guilford Press.

Tangney, J. P. (1999). The self-conscious emotions: Shame, guilt, embarrassment, and pride. In T. Dalgleish & M. Power (Eds.), *Handbook of cognition and emotion* (541–68). Chichester: Wiley.

Tangney, J. P., & Dearing, R. L. (2002). *Shame and guilt.* New York: The Guilford Press.

Tangney, J. P., Miller, R. S., Flicker, L., & Barlow, D. H. (1996). Are shame, guilt and embarrassment distinct emotions? *Journal of Personality and Social Psychology, 70*, 1256–69.

Tangney, J. P., Stuewig, J., & Mashek, D. J. (2007). What's moral about the self-conscious emotions? In J. L. Tracy, R. W. Robins & J. P. Tangney (Eds.), *The self-conscious emotions: Theory and research* (21–37). New York: The Guilford Press.

Tangney, J. P., Wagner, P. E., Fletcher, C., & Gramzow, R. (1992). Shamed into anger? The relation of shame and guilt to anger and self-reported agression. *Journal of Personality and Social Psychology, 62*, 669–75.

Tracy, J. L., & Robins, R. W. (2006). Appraisal antecedents of shame and guilt: Support for a theoretical model. *Personality and Social Psychology Bulletin, 32*, 1339–51.

Walster, E., Berscheid, E., & Walster, G. W. (1970). The exploited: Justice or justification? In J. Macaulay & L. Berkowitz (Eds.), *Altruism and helping behavior: Social psychological studies of some antecedents and consequences* (179–204). New York: Academic Press.

Weiner, B. (1985). An attributional theory of achievement motivation and emotion. *Psychological Review, 95*, 548–73.

Wicker, F. W., Payne, G. C., & Morgan, R. D. (1983). Participant descriptions of guilt and shame. *Motivation and Emotion, 7*, 25–39.

Xu, H., Bègue, L., & Bushman, B. J. (2012). Too fatigued to care: Ego depletion, guilt, and prosocial behavior. *Journal of Experimental Social Psychology, 48*, 1183–86.

Yu, H., Hu, J., Hu, L., & Zhou, X. (2013). The voice of conscience: Neural bases of interpersonal guilt and compensation. *Social Cognitive and Affective Neuroscience, 9*, 1150–58.

Zeelenberg, M., & Breugelmans, S. M. (2008). The role of interpersonal harm in distinguishing regret from guilt. *Emotion, 8*, 589–96.

Zhong, C.-B., & Liljenquist, K. (2006). Washing away your sins: Threatened morality and physical cleansing. *Science, 313*, 1451–52.

Chapter 8

How Guilt Serves Social Functions from Within

Darren McGee and Roger Giner-Sorolla

Guilt, together with shame, is one of the negative emotions that looks inward, on the actions and status of the self. But the status of the self is ambiguous in Western psychology. It is seen as the sovereign essence and regulator of the individual (e.g., Epstein 1973; Markus & Wurf 1987; Sedikides, Gaertner, & O'Mara 2011), yet formed and updated continually in interactions with others (e.g., Goffman 1949; Hermans, Kempen, & van Loon 1992). Likewise, the status of guilt is unclear. Is it a guide for the actions of the individual, coming from within, a constant voice against the exigencies of social situations? Or is it oriented toward the needs of others in relationships? We will argue that an accommodation between social and individual views of the self happens through *internalization*. Internalization is a process in which social concerns become mystified, their origin obscured, attributed to personal inner feelings rather than external, rational, social concerns. Guilt, as experienced in Western culture, is an emotion subject to internalization, but in it, the vestiges of its social function and origin can still be discerned.

We will begin by laying out arguments for the socially oriented versus the internal and individual nature of guilt, as psychological theorists and researchers have presented them. We will then describe our own integrative position. We grant guilt a social function and a social origin, but we explain its often-individualist phenomenology through processes of internalization (attribution to self) and mystification (elision of the rational forces at play in a social situation). Both processes aid guilt's function as a social-regulatory emotion. Finally, we will describe recent work in our lab that contributes to our understanding of guilt. This research identifies two types of internalized cognition that contribute uniquely to guilt feelings, above and beyond shame and other emotions: partially internalized social appraisals in which the self is treated like a relationship partner; and fully internalized standard-based appraisals. Both internalized appraisals are especially predictive of guilt in situations of individual self-control such as dieting or studying, in which no obvious social interactions are present.

IS GUILT SOCIAL BY NATURE? THE CASE FOR

In reviewing the empirical guilt literature, Baumeister, Stillwell, and Heatherton (1994) conclude that guilt is best viewed as an inherently social phenomenon, with guilt being experienced most frequently in small-scale relationships that are characterized by concerns involving fairness, respect, and welfare. Accordingly, guilt functions to help maintain these types of relationships by a) reducing self-interest, which shifts focus from the self to the partner, making the needs of the partner more salient; b) redistributing power inequalities, with elicitation of guilt being used as means to leverage influence over a more dominant partner; and c) restoring emotional equity within the relationship, so that the level of distress experienced by one partner is matched in the other partner who is responsible for causing the distress.

This idea of guilt functioning to preserve close relationships is also shared by Gilbert (2003), who suggests that guilt initially evolved from a more primitive adaptation that functioned to encourage altruistic behaviour in parent-infant and close-kin relationships. Furthermore, guilt functioning to reduce self-interest and in turn promoting positive action toward another person is similar to Trivers's (1971) conceptualization of "reciprocal altruism," which, in more biological terms, describes how the initial cost incurred in being altruistic to another animal/individual is recovered at a later time when the situation is reversed. That is, it is beneficial to our biological fitness to be altruistic to another individual, as there is an expectation that the cost incurred will be repaid later. Guilt as the sense of owing something, in fact, is reflected in the German etymology of the word for guilt, *schuld*, which can also mean "debt" (Nietzsche 1887/1989). The prospect of guilt at such an unrepaid debt should discourage the person who feels it from selfishly planning to cheat rather than to reciprocate.

In support of the above, Baumeister, Reis, and Delespaul (1995) had participants recall six different personal experiences that elicited six different unpleasant emotions, one of which was the feeling of guilt (Study 2). Participants were asked to describe these emotional experiences in as much detail as possible, describing what caused the feeling; what occurred before, during, and after the feeling; and the overall intensity of the feeling. Participants' experiences were then coded for specific social features, with the aim of identifying the type of relationship that was responsible for eliciting the unpleasant emotional response. Results showed that feelings of guilt were, on average, quite intense, as most reported the intensity of the guilt feelings as being either a 5 or 6 on a 7-point Likert scale. Crucially, interpersonal involvement was shown to be significantly more prevalent in the guilt experiences, when comparing guilt experiences with the other five unpleasant emotion experiences. Furthermore, the guilt experiences were significantly more likely to involve intimate relationships than the other emotion experiences. Interestingly, although private experiences of guilt were less common than for the other emotion experiences, when guilt was felt in private it involved instances of personal self-control failure. This will be relevant to our research on the social roots of guilt in "private" contexts, discussed later.

In a parallel set of studies, Baumeister, Stillwell, and Heatherton (1995) had participants recall and then describe two scenarios in which they angered another person, with one scenario resulting in participants experiencing feelings of guilt and the other scenario resulting in participants not experiencing feelings of guilt. Importantly, scenarios involving guilt were significantly more likely to contain expressions of interpersonal concern, such as wanting to apologize and confessing the misdeed. Similarly, the scenarios resulting in guilty feelings were significantly more likely to involve close relationships, such as a family member or a romantic partner. In Study 2, Baumeister, Stillwell, and Heatherton (1995) had participants recall either an instance in which another person made them feel guilty or an instance in which they induced feelings of guilt in another person. Coders then differentiated between the type of relationship involved in these scenarios, coding for four different types of relationships: strangers with or without an expectation of future interactions, casual acquaintanceships, or intimate relationships. The results were quite clear: Almost all instances of guilt involved an intimate relationship, with only one participant out of the 104 describing a guilt scenario involving a stranger. Furthermore, interpersonal neglect was the most often-cited motivation behind the guilt induction, further supporting the idea that guilt functions to regulate and maintain close relationships.

Research from different labs has also found support for this view of guilt. Tangney, Miller, Flicker, and Barlow (1996), for example, asked participants to recall a time when they experienced feelings of guilt, shame, and embarrassment and then had them describe these experiences in as much detail as possible, using prompts such as "Why did it happen?" and "What were you thinking and feeling?" etc. Of interest, these experiences were coded for whether other people were present or not. Although experiences of embarrassment had, on average, more people present compared with shame and guilt, the vast majority of guilt experiences occurred in the presence of another person, with only 10 percent of guilt experiences occurring in private. Furthermore, these guilt experiences typically occurred in the presence of someone who was known to the participant and whom they highly regarded.

In addition, there is experimental research showing that guilt functions to promote positive interpersonal behavior. Ketelaar and Au (2003), for example, experimentally manipulated (in one group) or assessed (self-report in another group) participants' levels of guilt feelings after behaving noncooperatively in a social bargaining game, which involved participants choosing either a cooperative strategy, so that they and another individual were both rewarded, or a noncooperative strategy, in which the participant intended to be rewarded at the expense of the opposing player. The authors then examined the relationship between guilt feelings and the likelihood of cooperating in a second round of a social bargaining game. As expected, those who experienced guilt feelings after initially adopting a noncooperative strategy in the first round were significantly more likely to cooperate in the second round. In other words, the elicitation or the experience of guilt feeling appeared to reduce self-interest, to the extent that participants switched from selfish (noncooperative) behavior to a more selfless (cooperative) behavior.

In fact, it has been shown that guilt reduces self-interest to the extent that highly guilt-prone individuals will avoid forming partnerships with other people; particularly when they perceive the other person as being more competent than themselves. Wiltermuth and Cohen (2014), across five studies, examined whether guilt-prone participants were more likely to reduce their financial gain after being partnered with a more competent partner. In their first study, for example, participants were told that they would be working with a partner to complete a trivia-based task about accounting, and that they would be paid for their participation. They were then presented with a sample trivia question and, after indicating whether they could successfully answer the question or not, were presented with the correct answer. Participants then completed two measures of self-efficacy, which measured how confident they thought they would be in successfully completing the full trivia task. After reading a description of their partner, who was described as being highly competent in this field of trivia, participants decided whether they should be paid based solely on their own performance or on an average of their own and their partner's performance. Results showed that highly guilt-prone participants who lacked belief in their own competency were less willing to be paid based on their joint performance with their partner.

The overall findings from Wiltermuth and Cohen (2014) suggest that highly guilt-prone individuals tend to avoid putting themselves in positions where they might be unable to respond in kind. Earlier research from Cohen, too, showed that a proneness to experience guilt was associated with reduced self-interest. Cohen, Wolf, Panter, and Insko (2011, Study 2), for example, showed that guilt-proneness was negatively correlated with making unethical business decisions and was positively correlated with altruism. In this same study, a subset of participants was also presented with a potential opportunity to earn money from acting dishonestly, at the expense of a random counterpart on the internet. The findings showed that those higher in guilt-proneness were less likely to act on self-interest, choosing to allocate potential earnings based on honesty rather than dishonesty.

Other theories argue that both guilt and shame are inherently social in nature, most notably Gilbert (2003), who characterizes guilt and shame as equally social emotions that emerged over evolutionary time in response to different social challenges. Gilbert describes shame as a response to challenges to social rank and reputation, which can affect how people are perceived and accepted in social groups. In this view, shame is adaptive, helping people regulate their standing within a social hierarchy. By contrast, Gilbert's (2003) account describes guilt as rooted in challenges to equity in smaller-scale, one-on-one social relationships, centered on harm-avoidance and fairness-related concerns. However, research supporting this evolutionary account is mainly correlational, and it is mainly focused on shame. There are associations between self-perceptions of low social rank and shame (Cheung, Gilbert, & Irons 2004; Gilbert, Allan, & Goss 1996; Gilbert & Miles 2000), while social anxiety disorder, which embodies concerns about low social rank, has also been consistently found to be associated with shame (Gilbert 2000; Hedman, E., Ström, Stünkel, & Mörtberg 2013; Michail and Birchwood 2013).

IS GUILT SOCIAL BY NATURE? THE CASE AGAINST

Possibly the longest-standing view of guilt is that it is an inherently personal emotion, drawing on one's inner conscience. For example, Benedict, in her 1948 book *The Chrysanthemum and the Sword*, contrasts U.S. culture, which is described as being predominantly guilt-oriented, with Japanese culture, which is described as being predominantly shame-oriented. Accordingly, in a "guilt culture," people are chiefly motivated by their own internalized moral concerns, which are largely unaffected by direct external influence. In a "shame culture," by contrast, an individual's behavior is more responsive to, and modulated by, external pressures, which take the form of social hierarchies and threats to honor. In other words, an audience is not required for the elicitation of guilt, but it is required for the elicitation of shame. Aside from this distinction representing an overly simplistic comparison of U.S. and Japanese cultures, which unfairly portrays the people of Japan (Creighton 1990), there is, nevertheless, some evidence supporting this view of shame and guilt.

Smith, Webster, Parrott, and Eyre (2002), across five experiments, tested the idea that guilt, but not shame, would remain largely unaffected after manipulating the level of public exposure associated with committing a moral or non-moral transgression. That is, that shame but not guilt would be more responsive to public exposure following an act of fault. Their first experiment, for example, had participants read scenarios involving moral transgressions (e.g., cheating on a test) and then had them imagine what the individual in the scenarios would be thinking and feeling. The amount of public exposure associated with the moral transgressions was manipulated (private, implicit public, and explicit public), as was the level of moral belief of the individual in the story: For example, the individual committing the transgression would either believe the act was very wrong (high moral belief) or would believe the act was wrong but had some justification (low moral belief), such as believing that other students had an unfair advantage. The results showed that shame was significantly higher in the explicit public exposure condition compared with the other two conditions and was significantly higher in the implicit public exposure condition compared with the private condition. Conversely, as expected, guilt was unaffected by the public exposure manipulation, as guilt did not significantly differ between any of the conditions. However, moral belief affected both emotions similarly, with low moral beliefs leading to less shame and guilt. Overall, Smith, Webster, Parrott, and Eyre (2002) showed that shame was more socially oriented than guilt, which was shown to be unaffected by public exposure.

Further supporting this, Combs, Campbell, Jackson, and Smith (2010, Study 1) had student participants read about a fellow student who was caught plagiarizing and had them imagine how this student would think and feel. The level of public exposure was also manipulated, with the plagiarizing student getting caught either in a one-to-one setting (low public exposure) or in a group setting in front of multiple lab assistants (high public exposure), or not getting caught at all (private condition). In addition, the level of reprimand was manipulated, with the plagiarizing student either receiving severe (accused of cheating and shouted at), mild (told that plagiarizing is wrong but "let off"), or no reprimand. Results showed that shame, but not guilt, significantly increased from the private (no exposure) condition to the low and high public exposure conditions, with no significant difference found between low and high conditions. However, neither shame nor guilt were affected by the level of reprimand. As such, these findings further support the idea that, while shame responds to any kind of social exposure, guilt is unaffected by public exposure manipulations.

In addition, there is evidence showing that an inclination to adhere to self-imposed restrictions, such as those found in individual self-control dilemmas, is more strongly associated with a propensity to experience guilt than shame. Tangney, Baumeister, and Boone (2004), for example, examined the relationship between a measure of self-control—which encompassed multiple aspects of self-control, such as habit breaking, impulse control, control over thoughts, etc.—and a host of other measures, one of which was the Test of

Self-Conscious Affect (TOSCA), which is a dispositional measure of shame and guilt. Their findings showed that higher scores in self-control were positively associated with guilt-proneness and negatively associated with shame-proneness. In other words, those high in self-control had a greater propensity to experience guilt, whereas those low in self-control had a greater propensity to experience shame.

FROM SOCIAL TO PERSONAL: INTERNALIZATION AND MYSTIFICATION

Despite the seeming contradiction between guilt's social and individual aspects, it is possible to understand how both strands of evidence can be accurate characterizations of guilt. Most evidence for guilt's social nature points to the contexts in which it arises, or the pro-social behaviors it functionally promotes. Evidence of guilt's individual nature is rooted in reports of the subjective experience of guilt, which seemingly comes from inside a person rather than being traceable to the input of other persons. In other words, it seems that guilt is an emotion with social input and output, but with a phenomenology that can be dissociated from explicit awareness of social presence. This process can be explained as internalization, and when it occurs, it serves a supremely important social function.

Our analysis is guided by the insights of Frank (1988), who explained many features of emotion as *commitment devices*. Emotions are often seemingly irrational, command our motivation and attention, and are communicated with a less-than-perfect ability to turn these signals on or off. While we may curse these intractable traits, in Frank's analysis, they serve two purposes. First, emotions such as guilt and shame levy painful costs on actions that break a commitment for a person's short-term gain at the cost of others' interests and their own long-term interests. Likewise, emotions such as love and pride make it rewarding to keep a commitment. These costs are adaptive in a social environment and in an environment that rewards planning.

Second, emotions communicate to others that those who have them are governed by pro-social rather than antisocial considerations. The communicative nature of emotion itself has been recognized at least since Darwin's treatise on the emotions (1965/1872). In Frank's analysis, seeing someone else's emotional expression can be a useful prelude and shortcut to cooperation decisions. A pro-social emotion such as guilt or affection, perceived in context, sends a signal about one's motives that encourages cooperative relationships and mutual emotional investment.

But the more controllable emotions are, the less useful they are as commitment devices. If guilt, whether occasioned by breaking one's own standards or harming another, could simply be turned off at will, what good would it be in motivating self-control? Emotional expressions, too, lose their value as a signal the more they can be controlled and faked. Some individuals are able to mimic true feelings, but they are necessarily rare in a population that relies on emotional signals to cement cooperation (Frank 1988). The uncontrollable and spontaneous nature of emotions is thus adaptive in the longer view, as social bona fides that encourage others to bond and help. More recent research supporting this view has shown that immediate, emotional, and spontaneous moral acts are not discounted the way that unpremeditated harmful acts are (Pizarro, Uhlman, & Salovey 2003) and increase perceptions of warmth and cooperativeness (Rom, Weiss, & Conway 2017). Similarly, inflexible moral judgments and uncalculated cooperative decisions, which might not be short-term adaptive to an individual, are positive signals of trustworthiness (Everett, Pizarro, & Crockett 2016; Jordan, Hoffman, Nowak, & Rand 2016; Rom et al. 2017).

Many psychologists, starting with Kohlberg (e.g., 1964), have observed that the development of moral motivations starts out with completely external reasoning about the consequences for behavior. Over time, these motivations evolve through internalization, potentially leading to a morality that responds to fully internalized rules. In further development, these rules become less rigid with maturity. They can focus on ultimate principles rather than hard-and-fast prohibitions (Kohlberg 1964) or become capable of imagining different perspectives and consequences for other people (Gilligan 1982).

Both these moral processes depend on internalization, in that the person proactively compares their behavior to a standard rather than explicitly modeling a process of punishment and reward. Imagination has to do less work in following an internalized morality. It is only necessary to judge a proposed action against the rule it would violate, or the harm it would cause, not to further envision the punishment that would follow. By this yardstick, an abstracted morality is even more internalized than one that is rooted in concrete social consequences, in the sense that it does not require explicitly envisioning even the thoughts of other people. It takes less effort to judge an action because it fits the category of something that is inherently bad, than to judge it in light of imagined harm to someone else, or to imagine their anger. An abstracted rule or principle, then, has a *mystified* social origin. That is, although it is experienced as a personal and individual phenomenon, it actually serves a social function, unbeknownst to the person who follows it. The principle serves as a shorthand for unexpressed concerns about other people, condensing, for example, "This would hurt someone else" into "This is wrong."

A mystified, abstracted rule is not only cognitively easier to apply, but harder to justify breaking. Many moral decisions that benefit other people can be overridden by mechanisms of moral disengagement (Bandura 1999).

In moral disengagement, a person who has harmed or is going to harm another person deploys cognitions that minimize the wrongness of their immoral actions. In doing so, they short-circuit the knowledge that the action is wrong, and avoid the guilt and remorse that might prevent the action from taking place, or that might follow having done the action. Moral disengagement mechanisms identified by Bandura's theory include minimizing harm done to others, denying that they are worthy of moral regard, deflecting personal responsibility, pointing out that other people have done things that are just as bad if not worse, and using euphemistic labels for the immoral acts. Moral disengagement strategies have been shown to operate in diverse contexts of personal criminality, interpersonal harm, and collective responsibility (e.g., Bandura, Barbaranelli, Caprara, & Pastorelli 1996; Castano & Giner-Sorolla, 2006).

Most moral disengagement mechanisms operate by altering the details of an action's actual or likely social consequences in the actor's mind. In a way, they encourage the actor into the act by directly minimizing the harm done, but also by minimizing the reputational harm anticipated (through making available euphemistic terms for the act, denying responsibility, and diverting criticism by comparison to other acts that could instead be condemned). But if an act is categorically prohibited, if the standards are internalized to the point where they become an abstracted, deontological mandate, many of these disengagement tools become ineffective. Euphemistic labeling, perhaps, might work: Instead of "murder" one commits "cleansing" or exacts "collateral damage." But because the other mechanisms refer to consequences of the act or motives for the act, when we adopt a moral principle that is sufficiently internalized to condemn the act in itself for no apparent reason, it is guarded against most of the tricks of moral disengagement.

Going one step further, *emotions* have an associative function that allows them to arise in response to cues that have only been associated with a situation (Giner-Sorolla 2012). This means they can respond to a moral situation automatically, without explicit processing of exactly what is wrong about the situation, what rule it breaks, or even how it is labeled. In general, the more a motivation depends on deliberative thought, the more a person is able to control it and the less useful it becomes as a long-term valid signal. If a feeling becomes associatively automatized, then it can have deterrent value even if its nature should somehow become known.

Associated emotions do not need explanations, especially visceral ones like disgust (Russell & Giner-Sorolla 2011). Even euphemistic labeling falters when an act is considered "disgusting" or "shameful" on the basis of intuition, terms that describe an immediate and aversive emotional reaction unmediated by reasoning. In this regard, we can see the associative function of emotions as the final step in the ladder of internalization, taking emotional

Table 8.1 Proposed Levels of Internalization in Dealing with Moral Situations That Can Lead to Guilt and Related Emotions

Internalization Level	Mental Representation	Emotional Experience	Subjective Origin
None	Punishment as a result of harming another	Anxiety	Other people who can punish the self
Superficial representation of others' reactions	Anger in the other from being harmed	Anxiety or guilt	Self, responding to other people who are or might be harmed
Explicit mentalization of others	Harming another, evaluated as an effect on that person	Guilt	Self, responding to own action as it relates to another person
Implicit mentalization of others' reactions	Harming another, evaluated as a negative consequence in itself	Guilt	Self, responding to own action as it relates to an abstract standard
Emotional internalization	Harming another is directly associated with guilt	Guilt	Self, origin implicit

reactions to one's own wrongdoing into a deep place that neither circumstance nor rationalization can uproot. Of course, emotions can arise from appraised experiences in which the basis for appraisal is consciously known, but they can also arise in its absence.

This downward-leading ladder of internalization in the case of guilt is shown in Table 8.1. As a self-critical feeling becomes more internalized, the mental representation needed to elicit it becomes more minimal. The subjective origin of the feeling—where it is experienced as coming from—also changes, and notably, so the quality of negative emotional experience also changes. When social standards—for example, about the need to avoid prejudiced expression—are experienced as coming from outside, from concern about the opinions of other people and social consequences, they are felt more as anxiety, while more internalized standards are those that lead to guilt (Plant & Devine 1998). In other words, the emotion shifts from one whose appraisal deals with threats from the outside world, to one that appraises faults in the self. With further internalization, the eliciting stimulus becomes more implicit, moving from the imagined anger of people one has harmed, through imagining the harm and injustice itself as it impacts the person, toward a direct, empathetic response to the fact or likelihood of the harm. At the ultimate level of internalization, thinking of doing wrong or breaking one's own moral standards leads immediately to the prospect of guilt, without any intervening cognition.

Even though shame depends more on the explicit concept of other people's disapproval compared to guilt, it is also prone to some degree of internalization. Smith et al. (2002) concluded that what is necessary to experience shame is not exactly the actual situation of having one's fault or misdeed exposed in public, but the internalized sense of being exposed and judged by others. One difference between shame and guilt, however, is that we can feel shame without accepting that we have done a moral wrong—shame can be felt on the basis of a stigmatized identity, an accusation, or an incompetent performance that is worse for ourselves than for others (Haidt 2003; Smith et al. 2002).

This scheme involves a few critical differences between internalization of shame and guilt. When imagining people's mentalized reactions at an early stage of internalization, it is likely, based on experimental evidence, that shame reacts more strongly to expressions of disgust (and possibly the related emotion contempt) and that guilt reacts more strongly to anger expressions (Giner-Sorolla & Espinosa 2011). Also, when the mentalization of others becomes implicit in shame, we think the relevant appraisal is not harm, but a comparison of status. In comparing status socially, even though other people are still represented, slipping beneath the ranking of others is the main concern, rather than imagining their mental states. The final stages, as with guilt, connect shame directly to the fault, with or without a conscious negative evaluation of the fault itself.

Indeed, the appraisal of self-harm to reputation is more characteristic of shame, and the appraisal of damage to another is more characteristic of guilt (Fontaine, Luyten, et al. 2006). The importance of concerns about harming others in guilt, and concerns about reputation in shame, is shown in two additional unpublished experiments of ours that studied the "explicit mentalization" level of internalization. One experiment had participants imagine inducing shame/guilt in another person. A second experiment shifted the target of the induction, having the participants imagine themselves as a person in whom someone else was trying to induce shame/guilt. When asked to imagine how they would induce shame (or guilt) in another person, or have shame (or guilt) induced in themselves, participants choose one of three possible statements: a public exposure statement ("look at how others see you"), an interpersonal harm statement ("look at how you've hurt me"), and a harm-self statement ("look at how you've hurt yourself"). The social context was also manipulated, so that the target of the emotion induction or the person inducing the emotion was either a friend or a stranger.

The findings were remarkably clear in both studies: Participants were shown to choose the public exposure statement ("look at how others see you") significantly more often in the shame-induction condition, particularly when asked to imagine interacting with a stranger versus a friend. Conversely, participants were shown to choose the interpersonal harm statement ("look at how you've hurt me") significantly more often in the guilt-induction condition, particularly when asked to imagine interacting with a friend versus a stranger. These findings are entirely consistent with Baumeister, Stillwell, and Heatherton (1995), who found similar findings when inducing guilt, and offers strong support to the idea that guilt functions to preserve close relationships.

Whether they deal with shame or guilt, these schemes give a view of how social consequences may be reduced to shorthand and automated through internalization—from the punishment that can be anticipated to follow a misdeed, to the reactions of others that signal punishment, to the conditions of harm or personal fault that themselves anticipate negative reactions. It is through these processes, we argue, that emotions with a social function and origin may seem to come from within. Notably, the schemes are parallel, in that an ultimate level of internalization can, in theory, be reached in both shame and guilt. Whether both emotions are equally prone to internalization in any given culture is a matter of empirical test. Before describing our research on this matter, we should also discuss what is known about the development of internalization through childhood and adolescence.

SOCIAL ORIGINS, INTERNALIZED DEVELOPMENT?

Evidence from developmental psychology supports the view that social emotions come about through increasing internalization of external standards. Recent reviews of the child development literature as it relates to shame and guilt (Malti 2016; Muris and Meesters 2014) bear this analysis out. Guilt is difficult to detect until children are able to talk about their feelings, but there is research identifying behavioral precursors of guilt in toddlerhood, namely, the tendency to help after a personal fault (e.g., Drummond, Hammond et al. 2017). Supporting the idea that guilt represents a development and internalization of anxiety, fear expressions in childhood relate to verbal guilt responses, which increase with age (Dys & Malti 2016). With age, guilt is more explicitly felt and talked about, and serves an important function in the development of personal moral standards (Malti 2016).

More comprehensive studies such as those by Ferguson, Stegge, and Damhuis (1991) directly show a developmental internalization of standards in middle childhood, with older children relying more on personal standards more than the reactions of others when discussing guilt and shame. A similar internalizing trend was shown by Gavazzi, Ornaghi, and Antonotti (2011) when comparing children's reasoning about guilt to adolescents'. Even as standards become more internalized, though, there is also more consideration

Table 8.2 Proposed Levels of Internalization in Dealing with Moral Situations That Can Lead to Shame and Related Emotions

Internalization Level	Mental Representation	Emotional Experience	Subjective Origin
None	Ostracism as a result of showing a fault	Anxiety	Other people who can sanction the self
Superficial representation of others' reactions	Disgust or contempt in other people from showing a fault	Anxiety or shame	Disapproval of other people
Explicit mentalization of others	Accepting and imagining being judged by other people for the fault	Shame	Self, responding to own action as it relates to another person
Implicit mentalization of others	Showing a fault by negative comparison to other people	Shame	Other people, who might disapprove on the basis of comparison
Abstract internalization	Showing a fault, evaluated as a negative consequence itself	Shame	Self, responding to inherent negativity of the fault
Emotional internalization	Showing a fault is directly associated with shame	Shame	Self, origin implicit

of the minds and perspectives of other people, responding directly to inferences of harm and suffering. In the scheme above (Table 8.2), this shift represents a move from explicitly modeling the angry responses of the harmed, to implicitly modeling the psychological harm itself, on the basis of empathy and perspective-taking. The overall picture demonstrates the dual nature of guilt—it may be responsive to social input, but that response is experienced as rooted deep within the person.

THE INTERNALIZATION OF SOCIAL CONCERNS IN SELF-CONTROL SITUATIONS: THEORY AND EVIDENCE

While it may be trivial to show the social nature of guilt and shame in explicitly social situations, a greater challenge comes from the undeniable experience of these emotions in non-social situations of self-control. In self-control dilemmas, an individual seeks to overcome short-term indolence or indulgence and achieve a painful but long-term goal. The anticipation of guilt, shame, and related emotions has been shown to support the self-controlled over-impulsive choice in such dilemmas (Giner-Sorolla 2001). At the same time, feelings of guilt often follow self-control failure as well as preceding it (Hofmann & Fisher 2012; Sanftner & Crowther 1998). However, in self-control situations such as dieting, studying, and personal money management, there is often no immediately social element. If guilt is fundamentally a social emotion, how can it make an appearance in such solitary dramas?

We argue that internalization of social concerns can explain why guilt appears in purely personal dilemmas. In effect, the self-control task is envisioned as a personal relationship between the active self and a "better self"—a dynamic similar, at least in superficial terms, to Freud's well-known distinction between the ego and superego. To the extent this relationship is explicitly internalized, people who experience guilt from failing at self-control should feel as though the reciprocal relations with the self have been broken. For example, one might envision that one has broken a bargain with one's self, that one has not been fair to one's self, and other threats to an internalized relationship with the better self. These appraisals would fit with the explicit internalization level of our model of guilt, in that another person—or persona, within the self—is explicitly imagined. However, it is also possible that guilt becomes internalized at a more implicit level, in which case the failure would be represented as an abstract failing to meet standards that are experienced as personal.

Shame in personal self-control situations is not as amenable to explicit internalization, because the act of imagining the self judging the self is hard to separate from an actual judgment of the self. We considered the possibility that shame in non-social situations might be elicited by implicit internalization of social input through social comparison. That is, seeing oneself as having fallen down a ranking compared to other people might be a shorthand for concerns about how people in general would react to this decline in status. Alternatively, we considered the possibility that shame in self-control situations might also react to fully internalized failure to meet personal standards, just as guilt does.

In the following section we will discuss evidence from our lab from nine unpublished studies. Data from these studies, conducted on undergraduate participants and online workers, show that, in individual situations of self-control, guilt consistently draws on two independent internalized sources: comparisons to implicitly internalized standards, and an explicitly internalized reciprocal relationship with the self. This research also shows that reciprocal items involving other people only draw on guilt in contexts involving interpersonal harm, as opposed to contexts involving individual self-control failure, which show these same reciprocal items drawing on shame. Our studies used a variety of self-control situations: either dieting among people who had previously indicated they were on a diet to lose weight, studying among university students, or self-chosen situations of self-control. This latter setting was explained to participants as a situation in which we forgo a short-term pleasure in order to gain a long-term reward, and it allowed them to choose the self-control challenge most relevant in their life at the moment.

In our research, shame and guilt were measured using multiple semantic emotion terms, with the exception of the two shame/guilt induction studies, which used the singular terms "ashamed" and "guilty" as shame and guilt measures. In the studies that used multiple semantic terms, there were typically thirteen emotion items used. Factor analysis was used in each study and two factors were consistently found, with the same emotion terms loading on the same factors in each study, with some minor exceptions. Typically, six emotion terms consistently loaded on the shame factor ("I would feel ashamed"; "it would be embarrassing"; "it would be humiliating"; "I would feel exposed"; "I would feel sickened at myself"; and "I would be disgusted with myself"), and six emotion terms consistently loaded on the guilt factor ("I would feel guilty"; "I would feel regretful"; "I would feel remorse"; "I would wish I had been more careful"; "I would feel annoyed at myself"; and "I would get angry at myself"). One "guilt" item, "my conscience would be hurt," was not included in the guilt scale because it consistently cross-loaded on both shame and guilt factors.

There were three main kinds of appraisals measured in these studies:

- "external hierarchical," representing the "implicit mentalization" level of shame appraisal, comparing the self to imagined others;
- "internal hierarchical," representing the "implicit mentalization" level of guilt appraisal, comparing the self to personal standards;
- "reciprocal-self," representing "explicit mentalization" in guilt appraisal applied to the self: that is, concerns about fairness to and from the self, imagined as a person.

A fourth type of appraisal, "reciprocal-other," which represented explicit mentalization of actual other people, was included in later studies.

Participants, after being presented with a scenario in which they were asked to imagine failing at self-control, were asked to rate how likely/unlikely each appraisal would be on a 7-point Likert scale. The external hierarchical appraisals measured how important a participant felt social comparison was to their engagement with their self-control dilemma (e.g., "I would feel like I have to increase my social standing with others"). The internal hierarchical appraisals measured how important a participant felt in comparison to an internal standard was to their engagement with their self-control dilemma. (e.g., "I would feel lower compared to my own standards"). The reciprocal-self appraisals measured the strength of the reciprocal bond construed between the participant and their self-control dilemma (e.g., "I would feel like I have broken a deal with myself"). The reciprocal-other appraisals mirrored the reciprocal-self appraisals, but the emphasis was shifted from the self to others (e.g., "I would feel like I have broken a deal with others").

In the first six studies, participants were asked to imagine how they would think and feel when failing at self-control. In all of these studies, participants' emotions and appraisals were measured using self-report, after reading hypothetical scenarios involving self-control failure. Other factors were manipulated in these studies, such as the degree of public exposure associated with the self-control failure, but findings relating to these manipulations are not the focus of this chapter and will not be discussed here. The purpose of the seventh study was to examine the relationship between these same appraisals and emotions in scenarios involving interpersonal harm, rather than self-control.

In all of our multiple regression analyses, the other emotion was entered into the model as a covariate: So guilt (or shame) was entered as a predictor along with all of the appraisal variables when shame (or guilt) was used as the outcome variable. Our findings showed that, across all of our studies involving situations of individual self-control failure, shame was consistently predicted by external hierarchical appraisals but not reciprocal-self or internal hierarchical appraisals. On the other hand, in these same studies, guilt was consistently predicted by reciprocal-self and internal hierarchical appraisals but not external hierarchical appraisals. In later studies of self-control dilemmas, with the introduction of reciprocal-other appraisals, shame was consistently predicted by both external hierarchical and reciprocal-other appraisals.

These findings were quite clear, showing that guilt draws on two independent sources: a fully internalized source, involving comparisons to internalized abstract standards and a partially internalized source, which involves recruiting the same cognitive heuristics that are used in close relationships with others when relating to the self. This latter point about guilt is further supported in our seventh study, which consisted of scenarios involving interpersonal harm, rather than self-control failure. Findings from this study showed that the reciprocal-other appraisals variable was the only significant predictor of guilt, in stark contrast to the self-control studies where this variable predicted shame. In particular, there seemed to be no effect of internal concerns on guilt, where external concerns were relevant to an actual other person harmed. This suggests that explicitly internalized social guilt is responsive to whoever is the target of the harm, whether it be the self, as was the case in self-control failure, or another person, as was the case in our seventh study.

CONCLUSION

How can guilt be personal, feel like it comes from within, operate even in matters of self-control, and still be social in nature and function? Internalization is the answer. Internalization is often hidden from conscious access, because a mystified process is harder to short-circuit. However, our research demonstrates the novel finding that vestiges of social guilt can be found even in personal settings. Specifically, explicit concern for others is recast in the role of explicit concerns for a part of the self that encourages better self-control and the achievement of long-term goals. This explicit internalization of social relationships predicts guilt uniquely, even when controlling for another predictor of guilt, internalized personal standards that represent norms for the self, and are only implicitly social. Although we believe such standards are also ultimately internalized from social evaluation and relationships, in the course of child and adolescent development, their social origin is less obvious in the form expressed.

Although our studies covered multiple explanations of internalized guilt, they also included shame, finding that its appearance in self-control situations was well predicted by comparisons of the self with other people. In self-control situations (but not situations of social harm), shame was also predicted by concerns about fairness and reciprocity with other people. While unexpected, this outcome is consistent with the possibility that thinking explicitly about other people, either in a reciprocal or a status-comparative way, aroused concerns that one's failure of self-control might be exposed in their eyes. This would have led to feeling shame rather than guilt. At the same time, we showed that the deepest form of internalization, where abstract personal standards are called on, belongs to guilt and not to shame. This is consistent with the overall finding in the previous literature that guilt is capable of deeper internalization than shame.

Despite these exciting findings, our full model as expressed in this chapter is much more comprehensive than the appraisal items used in our studies, and it deserves further exploration. We initially developed the appraisal questions with an aim to test theories derived from Gilbert's model of reciprocal and hierarchical social relations as determinants, respectively, of guilt and shame. Over the course of the studies, it became apparent that the level of internalization was also in play as a factor, and that distinctions could be drawn between more and less abstract forms of internalization. However, the complete model of internalization has yet to be tested in the context of shame and guilt. In particular, the less internalized appraisals, such as anticipating social sanctions or negative emotional reactions, might appear in both self-harming and other-harming instances of moral failure, bringing with them anxiety-related emotions in addition to guilt and shame. Also, the possibility that a situation might immediately activate guilt without the feeling of an intervening cognition is a speculative one, and probably one that should be studied in a controlled lab setting where the time course of mental events can be tightly tracked.

The next frontier, perhaps, is to apply the model of internalization to non-Western cultures. A recent systematic review concludes that shame in such cultures in more socially accepted and leads to relatively more pro-social actions (Sheikh 2014). It might also be that with greater facility with shame, comes greater internalization, so that abstracted standards support anticipatory feelings of shame. In other words, things are not done because they "would be shameful," on the basis of the twinge of anticipation of that unpleasant feeling. On a cultural level, it may be that ease of internalization is not a product of the natural characteristics of shame or guilt, but rather a product of the relative importance and practice given to those two feelings.

Overall, we believe we have brought a new perspective to the study of guilt and related emotions that attend personal and social moral failure. By demonstrating a form of internalization not often studied, in which the self is treated as a social object, our studies bridge the gap between the social context and function of guilt, and its use in the self-control of individual dilemmas. If one of the important emotions regulating the self is essentially social, this points also toward a general appraisal of the self as social. As humans, we cannot physically survive infancy without care, and it appears more and more clear that our psychological functioning is also essentially dependent on our interactions with other people.

REFERENCES

Bandura, A., Barbaranelli, C., Caprara, G. V., & Pastorelli, C. (1996). Mechanisms of moral disengagement in the exercise of moral agency. *Journal of Personality and Social Psychology, 71*(2), 364–74. https://doi.org/10.1037/0022-3514.71.2.364.

Bandura, A. (1999). Moral disengagement in the perpetration of inhumanities. *Personality and Social Psychology Review, 3*(3), 193–209. https://doi.org/10.1207/s15327957pspr0303_3.

Baumeister, R. F., Reis, H. T., & Delespaul, P. A. (1995). Subjective and experiential correlates of guilt in daily life. *Personality and Social Psychology Bulletin, 21*(12), 1256–68. https://doi.org/10.1177/01461672952112002.

Baumeister, R. F., Stillwell, A. M., & Heatherton, T. F. (1994). Guilt: An interpersonal approach. *Psychological Bulletin, 115*(2), 243. https://doi.org/10.1037//0033-2909.115.2.243.

Baumeister, R. F., Stillwell, A. M., & Heatherton, T. F. (1995). Personal narratives about guilt: Role in action control and interpersonal relationships. *Basic and Applied Social Psychology, 17*(1–2), 173–98. https://doi.org/10.1207/s15324834basp1701&2_10.

Benedict, R. (1946). *The chrysanthemum and the sword: Patterns of Japanese culture*. Boston: Houghton Mifflin. https://doi.org/10.2307/3537694.

Castano, E., & Giner-Sorolla, R. (2006). Not quite human: Infra-humanization as a response to collective responsibility for intergroup killing. *Journal of Personality and Social Psychology, 90*, 804–18. https://doi.org/10.1037/0022-3514.90.5.804.

Cheung, M. P., Gilbert, P., & Irons, C. (2004). An exploration of shame, social rank and rumination in relation to depression. *Personality and Individual Differences, 36*(5), 1143–53.

Cohen, T. R., Wolf, S. T., Panter, A. T., & Insko, C. A. (2011). Introducing the GASP scale: A new measure of guilt and shame proneness. *Journal of Personality and Social Psychology, 100*(5), 947. https://doi.org/10.1037/a0022641.

Combs, D. J., Campbell, G., Jackson, M., & Smith, R. H. (2010). Exploring the consequences of humiliating a moral transgressor. *Basic and Applied Social Psychology, 32*(2), 128–43. https://doi.org/10.1080/01973531003738379.

Creighton, M. R. (1990). Revisiting shame and guilt cultures: A forty-year pilgrimage. *Ethos, 18*(3), 279–307. https://doi.org/10.1525/eth.1990.18.3.02a00030.

Darwin, C. (1965/1872). *The expression of the emotions in man and animals*. London, UK: John Marry.

Drummond, J. D., Hammond, S. I., Satlof-Bedrick, E., Waugh, W. E., & Brownell, C. A. (2017). Helping the one you hurt: Toddlers' rudimentary guilt, shame, and prosocial behavior after harming another. *Child Development, 88*(4), 1382–97. https://doi.org/10.1111/cdev.12653.

Dys, S. P., & Malti, T. (2016). It's a two-way street: Automatic and controlled processes in children's emotional responses to moral transgressions. *Journal of Experimental Child Psychology, 152*, 31–40. https://doi.org/10.1016/j.jecp.2016.06.011.

Epstein, S. (1973). The self-concept revisited: Or a theory of a theory. *American Psychologist, 28*(5), 404–16. https://doi.org/10.1037/h0034679.

Everett, J. A., Pizarro, D. A., & Crockett, M. J. (2016). Inference of trustworthiness from intuitive moral judgments. *Journal of Experimental Psychology: General, 145*(6), 772–87. https://doi.org/10.2139/ssrn.2726330.

Ferguson, T. J., Stegge, H., & Damhuis, I. (1991). Children's understanding of guilt and shame. *Child Development, 62*(4), 827–39.

Fontaine, J. R., Luyten, P., De Boeck, P., Corveleyn, J., Fernandez, M., Herrera, D., & Tomcsányi, T. (2006). Untying the Gordian knot of guilt and shame: The structure of guilt and shame reactions based on situation and person variation in Belgium, Hungary, and Peru. *Journal of Cross-Cultural Psychology, 37*(3), 273–92. doi: 10.1177/0022022105284493.

Frank, R. H. (1988). *Passions within reason: The strategic role of the emotions*. New York, NY, US: W W Norton & Co.

Gavazzi, I. G., Ornaghi, V., & Antoniotti, C. (2011). Children's and adolescents' narratives of guilt: Antecedents and mentalization. *European Journal of Developmental Psychology, 8*(3), 311–30. https://doi.org/10.1080/17405629.2010.491303.

Gilbert, P. (2000). The relationship of shame, social anxiety and depression: The role of the evaluation of social rank. *Clinical Psychology & Psychotherapy: An International Journal of Theory & Practice, 7*(3), 174–89.

Gilbert, P. (2003). Evolution, social roles, and the differences in shame and guilt. *Social Research: An International Quarterly, 70*(4), 1205–30.

Gilbert, P., Allan, S., & Goss, K. (1996). Parental representations, shame, interpersonal problems, and vulnerability to psychopathology. *Clinical Psychology & Psychotherapy: An International Journal of Theory and Practice, 3*(1), 23–34.

Gilbert, P., & Miles, J. N. (2000). Sensitivity to social put-down: Its relationship to perceptions of social rank, shame, social anxiety, depression, anger and self-other blame. *Personality and Individual Differences, 29*(4), 757–74.

Gilligan, C. (1982). *In a different voice.* Cambridge, MA: Harvard University Press.

Giner-Sorolla, R. (2001) Guilty pleasures and grim necessities: Immediate and deliberative affective attitudes in dilemmas of self-control. *Journal of Personality and Social Psychology, 80*, 208–21. https://doi.org/10.1037/0022-3514.80.2.206.

Giner-Sorolla, R. (2012). *Judging passions: Moral emotions in persons and groups.* London: Psychology Press.

Giner-Sorolla, R., & Espinosa, P. (2011). Social cueing of guilt by anger and shame by disgust. *Psychological Science, 22,* 49–53. doi: 10.1177/0956797610392925.

Goffman, E. (1949). The presentation of self in everyday life. *American Journal of Sociology, 55,* 6–7.

Haidt, J. (2003). The moral emotions. In R. J. Davidson, K. R. Scherer, & H. H. Goldsmith (Eds.), *Handbook of affective sciences* (pp. 852–70). Oxford: Oxford University Press.

Hedman, E., Ström, P., Stünkel, A., & Mörtberg, E. (2013). Shame and guilt in social anxiety disorder: Effects of cognitive behavior therapy and association with social anxiety and depressive symptoms. *PloS One, 8*(4), e61713.

Hermans, H. J., Kempen, H. J., & Van Loon, R. J. (1992). The dialogical self: Beyond individualism and rationalism. *American Psychologist, 47*(1), 23. https://doi.org/10.1037/0003-066x.47.1.23.

Jordan, J. J., Hoffman, M., Nowak, M. A., & Rand, D. G. (2016). Uncalculating cooperation is used to signal trustworthiness. *Proceedings of the National Academy of Sciences, 113*(31), 8658–63. https://doi.org/10.1073/pnas.1601280113.

Ketelaar, T., & Tung Au, W. (2003). The effects of feelings of guilt on the behaviour of uncooperative individuals in repeated social bargaining games: An affect-as-information interpretation of the role of emotion in social interaction. *Cognition and Emotion, 17*(3), 429–53. https://doi.org/10.1080/02699930143000662.

Kohlberg, L. (1964). Development of moral character and moral ideology. *Review of Child Development Research, 1,* 381–431.

Malti, T. (2016). Toward an integrated clinical-developmental model of guilt. *Developmental Review, 39,* 16–36. https://doi.org/10.1016/j.dr.2015.11.001.

Markus, H., & Wurf, E. (1987). The dynamic self-concept: A social psychological perspective. *Annual Review of Psychology, 38*(1), 299–337. https://doi.org/10.1146/annurev.ps.38.020187.001503.

Michail, M., & Birchwood, M. (2009). Social anxiety disorder in first-episode psychosis: Incidence, phenomenology and relationship with paranoia. *The British Journal of Psychiatry, 195*(3), 234–41.

Muris, P., & Meesters, C. (2014). Small or big in the eyes of the other: On the developmental psychopathology of self-conscious emotions as shame, guilt, and pride.

Clinical Child and Family Psychology Review, 17(1), 19–40. https://doi.org/10.1007/s10567-013-0137-z.

Nietzsche, F. W. (1989). *On the genealogy of morals* (R. J. Hollingdale, trans.). New York: Vintage.

Pizarro, D., Uhlmann, E., & Salovey, P. (2003). Asymmetry in judgments of moral blame and praise: The role of perceived metadesires. *Psychological Science, 14*(3), 267–72.

Plant, E. A., & Devine, P. G. (1998). Internal and external motivation to respond without prejudice. *Journal of Personality and Social Psychology, 75*(3), 811–32. https://doi.org/10.1037/t03881-000.

Rom, S. C., Weiss, A., & Conway, P. (2017). Judging those who judge: Perceivers infer the roles of affect and cognition underpinning others' moral dilemma responses. *Journal of Experimental Social Psychology, 69*, 44–58.

Russell, P. S., & Giner-Sorolla, R. (2011). Social justifications for moral emotions: When reasons for disgust are less elaborated than for anger. *Emotion, 11*, 637–46. https://doi.org/10.1037/a0022600.

Sanftner, J. L., & Crowther, J. H. (1998). Variability in self-esteem, moods, shame, and guilt in women who binge. *International Journal of Eating Disorders, 23*(4), 391–97. https://doi.org/10.1002/(sici)1098-108x(199805)23:4%3C391::aid-eat6%3E3.0.co;2-d.

Sedikides, C., Gaertner, L., & O'Mara, E. M. (2011). Individual self, relational self, collective self: Hierarchical ordering of the tripartite self. *Psychological Studies, 56*(1), 98–107. https://doi.org/10.1007/s12646-011-0059-0.

Sheikh, S. (2014). Cultural variations in shame responses: A dynamic perspective. *Personality and Social Psychology Review, 18*(4), 387–403. https://doi.org/10.1177/1088868314540810.

Smith, R. H., Webster, J. M., Parrott, W. G., & Eyre, H. L. (2002). The role of public exposure in moral and nonmoral shame and guilt. *Journal of Personality and Social Psychology, 83*(1), 138. https://doi.org/10.1037//0022-3514.83.1.138.

Tangney, J. P., Baumeister, R. F., & Boone, A. L. (2004). High self-control predicts good adjustment, less pathology, better grades, and interpersonal success. *Journal of Personality, 72*(2), 271–322. https://doi.org/10.4324/9781315175775-5.

Tangney, J. P., Miller, R. S., Flicker, L., & Barlow, D. H. (1996). Are shame, guilt, and embarrassment distinct emotions? *Journal of Personality and Social Psychology, 70*(6), 1256. https://doi.org/10.1037/0022-3514.70.6.1256.

Trivers, R. L. (1971). The evolution of reciprocal altruism. *The Quarterly Review of Biology, 46*(1), 35–57. https://doi.org/10.1086/406755.

Wiltermuth, S. S., & Cohen, T. R. (2014). "I'd only let you down": Guilt proneness and the avoidance of harmful interdependence. *Journal of Personality and Social Psychology, 107*(5), 925. https://doi.org/10.1037/a0037523.

Chapter 9

One Reactive Attitude to Rule Them All

Nicholas Sars

> People incapable of guilt usually do have a good time.
>
> —Rust Cohle, HBO's *True Detective*

P. F. Strawson famously gives pride of place to the reactive attitudes in his account of moral responsibility, though he says little about guilt or any other self-reactive attitudes. This inattention is curious, given that on his view lacking capacity for self-reactive attitudes is grounds for exemption from the moral community. Perhaps because of Strawson's limited remarks regarding them, the self-reactive attitudes have not received much attention in commentaries on his view. In this paper, I will attempt to fill this lacuna by examining the role of the self-reactive attitudes within his approach to moral responsibility. I will focus in particular on reactive guilt to show that it plays a number of roles in our interpersonal lives, from reinforcing our important personal relationships to holding ourselves accountable with respect to our own personal ideals. A better understanding of these roles, I will argue, helps to clarify Strawson's notion of reactive attitude and to strengthen his overall argument, in addition to revealing some interesting aspects of the way various self-reactive attitudes operate within our lives.

I begin in section 1 with an overview of Strawson's approach that emphasizes the self-reactive attitudes and explains their status as exempting conditions. In section 2, I show that an emphasis on the communicative nature of the reactive attitudes helps to explain a variety of features implicit in Strawson's discussion of the self-reactive attitudes. In section 3, I claim that a faithful reading of Strawson should make room for the contextual nature of the personal reactive attitudes, and I argue that this reading reveals a heretofore overlooked role the self-reactive attitudes can play in understanding Strawson's view. In section 4, I compare guilt and shame as self-reactive attitudes and argue that guilt is better suited for holding ourselves accountable with respect to individual ideals. In section 5, I show that reactive guilt can help make sense of role-reversing arguments, the upshot being that a reactive sense of guilt is uniquely capable as a means of holding oneself to account based on standards ranging from the most individual to the most general. Finally, in section 6, I return to Strawson's overall approach to responsibility and show that a better understanding of guilt as a reactive attitude can strengthen an overlooked aspect of his argument's underlying structure.

1. SELF-REACTIVE ATTITUDES AMONG OTHERS

The context of Strawson's discussion in "Freedom and Resentment" is the traditional problem of free will and determinism. The problem dates (at least) to the Presocratics, and the two main sides in the modern debate have been entrenched since (at least) around the time of Hobbes. One side (the "compatibilists") thinks freedom and moral responsibility are compatible with a deterministic world; the other side (the "incompatibilists") thinks they are not. The second side can be further split into those (often called "libertarians") who think we have freedom and moral responsibility in our world and those (often called "free will skeptics" or "hard determinists") who think we do not. Strawson uses the terms "optimists," "pessimists," and "skeptics," and these are generally taken to correspond to compatibilists, libertarians, and hard determinists, respectively.[1] Perhaps the most significant feature of Strawson's discussion is that, instead of endorsing any particular camp, he attempts to reveal a significant misunderstanding presumed in the way the question is traditionally framed by claiming that the truth or falsity of the thesis of determinism is *irrelevant* to whether our "concepts of moral obligation and responsibility," "practices of punishing and blaming," and "expressing moral condemnation and approval are really justified."[2]

Strawson begins his inquiry with an invitation. He asks us to take note of "the very great importance that we attach to the attitudes and intentions towards us of other human beings, and the great extent to which our personal feelings and reactions depend upon, or involve, our beliefs about these attitudes and intentions."[3] Strawson initially identifies our attitudes that depend on the quality of the attitudes toward us of others as *reactive* attitudes. Consider a case of someone stepping on your foot. If that person is simply trying to cause you pain, you will probably resent the action; in contrast, if the person is trying to kill a spider that might harm you, your natural inclination toward resentment will likely be suspended. Only the former case would be an expression of poor quality of will.[4] Strawson includes resentment within his list of personal reactive attitudes, in addition to gratitude, forgiveness, reciprocal love, and hurt feelings.

Strawson describes the complicated ways that these personal reactive attitudes operate within our interpersonal practices, with an emphasis on the familiar excusing (e.g., accident, compulsion, ignorance) and exempting (e.g., insanity, immaturity) considerations relevant to withholding them, and he claims that a plea on the basis of the thesis of determinism is relevantly dissimilar to any such consideration, given that it would seem to entail universal application if the thesis were true.[5] Thus, nothing about our characteristic interpersonal pleas gives us reason to think that the truth of determinism would constitute either an excuse or an exemption.[6] Strawson then turns to discussing a "kindred" class of reactive attitudes that he says are "moral" because of their "impersonal or vicarious character."[7] His discussion of the moral reactive attitudes parallels his earlier discussion, and he concludes that the thesis of determinism is similarly irrelevant to whether we withhold the moral reactive attitudes. Within Strawson's discussion of the moral reactive attitudes, he also mentions the self-reactive attitudes:

But the picture is not complete unless we consider also the correlates of these attitudes on the part of those on whom the demands are made, on the part of the agents. Just as there are personal and vicarious reactive attitudes associated with demands on others for oneself and demands on others for others, so there are self-reactive attitudes associated with demands on oneself for others. And here we have to mention such phenomena as feeling bound or obliged (the "sense of obligation"); feeling compunction; feeling guilty or remorseful or at least responsible; and the more complicated phenomenon of shame.[8]

The reactive attitudes, thus, comprise three classes: personal, moral, and self. Strawson's description of the self-reactive attitudes implies that the three classes of attitudes operate within our practices similarly, and he goes on to explicitly claim that "all these types of attitude alike have common roots in our human nature and our membership of human communities."[9] He, further, states the following within his discussion of the moral reactive attitudes: "Though there are some necessary and some contingent differences between the ways and cases in which these two kinds of attitudes operate or are inhibited in their operation, yet, as general human capacities or pronenesses, they stand or lapse together."[10] The "two kinds of attitudes" Strawson refers to are the personal and the moral reactive attitudes, but I think that the context of the section—especially in the light of the previous quotation—implicates the self-reactive attitudes, as well. Regardless, as I will show in the following section, there is good reason to read Strawson this way, because doing so greatly aids in vindicating the claim of standing or falling together.

The similarities between the three classes of reactive attitudes, both implicit and explicit within Strawson's discussion, have led many commentators to characterize the three as simply first-, second-, and third-personal analogues of each other. According to R. Jay Wallace, "When you blame somebody, you are exercised by what they have done, insofar as you become resentful or indignant about it (or experience guilt in the reflexive case)."[11] Wallace emphasizes the perspectival basis of his interpretation, stating:

> To resent someone is to feel not merely that they have acted wrongly, but that they have wronged us in particular, violating the norms that constitute relations of mutual regard. Likewise, we are prone to guilt when we take it that we have wronged someone else in our dealings with them. . . . To feel indignation is to be exercised on behalf of another person, on account of a wrong that has been visited on that person in particular.[12]

However, glossing the three classes of reactive attitudes as analogues that differ merely in the perspective from which they are experienced should be avoided, because it hides a unique relation that the self-reactive attitudes have toward each of the other two classes of reactive attitudes.

Although it is perhaps easy to overlook, Strawson claims that an incapacity with respect to the self-reactive attitudes is an exempting condition with respect to the moral reactive attitudes.[13] In other words, if one was unable to ever experience guilt or other self-reactive attitudes, one could never be fittingly subject to indignation. One reason this feature is elusive is that Strawson only states it explicitly within his discussion of the moral reactive attitudes, which itself is much shorter than his discussion of the personal reactive attitudes. The explicit statement, though, is quite clear:

> But suppose we see the agent in a different light: as one whose picture of the world is an insane delusion; or as one whose behaviour, or a part of whose behaviour, is unintelligible to us, perhaps even to him, in terms of conscious purposes, and intelligible only in terms of unconscious purposes; or even, perhaps, *as one wholly impervious to the self-reactive attitudes I spoke of, wholly lacking, as we say, in moral sense.*[14]

Strawson does not explicitly include an imperviousness to the self-reactive attitudes within his earlier list of exempting conditions for the personal reactive attitudes; however, he does follow the previous quotation with a curious sentence: "Seeing an agent in such a light *as this* tends, *I said*, to inhibit resentment in a wholly different way."[15] What's curious, of course, is that he does not say "this" previously about the self-reactive attitudes; in the context of exemptions from the personal reactive attitudes, there is no reference to the self-reactive attitudes (or any "lacking . . . in moral sense"). One possible explanation for the earlier omission is simply rhetorical: When Strawson initially discusses the personal reactive attitudes, he has not yet introduced the self-reactive attitudes as an independent class. He does describe agents exempted from the personal reactive attitudes as "psychologically abnormal—or as morally undeveloped,"[16] which could be taken to implicate agents "wholly impervious to the self-reactive attitudes." Although I think the parallel discussions sufficiently implicate self-reactive incapacity as an exemption from the personal, as well as the moral, reactive attitudes, some readers are likely to disagree on this interpretive question. I will note for now that it is at least not *inconsistent* with the text to understand self-reactive incapacity as an exempting condition for each of the other classes of reactive attitudes; in the following section, I will show that reading the self-reactive attitudes as implicated on this question increases the plausibility of a popular interpretation that can help deliver on Strawson's explicit claim that the personal and moral classes stand or fall together. It also has a more straightforward consequence of shining helpful light on an exchange between Strawson and Jonathan Bennett.

Bennett challenges Strawson's use of "personal," "moral," and "self" as labels for the three classes of reactive attitudes by arguing that, "As for self-reactive attitudes: some of them are principled and some are not; for an attitude of self-censure or self-congratulation may, but need not, rest upon some principle which one holds."[17] By "principled," Bennett means "moral," and Strawson concedes the point: "Bennett is certainly right in saying that I was wrong so to use the word 'moral' as to exclude the self-reactive attitudes from its scope."[18] There is something "moral," then, about both the self-reactive and the moral reactive attitudes, and this naturally raises the question of what Strawson means by the term "moral." He is at first glance frustratingly ambiguous on this question; he transitions from discussing the personal reactive attitudes to the moral reactive attitudes by stating that, "The reactive attitudes I have now to discuss might be described as the sympathetic or vicarious or impersonal or disinterested or generalized analogues of the reactive attitudes I have already discussed."[19] Bennett claims that "generalized" is the key disjunct to understanding the moral class of reactive attitudes and concludes that, "Strawson assumes—rightly, in my view—that an attitude counts as 'moral' only if it rests on a general principle, or anyway on something which does not essentially refer to any particular item."[20] Strawson's favorable assessment of Bennett's commentary, then, has (at least) the following implication: The self-reactive attitudes can *sometimes* be based on violations of principles that generalize across all persons; however, the self-reactive attitudes are only *possibly* "moral" in this sense, because they are not *necessarily* traceable to violations of general principles. The self-reactive attitudes can, thus, be fitting in cases that correspond to either personal or moral reactive attitudes.

Summing up, then, Strawson's view includes personal reactive attitudes (e.g., resentment), moral reactive attitudes (e.g., indignation), and self-reactive attitudes (e.g., guilt), which, I have claimed, should be understood as in some sense *unified*, such that they stand or fall together; in addition, our capacity to feel the latter is necessary in some way for the others to ever be appropriate; finally, the self-reactive class can apply to violations of both moral and non-moral principles. As I will now show, these three elements fit together conveniently well when the communicative nature of the reactive attitudes is emphasized.

2. UNIFYING THE CLASSES OF REACTIVE ATTITUDES

Recall that Strawson's overall goal is to justify certain concepts, practices, and expressions. For him, this justification comes holistically, as evidenced in his appeals to the internal logic of the reactive attitudes as a whole to provide such justification.[21] Nevertheless, some critics suggest a piecemeal excision of individual reactive attitudes (such as resentment) on the basis of their distinctly unpleasant qualities.[22] One way to bolster Strawson's holistic picture is to follow many commentators who argue that the *expressive* nature of the reactive attitudes gives rise to intelligibility conditions, such that the attitudes must be related in precise ways. As Coleen Macnamara describes it, "The tendency is to suggest the other-regarding attitudes are conceptually connected to their self-regarding counterparts. Specifically, resentment and indignation are associated with guilt from the wrongdoer, and gratitude and approval with self-approbation from the benefactor."[23] Unpacking this approach to the reactive attitudes will help to give weight to the interpretive positions taken in the previous section.

Given their communicative nature, the (negative) reactive attitudes are often viewed as forms of blame, with resentment and indignation being means of blaming another and guilt being a means of blaming oneself. The notion of self-reactive incapacity as an exempting condition, then, might be glossed by saying that one is not eligible for blame—from *anyone*—if one does not have the capacity to blame oneself, that is, to feel guilt. As Stephen Darwall explains, "we can intelligibly address demands through reactive attitudes only to those we assume able to take the very same attitudes toward themselves. . . . [Addressees] hold themselves responsible through blaming themselves. In seeing themselves as to blame, they regard themselves as warrantedly blamed from the perspective of a member of the moral community."[24] Reactive guilt, thus, constitutes the right kind of "uptake" of what is being addressed to a blamee.[25] Commentators disagree on the precise content of what is addressed to addressees via the reactive attitudes, but a common view is that demands are addressed.[26] Thus, in the language of demands, one could say that the conceptual connection between blame and guilt provides a natural basis for "acknowledging the legitimacy" of the demand implicit in blame.[27]

This understanding of the relationship between the blame embodied in the other-directed reactive attitudes and the acknowledgment embodied in the self-reactive attitudes finds empirical support when examining the roles these attitudes play in our lives. The best predictor of the removal of anger—and resentment and indignation are widely considered to be forms of anger—is apology, amends, or remorse on the part of the object of the anger[28]; but the motivational tendencies most commonly associated with guilt just are apology, amends, and signs of sorrow or remorse, thus supporting the idea that guilt and anger are natural affective correlates.[29] Furthermore, both moral and non-moral transgressions have been shown to elicit guilt[30]; thus, Strawson's concession to Bennett seems correct. As Macnamara describes, the cohesive structure of the various classes of reactive attitudes allows them to play a crucial role in our interpersonal lives: "insofar as resentment and indignation elicit guilt in wrongdoers, they catalyze the reparative work that is so essential to healing the bonds we work so hard to build."[31] On this understanding, guilt is "the crucial motivational link" between acknowledgment and amends, and it "generates the sincere desire" for reparative action.[32]

Unpacking reactive guilt in terms of uptake and interpersonal acknowledgment helps support the interpretive positions suggested in the previous section.[33] An inability to feel reactive guilt would amount to an inability to recognize the demands and expectations that resentment and indignation express—at least to recognize them via the natural affective correlates of those attitudes.[34] Without even the possibility of the right kind of uptake, expressions of resentment or indignation would necessarily be inefficacious. Furthermore, in the absence of a compelling reason to think moral and non-moral guilt have distinct psychological mechanisms, it would seem that an incapacity for one is an incapacity for both; thus, an incapacity for either entails an exemption from both personal and moral reactive attitudes.[35] The communicative nature of these attitudes, thus, would seem to support understanding self-reactive incapacity as an exempting condition for both the personal and moral reactive attitudes; furthermore, this understanding would vindicate Strawson's idea that the personal and moral reactive classes stand or fall together by showing that those two classes fall—together—with a lack of self-reactive capacity. In addition, this reading opens room to explore relations between the various classes that are not as clear in the text, a task to which I now turn.

3. MAKING SENSE OF COMPLICATED RELATIONSHIPS

Strawson's approach is based on "commonplaces" within our interpersonal lives, and one obvious feature of our lives is that they involve relationships that can easily come into conflict. In one context, one's expectations as a parent might take priority over one's expectations as an employee; in another context, the opposite might be true. Some influential commentaries have tied the reactive attitudes as a whole to moral obligations, which by their nature would not allow corresponding expectations to be set aside based on context; however, there are textual grounds for resisting such a move.[36] In describing the personal reactive attitudes, Strawson explicitly acknowledges their potentially contextual nature:

> We should think of the many different kinds of relationship which we can have with other people—as sharers of a common interest; as members of the same family; as colleagues; as friends; as lovers; as chance parties to an enormous range of transactions and encounters. Then we should think, in each of these connections in turn, and in others, of the kind of importance we attach to the attitudes and intentions towards us of those who stand in these relationships to us, and of the kinds of reactive attitudes and feelings to which we ourselves are prone. In general, we demand some degree of goodwill or regard on the part of those who stand in these relationships to us, *though the forms we require it to take vary widely in different connections*. The range and intensity of our reactive attitudes towards goodwill, its absence or its opposite vary no less widely.[37]

In this section, I will argue that faithfully reading the fittingness of the personal reactive attitudes as varying based on context reveals an overlooked role the self-reactive attitudes can play within Strawson's view.

Given that our "many different kinds of relationship" are constituted by a wide variety of expectations between ourselves and our family, friends, lovers, and so on, we inevitably face competing expectations. As mentioned in the previous section, commentators tend to interpret reactive attitudes as addressing moral demands; however, this interpretation loses plausibility on the contextual reading, because on that reading interpersonal expectations will often conflict with each other. Michelle Mason has recently suggested that, instead of interpreting the reactive attitudes in terms of imperatives that are associated with deontic demands based in moral obligation, we should view the reactive attitudes as *appellative* in nature. On Mason's view, reactive attitudes are a way of appealing to each other in a special way, namely from *within* the relationships that are important to us. More specifically, they are appeals to recognize the expectations that constitute those relationships. Mason argues that the reactive attitudes "relate persons in reciprocal prescription and recognition of legitimate expectations of conduct or character regulation, accordance with which is necessary for aspiring to relationships of value to beings like us."[38] In contrast with views grounded in moral demands, Mason's view has no trouble accommodating the fact that our various relationships are apt to be constituted by different sets of expectations that will inevitably compete with each other. Admittedly, this creates complications, such as the question of which expectations we should uphold; however, the self-reactive attitude of guilt can help make sense of these complications.

Patricia Greenspan has discussed what she calls the identificatory mechanism of guilt. This mechanism is most straightforward in the case of wronging someone. Because of the reflexive connection between that someone's (fitting) resentment and your (fitting) reactive guilt, the latter is a means of identifying with that person's perspective and recognizing that, were you in the other's position, you could fittingly be the resentful one.[39] But the identificatory aspect of guilt can be informative in more than just cases of wrongdoing. As Greenspan describes, "to the extent that the guilty self identifies with the victims of the wrong it does, as well as with its judges, its responsibility ties it to others; and the connection is reinforced, of course, for nonmoral variants of guilt such as survivor's guilt that are imposed for benefits distinguishing an individual from other members of a group."[40] Your guilt over being the only member of your cohort to get a tenure-track job, for example, reinforces your identification within that group.

With respect to competing expectations within relationships, imagine that your roles as a colleague to A and a spouse to B result in a situation in which you must fail to satisfy a (legitimate) expectation of one to satisfy a (legitimate) expectation of the other. Let's say that the first time this happens, you decide to satisfy the expectation of your spouse; the next time it happens, you satisfy the expectation of your colleague. In both cases you are likely to feel some guilt over your failures to satisfy legitimate expectations—you might feel compelled to offer an apology or explanation, or to make some kind of amends—there is apt to be a (non-)moral residue.[41] However, let's also stipulate that, though the expectations are seemingly equally legitimate, in the second case you feel more guilt. Indeed, over time you continue to alternate satisfying the competing expectations of A and B, and you continue to feel much more guilt when failing to satisfy the expectations of your spouse. I suggest that this would be a sign that the expectations—and, therefore, perhaps the relationship as a whole—with your spouse are more important to you. Greenspan notes that, "Part of showing that one identifies with others in a way that makes inequalities unwelcome involves the willingness to make up for inequalities with self-inflicted emotional distress."[42] Greenspan has in mind situations in which one has some element of control over one's emotions, but the basis of her point is guilt's communicative nature; your guilt is a (perhaps nonverbal) sign of identification with the members of the relevant group. Non-voluntary guilt, then, will tend to serve the same purpose.

Guilt, thus, can be a means of *reinforcing* the most important of our interpersonal bonds. Your spouse can perhaps feel more secure in your relationship based on the implications of your differing degrees of guilt. This is not to say, however, that your colleague's expectations do not remain legitimate. The colleague can still fittingly resent you for failing to meet those expectations, and the corresponding guilt you continue to fittingly feel can "serve to protect and strengthen" that relationship as well.[43] The self-reactive class of reactive attitudes, then, helps to ameliorate the issue of competing expectations that arises under the contextual interpretation of the personal reactive attitudes. But, of course, the problem of competing expectations is something we simply do face as agents—its source isn't philosophical—and so we can see that in adding this "complication," the contextual reading allows Strawson's view to better match our lived experience. Furthermore, in explicating this overlooked role for the self-reactive attitudes I have relied on their expressive nature, so to the extent the account seems plausible, it also implicitly supports the communicative interpretation discussed in the previous section. We might wonder, though, whether commentators have been correct to emphasize the role of guilt, in particular, within communicative interpretations. Some theorists have noted that shame—an attitude Strawson refers to in the context of the self-reactive attitudes—can play an identificatory role similar to the one I have discussed above for guilt.[44] In the next two sections, I will shift my focus to discussing some features that make guilt unique among the self-reactive attitudes.

4. GUILT, SHAME, AND INDIVIDUAL IDEALS

In sections 1 and 2, I noted that the communicative interpretation of the reactive attitudes tends to emphasize a conceptual connection between reactive guilt and other-regarding reactive attitudes like resentment and indignation. However, Strawson also thinks that "the more complicated phenomenon of shame" is a self-reactive attitude, so one might wonder why commentaries focus almost exclusively on guilt. Sometimes the explanation is stipulative; for example, Wallace thinks that Strawson's view is best understood by narrowing the list of reactive attitudes in a way that excludes shame as a reactive attitude. On Wallace's interpretation, "the reactive attitudes are explained exclusively by beliefs about the violation of moral obligations (construed as strict prohibitions or requirements)."[45] Because shame, plausibly, has a broader scope than the morally obligatory, it is not a reactive attitude on this understanding. In contrast, the appellative reading of the reactive attitudes that I favored in the previous section is perfectly compatible with shame's broad scope. Similar to guilt, shame is closely tied to interpersonal expectations and "concerns failure to live up to norms, ideals, and standards that are primarily *public*."[46] Felt shame, then, would seem capable of expressing that one acknowledges the legitimacy of relevant norms and relationship expectations, and, thus, I think commentators do have the burden of explaining their emphasis on guilt as a self-reactive attitude within the communicative interpretation. In this section, I will begin to develop a response by discussing the phenomenon of holding oneself accountable for violating individual ideals. The discussion of guilt in the individual case will reveal important features that I will, in the next section, apply to the fully generalized case as well.

It will help to think in terms of some cases. Take Serena and Tiger. Serena plays tennis, and Tiger is a golfer. Imagine that Serena is the greatest-ever female tennis player and that Tiger is the best-ever male golfer. Let's say, further, that the margin between Serena and Tiger and the next-best individuals who have ever competed in their relative disciplines is vast. In fact, let's stipulate that Serena and Tiger's average performances are better than the best performances that any others have ever given in their respective disciplines.[47] Finally, let's say that, like many extreme outliers, Serena and Tiger consider any of their performances below their own personal average abilities to be unacceptable. I want to explore some of the differences between Serena and Tiger feeling shame and feeling guilt over their unacceptable performances.

I will first consider shame. The phenomenology of shame is vividly discussed by Bernard Williams. Williams writes that, "The basic experience connected with shame is that of being seen, inappropriately, by the wrong people, in the wrong condition."[48] Plausibly, in its most primitive version, the experience is being seen naked (by the wrong person), and this experience has a very familiar motivational tendency: to hide, to seek cover.[49] Williams characterizes shame in terms of wanting to avoid a gaze that comes from a particular perspective. He writes, "The other may be identified in ethical terms. He . . . is conceived as one whose reactions I would respect; equally, he is conceived as someone who would respect those same reactions if they were appropriately directed to him."[50] So how should we understand Serena being ashamed of a below (her own) average performance? We would have to think of Serena wanting to hide from herself or cover herself to avoid her own gaze.[51] But there is something puzzling about the notion of hiding from oneself, similar in a sense to the puzzle of self-deception. Perhaps Serena could project an idealized version of herself as a gazer and imagine shrouding her actual self from the gazer's view. That idea is not conceptually incoherent, and it, further, seems phenomenologically accurate in at least some cases of personal failure. But I have not picked the names Serena or Tiger randomly.

Serena Williams and Tiger Woods are athletes with millions of fans across the globe who admire—even revere—their competitive natures. Admittedly, the cases as stipulated are a bit exaggerated if intended to describe the real individuals; however, I take it that the general picture is accurate. And when we think of the real Serena and Tiger, the description above of concealing behavior seems an inapt characterization of how they would hold themselves to their highest individual ideals. As *extreme* outliers when it comes to both talent and competitiveness, I take Serena and Tiger to be athletes who stare at themselves transparently in the mirror and curse their own failures to win—precisely opposite of the hiding type of behavior associated with shame. Instead of avoiding the gaze of another, Serena and Tiger (as I imagine them) relish it; it drives them to improve on their already unprecedented abilities. Conveniently, nothing about the motivational tendencies associated with guilt is inconsistent with this picture. One can easily apologize to oneself or make amends by promising to do better next time (and one can do so while staring unblinkingly into a mirror). I take it that these phenomena are familiar to many who are dedicated to self-improvement.

Furthermore, there are empirical grounds for thinking that guilt is a better means than shame toward self-improvement. The "generally adaptive nature of guilt" can be contrasted with the "generally maladaptive nature of shame" based on their differing connections with anger and empathy.[52] In addition to shame's motivational tendency toward concealment or avoidance, shame is also associated with "a defensive, retaliative anger and a tendency to project blame outward," whereas guilt tends to be "associated with a tendency to accept responsibility."[53] Regarding empathy, "proneness to guilt consistently correlates with measures of perspective taking and empathic concern," as opposed to shame proneness being "associated with an impaired capacity for other-oriented empathy."[54] Each of these contrasts suggests that guilt is a more constructive means of improving oneself. Retaliative anger seems obviously counterproductive. A connection to empathy might not be as clearly related to achieving individual ideals; however, Nancy Sherman has argued that *self*-empathy can be a useful means "of holding oneself accountable that involves less reproach and more trust or confidence in oneself," which can be highly relevant in cases where individuals are much more receptive to that kind of positive engagement.[55] Guilt, then, seems to have a number of advantages over shame as a means of holding oneself to individual ideals.[56] Of course, one might wonder whether this discussion applies beyond the individualized case. In the next section, I will broaden the scope to fully generalized cases that involve other-regarding reactive attitudes, such as resentment and indignation.

5. THE ARGUMENT FROM RESENTMENT

Thomas Nagel uses the reactive attitude of resentment to help explain role-reversing arguments that are exemplified by the question, "How would you feel if that were you?" Nagel claims:

The essential fact is not only that you would *dislike* it if someone else treated you in that way; you would resent it. That is, you would think that your plight gave the other person a reason to terminate or modify his contribution to it, and that in failing to do so he was acting contrary to reasons that were plainly available to him. In other words, the argument appeals to a *judgment* that you would make in the hypothetical case, a judgment applying a general principle which is relevant to the present case as well. It is a question not of compassion but of simply connecting, in order to see what one's attitudes commit one to.[57]

Wallace has offered an interpretation of this type of "argument from resentment" to defend against the challenge that it either begs the question or illicitly violates an is-ought gap, and he attempts to do so by shifting from an analysis of the structure of the argument, per se, to an analysis of the role resentment plays as a "deliberative phenomenon."[58]

Wallace suggests we understand the argument not as using facts about our sentiments to draw normative conclusions about moral reasons (which would problematically jump the is-ought gap), but as using facts about sentiments to reveal implicit features within our practical deliberation. Wallace's examination of resentment, however, relies on his moralized understanding of that attitude. He claims that "resentment stands apart from the other reactions in being a moralizing response."[59] He further claims that "thoughts about *moral* wrongdoing . . . are *essential* to resentment in its paradigmatic form."[60] More specifically, Wallace thinks that the thoughts involved in resentment include "the moral judgment that we have been wronged by another, treated in a way that violates requirements or demands that are owed to us, as a matter of right or entitlement."[61]

Thus, on Wallace's interpretation of role-reversing arguments, when we take the perspective of the other, "our resentment commits us to the judgment that an agent who acted wrongly under these circumstances had good reason to comply with moral requirements in their treatment of us."[62] Because moral requirements apply equally to all persons, our resentment in the role-reversed position implies our recognition that a person in our actual position has good reason not to perform the act in question. On Wallace's interpretation, then, the argument from resentment is a means of revealing errors within one's own practical reasoning; it serves as "a reminder" of one's "unacknowledged normative commitments."[63]

I think Wallace's response is effective against those who would claim the argument from resentment illicitly violates an is-ought gap; however, Wallace is still susceptible to an accusation of begging the question in a sense relevant to my broader discussion. As I described above, a faithful Strawsonian would reject the idea that moral thoughts or judgments are "essential to resentment in its paradigmatic form." Nevertheless, I think Wallace's analysis in terms of a deliberative perspective that is implicit in the structure of our reactive attitudes is compelling. To retain the spirit of that move, but avoid relying on a problematic interpretation of Strawson, I suggest simply supplementing his discussion with additional classes of reactive attitudes.

Returning to Nagel's basic idea of reversing roles, the idea is that resentment would be fitting from the perspective of the other. But fitting resentment from the perspective of the victim implies fitting reactive guilt from the perspective of the perpetrator; thus, one's own natural sentimental nature provides the means of recognizing that reactive guilt would be fitting from one's own perspective if the action were carried out. Furthermore, because fitting reactive guilt implies the violation of some legitimate expectation (perhaps contextual and based on the particular relationship between the perpetrator and victim), the faithful Strawsonian can agree with Wallace that the argument from resentment should be understood as based on one's own practical deliberation. In particular, your sentimental nature reveals to you that you are in some sense committed to the expectation that tells against your performing the act in question; your role-reversed resentment reveals—via the reactive guilt that you, yourself, should think is fitting—that you have a reason not to perform the action.[64]

Wallace, of course, intends to defend the idea that the argument from resentment delivers a special kind of reason, namely a moral reason. Nagel originally uses the argument as a defense against moral skepticism, concluding in the end that "When they are wronged, people suddenly understand objective reasons, for they require such concepts to express their resentment. That is why the primary form of moral argument is a request to imagine oneself in the situation of another person."[65] The contextualized reading of resentment (qua personal reactive attitude) would not support such a conclusion; however, a faithful Strawsonian might be able to achieve Nagel's goal by taking recourse to the third class of reactive attitudes.

As described in sections 1 and 2, in Strawson's view indignation is "moral" in the sense that it is not based on the particular features of any given person; it is based on the characteristics of "persons as such." If we change the argument from resentment into an argument from indignation, then, if you reverse roles and think that indignation would be fitting, you are committed to thinking any person would fittingly feel indignant in the same situation. Indeed, shifting focus to indignation reveals that we need not limit ourselves to role-*reversal* arguments. You can simply ask whether, from *any* perspective, you would feel indignation toward the actor.[66] Because reactive guilt corresponds to indignation just as well as to resentment, if indignation is fitting, then so is reactive guilt on the part of the actor. In fact, recalling Bennett's point against Strawson, given that these attitudes are moral in the sense that they are based only on the characteristics of persons, as such, the argument from indignation yields a general conclusion that reactive guilt would be fitting for *any* person, were they to carry out the action. Thus, the argument implies that *anyone* would have reason not to perform the action. We see, then, that what makes guilt uniquely useful on Strawson's approach is that it need not involve any particular perspective to be intelligible. It can apply to the most individual and the most generalized expectations, and, for that matter, it can apply to any perspective in between, consistent with the contextualized role discussed in section three.

6. TO THERE AND BACK AGAIN

In this chapter I have examined the role of the self-reactive attitudes within Strawson's argument. This has involved explaining why Strawson considers a self-reactive incapacity to be an exempting condition and how self-reactive attitudes help to unify the reactive attitudes and vindicate Strawson's claim that they stand and fall together. I have identified how the self-reactive attitudes can help make sense of the complexity involved in reading the personal reactive attitudes as based in our contextual interpersonal roles. Additionally, a narrower examination of guilt has revealed its unique capability as a means of holding oneself to account from both the most individual and the most general perspectives.

What I want to do now is briefly return to Strawson's overall argument to show that the understanding of the self-reactive attitudes on offer can help to reveal and *strengthen* its underlying structure. Recall that Strawson's discussion involves first examining the personal reactive attitudes and then the moral reactive attitudes. One reason for doing so would be to support his conclusion that the truth of the thesis of determinism is irrelevant to considerations of moral responsibility based on the plausibility of its irrelevance in the case of the personal reactive attitudes. One might call this an *analogical* reading of Strawson's argument, and, accordingly, the strength of Strawson's final conclusions would rely in part on the similarity of the separate discussions. On such a reading, Bennett's point that the self-reactive attitudes can be both moral and non-moral in nature would gain additional relevance. Understanding reactive guilt as a conceptual correlate of both indignation and resentment—and taking self-reactive incapacity as an exempting condition for both the personal and moral reactive attitudes—increases the similarity between Strawson's two distinct discussions, thus strengthening the analogy. Indeed, *not* understanding the relations in those ways would stand as a significant dissimilarity that would threaten to undermine the argument. To the extent that this appreciation suggests an internal coherence perhaps stronger than has to this point been recognized, it suggests that guilt is the glue that binds the other classes together and is perhaps the class of reactive attitudes most crucial to understanding Strawson's overall view.[67]

NOTES

1. Familiar contemporary figures in the debate include John Martin Fischer and Daniel Dennett (compatibilists), Robert Kane and Peter van Inwagen (incompatibilists), Ted Honderich (hard determinist), and Derk Pereboom (free will skeptic). See Robert Kane, ed., *The Oxford Handbook of Free Will, Second Edition* (Oxford: Oxford University Press, 2011) for essays by each of these philosophers, in addition to many more.

2. P.F. Strawson, "Freedom and Resentment," in *Freedom and Resentment and Other Essays* (New York: Routledge: 2008), 1.

3. Strawson, "Freedom and Resentment," 5.

4. T.M. Scanlon, "The Significance of Choice," in *Free Will, Second Edition*, ed. Gary Watson (New York: Oxford University Press, 2003), 358-60.

5. See Gary Watson, "Responsibility and the Limits of Evil: Variations on a Strawsonian Theme," in *Responsibility, Character, and the Emotions: New Essays in Moral Psychology*, ed. Ferdinand Schoeman (Cambridge: Cambridge University Press, 1987) for the influential discussion that established "excuse" and "exemption" as terms for these importantly different categories within Strawson's discussion.

6. For an insightful explication of Strawson's strategy of addressing the problem of free will and determinism, see R. Jay Wallace, *Responsibility and the Moral Sentiments* (Cambridge, MA: Harvard University Press, 1994).

7. Strawson, "Freedom and Resentment," 15.

8. Strawson, 16.

9. Strawson, 17.

10. Strawson, 19.

11. R. Jay Wallace, "Dispassionate Opprobium: On Blame and the Reactive Sentiments," in *Reasons and Recognition: Essays on the Philosophy of T.M. Scanlon*, ed. R. Jay Wallace, Rahul Kumar, and Samuel Freeman (New York: Oxford University Press, 2011), 367.

12. Wallace, "Dispassionate Opprobium," 369.

13. See John Deigh, "Reactive Attitudes Revisited," in *Morality and the Emotions*, ed. Carla Bagnoli (Oxford: Oxford University Press, 2011) for a commentary that notes this aspect of the view.

14. Strawson, "Freedom and Resentment," 17–18 (emphasis added).

15. Strawson, 18 (emphases added).

16. Strawson, 9.

17. Jonathan Bennett, "Accountability," in *Philosophical Subjects: Essays Presented to P.F. Strawson*, ed. Zack Van Straaten (Oxford: Clarendon Press, 1980), 46.

18. P. F. Strawson, "P. F. Strawson Replies," in *Philosophical Subjects: Essays Presented to P.F. Strawson*, ed. Zack Van Straaten (Oxford: Clarendon Press, 1980), 266.
19. Strawson, "Freedom and Resentment," 15.
20. Bennett, "Accountability," 46. Contrast a definition of moral emotions that is more characteristic of the psychological literature: "those emotions that are linked to the interests or welfare either of society as a whole or at least of persons other than the judge or agent" (Jonathan Haidt "The Moral Emotions," in *Handbook of Affective Sciences*, ed. R. J. Davidson, K. R. Scherer, and H. H. Goldsmith (Oxford: Oxford University Press, 2003), 853. One of the most significant challenges in discussing emotions is navigating the various ways philosophers, psychologists, neuroscientists, and so on think of emotions as objects of study. For critical discussion of some influential psychological research on guilt, see Heidi Maibom's entry in this volume.
21. Strawson, "Freedom and Resentment," 25.
22. See, e.g., Margaret R. Holmgren, "A Moral Assessment of Strawson's Retributive Reactive Attitudes," in *Oxford Studies in Agency and Responsibility, Volume 2*, ed. David Shoemaker and Neal A. Tognazzini (Oxford: Oxford University Press, 2014) and Derk Pereboom, *Free Will, Agency, and Meaning in Life* (Oxford: Oxford University Press, 2014).
23. Coleen Macnamara, "Reactive Attitudes as Communicative Entities," *Philosophy and Phenomenological Research* 90, no. 3 (2015): 550.
24. Stephen Darwall, *The Second-Person Standpoint* (Cambridge, MA: Harvard University Press, 2006), 79.
25. Coleen Macnamara, "Blame, Communication, and Morally Responsible Agency," in *The Nature of Moral Responsibility: New Essays*, ed. Randolph Clarke, Michael McKenna, and Angela Smith (Oxford: Oxford University Press, 2017), 212.
26. I will go on in the next section to reject the idea that *all* reactive attitudes should be interpreted as addressing demands. See Coleen Macnamara, "Taking Demands Out of Blame," in *Blame: Its Nature and Norms*, ed. D. Justin Coates and Neal Tognazzini (New York: Oxford University Press, 2013) for an extended critique of analyzing the reactive attitudes in the language of demands.
27. Brendan Dill and Stephen Darwall, "Moral Psychology as Accountability," in *Moral Psychology and Human Agency: Philosophical Essays on the Science of Ethics*, ed. Justin D'Arms and Daniel Jacobson (Oxford: Oxford University Press, 2014), 43. Dill and Darwall's discussion of guilt is situated within an argument in support of an understanding of "morality as accountability," an approach to morality defended in Darwall, *The Second-Person Standpoint*. As I will argue in the next section, I think that a narrow understanding of the reactive attitudes as grounded in moral obligation is misguided. Although I don't have the space to defend the claim, I think that Dill and Darwall's central insights about guilt can be retained even if their narrow scope is rejected. The primary consequence of their narrow focus, I think, is that it prevents application of their conclusions broadly to both non-moral and moral guilt, thus inhibiting a fuller understanding of the reactive attitudes. Furthermore, I worry that their narrow focus increases their argument's susceptibility to the problem highlighted in note 33 below.

28. David Shoemaker, "You Oughta Know: Defending Angry Blame," in *The Moral Psychology of Anger*, ed. Myisha Cherry and Owen Flanagan (New York: Rowman & Littlefield International, 2017), 81.

29. See Dill and Darwall, "Moral Psychology as Accountability," 50, for an extensive list of supporting citations.

30. June Price Tangney, et al., "Are Shame, Guilt, and Embarrassment Distinct Emotions?," *Journal of Personality and Social Psychology* 70, no. 6 (1996): 1257.

31. Macnamara, "Reactive Attitudes as Communicative Entities," 561. See Ilona De Hooge's entry in this volume for further discussion of the many positive interpersonal consequences of guilt.

32. David Shoemaker, *Responsibility from the Margins* (Oxford: Oxford University Press, 2015), 110. See John Deigh's entry in this volume for further discussion of what distinguishes sincere guilt from mere pretense.

33. I use the term "reactive guilt" to emphasize that I'm appealing to a conceptual connection that many theorists have taken to exist between reactive attitudes. Reactive guilt is perhaps a form of guilt in the way that resentment is a form of anger. Commentators tend not to make this distinction; however, I think this elision is worrisome because it potentially hides the fact that empirical studies of guilt do not necessarily support philosophical conclusions about guilt qua reactive attitude.

34. Many philosophers would argue that affective incapacities are not sufficient to exempt agents from the moral community. See, for example, Matthew Talbert, "Blame and Responsiveness to Moral Reasons: Are Psychopaths Blameworthy?," *Pacific Philosophical Quarterly* 89 (2008) and Gary Watson, "The Trouble with Psychopaths," in *Reasons and Recognition: Essays on the Philosophy of T.M. Scanlon*, ed. R. Jay Wallace, Rahul Kumar, and Samuel Freeman (New York: Oxford University Press, 2011) for opposing views on the moral status of psychopaths. For the purpose of this chapter, I am agnostic regarding the extent to which such debates threaten Strawson's overall argument.

35. Here is one point where the distinction between guilt and reactive guilt is likely relevant. It seems plausible that there is one psychological mechanism (however complex) behind our emotional experiences of both moral and non-moral guilt. However, it seems much easier to draw conceptual distinctions between reactive moral guilt and reactive non-moral guilt. On Strawson's view, the former are grounded in transgressions of generalized expectations. Can an individual lack an ability to recognize generalized expectations, yet retain an ability to recognize individual or personalized ones? Perhaps agents with mild intellectual disability (MID) are an example (see Shoemaker, *Responsibility from the Margins*, 182–88, for discussion of the difficulty these agents face in forming abstract judgments). Would such agents be a devastating counterexample to Strawson's view? I don't think so. For one, Strawson says that being "wholly impervious" to the self-reactive attitudes is grounds for exemption, so it's not clear that MID agents would qualify as exempt. But even if the reactive attitudes are not as unified as Strawson seems to think, on the reading I am advancing, whereby guilt (normally) corresponds to both personal and moral reactive attitudes, we can still say that the personal reactive attitudes are appropriate in the case of MID agents, which retains Shoemaker's idea that such agents are "marginal" in the sense that they are proper targets of some, but not all, of our responsibility responses.

36. See Deigh, "Reactive Attitudes Revisited," Macnamara, "Taking Demands out of Blame," Michelle Mason, "Reactive Attitudes as Second-Personal Forms of Address," in *Ethical Sentimentalism: New Perspectives*, ed. Remy Debes and Karsten R. Steuber (Cambridge: Cambridge University Press, 2017), and Shoemaker, *Responsibility from the Margins*, 88–89, for discussions skeptical toward narrow or overly moralized interpretations of Strawson. Perhaps the best example of a moralized interpretation is Darwall, *The Second-Person Standpoint*.

37. Strawson, "Freedom and Resentment," 6–7 (emphasis added).

38. Mason, "Reactive Attitudes," 156.

39. This type of scenario takes center stage in section 5.

40. Patricia Greenspan, *Practical Guilt* (Oxford: Oxford University Press, 1995), 135.

41. The term "moral residue" is, of course, most often associated with genuine moral dilemmas. I employ it here because the relevant phenomenology seems at least prima facie similar in the moral and non-moral cases. For further discussion of the more standard case, see Bernard Williams, "Ethical Consistency," in *Problems of the Self* (Cambridge: Cambridge University Press, 1973).

42. Greenspan, *Practical Guilt*, 165.

43. Roy F. Baumeister, Arlene M. Stillwell, and Todd F. Heatherton, "Interpersonal Aspects of Guilt: Evidence from Narrative Studies," in *Self-Conscious Emotions: The Psychology of Shame, Guilt, Embarrassment, and Pride*, ed. June Price Tangney and Kurt W. Fischer (New York: The Guilford Press, 1995), 256.

44. See, e.g., John Deigh, "Shame and Self-Esteem: A Critique," *Ethics* 93, no. 2 (1983): 243.

45. Wallace, *Responsibility and the Moral Sentiments*, 38.

46. Heidi Maibom, "The Descent of Shame," *Philosophy and Phenomenological Research* 80, no. 3 (2010): 568 (emphasis in original).

47. This is not to stipulate that Serena and Tiger are unbeatable. It is, however, to stipulate that they must perform below their averages for a competitor to possibly beat them.

48. Bernard Williams, *Shame and Necessity* (Berkeley: University of California Press, 1993), 78.

49. As Williams notes, this can only be the most primitive sense within cultures in which nakedness is governed by privacy norms; however, Williams thinks there is an even more primitive idea of "loss of power" at issue that can be found in any culture that experiences shame, regardless of the particular norms that are associated with it (*Shame and Necessity*, 220). My point in the text turns only on the existence of a distinct difference in motivational tendency between guilt and shame, not the plausibility of any particular proposal for the most primitive source of those tendencies.

50. Williams, *Shame and Necessity*, 84. For further discussion of Williams on guilt and shame, see Laura Papish's entry in this volume.

51. Perhaps it is not Serena's gaze, but the gaze of an "ideally perfect" tennis player that she is compelled to hide from. On that picture, however, it's unclear what ideal Serena would be holding herself to. She doesn't think that *all* players must meet the relevant ideal, for that would entail that she thinks all (other) players should be ashamed of all matches they have ever played. Serena thinks that *she*—because of her

individual abilities—should always play up to her individual standards, and it isn't clear why an ideal tennis player would single Serena out as having that particular standard. An idealized perspective is much more plausibly the source of a generalized ideal of performing to one's best abilities, whatever those might be. However, on that picture, Serena's attitude would not be based on an *individual* ideal; it would correspond to a general ideal that everyone always should do their best.

52. June Price Tangney and Jeff Steuwig, "A Moral-Emotional Perspective on Evil Persons and Evil Deeds," in *The Social Psychology of Good and Evil*, ed. Arthur G. Miller (New York: The Guilford Press, 2004), 329–33.

53. June Price Tangney, et al., "The Relation of Shame and Guilt to Constructive vs. Destructive Responses to Anger Across the Lifespan," *Journal of Personality and Social Psychology* 70, no. 4 (1996): 798.

54. Tangney and Steuwig, "A Moral-Emotional Perspective," 330.

55. Nancy Sherman, "Self-Empathy and Moral Repair," in *Emotion and Value*, ed. Sabine Roeser and Cain Todd (Oxford: Oxford University Press, 2014), 191.

56. This, of course, is not to say that shame cannot also function as a means toward holding oneself to individual ideals (In addition to Deigh, "Shame and Self-Esteem," see Janice Lindsay-Hartz, "Contrasting Experiences of Shame and Guilt," *American Behavioral Scientist* 27, no. 6 [1984]: 700). Furthermore, if we have reason to abandon the Strawsonian reactive attitudes—e.g., if criticisms in Pereboom, *Free Will* are valid—other emotions, such as regret or sadness, might also serve as means toward the same end. These alternatives, however, would lack some of the features of guilt that make it particularly suited for the role (e.g., transparency, reparative motivation, and connection to a precise norm or expectation). I'm grateful to Brad Cokelet for prompting this clarification.

57. Thomas Nagel, *The Possibility of Altruism* (Princeton: Princeton University Press, 1970), 83.

58. R. Jay Wallace, "The Argument from Resentment," *Proceedings of the Aristotelian Society* 107, no. 3 (2007): 307. Wallace's discussion is motivated by Michael Smith, "The Resentment Argument," in *Exploring Practical Philosophy: From Action to Values*, ed. Dan Egonsson (Aldershot: Ashgate Publishing, 2001).

59. Wallace, "The Argument from Resentment," 300.

60. Wallace, 303 (emphases added).

61. Wallace, 304.

62. Wallace, 307.

63. Wallace, 312.

64. As David Shoemaker points out, these steps are also plausibly implicit in simply immediately feeling empathy (Shoemaker, *Responsibility from the Margins*, 111).

65. Nagel, *The Possibility of Altruism*, 145.

66. This shift to an argument from *indignation* is apt to call to mind the type of impartial spectator argument found in Adam Smith: "When he views himself in the light in which he is conscious that others will view him, he sees that to them he is but one of the multitude in no respect better than any other in it. . . . But if he should justle, or throw down any of them, the indulgence of the spectators is entirely at an end. . . . They readily, therefore, sympathize with the natural resentment of the

injured, and the offender becomes the object of their hatred and indignation. . . . As the greater and more irreparable the evil that is done, the resentment of the sufferer runs naturally higher; so does likewise the sympathetic indignation of the spectator, as well as the sense of guilt in the agent" (II.ii.2.1–2) (Adam Smith, *The Theory of Moral Sentiments* [Indianapolis, IN: Liberty Fund, Inc., 1982], 83–84).

67. I am very grateful to Olivia Bailey, Brad Cokelet, and Dave Shoemaker for insightful comments and suggestions on earlier drafts of this chapter and to Eric Brown and Marcus Hunt for discussion of some of the issues involved.

Section 3

EVALUATING GUILT

Chapter 10

Darker Sides of Guilt
The Case of Obsessive-Compulsive Disorder

Juliette Vazard and Julien Deonna

INTRODUCTION

Why do thoughts involving harm and damage trigger guilt in certain individuals and not in others? The significance of this question comes into view when considering the medical and psychological literature on patients with obsessive-compulsive disorder (OCD). Patients with OCD feel guilt in response to having certain recurring, negative thoughts whose content evoke scenarios of harm and damage. This, however—at least in most readings of what those thoughts consist of—is puzzling. The transition from having a thought about being the source of harm popping up in one's mind to feeling guilty is not straightforward, and it calls for explanation.

Indeed, OCD appears to challenge a traditional picture of what guilt is all about. According to it, guilt is an experience of a deed of ours as wrong, of an action (or an omission) as infringing a norm to which we adhere. As a consequence, guilt is associated with action tendencies aimed at making reparations or amends, perhaps in proportion to the wrong done. Now, if this picture is correct, then we should find it quite strange that the guilt experienced by obsessive patients has very little to do with any actual wrong nor with drives to repair any damage done. Indeed, the guilt of OCD sufferers seems to be a personal affair, which takes place between themselves and their thought processes.

This being the case, we think that the alleged existence of OCD guilt, inasmuch as it stretches our ordinary concept of guilt in interesting directions, allows us to ask anew some pressing questions regarding its applicability in test cases. While showing that the resulting discussion sheds light on what the deciding factors should be in reflecting about the limits of emotion concepts such as guilt (present-oriented, future-oriented, and anticipatory), shame, and other reflective and meta-emotions, we also hope to show how the philosophy of emotion can provide a framework for discussions in the medical and psychological literature on the disorder. Ultimately, we shall argue that the affective distress that OCD patients undergo calls for a re-description of what they experience rather than a radical revision of our best accounts of self-reflective emotions.

Specifically, we start by describing in very general terms the disorder and the way guilt features in it. We shall then remind ourselves of how guilt, quite independently of OCD, is commonly portrayed in the literature, and how it contrasts with shame. Having done that, we proceed to argue that it is fear of anticipatorily experienced guilt, rather than guilt *itself*, that best describes OCD patients suffering in response to their intrusive thoughts. The fear in question, we then suggest, is particularly upsetting in that the guilt it focuses on is interpreted by OCD sufferers as indicative of a defective self that cannot possibly be repaired. The focus on the defective self is in turn, we speculate, likely to generate guilt over character traits or even shame, maintaining in that way the subject in a spiral of negative self-oriented emotions. At the very end, we allow ourselves to suggest that the particularly severe patterning of negative emotions characteristic of OCD will be familiar, perhaps in lighter forms, to many who have not been diagnosed with the disorder.

DEFINING THE OBSESSIVE MIND

Obsessive-compulsive disorder (OCD) is one of the most prevalent of anxiety disorders, and it has been rated as a leading cause of disability by the World Health Organization (WHO 1996). It is often considered to be a form of emotion-related psychopathology, in which anxiety and guilt play central roles (Frost, Steketee, Cohn, & Griess 1994; Shafran, Watkins, & Charman 1996). OCD most often implies two elements: obsessions, "which are intrusive, unwanted thoughts, ideas, images, or impulses"; and compulsions, which are acts taking the form of "behavioural or mental rituals according to specified 'rules' or in response to obsessions" (Abramowitz, McKay, Taylor 2008, 5). The unwanted, intruding thoughts in OCD can be classified according to their specific themes: "(a) aggressive, sexual, religious, or somatic obsessions and checking compulsions; (b) obsessions concerned with symmetry and ordering and counting and repeating rituals; (c) obsessions with contamination and compulsions to clean; and (d) hoarding" (Abramowitz, McKay, Taylor 2008, 5).

Obsessions and compulsions are easily understandable because we may all be familiar with their variants: We double-check the door when we leave on vacation, we dislike it when our desk is not perfectly clean and tidy, etc. We are also familiar with the experience of thoughts and images popping up in our minds without them bearing any apparent connection with ongoing deliberation processes. However, when people spend entire days washing their hands, aligning chairs, and checking the windows for hours on end, we seem to be faced with something different, a behavior that is yet to be fully understood.

Intrusive thoughts and compulsive activities that characterize OCD are also present to a lesser degree in nearly 90 percent of the general population (Ladouceur et al. 2000; Rachman & de Silva 1978; Salkovskis & Harrison 1984). This includes experiencing thoughts as intrusive and disturbing. Even if they do not develop the debilitating disorder that OCD is, ordinary people sometimes experience thoughts as intrusive, disturbing, or in some way ego-dystonic, and they engage in some behavioral or mental attempts to suppress the thought or neutralize its power. How does guilt come into this picture?

GUILT IN OCD

While researchers and clinicians have paid little attention to addressing guilt in the treatment of OCD, it has recently been suggested that this emotion should be seriously considered as a maintaining factor of OCD symptoms. Several studies have demonstrated that OCD subjects experience higher state-guilt, that is, more episodes of guilt, but also higher trait-guilt, that is, a stable tendency to experience more guilt more often, than controls. It has also been shown that persons with high trait-guilt are generally more prone to developing OCD symptoms, which means that a disposition to experience this particular emotion constitutes one of the factors able to predict the onset of the disorder in individuals.

In the past, intense and persistent guilt was frequently mentioned as a major component of OCD scrupulosity, which is a particular subtype of OCD in which obsessions specifically involve religious or moral content. Today, however, it is believed that the impact of guilt on OCD extends well beyond this particular subtype. In fact, in their review of the literature on guilt and OCD, Stewart and Shapiro (2011) claim that "guilt may mediate most other obsessions, including aggressive, contamination, sexual, religious, symmetry/exactness, and other obsessions. It may also motivate nearly all compulsion subtypes, including cleaning, checking, repeating, counting, ordering, and miscellaneous compulsions." In fact, current literature suggests that guilt should be considered in the assessment and management of all OCD patients.

It appears then quite clearly from this literature that the emotion of guilt is particularly correlated with OCD symptoms. Moreover, as high trait guilt is a predictor for the development of OCD, a disposition toward guilt might even be considered as one cause of the disorder. But, and this is a pressing question, what do patients with OCD feel guilty about? The medical and psychological literature suggests that OCD patients feel guilty in response to thoughts whose content evoke scenarios of harm and damage. Thoughts of—for example—harming family members, having sex with inappropriate partners, making oneself ill (through contamination, for instance), etc., constantly invade awareness. We shall shortly examine in some details what these thoughts exactly involve, but let us first remind ourselves of how guilt is commonly portrayed in the literature.

GUILT IS GOOD SELF DOING WRONG THINGS

Guilt is characterized by psychologists and philosophers alike as a negative emotional state associated with the belief that one has broken personal norms. This is why guilt is thought to be a reflexive emotion: When undergoing guilt, we must view ourselves as the doer of a particular deed that exemplifies the violation of a personal norm (Taylor 1985; Miceli & Castelfranchi 2015).

Experiencing emotions such as guilt thus implies that we see ourselves as agents in the world who can succeed or fail to realize certain states of affairs that, typically but not necessarily, include other agents. Guilt hence requires a knowledge of certain norms, a grasp of the demands these norms impose on us, and an understanding of the actions and behaviors considered as conforming to or transgressing them (e.g., Helm 2001).

Guilt, then, is rational when it is felt in relation to things for which we can be held responsible. These are typically actions and omissions, but also character traits. Indeed, we may feel rational guilt in connection with our selfishness if we believe that this trait is the result of a failure on our part to cultivate more altruistic attitudes. Which traits are such that we can cultivate their presence or absence is, of course, a matter of controversy (see Meriste, this volume), but it seems fair to say that guilt starts to lack intelligibility when we fail to see how the subject could have had any power to contribute to what he feels guilty about.[1]

In this traditional portrayal of guilt, it appears then that the locus of evaluation is an action of mine, either related to how I treat others or to the way I expect to conduct myself, which I construe as an infraction, and for which I feel responsible. It is an emotion that is directly linked to the concern of performing "right" actions, and hence to morality in this sense (Deonna & Teroni 2008).

It is useful here to contrast guilt with shame. In guilt, the experience of violating a norm to which we adhere is not fatal to how we see ourselves, as the negative evaluation is really focused on one of our actions or behaviors. As Tangney et al. (1992, 100) note: "In guilt, the object of concern is some specific action (or failure to act) which violates internal standards." In shame, however, the focus is not on a specific action of mine, but rather on some feature of myself that cannot be easily removed. Although the person experiencing guilt may feel for the moment as if she or he is a "bad person," her or his self-concept and core identity remain for the most part intact (Deonna & Teroni 2009; Bruun & Teroni 2011). Shame by contrast appears to involve the experience of an undermined self, inherently imperfect and fallible. In guilt, one can wonder why one behaved badly while retaining the idea that one is a "good person." The failing is not perceived by the agent as sufficiently severe to affect his identity in some distinct way (Deonna, Rodogno, & Teroni 2011).

Keeping these distinctions in mind will help us identify more precisely in what terms we can articulate the distressing state caused by intrusive thoughts in persons with OCD. Before we embark on our attempt to understand the guilt allegedly experienced by OCD sufferers, some candidate objects of their guilt can be excluded from the start.

A first option is that the guilt is simply felt over the destructive or negative events represented in the obsessive thought. This is however clearly not the case. OCD patients are not deluded into thinking that they have committed the harm they imagine doing. It is also crucial to emphasize that OCD patients do not feel guilt over indulging in enduring imaginative projects in which they act badly. Intrusive thoughts are not active mental explorations of scenarios in which subjects harm other people. If that was the correct description of their experience, then we would have a ready explanation of their emotion: Feeling guilt over seeking satisfaction in mental scenarios of causing harm makes perfect sense. The guilt in OCD, however, is not a form of guilty pleasure, not a meta-emotion in this sense. As was suggested from the beginning, the immoral or harmful actions that pop up and intrude in OCD patients' mental lives are at no point experienced by them as intentional plans upon which they might want to act. As we shall now see, getting a clearer understanding of the nature of those thoughts and how they are received might enlighten us on how guilt exactly enters the picture.

TAKING THOUGHTS SERIOUSLY

As was just emphasized, the main characteristic distinguishing obsessions from other types of negative thoughts (such as depressive ruminations) seems to be their unwanted nature (Rachman & Hodgson 1980). The ego-distonicity of obsessions, the fact that their content immediately appears to stand in tension with the subject's values and norms, differentiates OCD from other disorders, such as paraphilias, in which the subject happily invites persistent thoughts into awareness. Obsessive thoughts are experienced as inconsistent with the beliefs about the kinds of thoughts she expects herself to have; they express evaluations that are frightening to the individual herself. Thoughts of harming one's children, having sex with inappropriate partners, and making oneself sick constantly invade awareness. Even an obsession that one has left an electric appliance on and caused a severe accident might be experienced as ego-dystonic in that it violates the individual's sense of himself as a conscientious, cautious, and responsible person. Furthermore, the knowledge that it is highly improbable that the feared event will actually occur may be inconsistent with the individual's view of himself as rational and sane.

While most of us might shrug our shoulders at the many silly fantasies that make their way into our streams of consciousness, subjects with OCD are characterized by their tendency to worry about their streams of consciousness, thereby revealing a belief that whatever appears in it should be "taken seriously." In Purdon and Clark's terms (1999, 102), "one of the most striking features in the presentation of individuals with OCD is their preoccupation with the contents of their stream of consciousness." However, once one attributes a profound meaning to the mere occurrence of a thought or a fantasy, one might start wondering: "Why would I have these ideas if they had nothing to do with me?" (de Haan, Rietveld, & Denys 2013).

This dimension of the disorder has fostered the emergence of so-called metacognitive models of OCD, models that emphasize the role of beliefs OCD sufferers have about their thoughts and thought processes. The idea here is that the persistence and idiosyncratic nature of the disorder can only be explained in reference to the assumptions that individuals make concerning the functioning and significance of their thought processes (Purdon & Clark 1999). The hypothesis brought forward by defendants of metacognitive models of OCD is that in the disorder, metacognitive knowledge may be inaccurate or dysfunctional, so that thoughts naturally occurring in the stream of consciousness are appraised as threatening (Wells 2002). Metacognitive processes then activate specific strategies for coping with the perceived threat. Such actions include thought suppression, neutralizing, checking, and ruminating, which result in a recurrence of that very thought. How does that work exactly? An example is a tendency that has been described as "Thought-Action Fusion" (TAF), and that refers to the belief that thought and behavior are linked in specific ways (Berle & Starcevic 2005, as cited in Garcia-Montes et al. 2008, 228). For instance, "probability TAF" corresponds to a person's assumption that a thought can increase the likelihood of an event happening. In other words, one of the defining elements of the disorder would be the fact that the occurrence of an intrusive thought about a possible future harm is appraised as indicating that one might cause this sort of damage, and that one is responsible for preventing the harm. On this metacognitive understanding of the disorder, one can make sense of the guilt experienced by OCD sufferers—at least on the background of the problematic metacognition—as a form of future oriented guilt, i.e., as bearing over a harm that might well come about because of me and that I have the power to prevent.[2] This inflated sense of responsibility in which a belief that one has influence over an aversive event translates in OCD patients into complete responsibility for preventing the occurrence of the event. Interestingly, for those patients, failing to prevent harm (omission) is felt as morally equivalent to deliberately causing harm (commission) (Wroe & Salkovskis 2000).

Now, the fact that a heightened sense of responsibility has indeed been found to correlate positively with the severity of OCD symptoms (Salkovskis et al. 2000) does not mean that the distress felt by OCD patients can generally and fruitfully be understood on the model of future oriented guilt just sketched. Most often than not, the responsibility and the distress felt by OCD patients is *directly over the content of their thoughts* and not about *what these thoughts indicate these patients are about to do (or fail to prevent happening)*. OCD sufferers appraise their thoughts as something they are responsible for—expressing evaluations such as, "How could I let myself think that!"—and the task of understanding this in connection with guilt is still ahead of us. Part of the literature suggests that it is perhaps not guilt that they feel, but rather a specific attitude toward guilt. We shall now examine this option.

GUILT AS A THREAT

What attitude do OCD sufferers have toward guilt? To answer this question, one needs perhaps to consider the specific way in which persons with OCD evaluate their own emotions. Indeed, if OCD subjects feel responsible for having their intrusive thoughts, they may have a similar approach to certain feelings, which they view as "forbidden" and unacceptable.

The term "sensitivity" with regard to emotions has been used in the psychological literature to refer to the individual's negative evaluation of her emotional state. Apart from being an evaluation itself, an emotion can also be judged by the person undergoing it in a positive or a negative way. For instance, a person with high levels of anxiety sensitivity perceives the manifestations of anxiety (such as accelerated heartbeat) as dangerous (triggering such thoughts as, for instance: "I will have a heart attack"), and she anticipates anxiety, thereby creating a vicious loop, since the evaluation of anxious symptoms worsen or maintain anxiety (Taylor 1995). Sensitivity often manifests itself as a tendency to overestimate the negative consequences of experiencing a specific emotion. It has been suggested that *guilt sensitivity*, or the tendency to overestimate the negative consequences of feeling guilt, might be what motivates patients with OCD to perform compulsive actions (Mancini, D'Olimpio, and Cieri 2003). The idea is that the distress that OCD patients feel toward their thoughts can be best characterized as a fear of guilt, a forward-looking emotion that anticipates the occurrence of guilt as a threat.

The authors have observed that an increase in perceived responsibility in nonclinical individuals induces obsessive-like behaviors (checking, hesitating, doubting), and that a fear of guilt regarding irresponsible behavior exacerbates these tendencies. They thus conclude that the way guilt enters into OCD is perhaps through the attitude the subject has toward this emotion, i.e., as an object of intense apprehension.

This seems to enlighten some aspect of the reaction of persons with OCD to their thoughts, and in particular the element of intense apprehension, which is not typically present in straightforward guilt. The intolerance or fear with regard to guilt, coupled with metacognitive beliefs regarding the power and meaning of the relevant thoughts, provide some explanation as to the way in which patients react to their intrusive thoughts by engaging in compulsive actions. Compulsive acts can, indeed, then be seen as precautionary, protective acts that aim at avoiding the dreaded state of guilt, at any cost. According to this view, the distress caused by intrusive thoughts seems more akin to an extreme fear of guilt, more precisely a fear born out of an episode of anticipatory guilt. On this picture, guilt enters into OCD as an anticipatorily felt state that is presently experienced as a great threat.[3]

While this seems promising—indeed, we now have a unified explanation of why anxiety and guilt are said to be the dominant emotions in OCD—the idea that one is afraid of one's guilt might be open to various interpretations.

BREAKING RULES

What is it, then, that persons with OCD fear, when we say that they fear guilt? Is it that they fear the deeply unpleasant hedonic sensations that accompany the emotion of guilt? Are they afraid of causing harm to others by thinking those thoughts, by perhaps making it more likely that these catastrophes happen (see previous section)? Or are they afraid of being an immoral person who would think those thoughts?

While it is difficult to provide a definite answer on that count, it looks like what we have so far defined as fear of guilt has more to do with a concern to conform to one's moral rules, rather than a fear of causing harm to others or doing wrong. Recent findings by Basile et al. (2014) have been interpreted through the prism of a related distinction between two kinds of guilt: deontological guilt and altruistic guilt. Deontological guilt (DG) is described in this account as an affective state elicited by the perception of the transgression of a moral rule (with no or little concerns for others to be damaged). Altruistic guilt (AG) is described as elicited by the belief that one has compromised an altruistic goal, by letting a friend down, for example (with no concern for the violation of an inner moral rule). Examples of deontological guilt include the kind of guilt elicited by breaking a religious rule, as may happen to a Roman Catholic who has sexual intercourse before marriage (Haidt et al. 1993). Whether there really are two kinds of guilt that warrant this distinction is arguable. Whether I let a friend down or I break a religious rule, I might always both feel that I have transgressed a rule, and that I have caused damage to some other—to my friend, or to God. It is through violating a personal norm that I have caused harm. Still, we may assume that our guilty feelings can focus our attention at times to the damage and harm caused, and at times rather to the rule that we have violated. In OCD patients, it seems to be the latter that dominates.

If that is right, then the following picture of the emotions felt by OCD patients seems to emerge. The guilt they feel is not actual, but anticipatory. This anticipated guilty state is what they fear, that is, what they experience as a great threat. The considerations just brought forward foster the idea that what they are concerned with in this guilty state is not so much the harm they might occasion, but the state of being someone who does wrong, the state of being a transgressor or, more generally, a morally fallible person. As we shall now see, the severity of the threat represented by guilt in OCD becomes intelligible in light of the fact that the prospect of this guilt is experienced as a state that cannot be forgiven or overcome.

UNACCEPTABLE GUILT

For OCD patients, the possibility of breaking a moral rule is viewed as serious, likely to happen, looming, and most importantly, unforgivable. In OCD, "the experience of guilt is not evaluated as an experience that can be overcome, even if painful, but as definitively compromising one's dignity as a moral individual" (Cosentino et al. 2012, 41).

Described in these terms, we understand that the fear of guilt (or fear of breaking rules) experienced by OCD sufferers is nothing like guilt *simpliciter*, an emotion in which the self is not affected in its core identity. While guilt gears action toward undoing or repairing the wrong that one has done, the fear of moral transgression manifested in OCD cannot find a resolution in any course of action. The dreaded state of being a transgressor of rules, which we have identified as a motivator for compulsions in OCD sufferers, is viewed as unforgivable and unalterable. Our final task is now to try to explain this belief. What is at stake in breaking rules for the person with OCD? One way in which we can understand the idea of a moral transgression as unforgivable and necessarily compromising one's identity is by emphasizing the idea that, behind the rule-breaking that the occurrence of the intrusive thought represents, is the fear *of the person one might be*, and of what this person might be capable of. If the fear of transgression is a fear of one's potential and *propensity* to act in irresponsible, immoral, and dangerous ways, then resolving it goes beyond repairing the damage caused by the act itself.

THE FEARED SELF: ALL THOSE THINGS I COULD DO

As has already surfaced in our discussion of metacognitive models, patients with OCD interpret the occurrence of the intrusion as revealing important and often hidden aspects of their character. These interpretations of intrusive thoughts lead patients to fear what they might be capable of in the future, and to suspect that deep down they are evil, dangerous, or insane (Rachman 2003). As Purdon and Clark (1999) suggest: "Given that thought occurrences may be perceived as evidence that the undesirable personality characteristic exists, the individual will develop a high stake in not having the thought." The idea is then that, because thoughts might represent evidence for the individual that he is not the reasonable, sane, loving person he thinks he is, controlling them becomes of uttermost importance. However, these beliefs regarding hidden traits are not limited to the way intrusions are interpreted; they reflect the more general assessment in patients with OCD "that the self possesses the potential to act immorally or harmfully" (Ferrier & Brewin 2005). When having thoughts about doing harm, the subject might take these as confirming his belief that he has sociopathic character traits. Implicit in this process are beliefs about the nature and importance of thoughts, of the type: "If I think about it, it means I want it to happen; it reveals my true nature."

"Actual self," "ought self," and "ideal self" are concepts that aim at providing a basis for explaining the discrepancies that can be felt between domains of one's self. With this in mind, the feared self has been defined as consisting in a set of attributes the person wants not to become but is concerned about possibly becoming (Nurius & Markus 1990). The concept of a feared self is useful in helping us understand the fear that we have identified as typical of OCD patients: The idea is that these patients obsess about manifesting certain unwanted personality traits.

Carver et al. (1999) developed a questionnaire measure that assessed discrepancies between the actual and the feared self, and compared OCD patients with anxious controls and non-anxious controls on this measure.

They found that the feared self of OCD patients typically consisted of traits that were dangerous to the self or others in virtue of being bad, immoral, and/or insane. In comparison, the feared self of non-anxious controls consisted of general character flaws, and the feared self of anxious controls was related to anxious traits such as fearfulness and hopelessness.

If guilt is usually thought to manifest a discrepancy between the actual self and the ought self, the fear of guilt experienced by persons with OCD seems to reveal a discrepancy between the feared self and the ought self. The conflict is one that takes place between two non-actual characters. The fear generated by the emergence of intrusive thoughts is not a signal that we are not behaving like the person we would like to be or believe that we should be, but that we are this person we fear to be.

All this is in tune with recurring themes in the literature according to which obsessional individuals are characterized and driven by a belief in their potential to act immorally or harmfully and display dangerous or immoral personality traits. In the background of OCD symptoms, we often find the assumption that one should not be trusted. Everything looks as if obsessive thoughts are taken as additional confirmation of the idea that one is likely to violate norms through one's future behaviors.

The anticipatory guilt that constantly brings back the individual to her character flaws reminds us of the idea that guilt can also be about character flaws. One can feel guilty, in some circumstances at least, not only about having done some harm, but also about being a selfish, cruel, immoral person, etc. One option then is that the anticipatory guilt felt by individuals with OCD is compounded by the guilt they feel over being an unreasonable, cruel, or out-of-control person who thinks such hideous thoughts. These feelings of guilt, we surmise, will play this all-domineering role when the character traits involved are such that one can think of them as—at least partially or indirectly—under one's control. Is being evil, dangerous, insane, or malevolent something I could have prevented from occurring? If I come to view myself in those terms, envisaging a specific course of action, trainings, amends, or reparations that could make up for it will seem both desirable and extremely arduous.

If guilt for character flaws might well be what dominates the experience of some patients, for others, the distress in question seems to run deeper, and carry an insoluble dimension that guilt alone cannot explain. We now turn to describing what blend of emotions might be involved in such cases.

INSOLUBLE GUILT AND SHAME

It is helpful at this juncture to consider how pathological guilt proper is described in the literature. Clinical guilt, according to Tangney, Wagner, and

Gramzow (1992, 476), "is an unusual form of guilt, quite distinct from that experienced in the normal range." A core-defining feature of pathological guilt, they observe, is that it is insoluble. It is not usually the kind of guilt that resolves after having made the necessary amends and reparations. Why is that?

It has been argued that the reason guilt comes to take such proportions in these cases is because it is fused with a form of shame in which the self is perceived as inherently faulty, deficient, and evil. In her seminal work, *Shame and Guilt in Neurosis* (1971), Helen Block Lewis proposed one of the few theoretical accounts of the way in which shame-proneness and guilt-proneness are linked to the development of different psychopathological symptoms. As Lewis (1971, 426) observed: "When shame and guilt are both evoked in the context of a moral transgression, the two states tend to fuse with each other, and to be labeled 'guilt.'" One can feel both guilty and ashamed about the same transgression; the first is characterized by an evaluation focused on the deed done, while the second is marked by a return to the self, which is then viewed as worthless, cruel, selfish, etc., for having caused or allowed the transgression. While shame-free guilt is more likely to find ways of resolving itself, guilt that is fused with shame is much harder to resolve, as "shame itself presents an insoluble dilemma because at issue is a malignant self, not a malignant behavior" (Tangney, Wagner, & Gramzow 1992, 476).

While we should be weary of transposing this directly to the case of OCD, it naturally invites the following reading on what happens in the cases that interest us. The fear of being guilty generates (or confirms) in OCD the belief in the possession of bad, immoral, malevolent personal qualities. The distress triggered by the intrusive thoughts is then more about being the type of person who could think (and do) such things, rather than about the harm they might cause by thinking and doing them. As fear of guilt reveals a self that is out of control, it is tempting to think that it is also the occasion to feel shame about being this self, i.e., to feel ashamed at being this person equipped with those traits that dispose one to actions of the worse type. That shame so conceived might play a role in the suffering felt by OCD patients is not an idea that is common in the relevant medical and psychological literature. If our discussion has provided reasons to explore this idea further, then we shall have succeeded in our goal.

CONCLUSION

Metacognitive models of OCD are keen to insist on the bias OCD patients exhibit while interpreting their obsessive thoughts. They believe these thoughts reflect who they are. In this article, we did not set out to provide an explanation of why they have such beliefs. However, following H. B. Lewis's contention that "shame of oneself is likely to be operating underneath guilt for transgression" (1979, 382), we might be tempted to conclude that shame is not only a consequence of the specific guilty scenarios envisioned by OCD sufferers but is also at the origin of their interpretative bias. Nothing we said in this paper warrants such a strong conclusion. We hope, however, to have done enough to suggest that OCD patients are likely to be caught in a spiral of negative emotions involving anticipatory guilt, fear of this guilt, and in all probabilities further guilt or straightforward shame at what this envisioned guilty state reveals of who they are.

We hope also to have done enough to illustrate a sequencing of emotions that many of us, although not diagnosed with OCD, are familiar with. It is reassuring to think that guilt is essentially outward-focused, interpersonal, and focused on our care for others (Tangney & Dearing 2002). The truth is, however, that the suffering we experience over the guilt we experience or anticipate experiencing connects critically with the threat to the view of ourselves that it poses. The guilt experienced is taken to reveal that one possesses the potential to act in ways that imply unacceptable violations of one's norms. It is then also a relationship with the self that is crucially at stake in resolving this kind of guilt. While the focus of the emotion is still on a particular action, when guilt arises in this context of diffused shame, the action will likely be apprehended as revealing (or confirming a belief about) a malevolent potential in the subject, making the negative evaluation and the accompanying feeling much harder to dissolve.

By signaling instances of bad, immoral, and dangerous actions or thoughts, guilt, actual or anticipatory, brings to light our potential to act in harmful ways. When it does, that is, when we take our mistakes as revealing of who we *are*, then guilt becomes fused with shame, and with it comes the danger of insoluble self-condemnation.

NOTES

1. Of course, this is the main theme of the various debates surrounding survival guilt. For an interesting, and according to us, correct verdict about this type of guilt, see Kerr, this volume.

2. See Meriste, this volume, for a convincing defense of the existence of future-oriented guilt.

3. Kerr, this volume, makes it clear how anticipatory guilt, as opposed to anticipated guilt for example, is a phenomenologically salient experience, i.e., it feels very much like guilt felt over wrongdoing we believe we have done. This is what we have in mind when we say that OCD patients suffer from anticipatory guilt.

REFERENCES

Abramowitz, J. S., McKay, D., & Taylor, S. (Eds.). (2008). *Clinical handbook of obsessive-compulsive disorder and related problems*. JHU Press.

American Psychiatric Association. (1994). *DSM-IV Sourcebook (Vol. 1)*. American Psychiatric Pub.

Basile, B., Mancini, F., Macaluso, E., Caltagirone, C., & Bozzali, M. (2014). Abnormal processing of deontological guilt in obsessive–compulsive disorder. *Brain Structure and Function*, 219(4), 1321–31.

Berle, D., & Starcevic, V. (2005). Thought–action fusion: Review of the literature and future directions. *Clinical Psychology Review*, 25(3), 263–84.

Berrios, G. E. (1989). Obsessive-compulsive disorder: Its conceptual history in France during the 19th century. *Comprehensive Psychiatry*, 30(4), 283–95.

Bruun, O. & Teroni, F. (2011). Shame, guilt and morality. *The Journal of Moral Philosophy*, 8 (2), 223–45.

Carver, C. S., Lawrence, J. W., & Scheier, M. F. (1999). Self-discrepancies and affect: Incorporating the role of feared selves. *Personality and Social Psychology Bulletin*, 25(7), 783–92.

Cosentino, T., D'Olimpio, F., Perdighe, C., Romano, G., Saliani, A. M., & Mancini, F. (2012). Acceptance of being guilty in the treatment of obsessive-compulsive disorder. *Psicoterapia cognitiva e comportamentale*, 18, 39–56.

De Haan, S., Rietveld, E., & Denys, D. (2013). On the nature of obsessions and compulsions. In *Anxiety disorders* (Vol. 29, 1–15). Karger Publishers.

Deonna, J. A. & Teroni, F. (2008). Distinguishing shame from guilt. *Consciousness and Cognition* 17(4), 725–40.

Deonna, J. A. & Teroni, F. (2009). The self of shame. In V. Mayer & M. Salmela (Eds.), *Emotions, ethics, and authenticity* (33–50). John Benjamins.

Deonna, J. A. & Rodogno R. & Teroni, F. (2011). *In defense of shame*. New York: Oxford University Press.

Ferrier, S., & Brewin, C. R. (2005). Feared identity and obsessive-compulsive disorder. *Behaviour Research and Therapy*, 43(10), 1363–74.

Flavell, J. H. (1979). Metacognition and cognitive monitoring: A new area of cognitive–developmental inquiry. *American Psychologist*, 34(10), 906.

Frost, R. O., Steketee, G., Cohn, L., & Griess, K. (1994). Personality traits in subclinical and non-obsessive-compulsive volunteers and their parents. *Behaviour Research and Therapy*, 32(1), 47–56.

García-Montes, J. M., Álvarez, M. P., Sass, L. A., & Cangas, A. J. (2008). The role of superstition in psychopathology. *Philosophy, Psychiatry, & Psychology*, 15(3), 227–37.

Haidt, J., Koller, S. H., & Dias, M. G. (1993). Affect, culture, and morality, or is it wrong to eat your dog? *Journal of Personality and Social Psychology*, 65(4), 613.

Helm, B. W. (2001). Emotions and practical reason: Rethinking evaluation and motivation. *Noûs*, 35(2), 190–213.

Ladouceur, R., Freeston, M. H., Rhéaume, J., Dugas, M. J., Gagnon, F., Thibodeau, N., & Fournier, S. (2000). Strategies used with intrusive thoughts: A comparison

of OCD patients with anxious and community controls. *Journal of Abnormal Psychology*, 109(2), 179.
Lewis, H. B. (1971). *Guilt and shame in neurosis*. International.
Lewis, H. B. (1979). Guilt in obsession and paranoia. In *Emotions in personality and psychopathology* (397–414). Springer.
Mancini, F., D'Olimpio, F., & Cieri, L. (2004). Manipulation of responsibility in non-clinical subjects: Does expectation of failure exacerbate obsessive–compulsive behaviors? *Behaviour Research and Therapy*, 42(4), 449–57.
Miceli, M., & Castelfranchi, C. (2015). *Expectancy and emotion*. Oxford University Press.
Niedenthal, P. M., Tangney, J. P., & Gavanski, I. (1994). "If only I weren't" versus "If only I hadn't": Distinguishing shame and guilt in conterfactual thinking. *Journal of Personality and Social Psychology*, 67(4), 585.
Nurius, P. S., & Markus, H. (1990). Situational variability in the self-concept: Appraisals, expectancies, and asymmetries. *Journal of Social and Clinical Psychology*, 9(3), 316–33.
Purdon, C., & Clark, D. A. (1999). Metacognition and obsessions. *Clinical Psychology & Psychotherapy: An International Journal of Theory & Practice*, 6(2), 102–10.
Rachman, S. (2003). *The treatment of obsessions*. Oxford University Press.
Rachman, S., & de Silva, P. (1978). Abnormal and normal obsessions. *Behaviour Research and Therapy*, 16(4), 233–48.
Rachman, S. J., & Hodgson, R. J. (1980). *Obsessions and compulsions*. Prentice Hall.
Salkovskis, P. M., & Harrison, J. (1984). Abnormal and normal obsessions: A replication. *Behaviour Research and Therapy*, 22(5), 549–52.
Salkovskis, P. M., Wroe, A. L., Gledhill, A., Morrison, N., Forrester, E., Richards, C., & Thorpe, S. (2000). Responsibility attitudes and interpretations are characteristic of obsessive compulsive disorder. *Behaviour Research and Therapy*, 38(4), 347–72.
Shafran, R., Watkins, E., & Charman, T. (1996). Guilt in obsessive-compulsive disorder. *Journal of Anxiety Disorders*, 10(6), 509–16.
Stewart, S. E., & Shapiro, L. (2011). Pathological guilt: A persistent yet overlooked treatment factor in obsessive-compulsive disorder. *Annals of Clinical Psychiatry*, 23(1), 63–70.
Tangney, J. P., & Dearing, R. L. (2002). *Shame and guilt*. Guilford Press.
Tangney, J. P., Wagner, P., & Gramzow, R. (1992). Proneness to shame, proneness to guilt, and psychopathology. *Journal of Abnormal Psychology*, 101(3), 469.
Taylor, S. (1995). Anxiety sensitivity: Theoretical perspectives and recent findings. *Behaviour Research and Therapy*, 33(3), 243–58.
Taylor, G. (1985). *Pride, shame, and guilt: Emotions of self-assessment*. Oxford University Press.
Taylor, J. (1836). *The Whole Works of the Rt. Rev. Jeremy Taylor*. Frederick Westley and AH Davis.
Wells, A., & Matthews, G. (1994). Self-consciousness and cognitive failures as predictors of coping in stressful episodes. *Cognition & Emotion*, 8(3), 279–95.

Wells, A. (2002). *Emotional disorders and metacognition: Innovative cognitive therapy*. John Wiley & Sons.

World Health Organization. (1996). *The World Health Report*: Fighting disease, fostering development/report of the Director-General.

Wroe, A. L., & Salkovskis, P. M. (2000). Causing harm and allowing harm: A study of beliefs in obsessional problems. *Behaviour Research and Therapy*, 38(12), 1141–62.

Chapter 11

Nietzsche's Repudiation of Guilt

Reid Blackman

At the time of writing, this chapter was due to the editors two weeks ago. Thankfully, I was granted a three-and-a-half-week extension, though I'm not certain I'm going to get it done in time. I feel guilty about this. I told them months ago I would contribute a piece to this volume, and here I am contemplating just quitting on it. That makes me feel guilty too.

What if I don't hand it in? The editors would likely be justifiably upset. They would blame me for not getting it done in time. I would blame myself. In fact, that's what I take my guilt to be: self-blame. I might offer considerations that blunt the force of the blows of our respective blamings—I have a newborn in addition to a three-year-old, I have other pressing projects, I couldn't figure out what I wanted to say in the paper, and so on—but the blame would remain intact, and seemingly, justifiably so.

But perhaps the seeming is illusory. Nietzsche seems to think guilt and blame are out of place, or inappropriate, not just here or there, but everywhere.[1] Granted, he had bigger Friday fish to fry, like the guilt of betraying God, but the core claim is the same: We ought not to feel guilty.

Claims about what people ought to do, to the ears of many contemporary philosophers who work on normativity, are claims about where the balance of normative reasons lies. The idea is that there are normative reasons—roughly, considerations or facts that count in favor of a course of action, belief, or emotion—and that these normative reasons come with varying weights. What one ought to do, believe, or feel in a given instance is a function of the balance of the weights of the normative reasons that bear on one at that instant. The claim that we ought not to feel guilt, or that we ought not to blame people, is then understood as the claim that the balance of one's normative reasons favor not having a given emotion.

Nietzsche's claim is not of that kind. His claim that we ought not to blame people is not the claim that each individual has a set of normative reasons to suspend blame and that those reasons are the weightiest. His claim is not directed at this or that person, but at a people or a culture. Understood this way, his claim is that there ought to be a kind of moratorium on blame, whether it's directed at others or at our ourselves. We ought not to be the kind of society in which people blame others for their misdeeds or blame themselves for their own misdeeds.

Understood this way, Nietzsche's view is similar to that of hard determinists like Derk Pereboom. In Pereboom's view, justified praise and blame require that individuals possess free will, but we lack free will, and so there is no justified praise and blame. Put into the language of normative reasons, a necessary condition for the existence of a normative reason to blame someone—be it someone else or oneself—is that people have free will. Since that condition is not met, no one has a normative reason to blame.

But Nietzsche's view is unlike Pereboom's view in an important respect. While Nietzsche arguably agrees that we lack free will of the sort that is needed to underwrite justified ascriptions of blame, that is not the primary driver of Nietzsche's call for a moratorium on blame. Instead, Nietzsche thinks what justifies the claim that we ought to have a moratorium is that we would be better off were we to do so. His argument is consequentialist in nature: People would be better off were we to live in a society free of blame and guilt.

There are two ways to resist Nietzsche's claim. The first is John Skorupski's: It cannot be the case that we ought not to feel guilty because it's not the case that we can stop feeling guilty. Nietzsche's proposal is just not psychologically possible for creatures like us. The second way is to allow that we could eradicate it from our lives, but that it would be a mistake to do so. Nietzsche got the calculation wrong, this second path of resistance maintains.

The remainder of the paper unfolds as follows. I begin by discussing Skorupski's claim, and then, drawing from the second treatise of *The Genealogy of Morality* (GM), I proceed to articulate why Nietzsche thinks guilt and blame are eradicable. For the sake of argument, I will assume Nietzsche's basic account of the contingency of the presence of guilt is correct. I'll then turn to Brian Leiter's approving account of what things would look like without blame and guilt and offer reasons for thinking both that Leiter gets Nietzsche wrong and the account is not an independently attractive one. That is, if this is Nietzsche's picture, then we should think Nietzsche got the calculation wrong. I'll then defend an interpretation of Nietzsche according to which ridding ourselves of guilt and blame is good for us, but it requires the support of an entire culture. Finally, I self-servingly conclude that my guilt surrounding this paper is misplaced.

GUILT'S CONTINGENCY

It's difficult to see how the phenomenon of blaming others and ourselves could be contingent in any society comprised of creatures like us. Skorupski puts the point well:

> It seems to me that the relations of blame, reconciliation etc. are universal in all societies. Priests may place their own magical and religious interpretations on them, but in themselves they are an inbuilt and ineradicable element in the range of human emotions. The sentiment of blame, and guilt or self-blame, is not reducible to any other sentiment, such as resentment, fear or shame. Its distinctive disposition is withdrawal of recognition, exclusion from the moral community. Atonement is the recovery of recognition—at-one-ment with others and oneself through remorse and ethical punishment. I believe that this pattern exists, through varying interpretations and institutions, in all societies, tribal, hierarchical or modern.

There is a lot in this passage to unpack, but here I only want to focus on Skorupski's claim that blame and guilt (and related emotional phenomena) are "inbuilt and ineradicable elements in the range of human emotions." This is a claim Nietzsche flatly denies, and it is important to see why.

Let's look at Nietzsche's account of the contingency of blame and guilt in broad outline. The key ingredient to guilt is the internalization of aggressive instincts, which becomes more or less a necessity once people are locked into a state of laws and customs. The idea is that humans have a natural instinct to aggression that can be expressed "in the wild" but cannot be expressed in the state, the primary deterrent being legal punishment. The most immediate result of failing to express the aggressive instinct is simply depression; not getting what you're built to go after is a demoralizing and frustrating experience. But no one wants to stay sick and depressed, and these instincts demand satisfaction.

If one is not permitted to be outwardly aggressive, then the only solution is that one must be internally aggressive; one must attack oneself. And for this, one needs some grounds for the attack. On the basis of what do I attack myself? I can't simply just start punching myself for no reason. That won't satisfy the instinct for aggression either. Enter the priests of the first treatise of the genealogy, the Jews. They tell us we are evil for breaking God's commandments, and now we have a reason to hurt ourselves: We *deserve it*. The Christian priests turn up the heat by throwing hell and original sin into the mix. Now you *really* deserve a lashing.

This account, or most of it, is clearly expressed in GM II:16.

> I look on bad conscience as a serious illness to which man was forced to succumb by the pressure of the most fundamental of all changes which he

experienced,—that change whereby he finally found himself imprisoned within the confines of society and peace. . . . I do not think there has ever been such a feeling of misery on earth, such a leaden discomfort,—and meanwhile, the old instincts had not suddenly ceased to make their demands! But it was difficult and seldom possible to give in to them: they mainly had to seek new and as it were underground gratifications. All instincts which are not discharged outwardly *turn inwards*—this is what I call the *internalization* of man.

Not everyone is subject to this fate. It can be avoided as the ancient Greeks avoided it: Allow the external expression of the aggressive instincts in pockets. For instance, if you allow the nobles to treat the plebeians with impunity and then attribute their vicious behavior to the influence of some meddlesome god, you get both the absence of self-blame by the noble, since he is not in need of attacking himself because he got to express his aggression on the plebs, and you have the absence of blame of the noble by others, since they attribute the source of his action to a god. As Nietzsche put it in GM II:23:

[T]here are *nobler* ways of making use of the invention of gods than man's self-crucifixion and self-abuse [as Christianity does] . . . this can fortunately be deduced from any glance at the *Greek gods*, these reflections of noble and proud men in whom the *animal* in man felt deified, did *not* tear itself apart and did *not* rage against itself! These Greeks, for most of the time, used their gods expressly to keep 'bad conscience' at bay so that they could carry on enjoying their freedom of soul: therefore, the opposite of the way Christendom made use of its God. They went *very far* in this, these marvelous, lion-hearted children; and no less an authority than the Homeric Zeus gives them to understand that they are making it too easy for themselves. 'Strange!', he says on one occasion. . . . *Strange how much the mortals complain about the gods!* We alone cause evil, *they claim, but they themselves, through folly, bring about their own distress, even contrary to fate!*

That we are locked up in a state that does not allow us to express our aggressive instincts is a contingent state of affairs. We could be in the kind of state the ancient Greeks created: one in which we find outlets for our aggressive instincts so they aren't turned against ourselves. This is why Nietzsche thinks Skorupski is wrong.

But this isn't particularly satisfying. The ancient Greek solution was to abuse others publicly and then proclaim it wasn't their fault because they were seduced to violence by the gods. That's a hard sell in today's society. We're going to need another option.

LEITER ON THE INNOCENCE OF BECOMING

Brian Leiter tackles this issue head-on, calling our attention to Nietzsche's consequentialist argument against blame and guilt:

> Nietzsche's crucial thought appears to be this: a world conceived in terms of responsibilities, justified rewards and punishments, warranted praise and guilt, is horrible, one that would hardly be worth living in. (17)
>
> Imagine the grotesque horror of believing one's adultery explained the storm that ravaged one's community? Or that a killing committed in anger explained the descent of locusts on one's village? Much that happens has been restored to innocence in Nietzsche's sense: we, in fact, employ the phrase "natural disaster" precisely for that reason. A natural disaster is an *innocent* disaster, one that is not the product of anyone's will, anyone's end or purpose. No one is *really* to blame for the horrors that befall those in the wake of a natural disaster. (17–18)

Leiter is right that seeing all the occurrences of the world as rewards and punishments from an all-powerful, ever-watchful deity can be distressing. And the idea is supposed to be that if we see the actions of humans in the way we now see natural disasters, then we will similarly be less distressed by the wrongful actions of others.(Of course, seeing natural disasters as nontheistically caused also has the benefit of being true). But how, exactly, are we supposed to make this kind of transition?

Leiter makes much of an important passage from *Thus Spoke Zarathustra*: "'Enemy' you shall say, but not 'villain'; 'sick' you shall say, but not 'scoundrel'; 'fool' you shall say, but not 'sinner' . . ." (18). When someone is our enemy, we need not blame her for it. She may have interests diametrically opposed to our own, and we may think that, were we in her circumstances, we would have those same interests. But as it stands, she grew up on that side of the wall, I grew up on this side, and so we are enemies, even if we could have been friends or even comrades in another life. Similarly, I can truly say of someone that she is sick even though she has done nothing to be in that condition, and I can attribute the misdeeds of someone to being foolish, to exercising bad judgment, even if I think that she couldn't have known better given her upbringing.

The explanation for why this causes less misery cannot, however, be the same as why seeing natural disasters for what they are decreases misery. Seeing disasters as caused by an all-powerful, ever-watchful deity is distressing because a) you are powerless relative to that deity, b) the deity seems to be merciless, c) the deity has no problem inflicting punishments that are disproportionate to the crime, d) those punishments cause great harm to people other than the offender (e.g., the offender's neighbor's children who now have nothing to eat), and e) *constantly* making sure one doesn't step over the line can be exhausting. It's particularly nerve-racking when you can cross the line involuntarily, e.g., by having impure thoughts. This is not at all the situation we are in relative to other people's actions, however, and so our question remains: Why would seeing people's actions as part of a string of cause and effect over which they have no control result in less distress on our part?

Leiter thinks we find Nietzsche's explanation in GM III:15:

> [E]very sufferer instinctively looks for a cause for its distress; more exactly, for a culprit, even more precisely for a *guilty* culprit who is receptive to distress,— in short, for a living being upon whom he can release his emotions, actually or in effigy, on some pretext or other: because the release of emotions is the greatest attempt at relief, or should I say, at *anaesthetizing* on the part of the sufferer, his involuntarily longed-for narcotic against pain of any kind.

Drawing from this passage Leiter claims, "The thought here seems to be that false ascriptions of guilt and blame increase the amount of misery in the world by inciting those so accused to inflict suffering on others. The mechanism Nietzsche identifies—those who suffer want to inflict suffering—does not seem an implausible one in the history of our particular species, but notice that the ascription of guilt does not even have to be false to cause the harm" (20). And "[w]hy not," Leiter asks, "'liberate' and 'redeem' humanity from this cycle of suffering and blame and then more suffering by expanding the scope of natural cause and effect all the way to alleged human agency itself?" (21).[2]

We now have Leiter's view of Nietzsche's account of *why* we should have a moratorium on blame and guilt. But what is the picture we are left with? The short answer, for Leiter, is that an anger that does not expand to full-blown blame is better for everyone. It's the kind of anger, he says, that one has toward one's dog that urinates on the carpet, and that anger is justified by the two purposes it serves. First, yelling at my dog serves the cathartic purpose of venting my rage. Once vented, there is no need to internalize it, and so no need to attack myself. And second, it can causally impact the dog such that the dog doesn't commit the offense again. Punishment, Nietzsche tells us, is a great way to create a memory of five or six "thou shalt not's."

This anger is not reserved for non-human animals. Leiter recounts a story in which his grandfather is verbally abused by a teacher when the grandfather was a young boy. Leiter says,

> This story fills me with rage, and my immediate reaction is I would like to kill this teacher, at least figuratively. I have no reason to think this teacher could have done otherwise than act out her nasty bigotry in humiliating a child. I do

> not resent her, and I do not feel a *moral* indignation towards her. She is, by my lights, not much different from my dog (probably less endearing, but I don't have enough information), despite walking on two legs and possessing language. Something was *wrong with this person*, and her deformities of character caused her malicious behavior. Her conduct enrages me, not because I think she made a free choice to be a sadistic bastard, or that she was wrongly responsive to "sadistic bastard" reasons rather than good moral reasons (to talk the language of recent academic ethics). Her conduct enrages me because of its harmful cruelty to a defenseless child—in this case, a defenseless child I care about, at least counterfactually! Perhaps my rage, if it had been acted on counterfactually, might have causally dissuaded her from "urinating on the carpet" again as it were, but my overwhelming emotion—about which philosophers, in their bourgeois moral propriety, have little to say—is for vengeance. (23)

The desire for vengeance doesn't face the same conditions of justification as blame does, Leiter tells us, because the former is independent of any attributions of free will or moral responsibility.

> The network of ethical concepts in which revenge is located includes well-being, honor and respect, not blameworthiness and responsibility. If you intentionally harm my well-being, you become a target for revenge; if you do so in a way that impugns my honor or shows lack of respect for my status, then vengefulness looms larger as an emotional response. In either scenario, the wrongdoer is, in Zarathustrian terms, an "enemy," not a "sinner."

What we get from Leiter is an account that recognizes the contingency of blame and guilt and, roughly, an account of the conceptual and practical shift that is involved in leaving them behind. I am not persuaded, however, that Leiter has answered some of the most important questions about Nietzsche's view.

On Leiter's view, we can suspend blame and go in for vengeance, and let's suppose for the sake of argument we can do that. But that doesn't answer one of the central problems the genealogy presents us with, viz. what are we to do with our aggressive instincts given that a) we're getting out of the blame game, including self-blame (aka guilt), and b) we can't vent our aggressive instincts willy-nilly like pre-society savages or the plebian-beating nobles of yester-year? To bring this to the everyday, what am I supposed to do with my aggressive instincts instead of directing them at myself for sending the paper later than the due date? Leiter has an answer for the editors: They can bludgeon me in a way that doesn't presuppose an attribution of moral responsibility (phew!), but what am I to do? Submit the paper late and . . . attack them?

Another issue with Leiter's interpretation is that it doesn't solve the problem Nietzsche allegedly set out to solve. Leiter's idea is that we should cease to blame people not (only) because it falsely presupposes that people have free will and are morally responsible for their acts, but (primarily) because it leads to bad consequences overall. The argument is as follows:

i. Blaming x causes x pain.
ii. Those in pain look to blame other people (especially those on whom they can vent their rage).
iii. This leads to a continuous cycle of blame.
iv. This is conducive to human misery/is inimical to human flourishing.

Let's grant all of this and ask, "Are things better if blame is replaced with acts of vengeance?" Surely the answer is "no." Acts of vengeance cause pain for those on whom such vengeance is expressed, and an animal in pain looks to get vengeance on *someone* or something (e.g., as portrayed perfectly in the movie *Office Space*, people want to smash printers that refuse to print), and so now we have a cycle of vengeance-seeking and pain. This seems no better than a cycle of blame-seeking and pain.

Lastly, suppose Leiter is right that we should just see people as bystanders in the natural chain of cause and effect. This is how Leiter claims to see the teacher that abused his grandfather. "There is something wrong with her," Leiter tell us. She's "sick," Zarathustra suggests. And this explains, Leiter tells us, why he doesn't blame her but wants vengeance instead.

Perhaps Leiter lives in ancient Greece, but by contemporary lights, this is a morally bizarre reply. Usually when someone is sick, when there's something wrong with them, and the person is not morally responsible for their deeds, an appropriate reply is compassion or forgiveness. It's simply not clear why Leiter concludes from his characterization of the teacher that compassion is not in order and that vengeance is. Of course, the desire for vengeance is *intelligible* in light of what's going on. If someone hurts someone you love, anger at them is a perfectly natural reply given the way we've been raised, that is, given that we have been raised in a culture that does not condemn, and certainly empathizes with, that kind of anger. But our culture is also one in which we are cultivated to believe that people are morally responsible for their actions. None of that tells us what our "natural" replies would be if we were raised in, and fully internalized, an understanding of people as bystanders in the chain of cause and effect, bereft of free will and moral responsibility.

Happily, I think Leiter's interpretation of Nietzsche is misguided. In the next section I'll offer a novel account of Nietzsche's view of what a society looks like without blame and guilt. It must be stressed at the outset, though, that Nietzsche is notoriously elusive when it comes to positive proposals and Nietzsche doesn't leave us with a lot to go on. Most of what I say will be straightforward interpretation, but some of it will have to be extrapolations that I think one could reasonably draw from Nietzsche's scant remarks about the topic.

AN ALTERNATIVE INTERPRETATION

You cannot solve the problem of guilt and blame, in Nietzsche's view, without solving the problem of the aggressive instincts. If they are not expressed at all but bottled up, we are left with depression, a kind of sickness, a "leadenness." If they are expressed in an overtly aggressive manner, we'll run afoul of the laws and cultural norms. If we direct them at ourselves, we become ridden with guilt, resulting in misery. And we've learned that whatever the solution is, it is not one directed at individuals. "You ought not to feel guilt" is shorthand for "we ought to cultivate a culture in which guilt is discouraged." Our question is thus: What sort of thing should a culture encourage such that the aggressive instinct is expressed but neither as outward aggression nor self-annihilation?

Nietzsche gives us a glimpse in GM II:24:

> For too long, man has viewed his natural inclinations with an "evil eye," so that they finally came to be intertwined with 'bad conscience' in him. A reverse experiment should be possible *in principle*—but who has sufficient strength?—by this, I mean an intertwining of bad conscience with *perverse* inclinations, all those other-worldly aspirations, alien to the senses, the instincts, to nature, to animals, in short all the ideals which up to now have been hostile to life and have defamed the world.

The idea is that the aggressive instincts have been intertwined with the "natural inclinations" and they should be untangled. I take it that by the "natural inclinations" Nietzsche means the set of desires that are condemned by the Judeo-Christian system, e.g., desires for sex, retaliation, superiority, even happiness. All those things that are animal in us, in contrast to that which is part of our Christian soul. And his suggestion is that we redirect that aggression to whatever in us seduces us to condemn the natural world and to praise and long for the otherworldly, the divine, the afterlife. Direct one's aggression toward the priests, for instance, as Nietzsche clearly does throughout his career.

Another possibility—and I do not see this directly in the text, but I think it is a reasonable extrapolation from it—is that Nietzsche thinks we ought to direct our aggressive instincts into enterprises that require creativity, like the arts, and to acts of self-overcoming, as people do in sports. For instance, I can take the "energy" of my own aggressive instincts and rather than use it for beating myself up for sending the paper late, I can devote it to working on the paper. And the editors, rather than expressing their aggressive instincts by berating me, could use it to find ways to encourage me to not be hard on myself and instead encourage me to work hard on getting it in soon.[3]

This example is utterly mundane. But applied to life more generally, it's a tall order. Rather than condemn the person who has wronged you, encourage them to be better in the future. Don't work for them to be punished, or spend your time wishing for them to fail. In fact, Nietzsche tells us in GM I:10 that the ability to do this is an expression of *strength*:

> To be unable to take his enemies, his misfortunes and even his *misdeeds* seriously for long—that is the sign of strong, rounded natures with a superabundance of a power which is flexible, formative, healing and can make one forget (a good example from the modern world is Mirabeau, who had no recall for the insults and slights directed at him and who could not forgive, simply because he—forgot.) A man like this shakes from him, with one shrug, many worms which would have burrowed into another man; actual "*love*" of your enemies" is also possible here and here alone—assuming it is possible at all on earth. . . . Against this, imagine "the enemy" as conceived of by the man of *ressentiment* —and here we have his deed, his creation: he has conceived of the "evil enemy," "*the evil one*" as a basic idea to which he now thinks up a copy and counterpart, the "good one"—himself!

The idea here is that people like Mirabeau are so strong, confident, able to keep pressing forward despite the slings and arrows directed at them, that they have no need to think about those who shot those arrows. Mirabeau is, in what is surely hyperbole, so strong that people cannot hurt him, and if they do, his eye is so focused on other tasks that he forgets they even did any harm to him in the first place. Dwelling on how people wronged you and seething with resentment is for the weak. The strong don't dwell; they just keep moving forward.

The same claims are made about entire communities in GM II:10:

> As a community grows in power, it ceases to take the offence of the individual quite so seriously, because these do not seem to be as dangerous and destabilizing for the survival of the whole as they did earlier: the wrongdoer is no longer "deprived of peace" and cast out, nor can the general public vent their anger on him with the same lack of constraint,—instead the wrongdoer is carefully shielded by the community from this anger, especially from that of the immediate injured party, and given protection. . . . As the power and self-confidence of a community grows, its penal law becomes more lenient; if the former is weakened or endangered, harsher forms of the latter will re-emerge. . . . It is not

impossible to imagine society *so conscious of its power* that it could allow itself the noblest luxury available to it,—that of letting its malefactors go *unpunished*. "What do I care about my parasites," it could say, "let them live and flourish: I am strong enough for all that!" . . . Justice, which began by saying "Everything can be paid off, everything must be paid off," ends by turning a blind eye and letting off those unable to pay,—it ends, like every good thing on earth, by *sublimating itself*. The self-sublimation of justice: we know what a nice name it gives itself—*mercy*; it remains, of course, the prerogative of the most powerful man, better still, his way of being beyond the law.

Here, too, we have a picture according to which a community can be strong, move forward, and be lenient on its wrongdoers because either it cannot be harmed or the harm is minimal relative to the strength and resiliency of the community. By contrast, societies that are unstable, given to infighting and stagnation, are those that punish harshly in a panicked attempt to maintain control.

And the view is repeated in II:11:

[T]he *last* territory to be conquered by the spirit of justice is that of reactive sentiment! If it actually happens that the just man remains just even towards someone who has wronged him (and not just cold, moderate, remote and indifferent: to be just is always a *positive* attitude), if the just and *judging* eye, gazing with a lofty, clear objectivity both penetrating and merciful, is not dimmed even in the face of personal injury, of scorn and suspicion, well, that is a piece of perfection, the highest form of mastery to be had on earth,—and even something that we would be wise not to expect and should certainly find difficult to *believe*. Certainly, on average, even a small dose of aggression, malice or insinuation is enough to make the most upright man see red and drive moderation *out of* his sight.

In this passage, Nietzsche portrays "the spirit of justice" as something that combats and, in a final battle, beats the "reactive sentiment." Being just—searching for the truth even in the face of personal injury—requires a great deal of energy, and not merely the passive ability to withstand the assaults. It is a "positive" attitude that is an expression of strength.

How can a society attain something approximating this picture? The culture has to encourage people to not be hard on themselves, and this in three ways.

First, the culture needs to encourage people to move on from their "sins," not by going to confession, not by self-flagellation, but by pressing on and attempting to do better, to be better; in short, to overcome oneself.

Second, people simply need to not take things—including the misdeeds of others *and oneself*—so seriously. The attitude is not borne of apathy, but as an expression of strength. "Their misdeeds can do no great harm to me—I can move on."

And third, by not seeing one's own aggressive instincts (including desires that those instincts express, e.g., ambition, beating the competition, contempt for the incompetent) as intrinsically evil, as instances of insurrection against God or against the community or even against oneself. One can recognize these desires as simply another part of being human in this society, and should one slip every now and again and act on those desires when one would rather not, well, "these things happen, but I'm not going to beat up other people about it, and I'm not going to beat myself up about it either."[4]

This picture is a surprisingly humane one to be found in Nietzsche. But given his praise for the natural and his disdain for demanding of humans that they be divine, perhaps it is not so surprising after all. We are human, after all, all too human, and we should not demand of ourselves or each other that we be more than this. Indeed, to demand that we be more is part of what the cruelty of Christianity consists of.

It might be thought that this is all well and good, but the message is coming, at least for contemporary secular readers, a bit late. We've already moved on, it might be thought, from the kind of punishing guilt Nietzsche is attacking.

But recall Skorupski's position. The "distinctive disposition" of "the sentiment of blame, and guilt or self-blame," he said, "is the withdrawal of recognition, exclusion from the moral community. Atonement is the recovery of recognition—at-one-ment with others and oneself through remorse and ethical punishment."

While Skorupski conceives of blame and guilt stripped of priestly "magical and religious interpretations," the conception is still remarkably Christian by Nietzsche's lights. To see this, we can look at how Skorupski conceives of morality: "Morality, the system of recognition, exclusion and return that I have mentioned, is the essential element that gives individuals freedom and standing in society. It was Hegel, not Nietzsche, who got this right."

According to Skorupski, morality is a *"system of recognition"* that "gives individuals freedom and standing." But if at the core of morality is giving individuals freedom and standing—essential elements of a life worth living—and blame consists in the *withdrawal* of recognition, then blame is a fantastically brutal form of punishment we can inflict on others. And guilt or self-blame is a particularly brutal punishment we can inflict on ourselves. Further, Skorupski thinks blame and guilt are essentially tied to the demand from others that one "atones" for one's misdeeds through "remorse and ethical punishment." In truth, I'm not sure what ethical punishment is, but it likely involves at least withdrawing recognition of the person. They should be made to feel like an outcast, an other, who must grovel at the feet of the community and descry one's misdeeds in order to be let back in. By the grace of others do we recuperate our standing. None of this, Nietzsche tells us, is humane. In fact, seen from the perspective of one who sees letting these things go as a symptom of strength and the inability to let them go as a sign of weakness, it's all pretty pathetic.

We also see Nietzsche's view at work in the criminal justice systems of varying countries. In the United States, the criminal justice system punishes onetime and habitual users of drugs. They are fined and incarcerated, and in those cases in which a drug-related felony has been committed, the United States withdraws recognition of the offender as a citizen of equal standing. They are stripped of a variety of rights, including their right to vote, the right not to be discriminated against for the purposes of hiring and housing, and the right to serve as a jury member.

While the United States sees drug use as a criminal problem, Portugal sees it as a medical problem for which people need help, not punishment. As a result, the contrast between America's results from the war on drugs and Portugal's decriminalization of drugs in light of seeing drugs as a medical problem is stark.

> Seventeen years on [from 2001, when Portugal decriminalized drugs], the U.S. is suffering its worst addiction epidemic in American history. In 2016 alone, an estimated 64,000 Americans died from opioid overdoses—more than the combined death tolls for Americans in the Vietnam, Afghanistan, and Iraq Wars. In Portugal, meanwhile, the drug-induced death rate has plummeted to five times lower than the E.U. average and stands at one-fiftieth of the United States'. Its rate of HIV infection has dropped from 104.2 new cases per million in 2000 to 4.2 cases per million in 2015. Drug use has declined overall among the 15- to 24-year-old population, those most at risk of initiating drug use.[5]

This serves as a nice example in which blame is converted to compassion on a cultural level that is translated into legal and governmental structures. There is no withdrawal of recognition from those engaging in the problematic behavior. There is less a focus on how damaged the state is from their behavior and more a focus on how damaging the behavior is to those people. The result is assistance in stopping the behavior, which is better for the abusers and the state alike.

LETTING GO OF GUILT

I have a confession to make. Forgive me, reader, for I have sinned. I told you I feel guilty for submitting this paper late, but I lied. Prior to submitting the paper, I felt burdened: There's this thing I have to do and I'm finding it difficult, mainly for logistical reasons, to get it done. *Ugh*, I thought/felt. But there was no condemnation of myself or my (in)action.

If the editors resented me for my tardiness, they didn't show it, but had they, I still would not have felt guilty. Agreeing to write this paper is a commitment I voluntarily took on, and I have weighty normative reasons (or perhaps an obligation) to complete the task by such and such a time. I have lots of other normative reasons (and obligations), though, including those to my wife and children, and even those relating to my own overall life goals (e.g., projects more tightly connected to my long-term welfare than this particular paper). When I chose to put this paper off because of more pressing demands, that was the right—or to use a less morally loaded word, the wisest—thing to do, even if it meant defaulting on my obligation to submit this paper by such and such a time. I cannot see the sense, let alone the good, in beating myself up for that.

Perhaps this case is not completely fair. The real issue is whether guilt is required in those cases in which I had most reason to X and then I failed to X. In such cases, objectors to Nietzsche's view will contend that the people I have wronged will justifiably resent me and that, in order for me to "take up" this reaction to my action in the appropriate way, I will have to feel guilty. This is required in order for me to take them seriously, they say. My guilt is a recognition of the wrong I've done, the pain I've caused, and it moves me to apologize, to make amends, to seek reparation, and so on. [6]

I do not deny that experiencing guilt is *a* way of taking others, and the ways in which one has wronged them, seriously. But it is not the only way one can take others seriously, and it's a peculiar way of taking them seriously.

Other ways of taking those one has wronged seriously is, upon recognizing that one has wronged them, to desire to help them, to wish one had not done that thing, to be sad both that one did it and that they are suffering, and so on. But none of those psychological phenomena entail the kind of accusation and self-attack involved in guilt.[7] And it would be odd—in fact, *cruel*—for someone to say to me, "Look, I see you're sad you did that, that you wish you hadn't done it, that you're now eager to help me out and make it right. But if you really want me to believe you take me seriously and the wrong you committed, you need to make yourself suffer. You need to be a target of your own anger. Resent yourself like I resent you. *Blame yourself* with the anger that I blame you with." This person is sadistic, not someone with a strong grip on what constitutes ethical sensitivity. At the very least, this person is not a good friend, and to echo Nietzsche, identifying with their attitude would be a variety of self-doubt and self-loathing that constitutes a kind of sickness.

NOTES

1. Warning to those without children: Reading *Green Eggs and Ham* every night will affect your philosophical writing. And your sanity. Unconfirmed reports indicate this was the cause of Nietzsche's breakdown.

2. Leiter considers the "familiar Strawsonian rejoinder," which is the same as Skorupski's: Doing away with these attitudes is impossible for creatures like us. Leiter pithily replies: "One might worry that such an armchair generalization is a case of reifying a contingent sociological artifact into nomic necessity" (21).

3. For the record, this is exactly what they did!

4. This picture stands in stark contrast to the Christian/Kantian picture endorsed by Chappell (in this volume).

5. See http://time.com/longform/portugal-drug-use-decriminalization/.

6. This line of thought is pushed by Sars (in this volume), along with those he cites. He goes so far as to say this is a *conceptual* connection as opposed to a contingent fact about human psychology. To quote Nietzsche, "beware the seduction of language."

7. Again, see the Chappell piece in this volume.

Chapter 12

Conscience and Guilt from St. Paul to Nietzsche[1]

Sophie-Grace Chappell

My interest in this paper is the phenomenology of the ethical life. I have nothing at all against those who want to use experimental data drawn from clinical psychology, quantitative sociology, and so on to inform their discussions of the ethical phenomena; that's not my project. It can't be—I don't know enough psychology or sociology. What I do know a bit about, as, of course, do all of us, is our ordinary shared moral experience. In previous essays I have identified a number of phenomena as key to moral experience yet unrepresented, or seriously underrepresented, in moral theory: for instance glory, action for the sake of the beautiful, objectual and experiential knowledge, attention and contemplation, value-encounter, epiphany, and imaginative identification with others.[2] In this essay I want to talk about another phenomenon that is central to our ethical experience but, it seems to me, rather neglected by much contemporary moral theory. This is the very familiar phenomenon of conscience, and with it its commonplace concomitant, guilt. My big-picture question, or clutch of questions, about that phenomenon is something like, "What is conscience, and why don't the modern moral theories say more about it, and where did we get the notion from, and how much has the experience of conscience changed over time, so far as we can tell?" Within the scope of this paper, I can't hope to fill in the whole of this big picture, but I will do *some* of the requisite filling in.

The phenomenological profile of conscience as we know it, and as it most usually connects with guilt, is simply this: you do something wrong[3]; then having once done it, you find you are troubled by feelings of guilt and/or remorse. These feelings of guilt can become overwhelming, tormenting, unbearable, or they can just hang around in your mind like an unwelcome background noise or perhaps a mild discomfort. Violent or mild, they exert a psychological pressure on you, and the surest way to escape that pressure is to give in to it. Giving in to it feels like a relief. The relief here consists in examining what you did, and either admitting that what you did was wrong, or else—but this is usually harder to do—finding no fault in it and excusing yourself. Where admission of guilt is the correct solution as well as the psychologically easier one, it is, paradigmatically, not only that you have to admit that you did wrong: what you have to admit, to get relief, is that you knew it was wrong even at the time when you did it. It may also be necessary, in order to obtain relief, to take penitential or reparatory steps—to apologise to someone, to pay back the money you stole, or whatever it may be. Such steps are typically possible, though there can be special anguish of conscience where, atypically, they are not. Once completed, they bring relief to the burdened mind.

The experience of conscience being so familiar, the question arises why contemporary moral theorists do not have more to say about it. (They do not, for instance, talk about the very specific experienced phenomenon that conscience is just by talking, much more generally, about moral judgement or self-assessment.) One reason is I think very obvious: it is that there is a clear place in only one of the three main contemporary schools of moral theory for anything like this experience, or what it is an experience of, to occupy.

Indeed, one response to my question is to query whether *experience* is the proper concern of moral theorists anyway. Isn't this, it may be asked, psychology or sociology rather than moral theory? This dismissive response, which I confidently expect from at least some hearers, is thoroughly at home in a utilitarian setting. Utilitarianism can, basically, interest itself in our experience of conscience only as something that may or may not happen to help particular people, in this or that particular social and psychological setting, to have their dispositions and choices shaped in optimific ways. Hence, all that the utilitarian, as such, can say about conscience is the same as she will say about nearly all the other close-resolution phenomena of moral experience. If it helps make things go well overall if people have such experiences, then they are to be applauded (and promoted); if not, not.[4] It is this sort of deliberate refusal to engage with the detail of the texture of our moral life that makes it more than a mere jibe to call utilitarianism, with Anscombe, a *shallow* philosophy.

Both the history of virtue ethics and its theoretical structure and strategy mean that virtue ethics need not share this shallowness, and that it is on the contrary likely to be very much at home in engagements with the detailed texture of moral experience. However, as things actually stand, contemporary virtue ethicists do not typically include in their list of virtues even conscientiousness, or punctiliousness or the like—let alone conscience itself. The fact that most virtue ethicists are Aristotelian virtue ethicists, and that Aristotle apparently has nothing to say about conscience or the experience of conscience,[5] is obviously relevant here. And virtue ethicists have a familiarly worrying bias toward those who are "by the ecological standard of the bright eye and the gleaming coat, dangerously flourishing" (Williams ELP, 46). In this respect as in some others, there can be a surprisingly close alliance between virtue ethicists and Nietzsche, who often points out that there is something in the experience of being pricked by one's conscience that looks like a sign of *weakness*: there is something about it that is less than full, husky, bright-eyed-and-bushy-tailed zoological wellness. For these reasons, at least, it seems to be no accident that, in practice, virtue ethicists display next to no interest in the paradigm experience of conscience described above.

There are ways of being a Kantian, too, that have little or no use for the notion of conscience. Kantianism can be presented as a view simply about pure practical reason, and what actions are revealed as mandated, permitted, or forbidden by pure practical reason when we subject them to the tests that follow from the different formulations of the categorical imperative. So presented—as it may be by contemporary Kantians—it is not obvious why Kantianism should have any particular theoretical interest or investment in the psychological motif of conscience that I described above. To the contrary, a Kantian of this sort may say (at this point echoing her utilitarian foe), there can be no direct engagement between pure practical philosophy and any *particular* pattern of psychology or experience whatever.

This modern form of Kantianism contrasts starkly with Kant himself; of whom it would be wildly false to say that he has no use for the notion of conscience. Here are two key statements of Kant's view of conscience as laid out in the *Tugendlehre*, together with a third quotation from the *Lectures on Ethics*[6]:

> Conscience is practical reason holding the human being's duty before him for his acquittal or condemnation in every case that comes under a law. (*Metaphysics of Morals*: Ak. 6: 400)
>
> Every concept of duty involves objective constraint through a law (a moral imperative limiting our freedom) and belongs to practical understanding, which provides a rule. But the internal *imputation* of a *deed*, as a case falling under a law (*in meritum aut demeritum*), belongs to the *faculty of judgment* (*iudicium*), which, as the subjective principle of imputing an action, judges with rightful force whether the action as a deed (an action coming under a law) has occurred or not. Upon it follows the conclusion of *reason* (the verdict), that is, the connecting of the rightful result with the action (condemnation or acquittal). All of this takes place before a judicial proceeding [*Gericht*] (*coram iudicio*), which, as a moral person giving effect to a law, is called a court [*Gerichtshof*] (*forum*).— Consciousness of an inner court in the human being ("before which his thoughts accuse or excuse one another") is **conscience**. (*Metaphysics of Morals*: Ak. 6: 437–38)

> The inner judicial proceeding of conscience may be aptly compared with an external court of law. Thus we find within us an accuser, who could not exist, however, if there were no law; though the latter is no part of the civil positive law, but resides in reason. . . . In addition, there is also at the same time in the human being an advocate, namely self-love, who excuses him and makes many an objection to the accusation, whereupon the accuser seeks in turn to rebut the objections. Lastly we find in ourselves a judge, who either acquits or condemns us. (*Lectures on Ethics:* Ak. 27: 354)

The motif of a moral self divided into three sub-selves or homunculi raises a question, which we will come back to, about how literally Kant means us to see these three sub-selves—whether each of them is to be is taken seriously as something like a self in its own right. The motif and the ensuing question also remind us, of course, of the tripartite soul of Plato's *Republic*. But, in fact, the immediate background to Kant's remarks here is not Plato's triad of *logos*, *thumos*, and *epithumiai*. The immediate background is the moral psychology of the New Testament (NT).

It may come as a surprise to some readers to hear that the NT *has* a moral psychology, since they have never been exposed to the possibility that the NT might be, or contain or imply, some seriously interesting philosophy. Nowadays many people regard it as an unforgivable indecency to use the word "Jesus" in any grammatical case except the vocative; and it is not only students who know about Christianity, if at all, only via Nietzsche's critique of it, which is a bit like knowing about the Roman Empire only via the table-talk of Attila the Hun. But the NT does have an interesting, if decidedly pre-modern, moral psychology, central to which is a notion of conscience. Why does modern philosophical ethics largely miss that fact, and indeed sideline the notion of conscience itself? I suspect an allergy to theology, especially Christian theology, is at work. So if you share this allergy, please bear with me in what follows; to make up for the Christianity there will, I promise, be some Nietzsche too.

Kant himself underlines the New Testament background of his courtroom picture of conscience by virtually quoting the NT within the second passage from the *Tugendlehre* that I cite above. Kant's bracketed phrase "('before which his thoughts accuse or excuse one another')" is a clear allusion to Romans 2:14–15:

> For when the nations that do not have the law do by nature what the law requires, then they are a law unto themselves. They bear testimony to the work of the law written in their hearts, inasmuch as their conscience also witnesses with them, taking its place among the thoughts which accuse them or else excuse them. (My own translation)

(Comparing the two German texts quickly confirms this. In the Luther Bible, the version that Kant would have known all his life, these verses read: "*Denn so die Heiden, die das Gesetz nicht haben, doch von Natur tun des Gesetzes Werk, sind dieselben, die weil sie das Gesetz nicht haben, sich selbst ein Gesetz, als die da beweisen, des Gesetzes Werk sei geschrieben in ihren Herzen, sintemal ihr Gewissen ihnen zeugt, dazu auch die Gedanken, die sich untereinander verklagen oder entschuldigen . . .*"; and at Ak. VI: 437–38 the last sentence of the second passage that I quoted above in English runs: "*Das Bewußtsein eines inneren Gerichtshofes im Menschen ('vor welchem sich seine Gedanken einander verklagen oder entschuldigen') ist das Gewissen.*")

The most prominent triad in NT moral psychology is the triad that Kant identifies in the third quotation above: accuser (*diabolos*), defence-advocate (*paraklêtês*), and judge (*syneidesis* or conscience). This is indeed, as Kant brings out, a forensic triad, and it is one in which God and the devil of traditional orthodoxy have interesting roles to play. *Diabolos*, accuser, and "devil" (or "*Teufel*") are the same word, and *paraklêtês*, defence-advocate, is a familiar title of the Holy Spirit (see John 14:16). The picture is then that "the devil" is the one who condemns us with as many accusations as he can find—the guilt aspect of the experience of conscience; whereas the *paraklêtês* pleads within us, not for condemnation, but for mercy and/or innocence. And in this inner court it is the conscience that has to choose between the defence and the prosecution: the conscience is the judge.

In the NT the interplay of these three forces within us is simply one battlefield in a universal cosmic conflict between God and the rebel angels. The accuser (Satan), the advocate (the Holy Spirit), and the judge (Christ in glory) are all essentially external beings. They (can) appear as psychological forces within us only because they are already spiritual realities outside us, "in heavenly places" (Ephesians 6:12). If and when the self is divided into three in the NT, it is because these spiritual forces are in conflict within the individual's psychology, a conflict that can only be ended either by confession and forgiveness (notice here that the NT Greek for "confess" is *homologeisthai*, "agree with"; i.e., agree with the accuser, accept the justice of his charge: see e.g., Matthew 3:6), or else by the successful dismissal of the accuser as, on this occasion, a *lying* accuser (see 1 John 3:20: "For even if our heart condemns us, God is greater than our heart, and knows all things"). Caught between *diabolos*, *paraklêtês*, and *syneidesis*, the one self is exposed to three different kinds of heavenly influences, as it were, three "tidal" pulls on it, just as, in the thought of the Graeco-Roman world in the first century AD, it was natural to suppose that all selves at all times were exposed to the kind of planetary influences that were studied by astrologers. (The language of Ephesians 6:12 is strikingly close to astrological language; though, of course, there are differences too.) The inner divisions caused by these different forces were felt as close to unbearable by Paul, documenting them in Romans 7:24: "Wretched man that I am, who will deliver me from the body of this death?" For many others the conflicts evidently became actually unbearable. Perhaps we are meant to understand the afflicted souls that the gospels describe as "possessed by devils" to be psychologies that are overwhelmed by a cacophony, or a legion, of accusing inner voices of tormenting guilt.

While taking over the NT authors' forensic schema of accuser, defence-advocate, and judge to describe conscience, Kant, of course, does not take the courtroom schema, as they clearly did, also as literal cosmology. But then, how *does* Kant take the *Gerichtshof* motif? Is it meant as literal psychology—does he suppose that there are actual homunculi within us that play the roles of accuser, defence-advocate, and judge? Whether or not he does so, presumably Kant's metaphor is meant as a phenomenological description: what goes on in our psychological life when we have the paradigm experiences of conscience *feels like* the courtroom process (or indeed *Prozess*) that he describes. That much seems true, or it can seem true. But the courtroom metaphor remains unclear to the extent that it is unclear what real entities in our psychology are supposed by Kant to *make it* seem true.

This is not just a question for curiosity. The paradigm experiences of conscience, as described above by me and Kant, are or can be *traumatic*. Guilt, seeing oneself as having done something, say, cruel or arrogant or deceptive or spiteful or shameful, can be extremely distressing. A key part of the distress here has to do with the inner division that is involved in experiences of conscience. Some of these divisions are brought out very vividly by the courtroom metaphor. To see oneself as accused, and as convicted, of doing something really bad is painful in any case; when the accuser and the sentence are *within oneself*, even more so. It is natural to think that the experience of being divided in this way is a threat to one's coherence, one's unity, as a person. As the way out of the experience of conscience, to regain its own self-respect, the self naturally seeks reintegration, it seeks to be made whole again, to be once more at-one (and so, perhaps, to atone). But exactly what the self needs to *do* to atone, to achieve this reintegration, to return to coherence, naturally depends on the exact nature of the *dis*integration, the incoherence, that the experience of conscience has introduced.

On this the NT writers give us very specific guidance ("repent, believe, and await the Holy Spirit"), but guidance of a kind that most secular moderns will find too freighted with supernaturalist Christian metaphysics to be something that they can appropriate for themselves. Such secular moderns will find Kant more helpful than the NT inasmuch as he eschews the Christian cosmology; but also less helpful inasmuch as he gives us no definite guidance about how to understand his courtroom metaphor, and so about how to apply it to the task of reintegration.[7]

There is in any case another aspect to the traumatic experience of bad conscience that is not captured by the courtroom metaphor, either in its Kantian or in its NT version. This is an inner division, not between accuser, defence-advocate, and judge, but between me at the time of my wrong action and me at the time of my later regret, or remorse, or repentance.

For the point about bad conscience is not simply that my moral understanding can change, and improve by changing. Certainly there is the experience of doing something and only later changing your values in a way that makes you realise *now* that what you did *then* was wrong. But the focal case of bad conscience is not this retrospective case. In the focal case, as I put it in my initial characterisation, it is "not only that you have to admit that you did wrong: what you have to admit, to get relief, is that you knew it was wrong even at the time when you did it." The pain of conscience is the pain of admitting that when I acted wrongly, *I already knew it was wrong*. When I experience the guilt of conscience in this full form, the question that tortures me is the question how it was possible for me-then to see the same moral data as me-now sees, *and yet disregard them*.

This seems to have been a significant part of Augustine's self-torturing over the stolen pears in *Confessions* II; despite its absence from the NT's courtroom metaphor, it is clearly there when St. Paul writes that "I do not do the good that I want to do; the evil that I do not want to do, that is what I do" (Romans 7:19, discussed further below). For, as St. Paul thinks, everybody does know right from wrong—in their hearts: consider here the implications of the famous phrase of Romans 2:14, "the writing of the law in their [the gentiles'] hearts," a phrase that in its turn is clearly alluding to the Old-Testament promise of Jeremiah 31:31–34, that "in the latter days" the God of Israel would write a new Torah, not on tablets of stone, but on his people's hearts.

This question how I can see the same moral data as two different times, and at one time respect and the other disregard them, has a self-disintegrating momentum. In contemplating it, I become, as Augustine and Paul did, a riddle to myself, an alien being, an incomprehensible monstrosity. One way to bring out what is puzzling here is a parity argument. There is nothing in the moral data that me-now can see, that was not equally available for me-then to see; how is it then that I have, at those two times, drawn two such different conclusions about what I should do?[8]

Alongside the puzzling moral epistemology of the clear-eyed wrongdoing that is central to the paradigm cases of bad conscience, there is the vital practical question of how I am to respond to myself when I find that I am guilty in the way described in such riddling cases. If I am to do justice to what my conscience is telling me, it can easily seem to become necessary for me-now simply to disown me-then. But this choice of simple rejection of the me, or the part of myself, that chose the bad comes at a high price. It seems to mean that I must reject the possibility of ever achieving full self-integration; it seems to mean cutting off part of myself from part of myself. Perhaps the lesson of Jesus's famous saying, "If thy right hand offend thee . . ." (Matthew 5:30) is that this kind of radical extirpation can be called for? In Romans 7:19–25 St. Paul at any rate does not hesitate to draw the self-disowning conclusion:

> I do not do the good that I want to do; the evil that I do not want to do, that is what I do. But then, if I do what I do not want to do, it is not me who works this deed, but the sin that lives in me. Thus I find that the Law, to me who wants to do the good thing—that it brings about evil in me. For my conscience agrees to the Law of God—as far as my inner man goes. But I see a different Law fighting against the Law of my reason, which takes me hostage in the Law of sin, which is in my physical members. Wretched man that I am! Who will deliver me from the body of this death? Grace be to God—through Jesus Christ our lord. And thus I myself serve the Law of God with my reason, but with my flesh, the Law of sin. (My own translation)

St. Paul's disowning, in these words, of the part of himself that chooses the bad is not only thoroughgoing. It also seems very close to Manichaean: in tension with the orthodox Christian teaching that there is only one divine lawgiver, Paul tells us that there are two whole systems of law in conflict in him, the Law of God and the law of sin. And it seems very close to dualistic: in conflict with the orthodox Christian teaching that body and soul are an indivisible unity and that both of them are essentially good, Paul tells us that while his reason (*nous*) blamelessly contemplates the goodness of God, it is his flesh (*sarx*) or physical parts (*melê*) that are responsible for his *hamartia*, his bad or sinful choices.

These theological flaws mean that this solution to our riddle is not philosophically stable either. The question that sets our riddle is this: how could me-then *with open eyes* and *fully responsibly* choose the bad that me-now rejects? And if we now say, apparently with St. Paul, that me-then, in choosing them, was actually overborne by the forces of "flesh" and "sin," then it is no longer clear that the me that chose them was either fully me or fully responsible after all. Apart from its other difficulties the extirpatory alternative, the alternative of demonising me-then as a chooser who is simply wicked and as such should just be rejected, apparently makes no progress with this riddle.

One way to respond to this difficulty is to rephrase what St. Paul is saying in the terms of a modern psychology informed by evolutionary considerations.[9] In humans, we might say, there is an overlaying of different systems of response and reaction. Going below the level of the fully conscious and rational mind, we may find ourselves drawn to respond to situations in ways that reflect our pleistocene or earlier ancestry more than they reflect the needs of our current social and ethical contexts. *Our history bubbles up in us*, often to destructive or even calamitous effect (Jung, EJ, 223: "Just as the human body is a museum, so to speak, of its phylogenetic history, so too is the psyche"). That history is just as much a genuine part of us as is our best and most rational judgement of how we ought to act and live; nonetheless, it is not always a good thing for us to act on its promptings. We do not need, indeed we need not, to *extirpate* the caveman who still lives in us; but we do need to listen to him and understand him and tame him.[10] Just as if we were in charge of a powerful wild animal—cp. *Republic* 588c-d—there are energies in the caveman that we can use, but only if we learn to channel and direct his abundant energies, and are always aware of those energies' dangerous potential.

To take this route would be to offer, perhaps against the grain of the text, a suggestion about "what Paul really meant" in Romans 7:19–25 that does not indict him of either Manichaeism or mind-body dualism. It would also be to show how internal reintegration might come back into focus as a real possibility on the, or a, Christian view of conscience, and how we might even keep a more or less complete recognition of the agent's responsibility for clear-eyed choices of the bad. In brief: the bad choices that me-then made really were *my* choices; for all that they can be choices that I do well to reject, because it is possible that me-then, though truly and genuinely *me*, was acting, perhaps not entirely realising it, out of the untamed Stone Age rather than out of well-thought-through civilised values. Yet the key to the manoeuvre is its recognition that we are not *naturally* integrated within. Integration is an *achievement*. We do not start off that way, and we have work to do to get there.

As may be evident by now, this, or something like it, would be my own preferred solution to this riddle about the conscience. Another way to go is not a Christian solution, as mine is, but an anti-Christian dissolution: a response that dissolves not only the riddle, but indeed the whole concept of conscience that generates it in the first place. And this is Nietzsche's response.

In the debate about conscience, Nietzsche is Luther's punk grandson. (He was a Lutheran himself, after all, and the son of a Lutheran manse.) For Luther,[11] the whole Catholic system of compunction (literally, of being pricked by conscience), of remorse (literally, of conscience biting back), and of penance or penitence (literally, of putting oneself to pains or repeated pains) was a system of *terrorism*. A structure of power, institutional Catholicism, was tyrannising the individual by terrorising his conscience. This, Luther judges, is an abuse both in itself, since the fears drummed into the individual believer are groundless, and also because of its political context, since the church's motive in this terrorisation of the conscience is the obviously ulterior one of maintaining its own power over individuals. Whatever their other differences, on these points Luther and Nietzsche simply agree. And Nietzsche will see the contortions of a St. Paul or Augustine, as briefly described above, simply as exhibits in the parade of evidence that supports this damning conclusion.

Despite Luther's individualism, one place where Luther and Nietzsche will of course *not* agree is over Nietzsche's rather Hobbesian view of the origin of conscience. (This is a view to which I might seem quite close myself, given my own evolutionary solution of the riddle of akrasia.) Nietzsche's hypothesis is that the origins of conscience lie in the origins of civil society, when humans, as they learn to live together, have to learn also to repress and sublimate the animal violence endemic to a Hobbesian state of nature (*Genealogy of Morality* Essay 2, paragraph 16):

> I look on bad conscience as a serious illness to which man was forced to succumb by the pressure of the most fundamental of all changes which he experienced—that change whereby he finally found himself imprisoned within the confines of society and peace. It must have been no different for these semi-animals, happily adapted to the wilderness, war, the wandering life, and adventure from how it was for the sea animals when they were forced to either become land animals or perish—at one go, all instincts were devalued and "suspended." Now they had to walk on their feet and "carry themselves," whereas they had been carried by the water up till then: a terrible heaviness bore down on them ... the poor things were reduced to relying on thinking, inference, calculation, and the connecting of cause with effect, that is, to relying on their "consciousness," that most impoverished and error-prone organ! I do not think there has ever been such a feeling of misery on earth, such a leaden discomfort—and meanwhile, the old instincts had not suddenly ceased to make their demands! But it was difficult and seldom possible to give in to them: they mainly had to seek new and as it were underground gratifications. All instincts which are not discharged outwardly *turn inwards*—this is what I call the *internalisation* of man: with it there now evolves in man what will later be called his "soul." The whole inner world, originally stretched thinly as though between two layers of skin, was expanded and extended itself and gained depth, breadth and height in proportion to the degree that the external discharge of man's instincts was *obstructed*. Those terrible bulwarks with which state organisations protected themselves against the old instincts of freedom—punishments are a primary instance of this kind of bulwark—had the result that all those instincts of the wild, free, roving man were turned backwards, *against man himself*. Animosity, cruelty, the pleasure of pursuing, raiding, changing and destroying– all this was pitted against the person who had such instincts: *that* is the origin of "bad conscience." Lacking external enemies and obstacles, and forced into the oppressive narrowness and conformity of custom, man impatiently ripped himself apart, persecuted himself, gnawed at himself, gave himself no peace and abused himself. . . .

This sublimation and repression, Nietzsche continues, takes its most acute form in religious versions of conscience, the most extreme and demanding of which is the Christian version (o.c. para.22):

> that will to torment oneself, that suppressed cruelty of animal man who has been frightened back into himself and given an inner life, incarcerated in the "state" to be tamed, and has discovered bad conscience so that he can hurt himself, after the *more natural* outlet of this wish to hurt had been blocked,—this man of bad conscience has seized on religious presupposition in order to provide his self-torture with its most horrific hardness and sharpness.

So, for Nietzsche, beings like St. Paul and St. Augustine do not propound any philosophically interesting riddle about akrasia. They are merely screw-ups, symptoms of a malaise—a rich, fruitful, and interesting malaise, but a malaise nonetheless: the malaise of civil society that is called *conscience,* in which the agent compensates for the unavailability of literal violence against others by indulging in sublimated violence against herself. And no doubt, in his talk of sublimated violence as the origin of conscience, Nietzsche has more than half an eye on Kant's image of the courtroom. There can hardly be anywhere in society that is more obviously a locus of sublimated violence than a court of law.

As so often with Nietzsche, there is a pressing question here about the practical consequences of his diagnosis. Suppose that someone accepts this state-of-nature story of Nietzsche's as the truth about the origin of the conscience. Then what is she to do with the often-alarming new insights that Nietzsche's story offers? It plainly is not a serious alternative for us now to return to the instinctive pre-social world, with its merry, carefree, unself-conscious externalisations of violence, even if that were desirable. Nor is Nietzsche to be read as saying either that it is a serious alternative, or that it would be desirable. (Though it has to be said that Nietzsche's romantic encomiums of the innocent violence of primal man read rather differently after Hitler.)

Nietzsche's own answer to the question how his sort of moral sceptic is to live his scepticism is, I take it, a call to some prototype of Rortyesque irony. He thinks that insofar as we can "healthily" do so (whatever that means), we should carry on living in our noninstinctive and fully social world, playing along with the roles, routines, and reactions that, on the basis of an ancient pious fraud, it demands of us; but without *being taken in* by them.

The best testimony to the plausibility of this answer is, presumably, the plain fact that something strikingly like this is exactly how so many of us now live. But that might not be enough to make the answer *fully* plausible.

For one thing, Nietzsche's account, like Hobbes's and indeed Rousseau's, presupposes the historical and causal priority of the *individual* human to the *group* of humans. But plenty of what we know about palaeoanthropology, and the comparative sociology of other hominid and great-ape species, tends to reverse this order of priority: much of the evidence now says that the *group* came first, not the individual. (For references on this, see Ian McGilchrist, *The Master and the Emissary*.)

For another, Nietzsche's extreme and pessimistic account is susceptible of a rewriting that seems at least as well-grounded as his in historical fact, and yet is neither extreme nor pessimistic in the way that his account is. This account simply agrees with Nietzsche that the altering demands of an increasingly complex social world must have imposed new pressures on individual humans to repress, and therefore sublimate, instinctive urges that are now increasingly understood, in her changing society, as destructive and antisocial. Where it differs from Nietzsche is simply in replacing his pessimism with optimism.

For what this story says is that when we learned that we can't live together successfully as social beings if, for example, we are constantly giving in to our instinctive liking for swiping off each other's heads; and when as a result of learning this, we learned to redirect the psychic energies that went into such casual violence, perhaps into standing up for our own group of humans by attacking other groups of humans, perhaps into primitive sports a bit like those of *Iliad* 23, perhaps even into activities of accusing and judging and censuring; when we learned these things, *that was progress*. And if we developed consciences along the way—if, that is, we learned as individuals to see for ourselves, merely by inner reflection, when for example we were hurting someone else, and to register this hurting as a bad thing that we ought to stop, without the need for any external monitor to point this out to us—if this happened, then this was progress too. What we are learning through such processes is to see, for ourselves, the interpersonal significance of the things we do. And there need be nothing fraudulent about this process whatsoever. For all that *this* developmental story says, the process can equally well be called the evolution of a capacity for moral perception.

Another way of putting this point is to note that, throughout Nietzsche's critique of conscience in the Second Essay of the *Genealogy*, he leaves out what might easily be said to be the most important thing of all about conscience: its *content*. When I feel a guilty conscience, then—at least in cases that are not thoroughly pathological—I feel guilt *about something I have done*. Nietzsche would of course agree that bad conscience does not present itself phenomenologically as an experience of self-laceration: it is part of his own account that, for the trick that bad conscience works on us to be successful, it has to be hidden. But he does not have enough to say about how bad conscience *does* present itself phenomenologically. As we experience it, bad conscience is about my own failures to respond adequately to the situations that I am presented by: I feel guilty *because* I did not respond to the beggar at my door, *because* I stole your watch, *because* I wounded your feelings by my childish tantrum, and so on. Or as we could also say: bad conscience is about my own failures to respond adequately to the *values* that I am confronted by.

Here I want to propose that—at least sometimes—the experience that Nietzsche calls *das böse Gewissen*, "bad conscience," is in essence just self-critical awareness that I have responded inadequately to some value or values that I am confronted by.[12] Bad conscience, therefore, is part of a continuum of moral awareness; because there is also the possibility that I respond *adequately* to those values. If bad conscience is distress caused in me by the knowledge that I have hurt or offended a value that deserves my recognition, then it is a form of moral awareness of a piece with the awareness that, at other times, makes us respond positively or appropriately or accurately to values. (Such awareness is, like almost everything else that is ethically interesting, culturally modulated and mediated; writing the history of these modulations and mediations would be a huge and fascinating task, but I can't even start on that task here.)

There are two components here, the inward-looking and the outward-looking. There is my response to the values that confront me, and there is my assessment of the quality of that response. Conscience is not *only* about those values; it is also about me, about how I respond to them. In typical cases of "bad conscience," I respond inadequately to them, and am pained by the awareness of my own inadequate response. But good conscience is also possible. That possibility is fraught with the danger of smugness, and perhaps we are, as a rule, never more self-forgetful than when we are focused on the goods around us. Still it does seem possible for someone to respond well to values, and know that she does so, and be pleased in the knowledge, *without* falling into smugness. The key point is that there is a virtuous mean here between the inward and outward directings of attention, between loving contemplation of the world around us, and honest recognition of our own failures to value it as it deserves. And it is important to insist on this mean, against those who like Nietzsche misunderstand conscience only as self-laceration, just as much as against those writers and writings that encourage this misunderstanding: such as Augustine's famous rant about the pears, or King David's "Against thee, thee only I have sinned" (Psalm 51:4, about an episode in which, pretty patently, he had actually sinned against Uriah the Hittite and Bathsheba as well as against God).

This honest recognition of our own failures to value the world around us as it deserves is the virtue of humility. Refusing to recognise, or care enough, about these failures is the vice of callousness or carelessness; caring about them too much, in an obsessive and self-focused way, is the vice of self-laceration. So understood, humility is a virtue that lies in a mean.

Though we might also think of humility more epistemically, and so as a virtue for which the mean is not so much a midpoint on a one-dimensional line, as a bull's-eye in a circular or otherwise two-dimensional domain ("getting it right"): so understood, humility for me is the true view of my place in the world, which is not that of the centre of the world. Both direct awareness of the values around me, and self-involving awareness of myself as a responder, adequate or inadequate, to those values, of the kind that conscience can bring home to me, will help me to "get it right" in this sense. There might be indefinitely many other ways of illuminating the virtue of humility: there is no need for us to insist on any single understanding of it as uniquely correct, provided we at least are free of the usual banal misunderstandings of this important virtue, many of which derive more or less directly from Hume's breathtakingly inept and crude misunderstanding of pride as good opinion of oneself, and humility as bad.[13]

As a postscript, there is this speculative question to be asked about Nietzsche's polemic against conscience in the Second Essay of the *Genealogy*. For Nietzsche could have majored on another theme. Rather than treating conscience as ingrown debt-collection, he could have focused on the way in which conscience simultaneously disempowers me, and also rewards me for this disempowerment. Typically the payback for being weakened or broken by conscientious recognition of my own bad deeds is that by admitting them I simultaneously get to claim that it is *God himself*, or moral objectivity itself, that is so convicting me; by admitting (along lines already suggested) that I'm not the centre of the universe myself, I nonetheless get to be in touch with the centre of the universe, by my own self-displacement. That certainly looks like an interesting kind of psychic bargain. And there are plenty of characters in the Christian moral tradition—and beyond it—who seem prepared to strike this bargain. (Perhaps Emperor Henry IV made such a bargain in his walk to Canossa. The historical facts are both contested and, given their psychological nature, close to impossible to access.) But the bargain seems so plainly open to Nietzschean analysis, as a clear case of a deformation of the will to power. Nietzsche could have focused on this theme as a way of understanding conscience, and perhaps would have had a more plausible account to offer if he had, than the account he actually does offer. So why didn't he?

It may of course be part of the answer that sometimes he *does* at least hint at this analysis.[14] See for instance Essay III of the *Genealogy*, section 22:

> Humility and self-importance cheek-by-jowl; a garrulousness of feeling that almost stupefies; impassioned vehemence, not passion; embarrassing gesticulation; it is plain that there is no trace of good breeding. How can one make such a fuss about one's little lapses as these pious little men do! Who gives a damn? Certainly not God. Finally, they even want "the crown of eternal life," these

little provincial people; but for what? to what purpose? Presumption can go no further. An "immortal" Peter: who could stand him? Their ambition is laughable: people of that sort regurgitating their most private affairs, their stupidities, sorrows, and petty worries, as if the Heart of Being were obliged to concern itself with them; they never grow tired of involving God himself in even the pettiest troubles they have got themselves into. And the appalling taste of this perpetual familiarity with God! This Jewish and not merely Jewish obtrusiveness of pawing and nuzzling God!

Another possible locus is when he says, in "The Four Great Errors," that "the banker immediately thinks of business, the Christian of sin, and the girl of her love"; though in that context Nietzsche is fairly plainly making a point about the kinds of *causation* that appeal to these groups.

Be that as it may, what is the Christian likely to say about Nietzsche's charge that the activity of conscience is to make us strong by making us weak (2 Corinthians 12:10)? I think the Christian is likely to say simply that, in her experience, this is just what happens. In the Christian view, God really does come closest to those who are weakest and most downtrodden, by their own conscientious awareness of their own fallibility as much as anything else; in the Christian worldview, the weak and the conscience-ridden have a kind of power that is denied to the mighty and unscrupulous. Certainly it is one explanation of that datum to say, with Nietzsche, that in this respect the Christian worldview is a deformation of the will to power. But another explanation of the datum is also possible: namely that, in this respect at any rate, the Christian worldview is simply correct.

NOTES

1. For helpful discussion, I am grateful to Brad Cokelet, Cristian Constantinescu, John Hacker-Wright, Ann Jeffrey, Michael Morris, Bob Stern, and Jon Webber.

2. On glory, see *Knowing What to Do*, chapter 7; on action for the sake of the beautiful, *KWTD*, chapter 8; on objectual and experiential knowledge KWTD Ch.11; on attention and contemplation, *KWTD* chapter 12; on value-encounter, see "Encounters with values" on academia.edu\sophiegrace; on epiphany, see "Grace in the world," forthcoming; on imaginative identification with others, see "How to be someone else" on academia.edu\sophiegrace.

3. Something actually wrong, or something that you believe to be wrong: that distinction is obvious, but this paper is not centrally about it.

4. This point is a pretty clear corollary of what that deepest (so not most orthodox) of utilitarian thinkers, John Stuart Mill, says about conscience in *Utilitarianism*, chapter 3: "The internal sanction of duty, whatever our standard of duty may be, is one and the same—a feeling in our own mind; a pain, more or less intense, attendant

on violation of duty, which in properly cultivated moral natures rises, in the more serious cases, into shrinking from it as an impossibility. This feeling, when disinterested, and connecting itself with the pure idea of duty, and not with some particular form of it, or with any of the merely accessory circumstances, is the essence of Conscience; though in that complex phenomenon as it actually exists, the simple fact is in general all encrusted over with collateral associations, derived from sympathy, from love, and still more from fear; from all the forms of religious feeling; from the recollections of childhood and of all our past life; from self-esteem, desire of the esteem of others, and occasionally even self-abasement. This extreme complication is, I apprehend, the origin of the sort of mystical character which, by a tendency of the human mind of which there are many other examples, is apt to be attributed to the idea of moral obligation, and which leads people to believe that the idea cannot possibly attach itself to any other objects than those which, by a supposed mysterious law, are found in our present experience to excite it. Its binding force, however, consists in the existence of a mass of feeling which must be broken through in order to do what violates our standard of right, and which, if we do nevertheless violate that standard, will probably have to be encountered afterwards in the form of remorse. Whatever theory we have of the nature or origin of conscience, this is what essentially constitutes it. The ultimate sanction, therefore, of all morality (external motives apart) being a subjective feeling in our own minds. . . ."

5. Though as John Hacker-Wright reminds me, Aquinas does read the notion of conscience into Aristotle: see e.g., Aq. *De Veritate* 17.

6. Both quotations sourced from Allen Wood, "Kant on conscience," on his Stanford web.stanford.edu/~allenw/webpapers/KantOnConscience.pdf.

7. Thanks for discussion of this point to Cristian Constantinescu.

8. My PhD thesis and my first book were centrally about this riddle: Timothy Chappell, *Aristotle and Augustine on Freedom,* Routledge, 1995.

9. Two superb expositions of the kind of view of our own messy history and resulting contingency and fallibility that I have in mind here are Valerie Tiberius, *The Reflective Life: Living Wisely within Our Limits,* and Peter Goldie, *The Mess Inside.*

10. If some readers see echoes here of the popular-psychology book *The Chimp Paradox* (by Steve Peters: London, Vermilion, 2012), that's fine by me. I am not snobbish about popular books. Though I am not *following* that book here, there are some parallels.

11. On Luther on the terrorised conscience, see the learned and wide-ranging discussion in Sir Richard Sorabji, *Moral Conscience through the Ages* (OUP 2014), chapter 6. Later in his book (188–90), Sorabji also discusses Nietzsche, though he does not make the comparison with Luther that I am offering here.

12. On the idea of being confronted by values, cp. my "Encounters with Values," in Kuhle & van Ackeren, *Moral Demandingness.*

13. Hume, *Treatise* Book 2. Many of the principal flaws are nicely (albeit perhaps inadvertently) brought out by Davidson's famous attempt to salvage something from Hume's train wreck: Donald Davidson, "Hume's cognitive theory of pride," *Journal of Philosophy,* Vol. 73, No. 19, Seventy-Third Annual Meeting Eastern Division, American Philosophical Association (Nov. 4, 1976), 744–57.

14. Thanks for this reference to Edward Skidelsky.

Chapter 13

A Thomistic View of Conscience and Guilt

Anne Jeffrey

INTRODUCTION

According to the Conscience Principle, it is never morally permissible to act contrary to conscience. The plausibility of this being a genuine moral principle depends on what conscience is, whether it can be mistaken, and what its role is in general moral psychology. For instance, if conscience is the internalized law of right reason, as Cicero claims, then it would be unsurprising that acting contrary to conscience would always be wrong, and that the guilt inflicted by conscience would be appropriate.[1] If conscience is ingrained by societal pressures, however, producing a medley of moral beliefs—some true, some false—then we might do well to be skeptical of the Conscience Principle and eschew the guilty pangs of conscience.[2]

Thomas Aquinas endorses and defends a unique version of the Conscience Principle. What's especially interesting about his unorthodox (for his time) view on conscience is that it seems to split the difference between the views we might expect to support the Conscience Principle: On the one hand, thoroughgoing subjectivism on which all moral facts and obligations are a function of agents' mental states, and on the other hand, objectivist intuitionism on which there is an external moral law but a faculty of conscience gives us inerrant access to it. Aquinas claims that there are objective moral truths, that conscience *fallibly* represents those truths, and yet, conscience *always* generates moral obligations, whether it is correct or incorrect.

Aquinas's view will strike many initially as puzzling, perhaps even incoherent. To make sense of it, we must understand that for Aquinas the Conscience Principle is not just one moral principle among many; instead, it falls out of a novel and philosophically powerful metaethical view of moral obligations (or what we might call requiring moral reasons). That metaethical view has significant implications for the moral psychology of guilt. This essay aims to explain Aquinas's views on conscience, guilt, and moral obligations or requirements and to show how they might be compelling in their own right, not simply interesting artefacts in the history of philosophy.

By the end of the essay, we'll see that Aquinas's account of conscience and guilt is at home in moral theories that place importance on cultivating a good will or moral virtue. For cultivating a good will or virtue requires a disposition to respond appropriately to reasons and values *as they appear to us*. On Aquinas's view, conscience is the vehicle for such appearances. The feelings of guilt that follow violations of conscience register a failure to respond appropriately to apparent values and normative requirements, even when those appearances aren't veridical. Guilt can thus help us identify defects in our will or character and has a critical role to play in the process of moral improvement.

WHAT IS CONSCIENCE?

It is common to think of conscience as a psychological faculty or power— a capacity for discerning what ought to be done, admonishing against a wrong course of action, and condemning or vindicating oneself for past actions.[3] Indeed, most medieval Christian theologians and philosophers until the middle of the thirteenth century share this view. For them, conscience is either a faculty or a habit of practical reason that issues judgments about what ought to be, or ought to have been, done.[4] These judgments are based on God's law (which for them is equivalent to the moral law). So we can think of conscience on the standard medieval view as a psychological faculty or habit that generates moral judgments. Aquinas's view is revisionist (as compared to his predecessors) in multiple respects, and the difference in the psychology has important ramifications for his moral theory. In this section, I'll aim to make Aquinas's view clear by contrasting it with earlier accounts and examining two of the normative implications of the distinctive moral psychological picture.

The etymology of the term *conscience* sheds light on standard the psychological characterization of conscience in late Stoic and early medieval Christian thought. The Greek root, συνείδησις, means something known (είδησις from οἶδα) in common with (συν). Early contexts of use indicate that this kind of knowledge is about another person, and it can be used in witness for or against him. Hence σύνοιδα comes to mean "I bear witness."[5] Philosophers interested in self-awareness begin using the term with a special ethical connotation, so that σύνοιδα refers to the internal faculty by which one accuses or absolves oneself from moral wrongdoing. Roman Stoics like Cicero then transliterate this into Latin as *conscientia*—*con-* meaning with and *scientia* meaning knowledge.⁶ Their general idea is that conscience acts as a witness regarding the moral goodness of one's own actions, judging whether those actions live up to the natural law of right reason and punishing the individual internally with guilt when her actions transgress that law.

Medieval theologians in the Christian tradition come to use another Latin term, *synderesis,* to signify conscience due to a reference in Peter Lombard's agenda-setting *Sentences*. In the *Sentences* II.39, Lombard is inquiring how it is possible for the will to be bad, given freedom of the will. Rather than decisively answer the question himself, Lombard surveys possible responses, one of which is the "two-wills" view: Perhaps humans have two wills, one that unerringly wants to do what is good and the other disposed to do what is bad. Lombard then cites Jerome as holding this view, citing a commentary on Ezekiel in which Jerome says that the *scintilla conscientiae*—the spark of conscience—cannot be extinguished in a person with a bad will. Jerome's text goes on to identify this spark of conscience with what the Greeks called synderesis; however, as there is no such word in the Greek lexicon at the time of this commentary, scholars now conclude that this was a corruption of the Greek συνείδησις. Nevertheless, Peter Lombard and, subsequently, commentators on his work, began distinguishing between *synderesis* and *conscientia.*

Thirteenth-century theologians such as William of Auxerre and Richard Fishacre argue that synderesis is unable to err. Fishacre calls synderesis the "aspect of the mind or soul that sees the rule of God," and is thus "always true . . . never erring and never sinning."⁷ He affirms that synderesis is the name for the part of reason that "sees the truth in its proper light," as Lottin explains; thus synderesis on this view is cognitive.⁸

Philip the Chancellor agrees that synderesis is unerring, but he challenges the view that it is a cognitive faculty. He argues that synderesis is an affective dispositional power in the soul, a kind of proto-desire for the universal good. Since it only takes one object—the general or highest good (these seem conflated throughout the text)—it can't be a faculty.⁹ Since it is affective rather than cognitive, whether or not it is part of reason depends on our conception of reason. If we take an expansive notion of reason, he explains, such that reason includes motives and affective elements of the psyche, then it is appropriate to include synderesis as part of reason; but if we take a narrower view of reason, such that it excludes affect and motivation, synderesis must be separate and above reason. In order to be motivated to pursue particular goods and to freely choose particular actions, we have to use synderesis in conjunction with lower reason perception, because these faculties supply the subject matter of the action or the particular features of the good being pursued. So, Philip says, when synderesis operates in concert with these other fallible faculties, sin (moral mistakes) can result.¹⁰

Albert the Great takes up Philip's suggestion that the object of synderesis is the universal good, but he rejects the idea that it is not a faculty or habit. In Albert's view, synderesis is a faculty coupled with a habit; it issues decrees about the universal good, which serve as the major premises in practical reasoning.[11] Just as theoretical (or speculative) reasoning requires a handle on certain starting points (like the principle of non-contradiction) in order to make judgments regarding what is true and false, so practical reasoning requires starting points (like that good is to be done, evil avoided) to make particular judgments about what is to be done or avoided—the first principles of practical reason. Albert then proposes that the distinction between conscience and synderesis consists in this: that conscience is an act of moral judgment about particulars, and synderesis makes the judgments about universals on which conscience relies.

Getting clear on the operative model of practical reasoning will help us understand both Albert's and Aquinas's views on conscience. Albert thinks of conscience as an act occurring at the end of practical reasoning about what to do in a particular circumstance. For instance, suppose you see someone on the side of the road with a sign that reads, "Out of work—please help." You might have a desire to do what's good, or a habit of believing that what's good is to be done. But for Albert, neither of those general dispositions alone can tell you what you ought to do here and now. The habit of believing the universal claim that good is to be done furnishes a major premise in practical reasoning:

(1) I ought to do good.
    But you need to add knowledge of the circumstances and particular moral directives, like
(2) It is good to help those in need with the resources you have.
(3) This person is in need, and I have business connections and a protein bar.
    Conscience is the act of applying moral knowledge expressed in (1) and (2) to the circumstances (3) to draw a conclusion:
(4) I ought to pull over, talk to this person, and give her a business card and protein bar.

Together, (1)–(4) constitute what the medieval call a practical syllogism. While many of Albert's predecessors think of conscience as supplying premise (1), Albert maintains that the act of conscience is expressed in premise (4).

Bonaventure, a contemporary of Aquinas but in the Franciscan order (rather than Dominican), also thinks of conscience as a premise of practical reasoning. But being concerned to show that the person who knows she ought to do something is also moved to do it, he maintains that conscience and synderesis are dispositions that supply both knowledge of what is to be done or what is good and desire for it.[12] The distinction, then, lies in the fact that synderesis inclines the will to the good in general and conscience inclines us to choose particular good actions.

So then only Albert and his most famous pupil, Thomas Aquinas, identify conscience with a cognitive act of moral judgment. We see his endorsement of Albert's view in his early work *Super Sententiae*, a commentary on Peter Lombard's *Sentences*:

> Reason, when choosing or rejecting, uses syllogism. . . . In working from universal principles, it makes a judgment about particulars. . . . The consideration of the conclusion drawn is the consideration of conscience.[13]

Aquinas's view of conscience is cognitivist: Conscience is the application of knowledge, and it can be true or false. Conscience aims to represent truths about the morality of particular human actions—that is, whether they contribute to a good human life or not. If giving to the needy is a good human action, and it is the case that the person with a roadside sign asking for assistance is in need, then my judgment that I ought to give to the person is true—I have a correct conscience. Conscience doesn't necessarily supply motivation to act as one believes one ought to. Aquinas claims that akratic action (incontinence) is certainly possible when one conscience is functioning well, but a person lacks virtues—dispositions that include affect and emotion that lead one to take the dictates of conscience to heart, so to speak.[14]

Later, in *De Veritate* (*Disputed Questions on Truth*), Aquinas explains that conscience can fall into error. While human reason at its best apprehends truths without dialectical inquiry—intuitively or by nature—this is the task of synderesis, not conscience. Natural or intuitive apprehension of certain fundamental truths is necessary in both theoretical and practical matters for us to reason, Aquinas thinks. We have to have a grasp of starting points, what Aquinas often calls principles, like the fundamental axioms of geometry, before we can reason about particulars. For Aquinas, synderesis is the grasp of starting points for practical reason: It is "a natural habit like a habit of principles, or names a certain power of reason with such habit."[15]

Aquinas offers two original arguments for the claim that synderesis is unerring. One starts with the foundationalist idea that we could have no certitude or stability in our judgments (theoretical or practical) unless they could be derived from some permanent, certain starting points. The infallibility of synderesis is a condition on the possibility of successful practical reasoning. Since we know practical reasoning can be successful, we can infer that the first principles of practical reason are firmly and permanently had in the mind.[16]

The second argument derives this conclusion from the Aristotelian maxim that nature always tends toward the good and conservation of order. Since synderesis is a natural habit, then, it must both have the good as its object and conserve the rational order.[17] Importantly, Aquinas does not hold the expansive view of reason considered by Philip on which desire and motive fall under the heading of reason. As synderesis is a habit of reason, it is not affective but rather cognitive.

Conscience, unlike synderesis, can be mistaken. Aquinas agrees with Bonaventure on this point. He says that conscience relies on the input of reason or perception, given its role in practical reasoning. And since reason and perception can err, thus supplying false premises in a practical syllogism, conscience is also liable to err.[18] But conscience can also fail to apply the form of reasoning that is fitting for a practical argument, and so reach the wrong conclusion or fail to reach the conclusion warranted by the syllogism. This can happen when a person's desires distract her attention from one of the premises in practical reasoning, for example when the wine lover is so drawn to its sweetness that she ignores her belief that drinking another glass would make her too intoxicated to drive home. The only instances of practical reasoning in which conscience is shielded from error are those in which reason supplies the minor premise and the premise is self-evident. For example, when he says, "this evil should be done," it is not a possible false conclusion of conscience when "this is evil" is self-evident, since through synderesis, a person cannot help but know that "evil should not be done." Since the vast majority of actions aren't self-evidently evil, though, the room for error in conscience is quite substantial.

Aquinas does not develop at length a psychological account of guilt (and things are complicated by the fact that the Latin for "guilt" can also mean "fault," and thus not indicate a psychological phenomenon). He does, however, discuss the *remorsus conscientiae*, or feelings of regret and sadness that follow a failure to act according to conscience, especially in connection to the practice of penance and forgiveness. Sometimes he uses "conscience" metonymically to refer to feelings of guilt, as when he describes conscience as keeping a person from feeling confident enough to approach God, or commenting on biblical passages like, "the blood of Christ cleanses our conscience" (since the sacrifice of Christ is meant to wipe away guilt, not do away with our moral judgments and reasoning).[19]

For Aquinas, guilt of conscience can be an appropriate form of punishment that a person's reason inflicts on her for wrongdoing.[20] Appropriate guilt of conscience performs two functions. First, it implements a kind of justice, distributing a proportionate punishment to compensate for the wrong done. Aquinas suggests that guilt of conscience is unwelcome for the person experiencing it, and since it is something she doesn't wish for herself, it is a kind of injury she suffers. Thus, it can contribute to or constitute compensation for her wrongdoing when it is proportionate to the wrong.

The second purpose of conscientious guilt, he says, is medicinal. Sometimes a person willingly bears the punishment for her wrongdoing; when someone patiently suffers the sorrow of guilt for past wrongs, she is said to bear a punishment in one sense (since she would not wish to have guilty feelings normally), but a medicine, rather than a punishment, in another sense. The person who willingly accepts a punishment like the remorse of conscience is like a person who takes a bitter medicine that is bad at the moment in order to obtain something better in the future, namely health. The person who patiently bears the remorse of conscience (and any other due punishments) experiences the punishment like a medicine because she bears something that is bad for her now in order to obtain a greater good—the health of her soul. This medicinal function of guilt is meant to help the wrongdoer to improve herself in ways she was defective and help her "progress in virtue."[21]

Summing up what we've learned thus far: Aquinas departs from traditional views in his basic psychology of conscience. Unlike most other medieval thinkers, he claims that conscience is an all-things-considered moral judgment about a particular action. It is strictly cognitive, with no affective component guaranteeing motivation to act as one believes one should. Further, he distinguishes conscience from synderesis, a natural habit infallibly grasping first principles of practical reason. Conscience draws conclusions from the major premises supplied by synderesis and fallible reason or perception, and so can be mistaken due to a mistake in the minor premise or by a failure to attend to the proper form of argument. Finally, the guilt of conscience is a kind of remorse or sadness, and can serve as a punishment and a medicine, something that aids the person in the cultivation of virtue.

THE CONSCIENCE PRINCIPLE

In the time Aquinas is writing, there are three canonical questions about conscience. The first two—what is conscience? and can conscience err?—are questions about the psychology of conscience. The third canonical question—does conscience obligate (*obliget*)?—is about the moral significance of conscience. Given the ways Aquinas departs from others in the medieval Christian tradition in his answers to the psychological questions on conscience, we might rephrase the third question: What kind of normative pressure do fallible moral judgments put on action? So understood, for Aquinas, this third question is a question about whether akrasia—acting contrary to one's moral judgments—is always bad.

In this section, I'll introduce Aquinas's answer to that question by means of contrast with standard contemporary responses. We'll see that his answer can be articulated in the form of a principle—the Conscience Principle—that is unlike the principles usually used to explain the badness of akratic action. Because he holds this nuanced varietal of the Conscience Principle, his position is unusual and unprecedented, but also subject to a number of worries that don't arise for other positions. I'll consider those worries in the subsequent section before moving on to his defense of his unorthodox view.

Do fallible normative judgments put normative pressure on actions? There is a strong pre-theoretic intuition that they put *some* normative pressure on us to do what we think we ought to do, and so acting contrary to such beliefs or judgments—acting akratically—is in some way normatively defective. Consider the following mundane case. Christy is the employer of two individuals, Ben and Leslie. Christy knows someone has violated a company policy and believes that the perpetrator is Ben. She concludes that she ought to fire Ben. Even if it turns out that Leslie is the perpetrator, not Ben, something is amiss if Christy avoids firing Ben when she thinks she ought to fire him. It seems that what's wrong with Christy's avoiding firing Ben is that it's an instance of a bad kind of action—akrasia.

An easy way to explain what's wrong with akrasia is to say that there is some first-order normative or moral principle that prohibits it. Such a principle could be a principle of rationality or a principle of morality.[22] Contemporary philosophers have proposed several such principles, and a brief look at these will help us get a handle on some initial options. First, there is the enkratic requirement of rationality:

> Enkrasia (E): "Necessarily, if N is within the domain of rationality, rationality requires of N that if (1) N believes at t that she herself ought that p and if (2) N believes at t that, if she herself were then to intend that p, because of that, p would be so and if (3) N believes at t that, if she herself were not then to intend that p, because of that, p would not be so then (4) N intends at t that p."[23]

So, in Christy's case, E says that so long as Christy believes she ought to fire Ben and that if she were to intend to fire Ben today, Ben would be fired today because of her intention, rationality requires Christy to intend to fire Ben today. When Christy fails to intend to fire Ben, she violates this rational principle. Moral rationalists who identify moral requirements with rational requirements can say that Christy's failure is a moral failure.

The requirement expressed in E has a wide scope; if we were to put it in deontic logical terms, the requirement R would govern a set of attitudes rather than each attitude independently:

Wide Scope: R [Believe(ought-φ)—> Intend(φ)]

Contrast this with a requirement with narrow scope:

Narrow Scope: Believe(ought-φ)—> R [Intend(φ)]

Others think of the problem with akrasia not as a violation of a strict rational requirement but rather as a failure to exhibit a slack normative relation between two mental states:

> Rational Commitment (RC): There is always something rational about forming the intention to x on the basis of your belief that you ought to x because doing so constitutes the satisfaction of a rational commitment.[24]

Here, one mental state stands in an objective normative relation to the other, such that the having of it contributes to the rationality of having the other mental state (without rationally requiring it). We could say of Christy that her mental life exhibits a certain defect in that she has a belief that she ought to fire Ben that would rationally support an intention to fire Ben, but she fails to have that normatively supported intention.

In contemporary discussion, some philosophers complain that wide-scope principles like Enkrasia or Rational Commitment have objectionable results. For these principles imply that it is equally rational to intend to φ as to give up the belief that one ought to φ.[25] Imagine, for instance, that I believe that I ought not eat meat. I feel guilty every time I succumb to my appetite for barbecue and deep-fried chicken. One day I decide I've had enough of all the guilt that weighs on me when I enjoy a delicious bite of chicken or spare ribs. So I resolve to give up my belief that eating meat is wrong. According to the wide-scope principle of rationality Enkrasia, rationality doesn't necessarily require me to intend to not eat meat; it is perfectly rational for me to simply abandon my moral belief and go ahead and eat meat. Rational and moral requirements thus look too easily escapable.[26]

Those who reject the formal rational principle approach for this or similar reasons will often instead appeal to substantive moral or rational principles that an agent violates when she acts akratically in a particular case. For instance, Christy, by her failing to intentionally fire Ben, may violate a substantive principle of epistemic rationality like the requirement to respond appropriately to the evidence one has. On these views, not every instance of akratic action exhibits moral or rational defect. For one could end up better approximating what substantive morality or reason requires by acting akratically, if one starts off with an incorrect moral judgment.[27] Philosophers cite the example of Huck Finn as someone who acts better, morally, by doing what his conscience tells him he ought not do; he conforms to the substantive moral principle to not perpetuate slavery by helping to free Ms. Watson's slave, Jim.

Where does Aquinas's view fall on the spectrum? Aquinas maintains that acting contrary to one's conscience, or moral judgments, is always morally bad. But he doesn't endorse a wide-scope formal principle of rationality like Enkrasia or Rational Commitment. Nor does he try to show that every akratic action violates a substantive moral principle. Instead, in response to the question "whether an erring conscience obligates," he proposes a nuanced moral principle—the Conscience Principle.

To formulate the Thomistic principle accurately, we need first to appreciate certain aspects of Aquinas's account of moral action and moral judgment that are operating in the background. We already know that the moral judgment of conscience is a mental act of concluding what one ought to do (all things considered) in a particular circumstance in light of universal moral principles and features of the circumstance. We also know that Aquinas is a cognitivist about moral judgments—they are truth-functionally assessable. So in answering the question whether conscience obligates, he needs to tell us whether both correct and incorrect conscience obligate.

What about moral action? Aquinas claims that the only actions subject to moral evaluation are what he calls human acts (*acta humana*). Human acts are intentional actions agents perform for reasons and with knowledge of what they are doing. Human acts always concern particulars. Aquinas contrasts the human act with an act of a humans (*actus humanis*). Acts of humans are like acts of other animals—the only thing human about them is that the animal performing the act is a human. But the act isn't performed in a characteristically human way; that is, its performance doesn't involve some intention or special exercise of practical reason of which only humans are capable.

We can get a handle on the distinction between human acts and acts of humans with some examples. Imagine you're throwing a dinner party for friends, and as you're cooking, your hand grazes the hot handle of a pan on the stove. You quickly withdraw your hand. This act is the act of a human; it is the operation of an instinctual reflex. Your withdrawing your hand isn't the product of a habit you've instilled through careful practice for the sake of keeping yourself from being burned. Had your cat brushed her tail up against the pan, it would have done the same thing. Contrast this with the act of slowly stirring vegetables in the pan, making sure they cook evenly, with just the right balance of crisp and tenderness. This you do intentionally, for the reason that you want to throw a memorable dinner party with a delicious meal. Your cooking the vegetables constitutes a human act on Aquinas's schema, while withdrawing your hand is simply an act of a human.

Imagine, further, that you have a cup of vegetable broth and a cup of chicken stock on the counter, one for the dish you'll serve to vegetarians and the other for the dish you'll serve to omnivores. As you stir the vegetarian dish, you reach for what you think is the vegetarian broth, but in fact, you end up mixing in the chicken stock. You go on to serve the vegetarians the dish with chicken stock unwittingly. On Aquinas's view, we might correctly describe you as performing a human act like serving a meal to your vegetarian friend, since you do this wittingly. But serving a meat dish to a vegetarian is not a correct description of a human act you perform since you lack knowledge that the dish you serve isn't vegetarian. Consequently, that is *not* an action that can be the appropriate subject of moral evaluation.

Now we can formulate Aquinas's principle about the badness of akratic action, keeping in mind which actions are eligible for moral evaluation at all and that a person can be mistaken in her moral judgments. Aquinas defends the following:

> Conscience Principle (CP): If someone concludes she ought not perform some action in circumstance C, then her knowingly and intentionally performing that action in C is morally prohibited.

According to this principle, what is morally prohibited is a certain kind of human act (not an act of a human), namely, intentionally performing an action she judges she ought not perform, independently of the correctness of the judgment. There are four things to note about the principle before moving on to the objections to it Aquinas considers.

First, the language of moral prohibition might be spelled out in terms of a requiring moral reason to not φ, the moral wrongness of the agent φ-ing, or the agent having a moral obligation to not φ. (Aquinas's terminology—*ligare*—is etymologically closest to the English world obligation.) What we should take away is that if conscience tells you that you ought not φ, then in some real sense, you ought not φ. Conscience puts significant moral pressure on action.

Second, the principle is a decidedly negative moral principle. It tells us that it's *im*permissible to act contrary to one's moral judgments. We can say that there is a requiring moral reason to not violate conscience. It doesn't tell us that acting in accordance with one's moral judgment is always morally *permissible*, much less required.

Third, the CP is unrestricted in an important (and perhaps puzzling) sense: Aquinas doesn't add any conditions a moral judgment has to meet to put normative pressure on action. But he believes in an objective moral law—the natural law—and believes that conscience is fallible with respect to it. We might have expected him to say that one shouldn't act contrary to her moral judgment so long as that judgment is correct, or not contrary to God's law. But Aquinas explicitly rejects such qualification, arguing that such a view would be rationally untenable, as we will see below.

Fourth and finally, while the principle is unrestricted, Aquinas does explain that the moral requirements generated by correct conscience differ in scope from those generated by incorrect conscience. According to Aquinas, a correct conscience binds, or generates a requiring moral reason, unconditionally, so the moral consideration it turns into a requiring moral reason is *narrow* in scope. That is, the requirement doesn't just govern the set of attitudes (believing I ought to φ, intending to φ) but the individual attitude of intending to φ. Giving up the conscientious judgment that one ought not φ isn't a valid way of escaping the requirement to not intentionally φ whenever conscience is correct:

> A correct conscience binds unconditionally because it binds absolutely and in all circumstances. For if one's conscience tells him to avoid adultery, he cannot change that conscience without sin, since he would commit a serious sin in the very error of changing such a conscience. Moreover, as long as it remains, it cannot actually be set aside without sin. Thus, it binds in all cases.[28]

When a person's conscience correctly concludes that some action is morally required, or prohibited, or that, all-things-considered it is good or bad, she apprehends a certain reality. The reality she represents is a relation between a certain human action and the end of human life—the human good. Some action types are good for human beings because they constitute the human good, for instance, "to understand the truth about God, and to live in society." Others are good because they contribute to the achievement of the human good, such as "to avoid ignorance, to not offend others with whom one should converse."[29] If conscience represents one of these action types as good or to be done, or action types that impede or undermine the human good as bad or not to be done, it is correct. Aquinas maintains that when a person's moral judgment or conscience is correct, she can't escape the subsequent requiring moral reason simply by ignoring or intentionally losing the knowledge she now has.

However, when one's conscience is incorrect, the moral requirements it generates are wide scope:

> A mistaken conscience does not bind except conditionally because it is under a certain condition. For that person whose conscience dictates that he is bound to fornicate, is not bound to fornicate in such a way that he is not able to dismiss conscience without sin, except if in his present condition this conscience persists. However, this condition is able to be removed without sin. Wherefore such a conscience does not bind on all occasions; for it can happen that someone puts down conscience, by which happening someone is not bound any longer.[30]

When a person's moral judgment falters, it doesn't accurately represent the action type's relationship to the human good. Still, on Aquinas's view, long as the person is in the grip of the idea that she ought to φ, or that it would be bad to not φ, she is required to φ. Unlike in the case of correct conscience, however, she can change her mind without moral mistake ("without sin").

And once she looses herself from the grip of that judgment, she'll no longer have a requiring moral reason to φ. The requiring moral reason generated by incorrect conscience thus has the same form as a principle like Enkrasia: so long as you believe p, you ought to φ—though there is no independent requirement to persist in belief that p.

We said earlier that Aquinas thinks of guilt as due or appropriate punishment for wrongdoing, and even an instrument in moral improvement. Now that we know he thinks one can do wrong by violating an incorrect or false conscience, we might be more skeptical about his stance on guilt. For if Aquinas is right about erring conscience obligating us, then the guilty feelings that follow from violating an erring conscience would serve as a punishment for genuine wrongdoing. But we might deny that it is appropriate to feel guilt about φ-ing when φ-ing isn't actually bad. Further, we might worry that guilt could be marshaled in the service of corrupting rather than healing the soul when the conscience that is the source of guilt is incorrect. The guilt and remorse of an incorrect conscience might reinforce negative feelings about permissible or good actions or positive feelings about prohibited or bad actions.

RESTRICTING THE CONSCIENCE PRINCIPLE

But there are worries that percolate upstream from these issues about guilt for Aquinas's view. He considers a slew of objections to his version of the Conscience Principle, and he eventually uses his responses to those objections to provide the full defense of his view. Below we'll review those objections and provide arguments that could be used to support them, as they help us understand what might have motivated Aquinas's opposition to adopt a restricted version of the Conscience Principle.

The first objection owes to Augustine's definition of sin, or moral wrongdoing, as whatever violates a law of God.[31] Even if we don't believe in a law of God, we can see how the objection would run. If there is a moral law that is objective and mind independent, then it shouldn't be possible to sin when acting *according* to that law. Aquinas accepts that there is an objective moral law—the natural law; he must in order for his account of conscience to be cognitivist. And yet if CP is true, and there is an objective moral law, then the following is possible. I might judge that I ought to not pursue education because more scientific knowledge will shake my religious faith; from this and CP, it follows that I have a requiring moral reason to not pursue education. Thus my pursuing education in this circumstance would be a sin—morally wrong or prohibited. Yet in Aquinas's view, God's law prescribes shunning ignorance and pursuing education. Now a certain action— pursuing education—is at once sin but decidedly not prohibited by God's law; and this would violate the analysis of sin or wrongdoing as a violation of the objective moral law, or as Augustine puts it, God's law.

This kind of objection fits well with views on which substantive moral principles can make some akratic acts, but not all, wrong. Surely Huck Finn, in helping free Jim, does what is morally good, even though his malformed conscience indicates it would be wrong.[32] If there are objective moral facts—whether it comes from an objective moral law or some other principles—it seems that conscience can't generate requiring moral reasons to act in ways expressly prohibited according to those objective moral facts. It would be a mistake to think that conscience always generated moral requirements while also maintaining that there is an objective moral standard to which actions ought to conform.

Aquinas considers another objection that would show that Huck's conscience fails to obligate: Only a probable conscience obligates. The passage shows that he is thinking of objective, rather than epistemic, probability, as he says, "erroneous conscience, especially about things which are bad per se, is in no way probable."[33] If Huck's conscience is incorrect about a moral principle as fundamental as the prohibition of slavery, we might say, it is not probable and so doesn't generate a moral obligation or requiring reason to not act contrary to it.

Finally, Aquinas considers the objection that if his view were correct, an erring conscience could create moral dilemmas. We can reconstruct the argument for the objection as follows. Suppose erring conscience generates genuinely requiring moral reasons. Those reasons will either prohibit actions prescribed by the moral law, require actions prohibited by the moral law, or require or prohibit actions that are morally neutral (*indifferens*) according to the moral law. If the act is already morally prohibited or required, then the reason of conscience will create a moral dilemma: The person both ought and ought not to φ. (For instance, if a parent judged that he shouldn't vaccinate his children on the CDC schedule because he feared harming his child, but there is an objective requiring moral reason to vaccinate his child on the CDC schedule, then the CP would generate a moral reason against vaccinating that conflicted with that objective requiring moral reason.) Aquinas quotes Augustine saying that these dilemmas are unacceptable because "no one sins in that which he cannot avoid."[34] If it's morally neutral, then it's not the case that there is a requiring moral reason to φ, but if CP is true, then there is a requiring moral reason to φ. That is, if CP were able to make it the case that one has a moral reason to φ, then it would not be true that φ-ing is morally neutral. Thus it would be impossible for the CP to satisfy the condition when it is supposed to apply in neutral cases.

If Aquinas didn't also hold the view that there is an objective moral law, then none of these objections would stick. A subjectivist view would easily avoid competing definitions of morally wrong acts or sins and the possibility of genuine moral dilemmas.[35] But since Aquinas does maintain that there is an objective standard for human action about which conscience can be right or wrong, these objections are especially threatening to his view.[36] For they seem to uncover a deep inconsistency in his view of normative authority. On the one hand, if divine law is normatively authoritative, then it shouldn't be able to be overridden or supplanted by conscience. On the other, if conscience is normatively authoritative, and it can contradict divine law, then it would seem to be able to override divine law or, at the very least, put one in a position where one is required to both follow and violate that law.[37]

In light of the worries above, as well as the worries I raised earlier about guilt, we might want to suggest a restriction on the Conscience Principle: Conscience binds just in those cases where it is correct, or the action under consideration is objectively morally neutral. According to Aquinas, this was in fact a common view among some Franciscans. Mistaken conscience can produce requiring moral reasons only in indifferent matters.

Take as an example of a morally neutral action covering one's mouth while yawning. Imagine that Francis is convinced that it is morally bad to yawn without covering one's mouth because it is disrespectful or disobedient. If CP applies to this action, then Francis has a requiring moral reason to not yawn without covering his mouth. There is no worry about moral dilemmas, since no objective moral requirement generates a requiring moral reason to leave one's mouth uncovered when yawning. The restricted version of CP endorsed by the Franciscans is:

> Restricted Conscience Principle (RCP): If one concludes that she ought not φ, then she ought not intend to φ IFF φ-ing is morally indifferent, antecedently.

Given the problems with the unrestricted CP, and Aquinas's commitment to objective moral truths that conscience can be mistaken about, we might anticipate that RCP fares much better than CP. It won't explain the badness of all cases of akrasia, but perhaps it shouldn't—for if Huck Finn's freeing of Jim is akratic, and we want to say it is nonetheless morally permissible (or even good), we have at least one case of akratic action that is not morally prohibited. The guilt that Huck feels can be dismissed, or a lack of guilt can be appropriate, and so his conscience won't reinforce morally bad beliefs and habits.

DEFENDING THE THOMISTIC CONSCIENCE PRINCIPLE

Aquinas thinks that despite appearances, RCP is unreasonable. He reconstructs what he takes as the best argument for RCP, and he identifies an assumption the defender of RCP must make in order to support two key premises in the argument. He then argues that the truth of that assumption actually points to a more fundamental metaethical truth about the nature of moral obligation and requirements. This truth, as it turns out, entails his unrestricted version of the CP. Thus, the argument for restricting the CP is self-defeating.

Aquinas's argument for his own view begins with an explanation of what would have to be true for RCP to be true—that is, for conscience to obligate in cases of antecedent moral indifference. He suggests that to support RCP, we must reason as follows:[38]

(1) There are three types of moral actions: good, bad, and indifferent.
(2) Suppose φ is a morally indifferent act.
(3) If a person judges she ought not to φ in the indifferent case, and she wills to φ, her will is bad.
(4) If the will that intends to φ is bad, then φ-ing is morally prohibited—one has requiring moral reason to not φ willingly.
(5) So the act of willing an indifferent action contrary to one's moral judgment that it is bad is morally bad.

Of course, whether this argument is persuasive turns on whether we can support (3) and (4).

The defender of RCP has to show that the action of φ-ing is morally bad, but the badness cannot be due to the type of action φ-ing is. For per hypothesis, it is neither intrinsically good nor intrinsically bad. The best explanation for the badness of φ-ing in such a case is supposed to be that it would exhibit a defect in the will. What exactly does the defect consist in? After all, if someone φ's in this case, but her will is generally oriented toward things that are good for human beings, should we really complain? The defender of RCP must assume that in morally neutral cases, what matters for evaluating a person's will is its relationship to the act *as it appears* to the person doing it, not the act as it is.

Aquinas points out that there is little to keep us from thinking that the act as it appears can make a difference to the moral valence of any action, once we admit that it can make a difference in the morally neutral case.[39] For from the first-person perspective, we are unable to distinguish between the good case and the bad case—that is, between the case where in fact, the thing we think is required or prohibited is neutral, on the one hand, and the case where in fact, the thing we think is required is prohibited or the apparently prohibited is required.[40] Moreover, if we gain evidence that we are in the good case—for instance, if Francis were to suddenly get evidence that his judgment about yawning etiquette is mistaken—that realization would make the action appear differently: It would appear morally indifferent. The phenomenology of erring conscience thus resembles that of nonveridical perception in general: As soon as the perceiver realizes her mistake, she no longer sees the object of perception in the same way. If I perceive a stick in water as bent, as soon as I realize the water creates an optical illusion it no longer seems bent to me, all things considered. Similarly, the moral seemings change as we make second order judgments about their veracity, probability, or reliability. Thus, there can't be a phenomenal difference between the case where we're correct and the case where we're mistaken.

This *lack of phenomenological difference* makes the Franciscan view untenable, Aquinas claims. Let's suppose the Franciscan is right to say that the problem with φ-ing when one's conscience says that φ-ing is bad in the morally neutral case is that the will of the person φ-ing would be bad, responding inappropriately to the apparent badness of the act. Now, given the lack of phenomenological difference between this case and the non-neutral case (say, where φ-ing is required by the natural law), what should we say about the will of the person who φs in the non-neutral case, also thinking φ-ing would be bad? The will in both cases is responding to the same apparent badness. So, we would think, it would be inappropriate in both cases for the will to choose the action, given its apparent badness. There is something incoherent in thinking that the will could be morally evaluated for its response to mere apparent badness in the former case, but not in the latter, despite the lack of phenomenological difference between them. Therefore, Aquinas maintains, a restriction on the conscience principle to cases of indifference would be objectionably ad hoc.

Aquinas uses the assumption the defender of RCP relied on in (3) and (4) to reveal something about the nature of moral requirements and their ineliminable relation to our moral perception:

> This, however, obtains not only in indifferent [acts], but even in those which are good or bad in themselves. For not only is one able to fall under the description 'good' or 'bad' accidentally on account of reason's apprehension of an object for the [act] which is indifferent; but even that which is good is able to be described as bad or that which is bad, as good, on account of reason's apprehension of it.[41]

To understand what Aquinas is claiming here, we need to appreciate the per se/*per accidens* distinction. Aquinas explains that here, he is simply taking a page from Aristotle's book on intemperance. Suppose a person is looking for honey but instead drinks scotch, thinking the scotch is honey because of its color; that person wills to have honey, essentially: her choice is per se a choice of honey; but because she replaced the appearance of scotch for honey, her choice is *per accidens* a choice for scotch.

When we have a false moral perception regarding some action, the action itself can take on the property of being bad or prohibited, or good or to be done, in virtue of our perception, but only *per accidens*. Usually, or in the normal case, say, the action is prohibited, so the action is prohibited per se; but *per accidens*, because of my false judgment, that action done by me right now would be *per accidens* bad or prohibited. Here comes the tricky part. Once an action has become prohibited or bad *per accidens*, on account of my incorrect conscience, my will is in a novel situation. If it clings to the action with knowledge that the action is prohibited or bad, then the will clings to what is morally bad under that description, and so is essentially, or per se, willing what is bad and only incidentally what is permissible or required. Aquinas says, "Therefore, there may be people considering a false argument is true. . . . If then he sticks by this false conclusion, really believing it to be true, he is *per se* standing by a true reason but *per accidens* by a false reason."[42] The person's will is essentially bad when she pursues what is even only *per accidens* bad because it appears that way to her. And her will is not bad if she is pursuing what she takes to be good, given how things appear to her. This will be so regardless of whether her moral perception is veridical, and regardless of whether the action in question is per se neutral, good, or bad.

Aquinas provides a neat framework for thinking about the nature of moral requirements or obligations that explains why the appearance an action has for an agent determines whether the agent is required to perform or abstain from performing the action. He explains that to obligate (*ligare*) just is for one thing to impose necessity on another. This can be done through coercion, as in the case of physical binding, or through conditional necessity, as when some act M is made necessary in becoming the only means to E where E is one's end—such as in the Enkratic principle. In his estimation, conscience obligates by imposing a conditional moral necessity on some action.

Conscience makes some action morally necessary for achieving our final end in the following way:

> No one is bound (*ligatur*) by a precept unless mediated through knowledge of that precept. And that person who doesn't have the capacity for knowledge of the precept is not bound by it; nor is someone ignorant of the precept said to be bound to act according to the precept. . . . Thus just as in the physical realm the bodily agent doesn't act unless through contact, so in the spiritual realm a precept doesn't bind unless through knowledge.[43]

Conscience supplies the contact needed for objective moral precepts about human action to obligate us. This provides a response to the Augustinian objection: the objective moral law actually doesn't generate requiring moral reasons or obligations for individuals on its own. It has to make contact with those individuals—it must be promulgated, just like any law has to be made known in order for it to have authority over the citizenry. So Augustine's definition of wrongdoing or sin is missing a crucial component, namely, that the person knowingly acts contrary to the law.[44]

But conversely, the objective moral law is important. There must be some standard for human actions for conscience to communicate. Otherwise we would be bootstrapping our way into moral requirements by thinking of them. Think of it this way: in the best case, conscience correctly communicates to us which actions are objectively good or bad, and the standard of human action thus makes the contact needed to impose moral necessity on our actions, making some right, some wrong. But we are often not in the best case, and we can't know whether we are in the best case or a bad case.

Now we can also reply to the objection that the CP generates moral dilemmas. Aquinas concedes that his view does allow for moral dilemmas, but they are only dilemmas in a qualified sense (*secundum quid*). For recall that the requiring reasons generated by incorrect conscience are wide in scope.[45] Someone who is under a wide scope requirement can escape that requirement without any moral mistake by changing the judgment of conscience. Additionally, whatever objective precept opposes the dictate of conscience can't generate a narrow-scope requiring moral reason for the person to do the opposing action. For the precept to generate a requiring moral reason, it has to make *contact* with her will via her conscience. Thus, we don't get a strict dilemma between requiring moral reasons when the person has a false but inculpably ignorant conscience. If someone is in a true dilemma created by a false judgment of conscience and a former true judgment of conscience, Aquinas explains, the dilemma is also qualified because it is of her own making. For Aquinas holds that one can't change her conscience when correct without making a moral mistake.

WHY THE SOLUTION FITS: GUILT, GOOD WILL, AND MORAL VIRTUE

Aquinas's views on conscience, guilt, and the CP assume that having a good will is morally important. His view will be most at home in a normative theory that places important on the will and character, or moral virtue. In this last section, I want to explain Aquinas's own rationale for thinking a good will is crucial for achieving the human good. I'll also show how on this view, it makes sense to think of conscience and guilt as lynchpins in moral development, even when they are mistaken.

What is the role of a good will in a good human life? As Aquinas tells the story, humans have an objective final end that is what our good or perfection consists in and is thus inescapably normative for us. This end is union with God. Union with God, as with any person, requires willing what God wills that we will, and not willing what God does not will us to do. On this view, the actions that are morally necessary to achieve our good or final end are the actions God wills us to do, and the avoidance of the actions God nils.

The obvious problem is that we can't infallibly know what God wills for us—that is the problem of erring conscience. And yet, "we *are* able to know what God wills, according to a *universal description*, as such. For we know that God wills whatever he wills under the description 'good.'"[46] Given our severe epistemic limitations in this respect, God decides to extend grace: God makes the only requirement for union with God that our will be right—that we will what we think God wills, namely, whatever falls under the description "good" and avoid what we think God nils, namely, whatever falls under the description "bad." In order to achieve the human good, we simply need to orient our wills toward what appears to us to be good and away from what appears to us to be bad. And as we saw, the will can be oriented toward the good *per se*, even if the action it chooses is bad *per se* and only good *per accidens* because of an incorrect conscience.

For instance, to modernize one of Aquinas's examples, suppose I'm at a crowded bar and I walk up behind someone who looks to me like my spouse, whom I'm supposed to meet there, and wrap my arms around them; but in fact, it is a stranger. It would be absurd to think of my action as adulterous or an instance of sexual harassment. Moreover, it doesn't seem that the hug displays a moral defect in my will—my will wasn't aiming at something bad *per se*, but rather *per accidens*. By contrast, if I think the person is someone I plan to cheat on my spouse with, and it turns out to be my spouse, the hug does display a moral defect in my will even though the action is per se good; since it is *per accidens* bad, and that *per accidens* appearance is what my will is clinging to essentially, my will is clinging to what is *per se* bad. Aquinas concludes that every time a person acts aiming at the *per se* bad, her will is bad. Sometimes she correctly judges what is bad so that what is *per accidens* bad and *per se* bad is the same act. But not always—perhaps not even often.

Aquinas thinks that our ultimate perfection, once we receive all of God's grace, involves cultivating not just a good will but also the moral virtues. Conscience and the guilt or remorse of conscience can steer us in the right direction, and we end up farther away from the ideal of virtue when we act contrary to conscience, even when it is a faulty judgment.

Commenting on Aristotle, Aquinas says that a person who clings to an object or action because she mistakenly perceives it as good is better than the person who pursues something knowing it is bad, but due to a recalcitrant desire for it. While a person who drinks too much wine because she's persuaded to falsely believe it's good, because pleasant, can be talked out of drinking too much wine by being talked out of thinking of it as good, not so for the person who goes in for more wine in full awareness of its badness. For she isn't principally motivated by the goodness of the wine: She wants what she desires regardless of whether it is good or bad. Similarly, the person who wraps their arms around a stranger at a bar due to the mistaken belief that the person is her spouse is not principally moved by that person, but rather by the thought of her spouse. All it takes to correct her behavior and attitudes is a correction of this judgment. Thus, Aquinas will argue, the person who thinks of the object she clings to "is more easily cured [*sanabilior*] because it is easier to dissuade him from what he currently believes."[47] It is much harder to cure the illness, so to speak, in a person who wraps her arms around the stranger planning to do something she knows is adulterous. For the defective element there is the will, and the way her desires are related to her choice, and for that there is no quick fix.

Does any of this help us assuage the worries about guilt and false guilt? I think it does. For responsiveness to one's guilt, even in the bad case, demonstrates a will oriented to what one thinks of as the good and away from what one thinks of as the bad. If Aquinas is correct, then paying attention to guilt can help a person cultivate a better will and subsequently virtue even if her judgment is mistaken. We should be clear that the guilt needs to be proportionate to the wrongdoing—the human act that was performed. Otherwise it will fail to be a just punishment and so even if taken on willingly, may not be healthy for the individual who feels its weight.

Contrary to the potential objection I considered earlier, what the guilt reinforces is the badness of doing what one knows or thinks to be bad. And this is, in fact, the worst thing we can do regarding our final end, on the Thomistic view. Guilt may accidentally reinforce certain habits or behaviors as long as we think of them as good or to be done; but as Aquinas says of the intemperate person, it is much easier to change one's bad habits based on false beliefs or judgments than it is to change bad habits that are rooted in a will indifferent to the goodness or badness of actions.

To wrap up: we saw that there is a deep-seated intuition that akratic action is defective. And yet, there is some resistance to adopting a principle like the Conscience Principle that would show all akratic action to be wrong. But if we try to restrict the Conscience Principle, say, to cases where the action in question is objectively morally neutral, we must make use of the assumption that the quality of a person's will is evident in how she responds to an action as it appears to her. The action as it appears to her is morally important, then, because it determines what someone can or can't do without marring her character or exhibiting a bad will. On closer examination, we saw that this idea acts as a camel's nose under the tent. If we accept it as a rationale for restricting the CP, then on pain of inconsistency we must also accept it in cases where the act types are morally good or bad as well, since there's no phenomenological difference between these cases for the agent.

We do not develop our character and will only when we're performing actions that could be described from some external point of view as good or bad, right or wrong. We are constantly shaping and exhibiting the quality of our will and character as we respond to the world as it appears to us. Since conscience and the guilt of conscience deliver those appearances, we do well to attend to them if we hope to progress in virtue.

NOTES

1. Cicero, *De Legibus* 1.40–41, 2.43.
2. See Arpaly and Schroeder (1999, 164–5); Arpaly (2003).
3. For instance, see Kant, *Metaphysics of Morals* 6:438–9.
4. See, for instance, John of Damascene 9 *coll.* 937, Peter Lombard *Sententiae* II.39, Bonaventure *In Sent.* II.39. The received view of conscience in the medieval period dates back to a Greek biblical commentary of St. Jerome on Ezekiel 1:4–14. In the neoplatonic tradition, earlier commentators had likened the three creatures in Ezekiel's vision to Plato's tripartite soul (Seek Kries 2002, 68–69). Jerome disputes this interpretation, arguing instead that the face of the eagle represents *synderesis*, the spirit within a human referenced by St. Paul in 1 Corinthians 2:11. The term *synderesis* is not in the Greek lexicon (at least, until Jerome), thus most scholars speculate that *synderesis* was a corruption of the Greek word *syneidesis*.
5. Cicero employed the concept earliest among the Stoics, with Seneca following him; prominent early Christian thinkers such as Origen and Lactantius, too, incorporated conscience in their account of human psychology. For discussion see Sorabji (2014).
6. For discussions of the development of the term *conscience* in the Greek and early Roman periods, see Marietta (1970), Atkins (2014). For overviews of medieval theories of conscience, see Langston (2001), Potts (1980); for a thorough history see Lottin (1948).
7. Quoted in Lottin (1928, 19 n. 1, translation mine).
8. Ibid., 19.
9. Philip the Chancellor, *Summa de Bono*, "Treatise on Conscience" I.B.3, translation from Potts (1980, 97).
10. Ibid., 24.
11. Albert the Great, *Summa de Creaturis* II.71 in Lottin (1928).
12. Thus we can think of him as holding an early version of motivational internalism. See Potts (1980, 33–34).
13. Aquinas, *Super Sententiae* d. 24, q. 2, a. 4, sol.
14. For brief discussion, see Hoffmann (2012, 258).
15. Aquinas, *De Veritate* 16.1, my translation.
16. Aquinas, *De Veritate* 16.2 co.
17. Ibid.

18. Ibid., 17.2 co.
19. Aquinas, *Summa Contra Gentiles* IV.90.9.
20. Aquinas, *Summa Theologiae* I.II 87.1 co.
21. Ibid. I.II 87.7 co.
22. Whether akrasia constitutes irrationality or moral badness is the subject of debate in the contemporary literature. Some think akrasia is a paradigmatic case of irrationality: for instance, Scanlon says, "Irrationality in the clearest sense occurs when a person's attitudes fail to conform to his or her own judgments," (Scanlon 1998, 25). Others go further and maintain that rational norms are subordinate to substantive moral norms (see, for instance, Audi 2013, 530).
23. Broome (2013, 425).
24. Shpall (2013, 733).
25. Notably, Schroeder (2004) and Kolodny (2005).
26. See Kolodny (2008) for an argument against several ways of supporting formal coherence principles governing beliefs and intentions.
27. Kolodny suggests that an akratic action could "merit positive evaluation, because one manifests certain valuable dispositions" in defying one's own normative judgments (2008, 461–62).
28. Aquinas, *De Veritate* 17.4.
29. Aquinas, Summa Theologica I.II 94.2 co.
30. Ibid.
31. Aquinas, De Veritate, VII.4.1.
32. See Arpaly and Schroeder (1999, 164–65); Arpaly (2003).
33. Aquinas, *De Veritate* 17.4.4.
34. Ibid., 8.
35. See King and Arlig (2018, sec. 6). To see this, contrast Aquinas's view with the subjectivism of Peter Abelard. Abelard argues that it's unreasonable to morally evaluate actions given the ubiquity of moral luck. Imagine two people want to build a house for the poor. One is wealthy, the second made destitute after being robbed. Now the first can carry out the action he intended but the second can't. To say that the wealthier person deserves moral praise because of her action and the destitute person does not, since she can't build the house for the poor now, seems to suggest that wealth could make someone morally better than another, which would be "the height of insanity!" Therefore, the only appropriate subjects of moral evaluation are an agent's character and intentions. Abelard's view ultimately supports an unrestricted, positive version of the conscience principle—one ought never intend contrary to one's moral judgment, and it is always permissible to intend to φ as long as φ-ing is not in violation of one's conscience. Aquinas explicitly rejects the positive view in *De Veritate* 17.4 co., reasoning that if acting rightly just consisted in acting according to conscience, then actions that are clearly right but done in accordance with advice or counsel would be required, which per hypothesis is absurd.
36. Aquinas, *De Malo* 2.2. ad.13. See also *Summa Theologiae* I.II 18.6 ad. 3, where he states that the interior act of the will "is compared to the exterior just as form is to matter" (my translation). For further discussion, see Brock (1998, 174–75), Hoffmann (2003, 73–94), Pilsner (2006), and Rhonheimer (2004, 461–516).

37. We can conceive of a reply on behalf of CP that moral dilemmas shouldn't be unwelcome in our moral theorizing because some of life's scenarios have a complex texture that naturally invites such dilemmas. But that, too, I want to suggest, is unsatisfactory. The moral dilemmas CP produces don't seem to be extensionally equivalent to those that the reply tells us we should accept. There's not much nuanced or intricate about the situation of the parent who continues to think, against the evidence, that vaccinating infants can cause the infant to be on the autistic spectrum, for example. It is hardly like Sophie's choice. The further worry is that such moral dilemmas entail a denial of ought implies can. Since no one can both phi and not phi at once, at least one of the oughts in the dilemma will not be possible for the agent to comply with; so if we admit such dilemmas it seems we must deny the intuitively plausible ought implies can principle.

38. Aquinas's argument for the Conscience Principle as it appears in both *Summa Theologica* I-II 19 and *De Veritate* 17 opens with a consideration of this kind of restricted conscience principle. Odon Lottin identifies the view as Franciscan in the second chapter of the second tome of his renowned Psychologie et Morale aux XIIe et XIIIe Siecles. See Odon Lottin, "Syndérèse et Conscience aux XIIe et XIIIe Siècles," *Psychologie et Morale aux XIIe et XIIIe Siècles*, vol. II/1: 103–349 (Louvain: Abbaye du Mont Cèsar; Gembloux: J. Duculot, 1948), 103–349. For excerpts on conscience from Jerome, Philip the Chancellor, Bonaventure, Peter Lombard, and Aquinas, and discussions of each, see Timothy Potts, *Conscience in Medieval Philosophy* (Cambridge: Cambridge University Press, 1980).

39. "And because the object of the will is the thing which is proposed by reason, as was said, from the fact that something is proposed by reason as bad, the will, while it carries this out, accepts the [thing] characterized as bad" (Ibid.).

40. Contemporary epistemologists call the analogue in theoretical beliefs the "New Evil Demon Problem." For discussion of this in contemporary metaethics, see Lord (2018).

41. Aquinas, *Summa Theologiae* I.II 19.5 co.

42. Aquinas, De Ethica VII.2, 1438.

43. Aquinas, *De Veritate* 17.3 co.

44. Some interpreters think Aquinas is saying that the actual judgment of conscience binds unless one ought to have known better or made a different judgment. That is, if Francis ought to know that driving over 30 mph is bad, because she passed a speed limit sign minutes ago, then she has a requiring moral reason to not go over 30 mph. Aquinas does accept that we can make moral mistakes on account of past ignorance for which we are guilty—when our conscience is incorrect due to an error for which we are morally responsible. However, if conscience failed to bind in every case where one ought to have known better, the view would face a vicious regress. For the ground of the requiring moral reason to know that driving over 30 mph is bad could itself be some further fact she ought to have known—for instance, that there is a requiring moral reason to look to the side of the road for speed limit signs, and she should have known that this is required of her because she should have listened closely to her driver's ed teacher in high school, and so on and so forth. But at a certain point, Francis's failure to comply with one of these supposed requiring reasons

makes her incapable of complying with reasons downstream. This kind of view would put no limit on the number of iterations of requiring reasons to know requiring reasons to know requiring reasons to know, et cetera. A more charitable interpretation of Aquinas here will simply note his discussion of culpable ignorance elsewhere gives him the resources to say that one may be disqualified from excuse from blame for an action if it resulted from willful ignorance because there was a requiring moral reason to know something that would have prevented one's blameworthy action. For instance, Aquinas, *Summa Theologiae* I.II 76.2.

45. Ibid.
46. *ST* IaIIae 19.10 ad. 1.
47. Aquinas, *De Ethica* VII.2, 1325.

REFERENCES

Aquinas, Thomas. (1882). *Summa Theologiae. Opera Omnia, iussu impensaque Leonis XIII.* (cura et studio Fratrum Predicatorum, Ed.). Rome.

———. (1882). *Quaestiones Disputatae de Veritate. Opera Omnia, Iussu Leonis XIII.* (P.M., Ed.). Rome: S.C. de Propoganda Fide.

Arpaly, N., & Schroeder, T. (2014). *In Praise of Desire.* Oxford ; New York: Oxford University Press.

Broome, J. (2007). Wide or Narrow Scope? *Mind, 116*(462).

Creighton, S., Chernausek, S. D., Romao, R., Ransley, P., & Salle, J. P. (n.d.). Timing and Nature of Reconstructive Surery for Disorders of Sex Development. *Journal of Pediatric Urology, 8*, 602–10.

Crouch, N. S., Liao, L. M., Woodhouse, C. R. J., Conway, G. S., & Creighton, S. M. (n.d.). Sexual Function and Genital Sensitivity Following Feminizing Genitoplasty for Congenital Adrenal Hyperplasia. *The Journal of Urology, 179*(2), 634–38. https://doi.org/10.1016/j.juro.2007.09.079.

Ewing, A. C. (1953). *Ethics.* London: English University Press.

Lottin, D. (1928). La syndérese chez albert le grand et saint thomas d'aquin. *Revue Néoscolastique De Philosophie 30*, 18–44.

Lottin, O. (1948). *Psychologie et Morale aux XIIe et XIIIe Siècles* (Vol. II/1). Louvain: Abbaye du Mont Cesar; Gembloux: J. Duculot.

Markovits, J. (2014). *Moral Reason* (First edition). Oxford, England ; New York: Oxford University Press.

Potts, T. (1980). *Conscience in Medieval Philosophy.* Cambridge: Cambridge University Press.

Rippon, S. (2011). In Defense of the Wide-Scope Instrumental Principle. *Journal of Ethics and Social Philosophy, 5*, 1–21.

Schroeder, M. (2014). Means-End Coherence, Stringency, and Subjective Reasons. In *Explaining the Reasons We Share* (173–200). Oxford: Oxford University Press.

Shpall, S. (2013). Wide and Narrow Scope. *Philosophical Studies, 163*, 717–36.

Sorabji, R. (2014). *Moral Conscience through the Ages.* Oxford: Oxford University Press.

Chapter 14

Kant and Williams on Guilt, Shame, and the Morality System

Laura Papish

If Bernard Williams is right, then Kant's account of what morality is and how it ought to shape our lives is deeply problematic. If, that is, a sense of obligation should not be influenced by one's social milieu, or if moral motivation must be driven by respect alone and not the dynamics of shame, admiration, and one's standing among peers, then Kant, it seems, has mistaken purity for strength and deprived human beings of the supports they need to live and act well. This would be worrisome enough, but there's also, for Williams, a strange irony at play here: Kant, in his efforts to promote the virtues of autonomous self-legislation, instead advances a private and lonely model of moral achievement, one promising a self-satisfaction that can't really be shared or created in concert with other human beings. Or, to put the point a bit differently, Williams detects something self-defeating about Kant's ethics. It inspires me to avoid the guilt that accompanies violating the moral law, but only to the extent that it encourages me to be shameless, to proceed unaware of and unmoved by other people and how they see me. At this point, the solipsism concurrent with a withdrawal into pure practical reason becomes bound up with, as Williams puts it, an "insensate degree of moral egoism."[1]

THE CHALLENGES POSED BY WILLIAMS'S CRITIQUE

In noting this, it may seem as though the next step is to respond to this critique, either by seeing if this reconstruction of Kant's ethics as a paradigmatic "guilt" morality is as damaging as Williams takes it to be, or by asking if Williams provides an accurate depiction of Kant's thought. But, at least as yet and for the reasons that follow, matters are too complicated to allow such questions.

First, what—or more specifically, what *else*—is at stake when Williams offers this critique of Kant? The claim that Kant offers a morality of guilt when we would be served better by a morality of shame is really a stand-in for a cluster of objections to not only Kant but also a host of other views that fall under the broad banner of what Williams calls the "morality system." This "morality system" includes most, if not all, forms of utilitarianism and consequentialism, as well as deontological approaches to ethics inspired by Kant (most notably contractualism).[2] Though he does not expressly list its features, for Williams the "morality system" characterizes those ethics that rely on either a particular type of moral vocabulary—one where legalistic concepts such as right, obligation, duty, or fairness are central[3]—or a certain set of presuppositions; these include the idea that human moral psychology permits or encourages a fine line to be drawn between emotional considerations and the verdicts of reason, and the belief that cool, detached, rational reflection is a better guide to ethics than culture, tradition, or literature.[4] Given these considerations, and Williams's own turn toward the Greeks for moral insight, more contemporary ethical theories than not will form part of the morality system. Given also Williams's insistence that we look really to Sophocles and Homer, and that even philosophy's most revered Greek thinkers—Aristotle and especially Plato—also appear taken in by this "system,"[5] it becomes clear that Kant is targeted really as a symbol of a movement as opposed to its catalyst or its sole contemporary figurehead.

Since this shows that Williams's historical target is in fact much broader and rather more elusive than it initially appears, narrowing one's focus on that target and asking questions about it becomes more challenging. Moreover, since it is reasonable to assume that there will be differences between Williams's Kant and the one found in, for example, historically informed Kant studies, we face a difficult task in assessing his critique: Should Kant-as-symbol be our focus, or Kant himself? Can the former be legitimately problematic for moral thought and practice even if the latter is not, or is at least less so? And most generally, how do we avoid, in thinking about Williams's critique of a Kantian morality of guilt, feeling the way Elizabeth Anscombe said one should if trying to engage Aristotle's ethics as a contemporary moral philosopher? As she famously noted, we should feel as we do when our jaws are out of alignment, since Aristotle's project and context are just so different from that typical of a contemporary moral philosopher.[6] With so much differentiating Kant's ethical thought from Williams's, can any attempt at sustained dialogue feel productive and fair to each thinker?

Second, along the same lines, matters are complicated further by the fact that Williams's philosophical objections to the morality system are complex. I've already mentioned that his worry about how the morality system, particularly as typified by Kant, relies on one reactive attitude—guilt—at the expense of others such as shame. But his claim is accompanied by a bundle of other concerns, some of which seem to amplify this moral psychological concern about guilt while others stake out its implications for ethical thought more generally.

If guilt is the reactive attitude that regulates our interactions with others, our moral imaginations, and our expectations for how unsound deliberation and action will be made palpable, then the following also holds for Williams. A morality of guilt will promote narcissism.[7] Guilt is the characteristic response to violating a moral law, and since the pronouncements of this law remain immune to details concerning whom I have mistreated or the social context we shared, then even if guilt often presupposes a victim, it's an attitude that inevitably, and perversely, directs attention back toward one's own wrongdoing and not toward others. Guilt experienced as moralists demand will also crowd out other reactive attitudes and other practical concerns. Guilt will be effective, and we will hear it as loud, when it's the only voice in the room. Shame, by contrast, is usually associated with metaphors of vision or with how we are seen, and it can be a response to a number of failures—small or large, positive or negative—that come into relief across one's practical horizon. Not winning the favor of someone I don't even like, realizing lettuce was stuck between my teeth at an event,[8] or never seeking my true vocational calling because of greed: All can occasion shame. Guilt, though, is tied to the idea that obligation—avoiding the forbidden, doing the required, and, per the dictum "ought implies can," bracketing that about us which is involuntary—is the basis of morality and that morality is the whole of what we can depend on to be good, valuable, or worthy of human concern.[9]

But even if all this allows Williams to expand and perhaps strengthen his critique, it also makes engagement with his criticisms more unwieldy. It is clear that, in his own alternative to the morality system, shame can accommodate guilt,[10] but it is less clear whether he sees the morality system, in its emphasis on guilt, as excluding shame altogether or just not giving it its proper due. So, does one respond adequately by simply pointing to where shame appears, or is more needed? More broadly, is the morality system's moral psychology, in both its prescriptive and descriptive aspects, Williams's true target? Is it also, or more, the theoretical apparatus—such as the focus on duty and obligation—that supports the morality system? Some further clarity here would be useful, since aside from digging in one's heels and defending the Kantian morality system exactly as it is depicted by Williams, one response that immediately suggests itself is to show that Williams's different objections to the morality system don't interlock with and support one another in the way he thinks they do. The morality system is, for Williams, philosophy's "peculiar institution."[11] With this quiet analogy to American chattel slavery,[12] we can see he views the morality system as enslaving us but also, it appears, as gaining support from its mutually reinforcing components, in much the way that any oppressive institution does. So to challenge Williams, one might try to show, for instance, that the charges of oppression against the morality system are overblown because a morality based on duty and obligation doesn't constrain our moral psychology in the way alleged. But this reply can only work if there is confidence that the ground will not shift beneath one's feet in trying to respond to Williams and that we know which aspects of his critique to put the most weight on. Absent this, it is difficult to proceed.

Finally, there is the added difficulty that Williams's concern is not only, and not, I think, primarily, the Kantian morality system or the philosophical lineage we're said to have inherited from Kant's morality of guilt. While we might put Williams's observations in terms of rival moral theoretical or moral psychological traditions—we might cite, that is, his proposals that we should make flourishing a more foundational concept than rightness, or that thick moral concepts better facilitate reasoning than thin ones[13]—this is an extremely narrow vantage point on his critique. Most essentially, Williams aims to put us "into honest touch with reality."[14] He is concerned with ethical and social practice. His questions are only indirectly questions regarding what professional philosophers call moral theory or moral psychology. Though we tend to situate his criticisms within certain philosophical subfields, Williams's foremost concern is whether real human beings have available to them the resources needed to live well and to understand themselves. What moral philosophers do or propose is subservient to this goal.

But even with this point clarified—or, more accurately, because this point has been clarified—the relationship between theory and practice will prove immensely complicated. For as much as Williams clearly thinks that Kant's morality of guilt has left us with a disfigured sense of what should count as an ethical failure, how to incorporate the beliefs or views of others into our practical reasoning, and how to feel in the face of mistreatment, Williams also recognizes that "almost all of us" now are, to a significant extent, Kantians.[15] Kant's morality of guilt and morality system have seeped into who we have become, and while we can find much to admire in, for example, Sophocles's vision of ethical deliberation, it would be deeply misguided to think we can return to this at will. But this symbiosis between theory and practice will cut both ways when assessing Williams's critique of guilt and the morality system. On the one hand, it gives Williams leverage. It lets us see that if we try to develop different ways of conceptualizing morality, then these will impact in real time how we feel, think, and act. But on the other hand, if we are indeed Kantians, then for as much as our moral practices are deficient, it's the case that they are still ours and we are used to them. We may wonder if we should take the dysfunction and self-enslavement that is comfortable and familiar to us over the promise of something new. Williams's argument is in fact structured to explain why we may be justified in standing by Kant, guilt, and the morality system, even if they prove to be defective in much the way Williams claims they are.

In sum, there are numerous difficulties inherent in an attempt to engage Williams's critique of Kant's morality of guilt and the broader morality system adjoined to it. We should appreciate and comment further on these difficulties, but the best way to do so is indirectly and through a set of questions more amendable to direct discussion. This paper will therefore ask: Even if Kant-as-symbol is likely too ambiguous a target to consider straightaway, is it accurate to claim that Kant valorizes guilt in the way alleged by Williams? Is shame absent or problematically marginalized in Kantian thought, perhaps such that it leaves us ill-prepared to navigate at least some important elements of practical life? I take it as a given that it would be misconceived to try to show that Kant does not privilege obligation, duty, and the moral "ought" above other ethical concepts; clearly, Kant does exactly this. I also take it as a given that Kant has good, if not unassailable, reasons for doing this, and that on this question regarding the very foundation of moral theory, it is generally best to leave Kant and Williams at a standoff.[16] But in regard to the issue of what sorts of feelings and attitudes help us make sense of ourselves, and how we should be tethered to other persons, it seems that there is here real room for nuance and debate. And if Kant can be shown to have a far more complex and plausible account of guilt and shame than it would initially appear, then this is significant. It would legitimate interest in Kant as a historical figure and would bode well for other guilt moralists or morality system advocates that wish to show, *pace* Williams, that certain theoretical commitments exclude neither a healthy moral psychology nor a complex and accurate vision of practical reality. Looking further forward, we might then refigure our ideas about the kind of morality Kant can be taken as a symbol of.

Before we turn to Kant directly, or assess how neatly his moral psychology aligns with Williams's understanding of it, it will help to build on the overview of Williams offered thus far and highlight its most relevant points. This is the first task of the next section.

GUILT AND SHAME, CONTINUED

To start, it should be emphasized that Williams's dichotomy between guilt and shame is not quite as sharply drawn as it may at first appear. Though he tends to associate the works of Homer and Sophocles with a shame ethic and Kant with a guilt ethic, we have already indicated that matters are in fact more complicated. While, in Williams's telling, Kant and the moralists see no real moral need for any emotion or attitude other than guilt, the Greeks in whom he is interested develop an account of shame that accommodates guilt. His contrast, then, is not between Kant and guilt, and the Greeks and shame, but between Kant's "guilt only" account and the Greek "shame, and then also guilt" account.

Guilt (alone) is said by Williams to be the paradigmatic and central moral attitude in Kant's thought because guilt encapsulates the way moral failure is experienced. We aim to live up to the categoricity demanded by the moral law, and never to make an exception to those maxims fit to hold as universal laws of nature. When we fail in this regard—and we invariably and often will—we understand this failure through the concept of guilt. Since guilt arises, on this picture, from moral acts or omissions, it is an emotion or attitude that stays relatively self-contained. An individual will feel guilt for her moral transgressions, and since the law that has been violated is within one's own reason, the experience of guilt doesn't connect us to other persons in any truly important or essential way. Guilt is also, on this picture, limited to the moral and thus the voluntary.

For Williams, shame, by contrast, has a much broader and more inclusive scope. I may feel shame for being exposed as a hypocrite and a liar, but I may also feel shame for something that has nothing to do with morality or even my actions (recall the lettuce in one's teeth). Shame is thus most typically experienced when some feature of one's character, perceived self, or self-conception is on display in an unfavorable, disadvantageous, or disempowering way. But since a person can also feel shame for moral acts and omissions—if, in my cowardice, I fail to protect you from harm[17]—and since these clearly can stem from the type of person one is, shame can accommodate guilt. In Williams's view, "shame can understand guilt, but guilt cannot understand itself" (I'll revisit this particular takeaway later).[18]

So, to summarize, Kant goes wrong, it's alleged, because he allows that the experience of guilt can be intelligible even if it doesn't occasion a deeper inquiry into one's self-conceptions or how others interpret her behavior; it's enough to know that the law was violated. With this, the question we now face is whether this "guilt only" moral psychology should in fact be attributed to Kant.

On its face, Kant's corpus challenges at least the ease with which Williams levels his critique and maybe the substance of his critique as well. Kant does speak of guilt (*Schuld*) or being guilty (*schuldig*) sometimes, but it is not a focal point or even an especially noticeable peripheral concept within his writings. Moreover, the uses to which Kant puts the notion of guilt, when he even bothers to name it directly, do not fit together in a systematic way. He does speak of guilt as attaching to particular transgressions on occasion,[19] and this may seem to support Williams's reading. But at other points Kant puts the concept of guilt either to an altogether different or an opposed use.

He relies on the concept of guilt, for example, to introduce certain moral pedagogical points. In a discussion of vengeance, for instance, he reminds us that each person has enough guilt all one's own such that vengeance is ill-conceived.[20] In one of the very few consistent, and therefore noteworthy, uses to which he puts the concept of guilt, he reminds us, in both *Religion within the Boundaries of Mere Reason* and the *Metaphysics of Morals*, that we are prone to confuse something like good moral luck—an idea Kant himself was tuned in to, even if his account of it would have to differ from Williams's—with having led a "guiltless life."[21] And in contrast to Williams's reading, Kant also references a more existential notion of guilt, one that attaches not to specific ways we've acted but to the fact that human beings suffer, invariably, from a radical evil that cannot be extirpated; he names guilt, not shame, as a fitting response to this feature of our characters.[22]

In citing guilt at this juncture, Kant shows at least that Williams's critique can't apply straightaway; guilt and shame do not appear to overlay with act and character in the way Williams proposes. We can add to this complication that it seems not to be the case that Kant has a "guilt only" view. Shame (*Scham* or *Schande*) is mentioned by Kant even less frequently than guilt, but it's not absent from his works. And, surprisingly, here his thought is more systematic than it is in the case of guilt. He consistently, in the pedagogy lectures, claims that while admonitions of shame should not be delivered to very young children who can't understand them, they should be delivered to those who have at least hit adolescence.[23] Moreover, shame is viewed by Kant as fairly indispensable for moral education and described in a way that is surprisingly parallel to contemporary conceptions, including Williams's own.

Shame is defined by Kant as an "anguish that comes from the worried contempt of a person who is *present*."[24] This is very close to Williams, who sees shame as having social awareness at its core. In contrast to guilt, which, for Williams, is a reactive attitude that connects a moral transgressor with an abstract moral law, shame is a reactive attitude that connects a given human being to an "other." This other, Williams notes further, is not necessarily an actual person or a fictitious one, but it has something like human character insofar as it represents an internalized but distinct and "genuine social reality," one whose insight we have to incorporate into our reflections and self-conceptions.[25] Kant, in arguing that shame is important to an individual's moral development,[26] and by adding that while the "presence of the person before whom he is ashamed" must be at least imagined, that person's physical or actual presence is not required,[27] anticipates Williams's account. And if we consider this connection a bit further, as well as some nearby points, then we can confirm that there is something shared between Kant and Williams. They are not merely both using the term "shame." They make some substantively similar proposals about how shame and social relations matter. The outline of Kant on shame that I provide in the next section will highlight what he and Williams share in common, and it will thereby put Kant's account of guilt in a different relief. However, as will become clear in the conclusion to this chapter, certain differences between the two philosophers on guilt remain meaningful and, in some respects, stark.

HONOR, RESPECT, AND CONSCIENTIOUS SELF-KNOWLEDGE IN KANT

Shame is a feeling or affect that is needed because, on Kant's view, it enlivens our sense of honor; honor must have already taken root for shame to occur.[28] But what is honor, and why is it important? And is it related to or reminiscent of other elements of Kant's moral psychology?

To address these questions, we can start by noting that Kant's account of honor—or more precisely, love of honor (*Ehrliebe*)—is interesting, in part, because of an apparent tension in it.[29] He presents, on the one hand, love of honor as a feeling, a "companion" of virtue, or inclination—he uses all of these descriptions,[30] as his account of honor is not especially systematic—that withdraws itself from the social realm and our tendency to indulge, in our relations with others, problematic inclinations for one-upmanship, domination, and zero-sum interpersonal comparisons. "True love of honor," then, is described by Kant as a type of self-esteem that derives not from social status but rather motivates and exemplifies living up to the dignity in human nature.[31] As such, love of honor must animate our actions, even in cases where we risk finding ourselves on the outs of society and vulnerable to the taunts, scorn, and ridicule that the masses may heap on the undeserving.[32]

Yet Kant also maintains that one who loves honor is appropriately concerned with the esteem shown to her by others. This is because our stance as agents and as knowers is implicated in the recognition of honor. If we are not received as honorable by others, and if they go so far as to view us with contempt, then this will make it difficult for us to extract the respect we rightly deserve and to achieve the ends we set as free, rational beings.[33] For these reasons, it is essential that we aim not only to do what is right or virtuous but that we try, when morally possible, to bring about conditions conducive to a certain type of social reception. We must, if we heed Kant's advice, take care to abide by the norms governing the behavior of each sex, avoiding, for instance, out of wedlock births and the types of vulgar jokes that invite shame.[34] Shame and a deterioration of social standing only imperfectly register a loss of proper self-esteem, but it nonetheless alerts a person to the fact that there is something remiss in the realization of one's moral vocation.

This account of shame and honor is important in light of Williams's critique, but it is further noteworthy because it offers a case study for a certain type of argumentative strategy. Kant stresses, first and foremost, the purity of moral motivation. One's social milieu and the other persons interacted with cannot displace one's own stance as a legislator of norms and the executor of action. But Kant also warns against becoming aloof or antagonistic toward matters of reception or one's social context. Moreover, that Kant is interested in phenomena such as or proximate to shame, and that this argumentative strategy is not a one-off, becomes further clear once we look for similar reasoning elsewhere in Kant's thought.

Consider, for example, Kant's account of respect, particularly in the second *Critique* but also in the *Metaphysics of Morals*. Much of the second *Critique*'s third chapter on the incentives of practical reason stresses that respect is an intellectual feeling produced by an a priori cognition of the moral law. As such, in feeling respect one's attention is led to a moral law that serves as a standard for both action and self-assessment. Concerning the former, we should act only on those maxims compatible with a system of universal laws. Concerning the latter, Kant is clearly distressed by the aforementioned "unsocial sociability" we exhibit and our propensity to color social comparisons with antagonism, envy, ungratefulness, and other dispositions that promote error, self-deceit, and cruelty. For this reason, Kant routinely emphasizes that the moral law itself, and not other human beings, should serve as our benchmark for self-assessment. Respect reveals to us this benchmark.

While Kant most often sticks with this account of what the proper object of our comparisons should be, he also expresses pronounced worries that this limited focus is morally detrimental. In a *Metaphysics of Morals* passage that is stunning for how lucidly it shows Kant attuned to Williams's *exact* worries about the "insensate egoism" implicit in his thought, Kant raises a "casuistical question" about his claim that the moral law alone should inform our self-assessments. Such causistical questions are not moments of devil's advocacy but instead real, tough, as yet unsettled questions about what sorts of practices are most likely to help us as we seek moral truth.[35] In this spirit, he questions his own commitment to the idea that we should compare ourselves to the law alone:

> Is not the human being's feeling for his sublime vocation, that is, his *elation of spirit* (*elation animi*) or esteem for himself, so closely akin to *self-conceit* (*arrogantia*), the very opposite of true *humility* (*humilitas moralis*), that it would be advisable to cultivate humility even in comparing ourselves with other human beings, and not only with the law?[36]

Here we see Kant entertaining, seriously, the idea that a genuine social reality, one independent of the moral law and oneself, is needed for a person to avoid, in her attempt to understand and improve her character, egoistic self-conceit. If we focus only on the moral law within us, is it not possible, he asks, that this elevating or ennobling idea will make us feel as if we are better than all those other persons not so adequately enlightened? We may rightly be worried that in comparing myself to other human beings, I'll bristle in a self-defensive posture and aim to take them down a peg. But we should also worry that in attending only to the underappreciated majesty of the moral law, I'll become fixated on the grandeur of my moral vision and lapse into a smug, self-satisfied arrogance.

This is, importantly, not the only occasion on which Kant fixes on this possibility. In the second *Critique*, Kant maintains that even though respect directs us to a law that is an appropriate object of comparison for us, it is also fitting that this feeling of respect be elicited by persons. While the law remains the standard bearer for conduct and provides the rule for judgment, this is, Kant acknowledges, only one element of the moral knowledge we need or seek. Another person can stir up a feeling of respect in me insofar as he serves as an example that depicts the "observance" of the moral law and allows the "practicability" of morality to be "proved before me in fact."[37] None of this experience, it is important to stress, is constructed voluntarily. No matter how much I may try, afterward, to uncover some defect of character in the person providing an example, Kant claims that before a "humble common man in whom I perceive uprightness of character" my "spirit bows": "*Respect* is a *tribute* we cannot refuse to pay to merit, whether we want to or not; we may indeed withhold it outwardly but we still cannot help feeling it inwardly."[38]

This means that the dynamic—finding oneself simultaneously and involuntarily elevated and humiliated, pleased and pained—that for Kant explains why the moral law itself can enliven good will can again be uncovered through an encounter with real human beings, as they, too, may be capable of having the same humbling effect on us. And to develop further this account of how respect can inform one's search for a comparative touchstone, Kant also considers a case where people learn that a man, once deeply and morally admired, suffers from a character that is in some manner deficient. So long as certain of his efforts are still in place—particularly the attempt to cultivate his own talents in line with the duty of self-perfection—the "common run of admirers" may give up on the man but the "true scholar" still feels respect. For the true scholar sees that this man cultivating talents is "engaged in a business and a calling that make imitation [*Nachahmung*] of such a man to some extent a *law* for him."[39] This clearly complicates Williams's contention that other persons are excluded from Kant's (and our) moral psychology in any complete or straightforward way. Even while Kant tends to maintain that only the moral law should inform self-assessments or guide action, his proposal that we can make, even if only in regard to the duty of self-perfection, another *person*—not the moral law in him but that person *himself*—a law for oneself is a significant concession to the idea that other persons can be directly implicated in one's understanding of how to live well. Similar to shame in that it reveals a point where morality and sociality meet, the experience of the other as to some extent a law for us can properly inform the standards we set for ourselves as we attempt to fulfill our moral vocation. Kant revisits this idea in his comparison of the feeling of respect with the feeling of the sublime in the third *Critique* as well, noting that when there is need to make "intuitable the superiority of the rational vocation of our cognitive faculty over the greatest faculty of sensibility," one may rely on a "subreption" wherein there is a "substitution of a respect for the object"—namely another human being—"for the idea of humanity in our subject."[40]

Finally, there is at least one other philosophical context—one that merges moral psychology with moral epistemology—in which Kant makes similar claims about the importance of other persons. Again, as noted earlier in this section, moral motivation must remain pure and free of empirical influence. But purity is not, for Kant, a desideratum in all other contexts. In particular, when he considers not volition but knowledge and self-knowledge—that is, when attending not to action itself but to the broader cognitive structures that frame volition—it becomes clear that self-knowledge must be impure or empirically conditioned. Consider Kant's discussion of conscience. Very roughly, Kant appears to develop a conception of conscience that focuses not on the "objective" question of what morality demands but on the "subjective" or "first-personal" questions regarding my mindset on the brink of action.[41] If, for instance, I adequately reflected on my proposed maxim and did due diligence to make sure that I considered the complexity of my circumstances, then I can be said to have acted conscientiously.

There are many noteworthy and suggestive elements of Kant's conception of conscience, but a particularly significant one is his confidence that we are capable of multiplying or splitting our sense of personality so that a person can question herself in much the same way—and to much of the same effect as—an external judge would. Kant continues, noting that the adoption of this second persona is facilitated if we imagine a certain type of other in its place. Most typically in Kant's corpus this is God,[42] but at least once Kant also acknowledges that for conscience to avoid being "in contradiction with itself" and to locate "someone other than himself," there is another possibility: "[t]his other may be an actual [*wirkliche*] person or a merely ideal person that reason creates for itself."[43] In other words, the other that provides the voice of conscience falls into the ontological categories proposed by Williams himself. In practical life, Williams insisted a person needs to avoid the "echo chamber" of her "solitary moral voice," but since we also need to avoid a crude heteronomy where another's opinions automatically shape my own, we need to find within an "internalised other."[44] Williams claims this other may be "abstracted and generalised and idealised, but he is potentially somebody rather than nobody, and somebody other than me."[45] This would appear exactly correct, by Kant's lights. And if Williams is right that the presence of this other dovetails with recognition of the role of shame in our lives, then it would seem that the same recognition may be found within Kant.

To conclude this section, we can note that this framing of Kant becomes only more pronounced if one looks past his account of conscience and toward his views regarding self-knowledge more generally. Self-knowledge is, by Kant's lights, essential; it is, in the *Metaphysics of Morals*, the "first command" of all duties to oneself.[46] But it is also a task made extremely difficult by the fact that each person actively obstructs her attempts to self-cognize. Kant notes, for instance, that without realizing it, we construct imaginary, post-facto accounts of what our motives or intentions were.[47] Even with the "keenest self-examination," we may still fail to detect a "covert impulse of self-love" in cases where we take ourselves to have acted from duty.[48] We must avoid the vice depicted in thinkers such as Haller, Lavater, and Pascal, all of whom indulge a misguided naval-gazing that Kant likens to moral hypochondria.[49] Admittedly, Kant does not always make clear either what, in trying to self-know, a person can rely on besides herself and the moral law within her, or what modes of thinking will better facilitate self-knowledge than these ill-conceived and indulgent forays into introspection.[50] I have, however, argued elsewhere that Kant likely believes we should instead envision self-knowledge as relational, as—like other forms of knowledge or cognition—revealed by considering ourselves in experience and in a network of (social) relations with others.[51,52] This alternative gains further support if we view it in light of the pattern that often animates Kant's discussions of moral psychology and that was laid out in this section. We may first see Kant as articulating a guilt morality, but there are important strands of a shame morality, where other persons are indispensably implicated in what's required to live up to our moral vocation, to engage in moral assessment, and to facilitate both conscientious self-reflection and moral self-knowledge.

CONCLUSION: GUILT, REVISITED

In this essay, I have explained where Kant's moral thought relies either on shame, explicitly, or on the practical commitments that, in at least Williams's view, underpin shame. In doing so, I have shown that at least one advocate of the morality system—Kant himself—has a view more complex than that attributed to him by Williams. Kant's morality may be a "guilt morality," but it is also a "shame morality"; each characterization is accurately applied to particular elements of moral theory and practice. Since other advocates of the morality system—like Mill in chapter 3 of *Utilitarianism*, or Rawls in part 3 in *A Theory of Justice*—have likewise offered a healthy and pro-social account of the moral sentiments and our inner lives, it stands to reason that one should have reservations about at least some of Williams's cynicism regarding the morality system. Instantiations of the morality system are not, *pace* Williams, "guilt-only" views.

But to bring this paper to a close, it is important to ask: even if we have made room for shame, how much have we really displaced Williams's suspicions toward the morality system? Guilt, as a reactive attitude that connects an individual with the moral law, still seems to have pride of place for at least Kant. We are to value, directly, only good willing. Autonomous action, or self-legislation and execution, remains the Archimedean point for Kant's morality system. And as Williams sees it, this point cannot bear the weight put on it. We can't make sense of the reasons and motives prescribed by Kant, though we could fuel motivation and find reasons for actions in our relations to other persons—real or idealized. Kant's moral thought doesn't have morality depend on social life in the way Williams's does, and so guilt cannot depend on shame in the way Williams says it must. As Williams said, and as noted earlier, "shame can understand guilt, but guilt cannot understand itself." In his view, the experience of shame makes our practical lives intelligible in a way that guilt cannot.

But in response to this concern, which touches on a foundational point of contention between the two thinkers, there can be no more conciliatory gestures to Williams. Instead, the Kantian should question whether shame can really bear the weight Williams puts on it. Developing this challenge will take some effort, but it may help to proceed by considering Kant and Williams's ethical views from a non-ideal vantage point, that is, from a perspective that takes stock of our moral failures and the threats we face when we try to live up to our ethical ideals.

Turning first to Williams, we might note his repeat example in *Shame and Necessity* of Ajax, who, once he realized how ridiculous he made himself by slaughtering sheep instead of his enemies, commits suicide. Another example, from "A Critique of Utilitarianism," is that of George, the chemist who must entertain whether to take a job that undermines his pacifist values. These two non-ideal scenarios are useful, for Williams, because they enable him to reveal features of his moral outlook. Particularly in the case of Ajax, whose suicide is prefaced by an intense encounter with shame, we see how the views of others—those who can look upon his foolishness—have normative currency for Ajax. And in both Ajax's case and that of George, we can observe a signature feature of Williams's thought that has not, as yet in this paper, been noted, namely his concern with integrity. Both men are enveloped by a set of attitudes and ground projects that give their life narrative shape and meaning, and while Ajax and George can only work out these projects in dialogue with others, real and idealized, both men are nonetheless reliably motivated to maintain (in the case of George) or restore (in the case of Ajax) integrity to their lives. This interest in integrity, informed by an acute sensitivity to social circumstance, permits them to navigate the ethical risks they face.

Williams thus envisions the delicate moments in practical life as those when a person loses her foothold temporarily but is generally able to restore it by keying back into the ground projects that matter and the empirical context that informs them. But Kant, and a number of those who find his writings compelling, would find this image of what most threatens us and how we can respond not only deeply misguided. They would also find it misguided in a way that has relevance for an account of guilt and shame. Two points can be noted.

1) Whereas Williams is confident that ethical reflection is productively informed by a continuity between the values endorsed by an agent and by his peers, Kantians see less reason to be placated. At the least, they will challenge any insinuation that Kant's emphasis on ethical self-reliance stems from a mere purity fetish or a nascent commitment to egoism. Such self-reliance is not valued for its own sake. Instead, it matters because of our susceptibility to moral disorientation. This feature of practical life may, admittedly, be underdiscussed in Kant's most well-known ethical writings, but in texts such as *What does it mean to orient oneself in thinking?*, we find a perspicuous account what such disorientation is like and how, to address it, a person may need recourse to values that can be detached from social context.

Drawing on a vivid and palpable example regarding physical space, Kant asks us to imagine approaching a city street where all buildings and other landmarks are newly reversed, with those that used to be on our right now on our left and vice versa. Were our only directional cues those that could come from these external markers, then we would be helplessly lost. But, Kant notes, a person in fact retains the ability to reorient herself. She has access to a subjective ground of differentiation, as she can rely on her internal sense of left and right to provide a point of stability in the midst of upheaval. And, Kant suggests, moral space can be like physical space in this regard. We can appreciate that if a person is surrounded by patterns of moral distortion and inversion—if, for instance, one's community commonly mistakes vulgarity for authenticity, nationalism for patriotism, or lack of empathy for a free-thinking independence—then a subjective ground of differentiation may be needed to right ourselves and prevent disorientation. Kantians, then, will see Williams as too sanguine about how disordered social life can become. They'll also argue that if an example like Ajax seems persuasive, it's likely because its readers—who are, as "almost all of us" are, Kantians—presume shame will guide Ajax only certain directions, implicitly confident that guilt works as an internal moral compass that will stop him from pursuing certain other paths.[53] They'll argue, then, that Williams's account of shame succeeds only if it is a foil to Kantian guilt and not its alternative.

2) Recall, also, Williams's emphasis on integrity. It animates Ajax, George, and still other examples found in Williams, like his famous treatment of Paul Gauguin.[54] But where Williams sees integrity as a robust and reliable motive in human life, Kant, in place of this, often presents an image of human beings as, to a surprising degree and for lack of a better way to put it, content to be sellouts. While Kant does stress that the competing incentives of hedonistic self-love and respect for the law present human beings with a crucial choice, in his most interesting moments he steps back from this and notes that the real problem isn't that self-love simply is highly attractive. The real problem is that human beings are generally willing to put a price on that which they know is beyond exchange or market value.[55] There may be the occasional Ajax, Gauguin, or George, but we should not overlook the banal, unglamorous cases in which we abandon our moral and personal values for things or experiences that please but that are unmistakably, and by our own lights, not worth it.[56] For Kant, this type of irrationality is ubiquitous, but that makes it no less profound and no more intelligible.

Kantians may rightly worry, then, that Williams, in his stress on shame, promises intelligibility where it would perhaps be out of place; shame, it seems, can't understand all that it promises to and it certainly can't understand a lot about guilt. While guilt or *Schuld* is not a concept that Kant puts to much direct use, if Williams is correct that it's a reactive attitude that starts and stops, as it were, with the individual and the violation of the law, then Kant's ethics is probably a guilt ethics and is so for a good reason. There's no insight others can provide to make comprehensible why in each person there is an "invisible enemy," one implicated in our eagerness to trade dignity or integrity for mere fancies or comparatively worthless goods.[57] Shame can't demystify this, and guilt at least has no pretense of being able to do so. Again, if almost all of us are Kantians now, this may be part of the reason why.

NOTES

1. Williams (1993), 100.
2. See, for instance, Williams (1985a), 83–84.

3. Williams's worries about the "quasi-legal" framework of much contemporary moral thought are noted in an interview (1985b). For the reference, I am indebted to Chappell (2018). The "quasi-juridical" character of the morality system is also noted in Sussman (2018), 790. Thanks to Michael Sigrist for his help on this point.

4. Here I am aided by A.A. Long (2007), 166–67.

5. Williams's scorn for Plato is especially strong in *Shame and Necessity*. See 99–101. Yet as noted by Long, Williams was more amenable to Platonic thought at points both early and late in his career. See Long (2007), 179.

6. Anscombe (1958), 2.

7. Williams (1993), 222.

8. In regard to this particular example, one might think it would occasion only embarrassment and not shame. But shame and embarrassment are not neatly distinguished in Williams's writings. See Williams (1993), 89–90.

9. I have chosen my words carefully here, leaving room for Kant's proposal that non-moral endeavors, like the attempt to find happiness, may be judged good under certain conditions even if they cannot be good *tout court*.

10. I offer further discussion shortly.

11. Williams (1985a), 174.

12. Williams's implied analogy is widely noted. See, among others, Darwall (2013), 89.

13. Williams (1985a), 200.

14. Williams (1981b), 252. For the reference, I am indebted to Long (2007), 158.

15. Williams (1985a), 174. For the reference, I am indebted to Long (2007), 159.

16. I do, though, weigh in a bit about this standoff in this paper's conclusion.

17. Williams (1993), 92.

18. Williams (1993), 93.

19. See Kant (1996c), 6:430; Kant (1996c), 6:490; and Kant (1996d), 6:117. See also Kant (1996a), 5:98, where he associates ethical misconduct with self-reproach and censure. Here and in the remainder of the paper, references to Kant cite the *Akademie* edition volume and page numbers, as these are reproduced in the Cambridge translation of Kant's works.

20. Kant (1996c), 6:460.

21. Kant (1996c), 6:392; see also Kant (1996d), 6:38.

22. Kant (1996d), 6:61.

23. See Kant (2007b), 9:465, 9:478, and 9:484. Note also that Kant's praise of shame includes the caveat that those who admonish the adolescents must be adults. Youth, he says, should never be admonished by someone of the same age. See (2007b), 9:491.

24. Kant (2007a), 7:255.

25. Williams (1993), 102.

26. Though he does not elaborate, Rawls claims that given Kant's account of moral education, it is shame, not guilt, that one feels in cases of moral failure. See Rawls (1971), 264.

27. Kant (2007a), 7:255.

28. Kant (2007b), 9:484. See also (2007c), 2:218.

29. My understanding of Kant on honor owes much to Sussman (2008), Thomason (2013), Bayefsky (2013), and Denis (2014).

30. Love of honor is described as a virtue or a companion to virtue at (2007c, 2:218) and (2007b, 7:257). It is described as a feeling at, for instance (2007b, 7:193). For an account of love of honor as an inclination, see (2007c, 9:492).

31. The expression "true love of honor" appears multiple times in the lectures notes taken by Johann Friedrich Vigilantius. See Kant (1997), 27:666, 27:695, and 27:696.

32. Kant (2007a), 7:257. See also Denis (2014), 201–02.

33. See Thomason (2013), 235–36 and Sussman (2008).

34. See Kant (1996c), 6:336, and (2007c), 2:234.

35. Kant (1996c), 6:411.

36. Kant (1996c), 6:437.

37. Kant (1996a), 5:77.

38. Ibid.

39. Kant (1996a), 5:78. My italics.

40. Kant (2000), 5:257.

41. See Moyar (2008) and Paton (1979).

42. See Kant (1996c), 6:439.

43. Kant (1996c), 6:438.

44. Williams (1993), 84–85.

45. Williams (1993), 84.

46. Kant (1996c), 6:441.

47. "[T]he human being comes to regard that which he has intentionally put in his mind as something that previously already must have been there, and he believes that he has merely discovered in the depths of his soul what he has forced on himself" (Kant (2007a), 7:162). The same concern about self-reflection is noted also at 7:133 and 7:143.

48. Kant (1996b), 4:407.

49. Kant (2007a), 7:133 and 7:162.

50. For further discussion of Kant's concerns regarding introspection, see Makkreel (2014) and my (2018), 162–64 and 171–72.

51. By "experience" here, I mean what Kant calls *Erfahrung*.

52. Papish (2018), 177–78.

53. Such as violence against others.

54. Williams (1981a), 24–25 and 36–38.

55. See, for example, Kant (1996b), 4:435.

56. I say "moral and personal values" here because in addition to sacrificing our moral principles, Kant makes it clear that we sacrifice our non-moral values too. We routinely jeopardize our prudential commitments by letting ourselves develop passions, which are deeply rooted dispositions characterized by a willingness to sacrifice happiness to indulge irrational desires—such as a desire for social dominance, or for lust—even though they promise to make us more miserable in the long run. On this point, see Sussman (2001).

57. Kant (1996d), 6:57 and 6:59.

REFERENCES

Anscombe, G.E.M. (1958). "Modern Moral Philosophy." *Philosophy*, 33 (124): 1–19.
Bayefsky, Rachel (2013). "Dignity, Honour, and Human Rights: Kant's Perspective." *Political Theory*, 49 (6): 809–37.
Chappell, Sophie-Grace (2018). "Bernard Williams." https://plato.stanford.edu/entries/williams-bernard/. Accessed September 21, 2018.
Darwall, Stephen (2013). *Morality, Authority, and Law: Essays in Second-Personal Ethics I*. Oxford: Oxford University Press.
Denis, Lara (2014). "Love of Honor as a Kantian Virtue," in Alix Cohen (ed.), *Kant on Emotion and Value* (London: Palgrave Macmillan).
Kant, Immanuel (1996a). *Critique of Practical Reason*, trans. Mary Gregor. In M. Gregor (ed.), *Practical Philosophy*. Cambridge: Cambridge University Press.
———, (1996b). *Groundwork of the Metaphysics of Morals*, trans. Mary Gregor. In M. Gregor (ed.), *Practical Philosophy*. Cambridge: Cambridge University Press.
———, (1996c). *Metaphysics of Morals*, trans. Mary Gregor. In M. Gregor (ed.), *Practical Philosophy*. Cambridge: Cambridge University Press.
———, (1996d). *Religion within the Boundaries of Mere Reason*, trans. George di Giovanni. In A.W. Wood and George di Giovanni (eds), *Religion and Rational Theology*. Cambridge: Cambridge University Press.
———, (1996e). *What Does It Mean to Orient Oneself in Thinking?*, trans. Allen Wood. In A.W. Wood and George di Giovanni (eds), *Religion and Rational Theology*. Cambridge: Cambridge University Press.
———, (1997). *Kant on the Metaphysics of Morals: Vigilantius's Lecture Notes*, trans. P. Heath. In Peter Heath and J. B. Schneewind (eds), *Lectures on Ethics*. Cambridge: Cambridge University Press.
———, (2000). *Critique of the Power of Judgment*, trans. Paul Guyer and Eric Matthews. Cambridge: Cambridge University Press.
———, (2007a). *Anthropology from a Pragmatic Point of View*, trans. Robert B. Louden. In Robert Louden and Günter Zöller (eds), *Anthropology, History, and Education*. Cambridge: Cambridge University Press.
———, (2007b). *Lectures on Pedagogy*, trans. Robert B. Louden. In Robert Louden and Günter Zöller (eds), *Anthropology, History, and Education*. Cambridge: Cambridge University Press.
———, (2007c). *Observations On the Feeling of the Beautiful and Sublime*, trans. Paul Guyer. In Robert Louden and Günter Zöller (eds), *Anthropology, History, and Education*. Cambridge: Cambridge University Press.
Long, A.A. (2007). "Williams on Greek Literature and Philosophy," in Alan Thomas (ed.), *Bernard Williams* (Cambridge: Cambridge University Press).
Makkreel, Rudolf (2014). "Self-Cognition and Self-Assessment," in Alix Cohen (ed.), *Kant's Lectures on Anthropology: A Critical Guide*. Cambridge: Cambridge University Press.
Moyar, Dean (2008). "Unstable Autonomy: Conscience and Judgment in Kant's Moral Philosophy." *Journal of Moral Philosophy*, 5 (3): 327–60.
Papish, Laura (2018). *Kant on Evil, Self-Deception, and Moral Reform*. Oxford: Oxford University Press.

Paton, H.J. (1979). "Conscience and Kant." *Kant-Studien*, 70 (1-4): 239–51.
Rawls, John (1971). *A Theory of Justice*. Cambridge, MA: Harvard University Press.
Sussman, David (2001). *The Idea of Humanity: Anthroponomy and Anthropology in Kant's Ethics*. New York: Routledge.
———, (2008). "Shame and Punishment in Kant's *Doctrine of Right*." *Philosophical Quarterly*, 58 (231): 299–317.
———, (2018). "Is Agent-Regret Rational?" *Ethics*, 128 (4): 788–808.
Thomason, Krista K. (2013). "Shame and Contempt in Kant's Moral Theory." *Kantian Review*, 18 (2): 221–40.
Williams, Bernard (1973). "A Critique of Utilitarianism," in J.J.C. Smart and Bernard Williams, *Utilitarianism: For and Against*. Cambridge: Cambridge University Press.
———, (1981a). *Moral Luck: Philosophical Papers 1973–1980*. Cambridge: Cambridge University Press.
———, (1981b). "Philosophy," in Moses Finley (ed.), *The Legacy of Greece: A New Appraisal*. Oxford: Oxford University Press.
———, (1985a). *Ethics and the Limits of Philosophy*. London: Fontana.
———, (1985b). "The Uses of Philosophy." An interview for the *Center Magazine* with Donald McDonald. November/December 1983, 40–49.
———, (1993). *Shame and Necessity*. Berkeley: University of California Press.

Chapter 15

Moral Autonomy and Relationality of Confucian Shame

Beyond Western Guilt and Shame

Bongrae Seok

GUILT, SHAME, AND CONFUCIAN SHAME

Guilt and shame are the two self-critical moral emotions that are often compared against each other. In many studies of psychology, guilt is characterized as a healthy sense of morality and a constructive and adaptive emotion, but shame is characterized as a feeling of failure and the stressful experience of the vulnerable self. Guilt is a "more articulated experience than shame and a more dignified one," but shame is "the affect of indignity of defeat, of transgression, and of alienation."[1] There are, however, less contrastive and more integrative approaches to the self-critical moral emotions. Although they have different moral psychological orientations, guilt and shame are often observed to have many characteristics in common.[2] Some scholars argue that guilt and shame can be felt together or they have overlapping boundaries.[3] Others argue that shame has positive and constructive properties.[4] They point out that the inner voice of conscience and repentance, typically ascribed to guilt, can be applicable to shame.[5] More broadly, they develop their arguments against the negative and inferior images of shame and highlight the constructive moral psychological roles played by shame in one's moral awareness and moral development.[6]

It seems that the two general viewpoints, i.e., the contrastive and the integrative interpretations, exhaust the whole possibility of explaining the moral psychological nature of guilt and shame.[7] Are there any other ways to explain self-reflective and self-critical moral emotions? Are guilt and shame fully and completely captured and explained by the two general viewpoints? In this chapter, I will discuss Confucian shame and analyze its moral psychological characteristics. Confucian shame refers to self-critical moral emotions such as *chi*恥, *xiu* 羞, *can* 慚, *kui* 愧/媿, and *zuo* 怍 discussed in the early Confucian texts. *Chi* (恥) is the most common character of shame in Confucian texts, and it shares general characteristics (i.e., being self-critical, strongly reactive, and affecting the whole self, etc.) of shame currently discussed in Western psychology and philosophy.[8] However, it is not an ordinary feeling of the vulnerable self or an emotion of self-condemnation. Nor is it easily explained by guilt, although Confucian shame shares many characteristics (such as inner, reflective, and moral self-awareness) with guilt. It is a unique form of moral emotion, not simply an emotion of self-condemnation and retrospective depression (i.e., regret), but an emotion of self-conscious and self-constructive enrichment that can be cultivated and refined. In fact, in many early Confucian texts, such as the *Analects*, the *Mencius*, and the *Xunzi* written in the Warring States period (475–221 BCE) of ancient China, shame is described as an emotion and a disposition that need to be cultivated, refined, and perfected for a virtuous life.

One can get, therefore, conflicting images of Confucian shame. On the one hand, Confucian shame is different from shame, i.e., a defensive, evasive, depressive, and self-condemning emotion. It is a constructive and responsive emotion that is self-reflective and self-cultivating. Confucius believes that shame is an ideal disposition one should cultivate (*Analects*, 13.20).[9] On the other hand, Confucian shame is different from guilt, i.e., an inner self-critical feeling against moral violations. Unlike guilt, Confucian shame concerns about the integrity of the whole self, not just particular actions or decisions. It is also sensitive and responsive to others' evaluation and criticism of one's self. In many passages of early Confucian texts, Confucian shame is described as an emotion that can be felt in front of or in relation to others (role models, counselors, mentors, imaginary moral figures, and ideally virtuous characters). In the book of *Mencius* (1A5, 2B18, 7A29), shame is often discussed in this interpersonal and communal context.[10] Because of these conflicting moral psychological properties, the clear and contrastive distinction between guilt and shame is hardly maintained in Confucian moral tradition. That is, Confucian shame has both guilt-like and shame-like characteristics.

The heterogeneous or ambiguous nature of Confucian shame, however, does not imply that Confucian shame is simply a delicate balance or an intriguing combination of guilt and shame for its moral psychological goals of self-regulation and moral development. Although it shares many characteristics with guilt and shame, it is not just a moral psychological hybrid of guilt and shame. Unlike guilt and shame, i.e., retrospective and self-critical emotions, Confucian shame has prospective and self-reflective properties. It is a unique moral emotion and disposition, a form of moral excellence one should develop and cultivate for one's ideal character.[11] This highly idealized, prospective, and developmental nature of Confucian shame takes one to the very different territory of self-reflective moral experience beyond guilt and shame.

In what follows, I will discuss and analyze Confucian shame and its philosophical and moral psychological significance by focusing on its unique characteristics that are not easily captured and explained by guilt or shame. I will take three steps to analyze Confucian shame. First, I will explore and survey three different theoretical approaches to shame. I will discuss how shame is understood in these theories and how it is compared with guilt. Second, I will discuss whether Confucian shame can be properly identified as an inner, self-critical moral emotion. Third, I will explain why it is a unique moral emotion that shares certain characteristics with guilt and shame yet different from them.

SELF-REPROACHING SHAME: SHAME AS A FEELING OF THE DISGRACED AND VULNERABLE SELF

Shame is often described as a negative and stressful feeling of the vulnerable self. Tangney and Dearing state that shame involves "fairly global negative evaluations of the self—the sense that '*I* am an inferior, inadequate, unworthy (or bad, immoral, unprincipled) person.'"[12] Shame is felt as an inner torment and a sickness of soul.[13] It is also a punishment, self-condemnation, and self-torturing in front of others. It is not only a dangerous but also socially and morally irresponsive emotion. Because it affects the whole person, shame can motivate a defensive, evasive, and protective concern for one's self without considering others and their well-being. Tangney and her colleagues characterize shame as a negative and unpleasant experience to one's *whole* self.[14] According to them, guilt focuses on a particular aspect of the self, such as one's action, decision, or attitude, but shame affects the whole self or person because in one's experience of shame, one feels that one's whole self is disgraced and criticized. Therefore, shame becomes a heavy psychological burden to shamed individuals and, as a result, they have no psychological room to consider others and their wellbeing or suffering.[15] As shame develops narrow self-interest and motivates self-protective or self-defensive actions, it becomes a more egocentric but less altruistic emotion.[16] Lewis explains shame from this viewpoint of the defensive and disgraced ego. When one feels shame, one becomes an object of scorn but others become a source of scorn.[17] For this reason, one tries to protect one's vulnerable self by avoiding others and hiding from their sight. Shame is, therefore, a socially maladaptive emotion: it focuses on one's own disgraced and depressed self and motivates hiding and escaping behaviors but does not pay attention to others who are affected negatively by one's action.[18]

It is important to note that both Tangney and Lewis contrast shame and guilt from the psychological viewpoint of one's relation to others. According to them, shame is not a moral emotion because it is a self-enclosed or self-centered emotion without any room for one's consideration of other. In contrast, guilt is a morally responsive emotion because it feels and considers others' suffering that might be caused by one's action. If shame is a feeling of "my whole self is disgraced" or "I am hurt by others," guilt is an empathic sense of others' suffering such as "others are hurt" or "they feel pain" because of my action. Whether it is because of the *scope* of self-criticism (i.e., part or whole) or one's *relation* to others (i.e., self-concerning or other-concerning), shame and guilt show two different moral psychological orientations. That is, shame is a self-centered experience of the vulnerable self in front of others, but guilt is a more discrete and dignified sense of one's moral self-awareness of others' suffering caused by one's moral violation.

Because of its obsession with the self-image and its narrow interest in self-interest, shame is often understood as an underdeveloped and immature emotion. Tangney states that shame is the immature emotion of narrow self-interest.[19] Creighton states that "Shame feelings precede the development of the superego [a Freudian sense of the broad self that includes one's narrow self in its relation to one's own self-consciousness and others], although they may later be integrated into the superego formation. Guilt develops later during the Oedipal phase and requires the presence of a superego."[20]

One can see this type of negative characterization of shame (shame as an immature and depressive sense of weak, inferior, and damaged self) in many psychological studies.[21] It is also a popular view of people in the WEIRD (Western, Educated, Industrialized, Rich, and Democratic) societies. Creighton states that "Shame, with its corresponding fear of rejection, is not a very effective sanction in American society, where individuals are encouraged to become independent."[22] Following the same line of reasoning, Scheff states that "Over the last 200 years in the history of modern societies, shame virtually disappeared. The denial of shame has been institutionalized in Western society."[23] That is, shame comes with an old system of repressive regulation that does not function effectively in a society that is founded upon the value of individual freedom and moral autonomy. Shame is not only an immature and depressive psychological state but also an outdated and ineffective way of regulating human behavior.[24]

Because of the negative, obsessive, and defensive tendencies of shame that are often harmful to the mental health of shamed individuals, some psychologists suggest the replacement of shame by a more mature sense of morality.[25] Creighton states that shame should be replaced by a more mature sense of morality, and Tangney and Dearing suggest a conscious shift from shame to a discrete sense of morality.[26] They all suggest that, because of the negative, maladaptive, and depressive characteristics, shame should be avoided, overcome, or replaced by a healthy and constructive moral emotions such as guilt.[27] As I will discuss shortly, however, both the contrastive distinction between guilt and shame and the negative characterization of shame are rarely seen in Confucianism. Confucian shame shares many moral psychological features with guilt and it, as a constructive moral emotion, plays important roles in the cultivation of ideal character traits.

ARISTOTELIAN SHAME: SHAME AS A REGULATIVE SENSE OF APPROPRIATENESS AND SELF-INTEGRITY

Aristotle defines shame and shamelessness (i.e., having or lacking a reactive and self-critical sense of appropriateness) as "Pain or disturbance in regard to bad things, whether present, past, or future, which seem likely to involve us in discredit; and shamelessness as contempt or indifference in regard to these same bad things" (*Rhetoric*, 1383b15). That is, shame is not simply a sense of one's compromised social reputation but a self-reflective sense of appropriateness. It is a sense of what is suitable, fitting, or relevant to a given circumstance and the opposite of shamelessness, not a feeling of ashamedness. It is important to note that the shame, Aristotle discusses here, is not just a retrospective emotion of regret (ashamedness) but also a prospective sense and concern of one's self-integrity (sense of shame). According to Aristotle, one can feel shame on future events where one's sense of appropriateness and one's self-integrity can be compromised. Shame can be prospective as well as retrospective. Additionally, in this interpretation of shame, the opposite of shame is not pride but shamelessness, i.e., lack of moral sense or moral integrity. Aristotle points out that this sense of how one should behave and feel in a given situation is critically important in the cultivation of virtue (*Nichomachean Ethics*, 1128b17-22, 1179b12-17). The reason one feels shame is not simply because one's wrongful behavior is seen by others (i.e., one is disgraced or dishonored in front of others), but because one's self-integrity is (actually or possibly) endangered.

Shame, in this context, is different from socially and externally imposed or inflicted emotions such as honor or pride because one can be ashamed of imaginary situations or future events with or without others' presence. That is, the essential nature of shame, according to Aristotle, is one's concern for one's self-integrity, not for one's honor and pride in front of others. Throwing away one's shield or taking to flight in a battle (*Rhetoric*, 1383b20) is an example of shame used by Aristotle. It is a shameful action not because others are watching it but because it threatens one's integrity and virtue: It is a cowardly behavior and a betrayal to one's community. Aristotelian shame, therefore, refers to this kind of self-conscious emotion for one's integrity and consistency that guard against any (past/future and monitored/unmonitored) irresponsible and irrespective behaviors.

As I explained in the previous section, shame, unlike guilt, is not empathic.[28] It focuses on one's shamed self in front of others but does not consider others' suffering caused by one's violation. For this reason, many psychologists believe that shame is not a moral emotion but a self-interested social emotion, i.e., fear of losing one's pride or face in front of others. Aristotelian shame, however, is a moral emotion, i.e., one's concern for one's self-integrity and virtuous character in one's interaction with others in one's community. In this sense, Aristotelian shame is not sharply distinguished from guilt. It shares empathic elements with guilt. It concerns for self-integrity, not for the sake of an individual's isolated self-interest but for the sake of her ideal character in relation to others in one's community. Aristotelian shame is also constructive and beneficial to young people who are in the process of developing their characters and virtues. He states that "the feeling of shame is suitable for youth. . . . For we think it right for young people to be prone to shame, since they live by their feelings, and hence often go astray, but are restrained by shame; and hence we praise young people who are prone to shame" (*Nichomachean Ethics*, 1128b17-22).[29] That is, Aristotelian shame, although not always a pleasant emotion, is not a destructive and immoral or amoral emotion. Rather it is a moral, constructive, and prospective emotion.

Aristotelian shame, of course, is a form of shame. It is a stressful feeling (i.e., fear, concern, or anxiety) of one's compromised self-integrity and bad reputation (*Nicomachean Ethics*, 1128b10–13; 1115a12–14). It affects the whole person, not an action or decision made by the person. It reflects one's sensitivity and responsiveness to others' opinions (*Eudemian Ethics*, 1233b26–28; *Rhetoric*, 1384b27-31). Guilt, however, is a discrete emotion. It is not caused by one's whole self being disgraced and exposed to others. Nor is it deeply involved with others' opinions. Guilt focuses more on one's own self-conscious inner voice than others' voices. However, Aristotelian shame is not necessarily a destructive or depressive emotion. It is a constructive, holistic, and active form of moral sense that does not cause deviant and depressive psychopathologies.

Ancient Greek culture celebrates military heroes and their honor and pride. Aristotle, however, carefully distinguishes shame from the heroic emotions of honor and pride that depends heavily on the public image. He explains shame as one's concern for virtue and self-integrity and shows how shame can be a genuine moral emotion that includes a broad category of constructive moral feelings, some of which can be comparable with guilt. If one can distinguish two forms of shame, i.e., social shame (i.e., fear of losing one's social status and prestige) and moral shame (i.e., fear of losing one's moral integrity),

Aristotelian shame belongs to the latter. It is a healthy sense of self-integrity, not narrowly focused and self-interested concern for one's endangered or compromised self in front of others.³⁰

RELATIONAL SHAME: SHAME AS A RELATIONAL MORAL SENSE

According to many Western psychologists, guilt and shame are distinct self-critical emotions. Guilt and shame have different targets (part of person versus whole person), inputs (others' pain caused by one's moral violation versus one's vulnerable and disgraced self), outputs (apology/reconciliation versus hide/escape), and evaluations (low evaluation of one's action versus low evaluation of one's self).³¹ Most important, guilt and shame have different moral psychological characteristics: guilt promotes "the progressive and adaptive development of the morally autonomous and responsible self but shame motivates "childish, regressive, and maladaptive reactions to moral or social failures."³² To simplify, guilt, by being criticized by the inner voice, comes out of the responsible and autonomous self but shame, by being disgraced by others, comes out of the heteronomous self. The third approach to shame challenges this contrastive characterization of guilt and shame.

In many psychological studies, guilt and shame are sharply distinguished on the matters of autonomy: Guilt is primarily an emotion of self-reflection of autonomous individuals but shame is primarily an emotion that derives from others' perception of one's disgraced self. A guilt-ridden self is a regulative or governing self, but a shame-ridden self is a weak and vulnerable self. At the heart of this dichotomous distinction (guilt-autonomy versus shame-heteronomy) lies a particular notion of moral agency. Moral agency refers to a set of properties that can make an individual a morally capable person. One of the conditions of moral agency is autonomy. A moral agent is an autonomous individual who can act and make decisions on the basis of her own thoughts independently of others' thoughts and viewpoints.³³ A classic view of autonomous moral agency can be found in Kant's moral philosophy. Kant states that "two things are required for inner freedom: being one's own master in a given case (*animus sui compos*), and ruling oneself (*imperium in semetipsum*)" (G6.407).³⁴ "Freedom" here means one's self-initiated ability to act morally and Kant designates autonomy as a key component of one's moral ability that can go beyond one's natural or emotional inclinations such as basic desires and passion that are passive and unregulated.³⁵

Many philosophers, however, criticize this narrow and restrictive notion of moral agency. Some argue that full autonomy is practically inappropriate. Instead, a partial (procedural or formal) notion of autonomy is suitable for moral agency.³⁶ Others criticize independence and isolation in the notion of autonomy. Lévinas for example, argues that autonomy promotes narrow individualism and it can reflect disguised self-interest and self-gratification.³⁷ One should, instead, be open and responsive to others and their needs. Feminist philosophers such as Donchin, Gilligan, Mackenzie, Stoljar, McLeod, and Sherwin argue that autonomy is an overly restrictive notion of moral agency because the self is an intrinsically relational and interdependent entity.³⁸ That is, one should understand agency not from the perspective of individual independence but from the perspective of the fundamental relationality and the interconnectedness of the self and others. They all argue that moral agency can be found in relational and interdependent individuals.

The same can be true of the moral agency involved in the experience of guilt and shame. According to the psychological interpretation of guilt and shame that I discussed in the previous sections, guilt, but not shame, comes out of one's autonomous moral sense. That is, guilt presupposes inner and autonomous moral agency, but shame only reflects the weak and heterogeneous self that is vulnerable and susceptible to external forces. The third approach challenges and criticizes this interpretation of guilt and shame. Since human beings are intrinsically and perhaps existentially relational and communal (or communo-nomous) beings, the autonomy based moral agency is not necessarily a good way to understand the distinction between guilt and shame and their moral psychological orientations.³⁹

From the perspective of the relationality and communality of moral agency, Williams criticizes the solipsistic orientations in many theories of moral agency.⁴⁰ He argues against ethical Cartesianism, i.e., ethics of inner independence or autonomy at the foundation of moral agency. He does not believe that abstract or absolute notions such as the inner self and the pure soul help us understand the intrinsically relational nature of moral agency and moral emotion.⁴¹ The same can be true of the unique moral psychological nature of shame. According to him, shame does not come out of the solipsistic, abstract, and independent self (i.e., the Platonic soul or Cartesian ego) but the interdependent and interconnected self of living individuals in their social, cultural, and political environments. He specifically argues that the modern concept of inner autonomous agency is not necessary when it comes to understand the moral significance of shame. He states that many scholars "see all Greek culture as governed by notions that are nearer to shame than to a full notion of moral guilt with its implications of freedom and autonomy; they believe that moral guilt was attained only by the modern consciousness [of inner autonomous agency].... These stories are deeply misleading, both historically and ethically."⁴² That is, the inner and autonomous moral consciousness developed in modern philosophy does not do full justice to the unique sense of morality developed in shame. According to him, shame is a moral sense of the interrelated, communal self, not the solipsistic Cartesian self.

Lacking autonomous moral consciousness, therefore, does not make shame a morally irresponsive and submissive emotion. Rather, shame, with its relational and communal sense of appropriateness, is a natural feeling of interdependent and interconnected human beings that can represent a unique form of moral sensitivity. Many scholars argue for this non-solipsistic, i.e., communal, sense of appropriateness as the foundation of morality and virtue. Morgan's, Nussbaum's, and Schneider's and Williams's interpretations of shame all emphasize the intrinsically social and relational side of shame in human moral psychology.[43] Nussbaum argues that the culturally variable and socially embedded nature of human existence should not be abstracted away for the sake of the universal autonomy of moral agency and the independence of the moral self.[44] That is, a sense of moral violation and a feeling of self-criticism do not necessarily derive from the pure and universal moral imperatives of the autonomous inner agency but from other sources that reflect the intrinsic interdependence and relationality of human being.[45] In this regard, Morgan even talks about a unique form of shame, i.e., collective shame. He states that "We normally think of shame as a private emotion, one that we have on our own, but . . . I speak of a shame that we share with others, with members of our group, of our nation, and of all humankind."[46]

According to the third approach, shame is a relational moral emotion concretely embedded in the moral and social habitat of human living. It can be felt without full autonomy in its strict sense. It represents the variable, vulnerable, and interdependent nature of human being yet it shows how our socially embedded moral sense can become a self-reflective moral emotion.[47] Although the distinction between guilt and shame is generally accepted in many academic disciplines beyond psychology, their exact moral psychological nature is not fully defined and fixed by abstract notions such the eternal soul, the solipsistic mind or the autonomous self.[48] Instead, guilt and shame should be understood by their open and interactive functions in the social, cultural, and political environments of human living that are always relational, interpersonal, and communal.[49]

CONFUCIAN SHAME AS AN INNER MORAL SENSE

As I discussed in the previous sections, shame is associated with social failure (a fear of losing one's reputation) or moral distress (a self-reflective sense of moral violation) in many schools of Western philosophy and psychology. Mostly, it is a stressful and self-critical feeling of social or moral violations.[50] In Confucianism (the school of *Ru* 儒, a Chinese philosophical tradition of moral cultivation and virtue), however, shame is not necessarily stressful experience of moral violation. It often refers to one's inner disposition and self-reflective moral ability. In fact, shame is one of the *important* Confucian moral emotions. In early Confucian texts such as the *Analects*, the *Mencius*, and the *Xunzi*, shame words (*chi*恥, *xiu* 羞, *can* 慚, *kui* 愧/媿, and *zuo* 怍) are mentioned and discussed more frequently than words of Confucian virtues such as courage (*yong*勇) and wisdom (*zhi* 智). Shame words appear fifty-eight times in the ancient Confucian texts, but courage (*yong*) and wisdom (*zhi*) appear only thirty-six and twenty-eight times, respectively.[51]

In the *Analects*, shame is an inner sense of morality and self-regulative ability. The following passage demonstrates that Confucius understood shame in this positive moral sense.

> The Master [Confucius] said, "If the people be led by laws, and uniformity sought to be given them by punishments, they will try to avoid the punishment, but have no sense of shame. If they be led by virtue, and uniformity sought to be given them by the rules of propriety, they will have the sense of shame, and moreover will become good." (子曰 道之以政 齊之以刑 民免而無恥 道之以德 齊之以禮 有恥且格, *Analects,* 2.3)

In this passage, shame is compared and contrasted with the external regulatory systems of human behavior such as the legal and punitive systems. Confucius believes in the superiority of the inner sense of regulation to the external enforcement. Shame is such an inner moral ability that motivates people to become virtuous independently of external regulations or coercive measures. In another passage of the *Analects*, Confucius praises Zi Lu (one of his disciples) who does not feel ashamed of his poor appearance (shabby dress, dirty face, etc.) in front of others (*Analects*, 9.27). Also, he openly criticizes fine words and excessive kindness to deceive others: he states that he is ashamed of these external decorations and hypocritical demeanors (*Analects*, 5.25). In these passages, shame is related to an inner moral sense, not a shameful feeling in front of others (external audience). That is, shame is not an experience of embarrassment or disgrace in an interpersonal interaction but of a self-conscious and inner moral sense.

Since Confucian shame works with internalized moral norms, it is often interpreted as internal shame, i.e., a self-critical emotion that functions independently of external audience or external authority. External shame, however, is caused or motivated by external audience or authority (i.e., others' presence, views, standards, or sanctions).[52] If Confucian shame is a form of internal shame, it shares the inner moral characteristics with guilt. As discussed in the previous sections, guilt is defined by its inner awareness of moral violation and, for that reason, the distinction between guilt and shame is typically made on the basis of their internal and external orientations. Simply speaking, guilt is an internally motivated emotion, but shame is an externally inflicted emotion. In Confucianism, however, this contrastive characterization of guilt and shame does not make sense. Confucius sees an inner sense of morality in shame that shares the inner orientation with guilt.

Many comparative scholars and sinologists, such as Ng, Roetz, and Santangelo point out the inner orientation of Confucian shame and its guilt-like properties.[53] Regarding Confucian shame, Ng states that "distinction between guilt and shame, expressed in series of contrasts such as guilt-internal and shame-external prevents us from a fuller and more accurate understanding of either, and better given up."[54] Although Santangelo is cautious in completely rejecting the distinction between guilt and shame in Confucian moral philosophy, he believes that Confucian shame has a strong inner orientation.[55] He states that "It is clearly stated in the *Analects* that what distinguishes Confucian morality from Legalist doctrines [doctrines regarding the effective use of regulatory enforcement held by the ancient Chinese school of *Fajia*法家] is the sense of shame. . . . This affirmation is interesting because while, on the one hand, it confirms the typology of the model that assigns traditional Chinese society to an orientation towards shame, on the other it makes clear the development of an internal conception of moral worth and of conscience."[56] Because of this internalizing tendency, he places Confucian shame in the middle point between guilt and shame.

Because of shame's external tendencies (i.e., its intrinsic relation to the external cause and authority), internal shame (shame that is felt and caused by an inner moral sense) seems to be an oxymoron or a contradiction. Roetz, however, believes differently. He interprets Confucian shame as an *internal* and *autonomous* sense of morality that is not affected by external values and regulations. He believes that this internal orientation is not only a unique but also an essential characteristic of Confucian shame. He states that "the genuine Confucian concept of shame . . . is by no means an expression of moral heteronomy."[57] That is, Confucian shame, according to him, is a strong emotion of inner autonomy and self-respect because the early Confucians, instead of emphasizing external sanctions such as punishment and disgrace as a means of moral cultivation, rely on "an inner feeling of shame and the self-reward of inner happiness." He adds that "For the genuine Confucian, there is no abode in the world without the seclusion in his self."[58] Perhaps, Confucian shame can be comparable to Stoic virtue or Kantian inner moral will that provides the unassailable inner autonomy and the peace of mind.

As many scholars point out, Confucian shame has a strong foundation in internalized moral awareness. It can be felt and motivated independently of external authority and enforcement. However, Confucian shame often comes with external (idealized, imagined, or actual) audience because it is not just a soliloquy of inner voice but more like a conversation with many voices. For example, in some passages of the *Mencius* (a major early Confucian text), the king of Qi says that he is ashamed *in front of* Mencius (吾甚慚於孟子) (2B18). In another passage (*Mencius*, 7A20), shame is elicited *in front of* others (俯不怍於人) and *in front of* an ideal authority such as Heaven, i.e., the ultimate, impersonal moral authority of Confucianism (仰不愧於天).[59] In these passages, external audiences are mentioned, and their norms and authorities are implicated. However, considering the relational and communal nature of shame discussed in the previous section and the intrinsically social and relational nature of moral agency in Confucianism, the externality of Confucian shame should be carefully understood. The externality does not imply that Confucian shame lacks moral significance. It simply discloses the communal and interpersonal dimensions of shame that are open to interpersonal relations and ideal moral authorities. Confucian shame has a strong inner and reflective orientation, but it also has the external and relational characteristics.

Although Roetz distinguishes internal (i.e., genuine and real) shame from its external conditions (such as external audience, bodily reactions of shame such as the blushed face), Confucian shame is not a solipsistic state of the mind.[60] The ultimate goal of Confucian ethics, according to Confucius, is not simply cultivating personal virtues for one's self but also establishing (立人) and enlarging *others* (達人), i.e., helping others to cultivate their virtues (*Analects*, 6.30). The most important lesson one should bear in mind throughout one's life, according to Confucius, is sympathetic understanding of *others* (*shu* 恕) (*Analects*, 15.24). The most important Confucian virtue is benevolent (*ren* 仁), which simply means, according to Confucius, *other*-concerning love (*Analects*, 12.22). In sum, *others* (人) always appear in one's moral virtue and moral emotion in Confucianism. Shame is no exception. Although Confucian shame can be felt and motivated internally, it is related to external audience (one's relation to others, their norms, and guidance) and their standards and expectations. It is important, therefore, to understand the essentially relational and external nature of Confucian shame.

The externality, however, does not imply that Confucian shame is a submissive and heteronomous emotion. It simply means shame's relationality and communal embeddedness in human moral ecology.[61] In fact, a prominent Confucian scholar Van Norden's interpretation of Confucian shame emphasizes this relational and communal orientation of Confucian philosophy.[62] Following Williams's view, Van Norden argues that Confucian shame is moral and communal.[63] Confucianism is not ethical Cartesianism and Confucian shame is not completely rooted in solipsistic inner autonomy.[64]

Because of its combination of inner moral awareness and external orientations (i.e., relationality and communality), Confucian shame can be understood as a moral psychological hybrid of Aristotelian shame and Kantian autonomy. Perhaps it can be called externalized guilt or communonomous self-reflection. If there exists a moral psychological middle point between Aristotelian or Greek sense of shame and Kantian inner moral autonomy, Confucian shame would take it as its natural base for self-cultivation and moral awareness. For this reason, one may call Confucian shame quasi-guilt or Confucian guilt.

Perhaps the best way to understand the relation between Confucian shame and guilt is to utilize an evolutionary viewpoint. According to several psychologists, shame is an effective appeasement or dominance negotiation strategy for social animals. According to them, shame is displayed by an individual to her socially or physically superior individuals to protect herself from their attacks. Subordination to authority is an evolutionary foundation of shame.[65] Beyond the protection from violence and sanction, it is also used to regulate socially inappropriate behaviors. Confucian shame adds another layer to this evolutionary process. Confucian shame can play ideal moral roles by extending its scope from subordination and social regulation to moral virtue.[66]

Therefore, shame, in its evolutionary origin, has to be explicitly or physically displayed so that others can see it as a signal of no-contest and subordination: particular forms of gaze, gait, or posture are important physical markers of shame. It is important to note that, although Confucian shame no longer serves the function of appeasement or subordination, it still retains these physical markers such as blushed face in front of external audience as an essential characteristic of self-reproaching emotion (*Mencius*, 7A20). Guilt does not have external expressions but shame, in Western psychology, typically comes with embodied markers. That is, despite the inner moral orientation, Confucian shame is a form of shame because it comes with embodied physical expressions (the blushed face, lowered body posture, etc.) and external audience (spectators or witnesses) that guilt does not have.

Other than these external features, however, Confucian shame and guilt share similar moral functions. How can one explain the similarity between Confucian shame and guilt discussed in this paper? From the perspective of evolutionary psychology, the close relation between Confucian shame and guilt can be explained by *homology*. Confucian shame is homologous (serving different functions but sharing the same origin, i.e., sharing the same vestigial physical features such as lowered body posture and the blushed face) to shame but analogous (sharing the similar function, i.e., moral self-awareness, with different origin) to guilt. In other words, shame and guilt are not homologous because they do not share the same origin but analogous because they share the similar functions: Confucian shame is non-homologous analogy of guilt.[67] From the perspective of moral psychological function,

Confucian shame is quasi guilt, perhaps, residing in the overlapping middle ground between Aristotelian shame and Kantian sense of guilt. It not only exhibits relationality and communality but also develops inner autonomous tendencies. However, it is not a simple moral psychological combination of Aristotelian shame and Kantian guilt. It retains the embodied externality as a key component of its identity perhaps because of its alleged evolutionary origin and, as a result, develops a form of shame that is different from both Aristotelian shame and Kantian guilt.

CONFUCIAN SHAME AS A DEVELOPMENTAL VIRTUE

I discussed three approaches to shame in the previous sections. In the first approach to shame (i.e., self-reproaching shame), guilt and shame are explained by the following characteristics: guilt is internal, moral, and autonomous but shame is external, social, and heteronomous.

Guilt	**Shame**
Internal	External
Moral (other-concerning)	Social (self-concerning)
Autonomous	Heteronomous

↘ ↙
Confucian Shame

Confucian shame resists this dichotomous characterization strongly held by many schools of philosophy and psychology. As Confucius (*Analects*, 2.3) states shame regulates human behavior by its inner moral disposition. Roetz and Tiwald believe that Confucian shame is an inner, autonomous, and moral emotion.[68] From this internal viewpoint, the sharp and contrastive distinction between guilt and shame cannot be maintained because Confucian shame is similar to and comparable with guilt.

Confucian shame, however, shares many characteristics with shame discussed in the second and the third approaches. Like Aristotelian shame, Confucian shame is a moral sense of self-integrity and a concern not just for failure but also for success. Like relational shame, Confucian shame has interpersonal or communal features often discussed in the Western philosophical contexts by such authors as Cairns, Konstan, Lansky, Morrison, Morgan, and Williams.[69] In addition, it is often interpreted as a moral disposition that derives from the metaphysical principle of Confucian harmony (和 he, the optimal, fluid, social, and moral interconnectedness to others and to the universe).[70] It seems that Confucian shame includes and integrates diverse characteristics of emotions and accommodates the broad spectrum of self-reflective and self-conscious feelings. Can Confucian shame be explained by a combination of these characteristics of self-conscious moral emotions? What is the unique moral psychological nature of Confucian shame?

Confucian shame is not simply a moral emotion but a moral virtue, a cultivated moral excellence and fully developed moral disposition.[71] A virtue is a fully established pattern of thought, feeling, and motivation that reflects one's character consistently and reliably expressed in varying conditions of life. Confucian shame is a virtue in this sense because it is one's disposition to develop ideal personal traits. The following passage of the *Analects* shows that shame has the property of moral excellence that an officer (*shi* 士, a morally straight and capable government official) should cultivate.

> Zi Gong asked, saying, "What qualities must a man possess to entitle him to be called an officer?" The Master said, "He who in his conduct of himself maintains a sense of shame...." (子貢問曰 何如斯可謂之士矣 子曰 行己有恥, *Analects*, 13.20)

In addition to the above passage, several passages of the *Mencius* (2A6, 6A6, 7A20) and the *Xunzi* (4.10) discuss shame (*chi* 恥, *xiu* 羞, or *lianchi* 廉恥) as a Confucian virtue.[72] Mencius takes shame (7A6, 7A7) as an important moral ability of human being. He states that one may not live as a human person without shame (7A6, 人不可以無恥) and shame is very important to human being (7A7, 恥之於人大矣). He also talks about shame (*xiu*) as the foundation of *yi* (righteousness) (*Mencius*, 2A6, 6A6).[73] Mencius compares king Wu's shame as his courage (*Mencius*, 1B10) and Xunzi (4.4) compares lack of shame with animals' (i.e., dogs' and pigs') courage (i.e., their impulsive recklessness). He (*Xunzi*, 6.12) also states that a virtuous person (the Confucian gentleman, *junzi* 君子) is not ashamed of being seen by others as dirty and clumsy but of not being fully matured and refined (i.e., not being fully virtuous).

Outside of Confucianism, shame, in whatever forms or styles, has never been recommended or suggested as an ideal character trait or a moral disposition. In some cultures, shame is perceived as an effective means to achieve regulative goals in education, management, and other social affairs, but it has never been recommended as a moral virtue.[74] Perhaps, Confucianism is the only philosophical tradition where shame is encouraged and commended as a stable disposition of moral excellence. If shame is one of the universal human emotions observed in any human culture, Confucianism is a moral tradition that maximizes shame's moral potential to its extreme.[75]

One way to understand the moral psychological significance of Confucian shame is to think of the special roles shame plays in Confucian learning (xue 學, the process of moral development and cultivation of virtue). According to early Confucian philosophers (Confucius, Mencius, and Xunzi), learning is not simply a process of obtaining factual information or acquiring practical skills. It is rather a holistic process of cultivating an ideal character. Confucian learning has unique developmental features. First, Confucian learning is not only a process of forming particular dispositions and traits, but it also develops and cultivates the whole self. For this reason, Confucian learning is often called the process of self-cultivation. It is a self-forming process, one's process of building one's own character. Second, however, Confucian learning is not only a process of formation but also of re-formation and trans-formation. It focuses on continuous renovation of the self and its moral potentials and, for that reason, it has no end point or ultimate climax of its developmental process. As Xunzi stresses, Confucian learning never ends (Xunzi 1.1, 學不可以已): it takes place consistently and continuously throughout the learner's life.

If Confucian learning aims at the excellence of the whole person and motivates both formative and transformative processes of development, one can understand why shame is important in Confucianism. Because of its self-reflective orientation and its influence on the whole person, shame can change a moral agent's actions and dispositions, but it can also change the self from which it originates. That is, shame is needed not only for formative development of character traits but also for *re*formative or *trans*formative change of the whole self. To achieve this type of comprehensive development, which Confucians believe as the ultimate goal of Confucianism, and to sustain the continuous motivation for self-cultivation, an ordinary virtue is not enough. Because modifying existing dispositions and giving them new foundations, a supervisory- or meta-disposition (i.e., an ability to modifying and removing existing dispositions) is necessary. That is, the transformative process of self-renovation requires a strong reflective force that only a virtue with a holistic and critical capability can provide. Shame fits this transformative moral psychological bill nicely because it is a disposition of self-cultivation via critical self-reflection that includes the process of changing and transforming existing dispositions. Therefore, shame is not only a virtue but also a developmental *meta*-virtue, a virtue of forming and transforming virtues at the level of the whole person. I believe that this continuously innovative and self-reflective ability is the moral psychological essence of Confucian shame.

The transformative power of Confucian shame can be compared with the developmental potential of Aristotelian shame. Aristotle believes that shame is important to young people because it can regulate their spontaneous and impulsive behavior. However, it becomes less important and meaningful once they grow up and mature: they no longer feel shame or concern about losing the sense of integrity and appropriateness. When the developmental process ends, "no one would praise them [i.e., fully developed individuals] for readiness to feel disgrace" (*Nicomachean Ethics*, 1128b17–22). According to him, shame is not a form of moral excellence but a form of developmental and self-reflective emotion. Unlike an actively functioning virtue, shame is felt passively and cannot become a stable personal trait (*Nicomachean Ethics*, 1128b10–16). He also points out that shame has a mean (a middle point between two extremes), not as a virtue but as a passive feeling (*Eudemian Ethics*, 1220b12–20, 1234a23–24). Simply, Aristotle does not believe that shame is a virtue worthy of full and continuous development. Confucian shame, in contrast, is a stable trait that Confucius asks his disciples to cultivate and maintain through their whole life. Typically, moral development culminates at a point of full maturation and stops there. In Confucianism, however, the developmental process continues throughout the life: it never ends. For this continuous process of development to be successful, a special virtue, one that is both formative, reformative, and transformative should be cultivated.

The *Great Learning* (*daixue* 大學, one of the four major texts of Confucianism) characterizes this transformative process as ceaseless daily renovation: "renew yourself one day and keep doing that every day (日日新 又日新)." The *Analects* (1.4) reports that Zengzi (one of Confucius's disciples) makes it a rule to self-reflect three times a day. Perhaps the unlimited potential of growth and innovation sets a virtuous Confucian agent apart from ordinary people and distinguishes Confucian ethics from other schools of moral philosophy. Therefore, shame is an important developmental virtue of Confucianism. The ability to sustain the continuous, innovative, and self-reflective process is the aretaic essence of Confucian shame. Here, the moral excellence does not lie in the end point but in the constructive and transformative nature and process of moral development. From this developmental perspective, Confucian shame is a unique form of shame that is rarely observed and discussed in other philosophical schools. This developmental and self-reflective uniqueness explains why shame, despite its seemingly negative and stressful characteristics, is a major virtue of Confucianism.

CONCLUSION

In this chapter, I discussed three major theoretical approaches to shame (self-reproaching shame, Aristotelian shame, and relational shame) and analyzed the unique moral psychological characteristics of Confucian shame.

Confucian shame (*chi* 恥) is a self-reflective emotion that cultivates the moral awareness of an agent. It is also a virtue, a form of moral excellence that should be cultivated and maintained throughout one's life to support continuous moral development of one's self. It is a stable and continuous disposition for innovative and transformative Confucian learning.

Confucian shame shares many moral psychological characteristics with guilt and shame, but it is different from guilt and shame. Like guilt, it is a critical emotion against one's moral violation. Like shame, it is a relational and social emotion and holistic and critical self-awareness. Unlike guilt and shame, however, Confucian shame is a moral virtue for continuous moral development for an ideal self. It is a developmental and self-innovative virtue that encourages and stimulates the self-reflective mind to go beyond the existing dispositions of the self. Socrates says that *know yourself* by cultivating wisdom. The early Confucian philosophers say that monitor, challenge, and continuously *develop yourself* by cultivating shame.

NOTES

1. See Helen Lewis, *Shame and Guilt in Neurosis* (New York: International Universities Press, 1971) 42, and Silvan Tomkins, *Affect, Imagery, Consciousness, vol. 2, The Negative Affects* (New York: Springer, 1963/2006), 118. Tangney and her colleagues state that "shame often leads to a desire to escape or to hide to sink into the floor and disappear. In contrast, the guilt experience is generally less painful and devastating than shame because guilt does not directly affect one's core self-concept." June Price Tangney, Rowland S. Miller, Laura Flicker, and Deborah Hill Barlow, "Are Shame, Guilt, and Embarrassment Distinct Emotions?" *Journal of Personality and Social Psychology* 70 (1996): 1257. Regarding the contrastive distinction between guilt and shame, see Paul Gilbert, "Evolution, Social Roles, and the Differences in Shame and Guilt," *Social Research* 70, 4 (Winter, 2003): 1205–30; Gershen Kaufman, *The Psychology of Shame: Theory and Treatment of Shame-Based Syndromes*, 2nd ed. (New York: Springer Pub. Co., 1996); Michael Lewis, *Shame: The Exposed Self* (New York: The Free Press, 1992); Thomas Scheff and Suzanne Retzinger, *Emotions and Violence: Shame and Rage in Destructive Conflicts* (Lincoln, NE: iUniverse, 1991/2001); June Price Tangney and Kurt Fischer, *Self-Conscious Emotions: The Psychology of Shame, Guilt, Embarrassment, and Pride* (New York: Guilford, 1995).

2. Olwen Bedford, "The Individual Experience of Guilt and Shame in Chinese Culture," *Culture and Psychology* 10, no. 1 (March 2004): 29–52; Olwen Bedford and Kwang-Kuo Hwang, "Guilt and Shame in Chinese Culture: A Cross-cultural Framework from the Perspective of Morality and Identity," *Journal for the Theory of Social Behaviour* 33, 2 (June 2003): 127–44; Jin Li, Lianqin Wang, and Kurt W. Fischer, "The Organisation of Chinese Shame Concepts?," *Cognition and Emotion*

18 (October 2004): 767–97; Martin Schoenhals, *The Paradox of Power in a People's Republic of China Middle School*. (Armonk, NY: M. E. Sharpe).

3. Martha Nussbaum, *Hiding from Humanity: Disgust, Shame, and the Law* (Princeton, NJ: Princeton University Press, 2004); Gerhart Piers and Milton Singer, *Shame and Guilt: A Psychoanalytic and a Cultural Study* (New York: Norton, 1971).

4. Seger Breugelmans and Ype Poortinga, "Emotion without a Word: Shame and Guilt among Rarámuri Indians and Rural Javanese," *Journal of Personality and Social Psychology* 91, 6 (2006): 1111–22; Michael Mascolo, Kurt W. Fischer, and Jin Li, "Dynamic Development of Component Systems of Emotions: Pride, Shame and Guilt in China and the United States," in *Handbook of Affective Sciences*, ed. Richard Davidson, Klaus Scherer, and Hill Goldsmith (New York: Oxford University Press, 2003), 375–408.

5. Gabriele Taylor, *Pride, Shame, and Guilt* (New York: Oxford University Press, 1985); Heiner Roetz, *Confucian Ethics of the Axial Age: A Reconstruction under the Aspect of the Breakthrough toward Postconventional Thinking* (Albany, NY: State University of New York Press, 1993); Barnard Williams, *Shame and Necessity* (Berkeley, CA: University of California Press, 1993).

6. Regarding the positive and moral functions of shame, see Fabrice Teroni and Otto Bruun, "Shame, Guilt and Morality," *Journal of Moral Philosophy* 8 (April 2011): 223–45. The main objective of Teroni and Brunn's discussion of shame is to argue against the well-received views of shame (i.e., shame is dirty, and shame is external). The negative view (the institutionalizing the denial of shame) is discussed by Thomas Scheff. See Thomas Scheff, "Shame in Social Theory," in *The Widening Scope of Shame*, ed. Melvin Lansky and Andrew Morrison (Hillsdale, NJ: The Analytic Press, 1997), 205.

7. See, for example, Maibom's summary of the standard distinction between shame and guilt broadly shared by many psychologists (Guilt and Shame: The Standard Picture) in her chapter in this volume.

8. In this chapter, "shame" without any specifier refers to the self-critical emotion of shame discussed and analyzed by Western psychologists. It is understandable, therefore, that Confucian shame and Aristotelian shame are different from shame.

9. "Zi Gong asked, saying, 'What qualities must a man possess to entitle him to be called an officer?' The Master said, 'He who in his conduct of himself maintains a sense of shame, and when sent to any quarter will not disgrace his prince's commission, deserves to be called an officer.'" See Confucius, *Analects*, https://ctext.org/analects (2018). In this chapter, I use the standard notation of early Confucian texts such as *Analects*, 13.20 that indicates the book, section, and passage number.

10. Mencius, *Mencius*, https://ctext.org/analects (2018).

11. Maibom in her chapter in this volume points out that shame can motivate long-term change in the whole person.

12. June Price Tangney and Ronda Dearing, *Shame and Guilt: Emotions and Social Behavior* (New York: The Guilford Press, 2002), 71.

13. Tomkins, *Affect, Imagery, Consciousness*, 118.

14. June Price Tangney, "Moral Affect: The Good, the Bad, and the Ugly," *Journal of Personality and Social Psychology* 61 (1991): 598–607; June Price Tangney,

Jeff Stuewig, and Debra Mashek, "Moral Emotions and Moral Behavior," *Annual Review of Psychology*, 58 (2007): 345–72.

15. Tangney and Dearing, *Shame and Guilt*.

16. Papish in this volume, however, reports that pure (Kantian) practical reason, including the sense of guilt, can be understood as self-contained and narcissistic egoism. Here I simply discuss the general views of psychologists who believe that guilt motivates the consideration of the victim, but shame focuses on the disgraced self.

17. Lewis, *Shame and Guilt in Neurosis*.

18. Regarding the ugly feeling of shame see Tangney, "Moral Affect," 600. Regarding the articulated and dignified feeling of guilt see Lewis, *Shame and Guilt in Neurosis*, 42.

19. Tangney, "The Moral Affect," 605–06.

20. Millie Creighton, "Revisiting Shame and Guilt Cultures: A Forty-Year Pilgrimage," *Ethos* 18 (September 1990): 286.

21. See Lewis, *Shame and Guilt in Neurosis*; Kaufman, *The Psychology of Shame*; Tangney and Dearing, *Shame and Guilt*; Paul Gilbert, "The Evolution of Social Attractiveness and Its Role in Shame, Humiliation, Guilt and Therapy," *The British Journal of Medical Psychology* 70 (June 1997): 113–47.

22. Creighton, "Revisiting Shame and Guilt Cultures," 296.

23. Scheff, "Shame in Social Theory," 205.

24. The psychological and social negativity of shame may be observed in Asian cultures. There are many reports on the negative mental health outcomes (psychological distress and life dissatisfaction) that are related to shame in Asian cultures. See Lei Wang, Joel Wong, and Barry Chung, "Family Perfectionism, Shame, and Mental Health among Asian American and Asian International Emerging Adults: Mediating and Moderating Relationships," *Asian American Journal of Psychology* 9 (June 2018): 117–26. It is important to note, however, that Confucian shame is a unique form of shame that is associated with a strong self-conscious moral sense. Although it shares certain characteristics of shame (social shame, family shame, external shame, etc.), it (as moral and internal shame) is not associated with psychological depression and political suppression. It is rather a stable and constructive moral disposition as I will discuss in the sections of Confucian shame.

25. Regarding the negative mental health implications of shame, specifically the correlation between suicidal thoughts and shame, see Marisa K. Crowder and Markus Kemmelmeier, "Cultural Differences in Shame and Guilt as Understandable Reasons for Suicide," *Psychological Reports* 121 (June 2018): 396–429.

26. Creighton, "Revisiting Shame and Guilt Cultures," 296; Tangney and Dearing, *Shame and Guilt*, 176.

27. It is important to note, however, even guilt can become inappropriate: It can be as dysfunctional and neurotic as shame can become. See Maibom's chapter in this volume. She argues that *both* shame and guilt can be dysfunctional and neurotic.

28. Lewis, *Shame and Guilt in Neurosis*; June Price Tangney, "Moral Affect"; Tangney and Dearing, *Shame and Guilt*; June Price Tangney, Jeff Stuewig, and Debra Mashek, "Moral Emotions and Moral Behavior."

29. Aristotle, however, does not believe that shame can be cultivated into a virtue. To mature (fully developed) persons, shame should not be praised. He states that no

one "would praise an older person for readiness to feel disgrace, since we think it is wrong for him to do any action that causes a feeling of disgrace" (*Nichomachean Ethics*, 1128b17-22). In contrast, Confucian shame can be cultivated and refined to form a stable moral disposition, i.e., a virtue.

30. Regarding the discussion of moral shame and social shame, see Bongrae Seok, *Moral Psychology of Confucian Shame: Shame of Shamelessness* (Lanham, MD: Rowman & Littlefield International, 2016), 39–40. Sometimes social shame is called "image shame" (shame deriving from one's compromised social image to others) and clearly distinguished from moral shame (one's internal moral sense). See Jess Allpress et al., "Two Faces of Group-Based Shame: Moral Shame and Image Shame Differentially Predict Positive and Negative Orientations to Ingroup Wrongdoing," *Personality and Social Psychology Bulletin* 40 (October 2014): 1270–84.

31. Seok, *Moral Psychology of Confucian Shame*, 34–35.

32. Ibid., 34.

33. An autonomous action or decision requires a particular type of self-governing abilities of an agent. An autonomous action is a voluntary and self-conscious action of an individual on the basis of her rational will and universal principles. A non-autonomous or heteronomous action is an action of an individual under the influence of external authorities or contingencies such as others' opinions or their perceptions. See Bongrae Seok, "Moral Agency, Autonomy, and Heteronomy in Early Confucian Philosophy," *Philosophy Compass* 12 (December 2017): https://doi.org/10.1111/phc3.12460.

34. Immanuel Kant, *Groundwork of the Metaphysics of Morals*, trans. Mary Gregor (Cambridge: Cambridge University Press, 1785/1998), 535.

35. According to Papish in her chapter in this volume, Kant (like Aristotle and perhaps Williams) believes that shame is indispensable to moral education. Shame stimulates moral thinking and gives the sense of how moral reality is embedded in personal relations and communal expectations. However, according to her, Kant does not believe shame can provide a solid moral compass that can deal with major moral disorientation or disintegration. That is, Kant's view on guilt, *in general*, is straight forward, i.e., deontological and juridical, but his discussion of shame is more complicated than what Williams and others think it would be. In this section, I discuss shame and guilt from the viewpoint of Kantian moral autonomy where the distinction between the shame and guilt is very clear. However, Kant seems to have a nuanced and complex view of shame as Papish points out in her chapter.

36. See Gerald Dworkin, *The Theory and Practice of Autonomy* (New York: Cambridge University Press, 1988); Gerald Dworkin, "The Concept of Autonomy," in *The Inner Citadel, Essays on Individual Autonomy*, ed. John Christman (New York: Oxford University Press, 1989), 54–62; Harry Frankfurt, *The Importance of What We Care About* (Cambridge: Cambridge University Press, 1988).

37. Emmanuel Lévinas, *Totality and Infinity* (Pittsburgh: Duquesne University Press, 1969). It is important to note, however, that Lévinas's idea of shame is not based on relational agency. According to him "shame" is associated with "the fact of being riveted to oneself, the radical impossibility of fleeing oneself to hide from oneself, the alterably binding presences of the I to itself." Emmanuel Lévinas, *On Escape* (Stanford: Stanford University Press, 1935/2003), 64.

38. Anne Donchin, "Autonomy and Interdependence: Quandaries in Genetic Decision Making," in *Relational Autonomy: Feminist Perspectives on Autonomy, Agency, and the Social Self*, ed. Catriona Mackenzie and Natalie Stoljar (New York: Oxford University Press, 2000), 236–58; Carol Gilligan, *In a Different Voice: Psychological Theory and Women's Development* (Cambridge, MA: Harvard University Press, 1982); Catriona Mackenzie, "Three Dimensions of Autonomy: A Relational Analysis," in *Autonomy, Oppression, and Gender*, ed. Andrea Veltman and Mark Piper (New York: Oxford University Press, 2014), 15–41; Catriona MacKenzie and Natalie Stoljar, ed., *Relational Autonomy: Feminist Perspectives on Autonomy, Agency, and the Social Self* (New York: Oxford University Press, 2000); Carolyn McLeod and Susan Sherwin, "Relational Autonomy, Self-Trust, and Health Care for Patients Who are Oppressed," in *Relational Autonomy: Feminist Perspectives on Autonomy, Agency, and the Social Self*, ed. Catriona Mackenzie and Natalie Stoljar (New York: Oxford University Press, 2000), 259–79.

39. Mead, Cooley, and Goffman all discuss shame from the perspective of the development of the social self. See Charles Horton Cooley, *Human Nature and the Social Order* (New Brunswick: Transaction Publishers, 1902/2006); Erving Goffman, *The Presentation Self of Everyday Life* (London: Penguin Books, 1959/1990); Herbert Mead, *Mind, Self, and Society* (Chicago: The University of Chicago Press, 1934/1967).

40. Williams, *Shame and Necessity*.

41. Ibid., 99, 217 n61.

42. Williams, *Shame and Necessity*, 5.

43. Michael Morgan, *On Shame* (New York: Routledge, 2008); Martha Nussbaum, *Hiding from Humanity: Disgust, Shame, and the Law* (Princeton, NJ: Princeton University Press, 2004); Carl Schneider, *Shame, Exposure, and Privacy*. (Boston: Beacon Press, 1992).

44. Nussbaum, *Hiding from Humanity*.

45. "I will argue that shame is an affect or a heteronomous feeling that results from the perception of a specific sort of social breakdown, in which the shamed person has her basic need to live unreflectively and trustingly with others thwarted." "For philosophical anthropology, emotions like shame are 'a personal confusion,' in which our 'significant relations to people and things' are disrupted . . ." Matthew Stewart Rukgaber, "Philosophical Anthropology and the Interpersonal Theory of the Affect of Shame," *Journal of Phenomenological Psychology* 49 (January 2018): 84, 106.

46. Morgan, *On Shame*, 2.

47. Rukgaber contrasts this communal, ecological, or interpersonal approach to shame with "the cognitivist, morally, rationally, autonomous view of shame as a negative judgment about the self." Rukgaber, "Philosophical Anthropology," 83–85.

48. Regarding how the distinction between guilt and shame is discussed and used in other disciplines of humanities and social sciences, see David Gilmore, *Shame and Honor and the Unity of the Mediterranean* (Washington, DC: American Anthropological Association, 1987); John Peristiany and Julian Pitt-Rivers, eds., *Honor and Grace in Anthropology* (New York: Cambridge University Press, 1992).

49. One may argue that shame does not necessarily need external audience (the presence of eyewitnesses, bystanders, and spectators. Deonna, Rodogno, and Teroni,

for example, state that social or interpersonal conception of shame is no longer dominant. However, the absence of external audience does not imply that shame is not a relational or social emotion. Even in one's experience of shame without external audience, one feels obligated to the standards or expectations of people whom one respects and emulates. This is particularly so in Confucian shame. Julien Deonna, Raffaele Rodogno, and Fabrice Teroni, *In Defense of Shame: The Faces of an Emotion* (New York: Oxford University Press, 2012), xi; Taylor, *Pride, Shame, and Guilt*.

50. Social and moral functions of self-conscious emotions such as embarrassment, pride, shame, and guilt, see Michael Lewis, "Self-Conscious Emotions: Embarrassment, Pride, Shame, and Guilt," in *Handbook of Emotions*, ed. Michael Lewis and Jeannette M. Haviland-Jones (New York: Guilford Press, 1993), 563–73.

51. Seok, *Moral Psychology of Confucian Shame*, 169.

52. See Margaret Ng, "Internal Shame as a Moral Sanction," *Journal of Chinese Philosophy* 8 (March 1981): 76. She states that "External shame is aroused by criticism by others, ridicule, gossip, embarrassment, public shaming, divesting of reputation, loss of face, and ostracism, all of which are 'set in motion by others' in the attempt to discourage behavior which deviates from or conflicts with what is socially accepted as proper. Internal shame is also a pressure to maintain good conduct, but it does not operate only when misdeeds are discovered by others and does not wait for others to minister the penalty. It operates autonomously, both the compulsion to good conduct and the standard of good conduct having been internalized, just as the external authority of the father and his decrees are internalized in internal guilt."

53. Ng, "Internal Shame"; Roetz, *Confucian Ethics*; Paolo Santangelo, "Human Conscience and Responsibility in Ming-Qing China," *East Asian History* 4 (1992): 31–80.

54. Ng, "Internal Shame," 84.

55. Santangelo, "Human Conscience," 41.

56. Ibid., 40.

57. Roetz, *Confucian Ethics*, 181.

58. Ibid., 184.

59. In Confucianism, Heaven (*tian*) does not mean sky or afterlife. Nor is it a personal god. It is the ultimate moral authority that affects the personal, social, and political course of life.

60. Ibid., 177.

61. A strongly relational interpretation of Confucian agency and Confucian ethics can be found in Roger Ames, *Confucian Role Ethics: A Vocabulary* (Hong Kong: The Chinese University Press, 2011).

62. Bryan Van Norden, "The Emotion of Shame and the Virtue of Righteousness in Mencius," *Dao, a Journal of Comparative Philosophy* 1 (2002): 45–77.

63. Ibid., 62 n27; Williams, *Shame and Necessity*, 99.

64. For example, non-Cartesian (i.e., non-internal but socially interactive) interpretations of Confucian shame is developed by other Chinese comparative philosophers. See Jane Geaney, "Guarding Moral Boundaries: Shame in Early Confucianism," *Philosophy East and West* 54 (April 2004): 113–42; Kwong-Loi Shun, "Self and Self-Cultivation in Early Confucian Thought," in *Two Roads to Wisdom? Chinese and Analytic Philosophical Traditions*, ed. Bo Mou (Peru, IL: Open Court, 2001), 229–44.

65. Regarding this evolutionary interpretation of Confucian shame see Seok, *Moral Psychology of Confucian Shame*, 59–78. Regarding other evolutionary approaches to social and moral emotions, see Paul Gilbert, *Depression: The Evolution of Powerlessness* (New York: The Guilford Press, 1992); Daniel Fessler, "Toward an Understanding of the Universality of Second Order Emotions," in *Biocultural Approaches to the Emotions*, ed. Alexander Laban Hinton (New York: Cambridge University Press, 1999), 75–116; Daniel Fessler, "Shame in Two Cultures: Implications for Evolutionary Approaches," *Journal of Cognition and Culture* 4 (June 2004): 207–62; Dacher Keltner and Randall C. Young, "Appeasement in Human Emotion, Social Practice, and Personality," *Aggressive Behavior* 23 (September 1997): 359–74; Dacher Keltner and Lee Ann Harker, "The Forms and Functions of the Nonverbal Signal of Shame," in *Shame: Interpersonal Behavior, Psychopathology, and Culture*, ed. Paul Gilbert and Andrew Bernice (New York: Oxford University Press, 1998), 78–98; Glenn Weisfeld, "Discrete Emotions Theory with Specific Reference to Pride and Shame," in *Uniting Psychology and Biology: Integrative Perspectives on Human Development*, ed. Nancy Segal, Glenn Weisfeld, and Carol Weisfeld (Washington, DC: American Psychological Association, 1997), 419–43; Glenn Weisfeld, "Darwinian Analysis of the emotion of Pride/Shame," in *The Darwinian Heritage and Sociobiology*, ed. Johan van der Dennen, David Smillie, and Daniel Wilson (Westport, Conn: Praeger Publishers, 1999), 319–33.

66. Seok, *Moral Psychology of Confucian Shame*, 64–71.

67. Ibid., 67–69.

68. Roetz, Confucian Ethics, 178; Justin Tiwald, "Punishment and Autonomous Shame in Confucian Thought," *Criminal Justice Ethics* 36, (2017): 45–60.

69. Douglas Cairns, *Aidos: The Psychology and Ethics of Honour and Shame in Ancient Greek Literature* (Oxford: Clarendon Press, 1993); David Konstan, "Shame in Ancient Greece," *Social Research* 70 (Winter 2003): 1031–60; Melvin Lansky and Andrew Morrison, *The Widening Scope of Shame* (Hillsdale, NJ: The Analytic Press, 1997); Morgan, *On Shame*; Williams, *Shame and Necessity*. Taylor, *Pride, Shame, and Guilt*.

70. Nathaniel Barrett, "A Confucian Theory of Shame," *Sophia: International Journal for Philosophy of Religion, Metaphysical Theology and Ethics* 54 (June 1, 2015): 143–63.

71. Ryan Nichols, "A Sense of Shame among the Virtues," *Journal of Moral Education* 45 (2016): 166–78; Bongrae Seok, "Moral Psychology of Shame in Early Confucian Philosophy," *Frontiers of Philosophy in China* 10 (2015): 21–57.

72. The four Confucian virtues are *ren* (benevolence), *yi* (righteousness), *li* (ritual propriety), *zhi* (wisdom). According to Mencius (2A6, 6A6), shame is related to the virtue of righteousness.

73. Regarding how shame and the virtue of righteousness are related in Confucian philosophy, see Yinghua Lu. "Shame and the Confucian Idea of 'Yi' (Righteousness)," *International Philosophical Quarterly* 58 (March 1, 2018): 5–18.

74. Regarding the culturally specific perception and use of shame in human affairs see Richard P. Bagozzi, Willem Verbeke, and Jacinto C. Jr. Gavino, "Culture Moderates the Self-Regulation of Shame and Its Effects on Performance: The Case of Salespersons in the Netherlands and the Philippines," *Journal of Applied Psychology* 88,

no. 2 (April 2003): 219–33; Ruth Benedict, *The Chrysanthemum and the Sword: Patterns of Japanese Culture* (Boston: Houghton Mifflin, 1946); Seger Breugelmans and Ype Poortinga, "Emotion without a Word"; Michael Casimir and Michael Schnegg, "Shame across Cultures: The Evolution, Ontogeny and Function of a 'Moral Emotion,'" in *Between Culture and Biology: Perspectives on Ontogenetic Development*, ed. Heidi Keller, Ype Poortinga, and Axel Schölmerich (New York: Cambridge University Press, 2002), 270–300; Gilmore, *Shame and Honor*; Kawng-Kuo Hwang, "Face and Favor: The Chinese Power Game," *American Journal of Sociology* 92, (January, 1987): 944–74.

75. See, for example, Ryan Nichols, "Civilizing Humans with Shame: How Early Confucians Altered Inherited Evolutionary Norms through Cultural Programming to Increase Social Harmony," *Journal of Cognition and Culture* 15 (2015): 254–84.

REFERENCES

Allpress, Jesse A., Rupert Brown, Roger Giner-Sorolla, Julien A. Deonna, and Fabrice Teroni. "Two Faces of Group-Based Shame: Moral Shame and Image Shame Differentially Predict Positive and Negative Orientations to Ingroup Wrongdoing." *Personality and Social Psychology Bulletin* 40, no. 10 (October 2014): 1270–84.
Ames, Roger. *Confucian Role Ethics: A Vocabulary*. Hong Kong: The Chinese University Press, 2011.
Aristotle. *Artistotle's Nicomachean Ethics*. Translated by Terence Irwin. Indianapolis, IN: Hackett Publishing, 1985.
Aristotle. *Eudemian Ethics*. Translated by Anthony Kenny. New York: Oxford University Press, 2011.
Bagozzi, Richard P., Willem Verbeke, and Jacinto C. Jr. Gavino. "Culture Moderates the Self-Regulation of Shame and Its Effects on Performance: The Case of Salespersons in the Netherlands and the Philippines." *Journal of Applied Psychology* 88, no. 2 (April 2003): 219–33.
Barrett, Nathaniel. "A Confucian Theory of Shame." *Sophia: International Journal for Philosophy of Religion, Metaphysical Theology and Ethics* 54 (June 1, 2015): 143–63.
Bedford, Olwen. "The Individual Experience of Guilt and Shame in Chinese Culture." *Culture and Psychology* 10, no. 1 (March 2004): 29–52.
Bedford, Olwen, and Kwang-Kuo Hwang. "Guilt and Shame in Chinese Culture: A Cross-cultural Framework from the Perspective of Morality and Identity." *Journal for the Theory of Social Behaviour* 33, 2 (June 2003): 127–44.
Benedict, Ruth. *The Chrysanthemum and the Sword: Patterns of Japanese Culture*. Boston: Houghton Mifflin, 1946.
Breugelmans, Seger and Ype Poortinga. "Emotion without a Word: Shame and Guilt among Rarámuri Indians and Rural Javanese." *Journal of Personality and Social Psychology* 91, 6 (2006): 1111–22.
Cairns, Douglas. *Aidos: The Psychology and Ethics of Honour and Shame in Ancient Greek Literature*. Oxford: Clarendon Press, 1993.

Casimir, Michael J., and Michael Schnegg. "Shame across Cultures: The Evolution, Ontogeny and Function of a `Moral Emotion.'" In *Between Culture and Biology: Perspectives on Ontogenetic Development*, edited by Heidi Keller, Ype Poortinga, and Axel Schölmerich, 270–300. New York: Cambridge University Press, 2002.

Confucius. "*Analects*." Accessed May 2018. Chinese Text Project. http://ctext.org/analects.

Creighton, Millie R. "Revisiting Shame and Guilt Cultures: A Forty-Year Pilgrimage." *Ethos* 18, no. 3 (September 1990): 279–307.

Cooley, Charles Horton. *Human Nature and the Social Order*. New Brunswick: Transaction Publishers, 1902/2006.

Crowder, Marisa K., and Markus Kemmelmeier. "Cultural Differences in Shame and Guilt as Understandable Reasons for Suicide." *Psychological Reports* 121, no. 3 (June 2018): 396–429.

Deonna, Julien A., Raffaele Rodogno, and Fabrice Teroni. *In Defense of Shame: The Faces of an Emotion*. New York: Oxford University Press, 2012.

Donchin, Anne. "Autonomy and Interdependence: Quandaries in Genetic Decision Making." In *Relational Autonomy: Feminist Perspectives on Autonomy, Agency, and the Social Self*, edited by Catriona Mackenzie and Natalie Stoljar, 236–258. New York: Oxford University Press, 2000.

Dworkin, Gerald. *The Theory and Practice of Autonomy*. New York: Cambridge University Press, 1988.

Dworkin, Gerald. "The Concept of Autonomy." In *The Inner Citadel, Essays on Individual Autonomy*, edited by John. Christman, 54–62. New York: Oxford University Press, 1989.

Fessler, Daniel M. T. "Toward an Understanding of the Universality of Second Order Emotions." In *Biocultural Approaches to the Emotions*, edited by Alexander Laban Hinton, 75–116. New York: Cambridge University Press, 1999.

Fessler, Daniel M. T. "Shame in Two Cultures: Implications for Evolutionary Approaches." *Journal of Cognition and Culture* 4, no. 2 (June 2004): 207–62.

Frankfurt, Harry. *The Importance of What We Care About*. Cambridge: Cambridge University Press, 1988.

Geaney, Jane. "Guarding Moral Boundaries: Shame in Early Confucianism." *Philosophy East and West* 54, no. 2 (April 2004): 113–42.

Gilbert, Paul. *Depression: The Evolution of Powerlessness*. New York: The Guilford Press, 1992.

Gilbert, Paul. "The Evolution of Social Attractiveness and Its Role in Shame, Humiliation, Guilt and Therapy." *British Journal of Medical Psychology* 70 (Pt 2), (June 1997): 113–47.

Gilbert, Paul. "Evolution, Social Roles, and the Differences in Shame and Guilt." *Social Research* 70, 4 (Winter, 2003): 1205–30.

Gilbert, Paul and Andrew Bernice. *Shame: Interpersonal Behavior, Psychopathology, and Culture*. New York: Oxford University Press, 1998.

Gilligan, Carol. *In a Different Voice: Psychological Theory and Women's Development*. Cambridge, MA: Harvard University Press, 1982.

Gilmore, David. *Shame and Honor and the Unity of the Mediterranean*. Washington, DC: American Anthropological Association, 1987.

Goffman, Erving. *The Presentation Self of Everyday Life*. London: Penguin Books, 1959/1990.
Hwang, Kwang-Kuo. "Face and Favor: The Chinese Power Game." *American Journal of Sociology* 92, 4 (January 1987): 944–74.
Kant, Immanuel. *Groundwork of the Metaphysics of Morals*. Translated by Mary Gregor. Cambridge: Cambridge University Press, 1785/1998.
Kaufman, Gershen. *The Psychology of Shame: Theory and Treatment of Shame-Based Syndromes*, 2nd ed. New York: Springer Pub. Co., 1996.
Keltner, Dacher and Lee Ann Harker. "The Forms and Functions of the Nonverbal Signal of Shame." In *Shame: Interpersonal Behavior, Psychopathology, and Culture*, edited by Paul Gilbert and Andrew Bernice, 78–98. New York: Oxford University Press, 1998.
Keltner, Dacher, and Randall C. Young. "Appeasement in Human Emotion, Social Practice, and Personality." *Aggressive Behavior* 23, no. 5 (September 1997): 359–74.
Konstan, David. "Shame in Ancient Greece." *Social Research* 70, 4 (Winter 2003): 1031–60.
Lévinas, Emmanuel. *On Escape*. Stanford: Stanford University Press, 1935/2003.
Lévinas, Emmanuel. *Totality and Infinity*. Pittsburgh: Duquesne University Press, 1969.
Lewis, Helen. *Shame and Guilt in Neurosis*. New York: International Universities Press, 1971.
Lewis, Michael. *Shame: The Exposed Self*. New York: The Free Press, 1992.
Lewis, Michael. "Self-Conscious Emotions: Embarrassment, Pride, Shame, and Guilt." In *Handbook of Emotions*, edited by Michael Lewis and Jeannette M. Haviland-Jones, 563–73. New York: Guilford Press, 1993.
Lansky, Melvin and Andrew Morrison. *The Widening Scope of Shame*. Hillsdale, NJ: The Analytic Press, 1997.
Li, Jin, Lianqin Wang, and Kurt W. Fischer. "The Organisation of Chinese Shame Concepts?" *Cognition and Emotion* 18, no. 6 (October 2004): 767–97.
Lu, Yinghua. "Shame and the Confucian Idea of 'Yi' (Righteousness)." *International Philosophical Quarterly* 58:1, no. 229 (March 1, 2018): 5–18.
Mackenzie, Catriona. "Three Dimensions of Autonomy: A Relational Analysis." In *Autonomy, Oppression, and Gender*, edited by Andrea Veltman and Mark Piper, 15–41. New York: Oxford University Press, 2014.
MacKenzie, Catriona and Natalie Stoljar, ed. *Relational Autonomy: Feminist Perspectives on Autonomy, Agency, and the Social Self*. New York: Oxford University Press, 2000.
McLeod, Carolyn and Susan Sherwin. "Relational Autonomy, Self-Trust, and Health Care for Patients Who are Oppressed." In *Relational Autonomy: Feminist Perspectives on Autonomy, Agency, and the Social Self*, edited by Catriona Mackenzie and Natalie Stoljar, 259–79. New York: Oxford University Press, 2000.
Mascolo, Michael F., Kurt W. Fischer, and Jin Li. "Dynamic Development of Component Systems of Emotions: Pride, Shame and Guilt in China and the United States." In *Handbook of Affective Sciences*, edited by Richard Davidson, Klaus Scherer, and Hill Goldsmith, 375–408., New York: Oxford University Press, 2003.

McKeon, Richard. *The Basic Works of Aristotle*. New York: Random House, 1941.
Mead, Herbert. *Mind, Self, and Society*. Chicago: The University of Chicago Press, 1934/1967.
Mencius. "*Mencius*." Accessed May 2018. Chinese Text Project. http://ctext.org/mencius.
Morgan, Michael. *On Shame*. New York: Routledge, 2008.
Ng, Margaret. "Internal Shame as a Moral Sanction." *Journal of Chinese Philosophy* 8 (March 1981): 75–86.
Nichols, Ryan. "Civilizing Humans with Shame: How Early Confucians Altered Inherited Evolutionary Norms through Cultural Programming to Increase Social Harmony." *Journal of Cognition and Culture* 15 (2015): 254–84.
Nichols, Ryan. "A Sense of Shame among the Virtues." *Journal of Moral Education* 45 (2016): 166–78.
Nussbaum, Martha. *Hiding from Humanity: Disgust, Shame, and the Law*. Princeton, NJ: Princeton University Press, 2004.
Peristiany, John and Julian Pitt-Rivers, eds. *Honor and Grace in Anthropology*. New York: Cambridge University Press, 1992.
Piers, Gerhart and Milton Singer. *Shame and Guilt: A Psychoanalytic and a Cultural Study*. New York: Norton, 1971.
Roetz, Heiner. *Confucian Ethics of the Axial Age: A Reconstruction under the Aspect of the Breakthrough toward Postconventional Thinking*. Albany, NY: State University of New York Press, 1993.
Rukgaber, Matthew Stewart. "Philosophical Anthropology and the Interpersonal Theory of the Affect of Shame." *Journal of Phenomenological Psychology* 49, no. 1 (January 2018): 83–112.
Santangelo, Paolo. "Human Conscience and Responsibility in Ming-Qing China." *East Asian History* 4 (1992): 31–80.
Scheff, Thomas. "Shame in Social Theory." In *The Widening Scope of Shame*, edited by Melvin Lansky and Andrew Morrison, 205–300. Hillsdale, NJ: The Analytic Press, 1997.
Scheff, Thomas and Suzanne Retzinger, *Emotions and Violence: Shame and Rage in Destructive Conflicts*. Lincoln, NE: iUniverse, 1991/2001.
Schneider, Carl. *Shame, Exposure, and Privacy*. Boston: Beacon Press, 1992.
Schoenhals, Martin. *The Paradox of Power in a People's Republic of China Middle School*. Armonk, NY: M. E. Sharpe, 1993.
Seok, Bongrae. *Moral Psychology of Confucian Shame: Shame of Shamelessness*. Lanham, MD: Rowman & Littlefield International, 2016.
Seok, Bongrae. "Moral Psychology of Shame in Early Confucian Philosophy." *Frontiers of Philosophy in China* 10 (2015): 21–57.
Seok, Bongrae. "Moral Agency, Autonomy, and Heteronomy in Early Confucian Philosophy," *Philosophy Compass* 12 (December 2017): https://doi.org/10.1111/phc3.12460.
Shun, Kwong-Loi. "Self and Self-Cultivation in Early Confucian Thought." In *Two Roads to Wisdom? Chinese and Analytic Philosophical Traditions*, edited by Bo Mou, 229–44. Peru, IL: Open Court, 2001.

Tangney, June Price. "Moral Affect: The Good, the Bad, and the Ugly." *Journal of Personality and Social Psychology* 61 (1991): 598–607.
Tangney, June Price and Ronda Dearing. *Shame and Guilt. Emotions and Social Behavior*. New York: The Guilford Press, 2002.
Tangney, June Price and Kurt Fischer. *Self-Conscious Emotions: The Psychology of Shame, Guilt, Embarrassment, and Pride*. New York: Guilford, 1995.
Tangney, June Price, Rowland S. Miller, Laura Flicker, and Deborah Hill Barlow. "Are Shame, Guilt, and Embarrassment Distinct Emotions?" *Journal of Personality and Social Psychology* 70 (1996): 1256–69.
Tangney, June Price, Jeff Stuewig, and Debra Mashek. "Moral Emotions and Moral Behavior." *Annual Review of Psychology*, 58 (2007): 345–72.
Taylor, Gabriele. *Pride, Shame, and Guilt*. New York: Oxford University Press, 1985.
Teroni, Fabrice, and Otto Bruun. "Shame, Guilt and Morality." *Journal of Moral Philosophy* 8, no. 2 (April 2011): 223–45.
Tiwald, Justin. "Punishment and Autonomous Shame in Confucian Thought." *Criminal Justice Ethics* 36 (2017): 45–60.
Tomkins, Silvan. *Affect, Imagery, Consciousness*, Vol. 2, *The Negative Affects*. New York: Springer, 1963/2006.
Van Norden, Bryan. "The Emotion of Shame and the Virtue of Righteousness in Mencius." *Dao, a Journal of Comparative Philosophy* 1 (2002): 45–77.
Veltman, Andrea and Mark Piper, ed. *Autonomy, Oppression, and Gender*. New York: Oxford University Press, 2014.
Wang, Lei, Y. Joel Wong, and Y. Barry Chung. "Family Perfectionism, Shame, and Mental Health among Asian American and Asian International Emerging Adults: Mediating and Moderating Relationships." *Asian American Journal of Psychology* 9 (June 2018): 117–26.
Weisfeld, Glenn. "Discrete Emotions Theory with Specific Reference to Pride and Shame." In *Uniting Psychology and Biology: Integrative Perspectives on Human Development*, edited by Nancy Segal, Glenn Weisfeld, and Carol Weisfeld, 419–43. Washington, DC: American Psychological Association, 1997.
Weisfeld, Glenn. "Darwinian Analysis of the emotion of Pride/Shame." In *The Darwinian Heritage and Sociobiology*, edited by Johan van der Dennen, David Smillie, and Daniel Wilson, 319–33. Westport, CT: Praeger Publishers, 1999.
Williams, Bernard. *Shame and Necessity*. Berkeley, CA: University of California Press, 1993.
Xunzi. *Xunzi, the Complete Text*. Translated by Eric Hutton. Princeton, NJ: Princeton University Press, 2014.

Index

Abraham, 81–91
action tendencies, 4, 38, 72–73, 79, 81–3, 88, 91n42, 98, 133,195
adaptation, 38, 41, 116–17, 124, 153–56, 182, 289, 295
adolescent development, 160, 165
affect, 19, 40, 119–20, 245, 247, 276, 289
aggressive instincts, 213, 214, 217, 219, 220, 222
akrasia. *See* weakness of will
altruism, 134–36, 138, 141, 150, 152, 198, 203, 291
amends, 38, 40–41, 45, 115, 117–19, 135–36, 141, 177, 179, 182, 195, 205–6, 224
anger, 17–18, 28, 31, 33, 39, 41–42, 56, 69n15, 113, 118, 158–59, 177, 182, 188n33, 216, 218, 224
animals (nonhuman), 32, 47, 125
anticipated emotions, 4, 15, 40, 87, 92n43, 95–110, 115, 117, 138, 160–61, 165–66, 195–96, 201–3, 205, 207
anxiety, 15–17, 25–26, 28, 30, 33, 39, 42, 54–56, 68n8, 153, 158, 160–61, 165, 196, 201–2, 294;
  disorder, 153, 196;
  internalization of, 160;
  moral, 55, 56;
  realistic, 56;
  Velleman's account of guilt as a family of emotions, united by, 25
apology, 23, 38, 40, 47, 64, 115, 135–37, 151, 177, 179, 182, 224, 228, 295
appearances, 244, 259–60, 262, 264
appraisal, 47, 131–34, 136, 149, 150, 158–59, 162–66, 200–1
Aquinas, Saint Thomas, 7, 242n5, 243–67;
  on the apprehension of moral obligations through conscience, 260–61;
  on the role of good will and the guilt of conscience in our moral experience, 261–64;
  on guilt of conscience, 248–49
Aristotle, 228, 270, 293–94, 304–5, 308n29
attachment, 63, 115
attitude, 6, 171–91, 198, 201, 221, 224, 250, 254, 265n21, 270–71, 273–75, 281–83, 291
Augustine, Saint, 233, 236–37, 256;
  on conscience and guilt, 233
authenticity, 282
authority, 8, 40, 56–63, 69n15, 261, 298–301, 311n52, 311n59
autism, 65

autonomy, 8, 38, 42–43, 269, 281, 289–317

basic emotions privacy, 18, 67, 151, 154, 241, 269, 297
belief, 14, 26–28, 30–32, 34n6–7, 48, 54–55, 69n14, 81–82, 85, 90n28, 96, 99–100, 105, 107n8, 114, 154, 172, 180, 198, 200–7, 211, 243, 248, 251, 263, 270
blame, 16, 39, 41–42, 44, 174, 176, 182, 211–19, 222–24, 266n43;
   self-blame, 211, 213–14, 217, 222
Brandt, R. B., 16, 17

cartesianism, 296–97, 311n64
character, 77–78, 85, 196, 198, 204–5, 217, 244, 261, 263–64, 274–75, 278, 293–94, 303–4
child development, 16, 19–21, 23, 32, 41, 57, 60–64, 66, 114, 122, 160
christianity, 7, 214, 219, 222, 230, 232, 234–35, 237, 240–41, 244–45, 249
chronic guilt, 40, 44
Cicero, 243–44
cognition, 33, 98, 119, 121, 134, 136, 149, 157–58, 166, 277, 280
cognitivism, 247, 252, 255
collective guilt or shame, 139, 297
compassion, 38, 183, 218, 223
compatibilism about free will, 172, 186n1
condemnation, 54, 55, 75, 157, 172, 207, 219–20, 223, 229–31, 244, 290–91
confession, 58–59, 221, 231
confucian ethics, 289–317
conscience:
   acquisition of, 59, 62;
   and empathy as distinct elements of the human personality, 65;
   Aquinas's cognitivist view of, 247;
   phenomenology of, 227–28;
   the distinction between *synderesis* and, 245–46;
   the etymology of the term, 244–45
consciousness, 53–54, 200, 229, 236, 292, 296–97
consequentialism, 212, 215
contractualism, 270
cooperation, 20, 67, 116, 123–26, 134–35, 138, 141, 155–56
crime, 53–54, 58, 75, 85
criminal justice system, 223
cross-cultural differences, 6, 9, 41
culpability, 28, 64, 261, 266n43
culture, 8, 14, 33, 65, 114, 123, 149, 153, 160, 212, 218–19, 221, 270, 304

decision-making, 97, 103, 107n7, 132
deontology, 178, 203, 250, 270, 309n35
depression, 38–39, 42, 44–45, 132, 213, 219, 290
desire, 22, 41, 47, 58, 97, 126, 135–36, 177, 198, 217–19, 222, 224, 245–48, 262–63, 285n56, 295, 306n1
disappointment, 21, 31–32
discipline, 19–20, 23, 56
dispositions, 30, 39, 44, 72–73, 76–79, 88, 155, 197–98, 213, 222, 228, 244, 246–47, 277, 285n56, 290, 298, 302–4, 306, 308n29
duty, 229, 241n4, 270–73, 278, 280
dysfunction, 37, 40, 41, 45, 200, 272, 308n27

ego, 8, 15, 55, 59, 60, 67, 68n9, 132, 162, 197, 199, 269, 277–78, 282, 291–92, 296, 308n16
embarrassment, 26–27, 40, 136, 151, 284n8, 298, 311n50, 311n52
emotions:
   anticipated, 97, 98, 99, 107n8;
   anticipatory, 95, 98, 99, 107nn6–8;
   backward-looking, 79–80, 90n20, 95–96;
   basic, 32, 101–2, 113, 115;
   beneficial, 19–20, 101–2, 150, 294;

cognitive component of, 25–26, 30, 38, 245, 247, 248–49;
evolutionary significance of simulated, 106;
fictional, 96, 97, 102, 103, 106, 107n4;
meta-, 96, 97, 102, 196, 199;
moral, 1, 3, 21, 33, 38, 42, 107n9, 113, 114, 115, 118, 119, 127, 131, 139, 140, 141, 289–94, 296, 297, 298, 300, 302, 303, 312n65;
occurrent (immediate), 30, 96–99, 102–3;
positive, 41, 84, 114, 127n1;
simulated, 99, 102–6, 108nn19–30;
temporal orientation of, 79–80
emotional maturity, 61, 292, 305
empathy, 19, 53–70, 161, 182;
and its role in facilitating solidarity, 67;
and perspective-taking, 161, 182;
developmental account of, 60;
fairness and justice in relation to, 66;
in the absence of conscience, 66;
lack of, 67, 282;
veridical, 61, 62
epistemology, 233, 279
ethics, 68, 217, 228, 230, 269–70, 283, 300, 305
evolution:
evolutionary account of existentialism, 73, 77, 89n2, 275;
See also *guilt*
experience. *See* phenomenology
expression, 19, 31, 53, 56, 62–64, 113–14, 118, 132, 151, 155–56, 158–60, 176–77, 214, 220–21, 299, 301

facial expressions, 113
failure, 2, 8, 21, 25, 38, 41, 45–48, 71, 73, 81, 83, 100, 114, 151, 161–62, 164–66, 179, 180–82, 238–39, 248, 250–51, 271–72, 274, 281, 284n26, 289, 295, 297, 302
faith, 24, 255

fallibility, 199, 203, 241, 242n9, 243, 245, 247, 249–50, 253, 262
family of emotions, 17, 25
fear, 25–26, 54–55, 79–81, 90n20, 95, 97, 100–1, 103–4, 138, 160, 196, 202–7, 213, 294
fittingness of emotions, 4, 72, 101, 103–4, 106–7, 178
forgiveness, 58–59, 64, 69n15, 117, 134–36, 173, 203, 218, 220, 231, 248
forward-looking emotions, 79–80, 90n20, 95, 202;
See also types of emotion freedom, 172, 214, 222, 229, 292, 295–96
free will, 172, 212, 217–18, 245
Freud, Sigmund, 15, 25, 53, 55–57, 59, 62, 68n8–9, 131–32, 162, 292;
on the historical/cultural origins of guilt, 15;
on guilt as a tension that arises between the ego and its conscience, 59
function of guilt, 6, 118, 121, 127, 131–32, 136, 141, 166, 249
future-focused guilt, 72, 73, 81–82, 87

Gauguin, Paul, 82, 283
God, 81, 86, 203, 211, 213–14, 222, 231, 233–34, 239–41, 244–45, 248, 254–56, 262, 279
Gordon, Robert M., 80, 81, 90nn21–25
group membership, 113, 116–17, 121
guilty pleasure, 76–77, 199
guilt:
a wrongdoer's consciousness of, 53;
altruistic, 203;
anticipatory, 4, 15, 87, 92, 95, 96, 106, 117, 202, 205, 207;
as a constitutive moral emotion, 121–23;
as a feeling, rather than an emotion, 28–29;
as a motivator of social approach of victims, 141;
as a self–reactive attitude, 174;

as an autonomous emotion, 42;
as an emotional experience that motivates relationship repair, 117;
as bad conscience, 14, 61;
as being rooted in the capacity for empathy, 60;
as involving a dramatic sense of irreversibility, 77;
as positively correlated with empathy, 19;
as the emotion resulting from doing a bad action, 25;
assessing the appropriateness of, 100–4;
associated with OCD symptoms, 197–98;
categorizing the consequences of, 134;
Catholic, 24, 203;
character-focused, 78;
culture, 38, 153;
deontological, 203;
disposition-, 77, 78;
empathy-based, 61–63;
evolutionary account of, 5–6, 106, 113–30, 153, 234, 301–2, 312n65;
existential, 73;
findings of behavioral studies on, 137–40;
Freud's omission of the social dimension of, 59;
future-focused, 72, 74, 75, 79, 81–88, 89nn5–8, 91n42, 92n43;
Greenspan's account of, 17;
Greenspan's discussion of the indentificatory mechanism of, 179;
Hoffman's error in taking reparative actions to be evidence of, 63;
identity-fidelity model of the experience of, 126;
in association with depression, 44, 45, 132;
similarities and contrasts with shame, 40–41, 114;
in relation to generosity, 15, 20;

in the Nietzschean sense of owing something, 150;
induction, 20, 23, 126, 137–39, 141, 151, 159, 160, 163;
interpersonal side of, 132;
Jewish, 24;
liability to, 61, 62, 64, 65;
omission-, 77;
other-directed, 28;
past-focused, 72, 78, 79, 83, 84;
pathological, 1, 44, 75, 205–6, 238;
phenomenology of, 79, 83–84, 133, 136–37;
present-focused, 4, 72, 74–79, 83–86, 88, 90n15;
problems with cognitive accounts of, 26–27;
proponents of, 16–17;
reactive, 171, 172, 176, 177, 179, 180, 184, 185, 188nn33–35;
retrospective, 4, 71–73, 75–77, 82, 87, 88, 89n13, 107n1;
self-directed, 24–26, 29;
sensitivity, 202;
simulation- (simulated), 84, 85, 87, 92, 103–7;
survivor's, 17, 24–26, 29, 31, 33, 101, 102, 179;
the Raskolnikov model of, 53–54;
transitional, 74;
unconscious sense of, 53, 57;
Williams's critique of a Kantian morality of, 269–73
guilt-proneness, 19, 20, 22, 39, 45, 77, 113, 115–17, 126, 127, 152, 153, 155;
as correlated with cooperation and pro-social behavior, 20;
as positively correlated with altruism, 152

habit, 126, 154, 244, 246–49, 252
harm, 2, 24, 26, 61, 63, 85, 103, 138, 140, 153, 156–62, 164–65, 195, 198–99, 201–6, 216–17, 220–21
hate, 45, 132

health, 1, 116, 249, 263, 289, 292–93, 295, 308nn24–25
hierarchy, 46, 126–27, 153, 163–65, 213
Hobbes, Thomas, 172, 236–37
human nature, 60, 173, 276
Hume, David, 60, 240
Hoffman, Martin, 3, 60–63, 66, 67, 69nn16–18

identification, 119, 121–22, 124–25, 127, 179, 227
identity, 5–6, 38, 57, 59, 117–19, 121–30, 159, 199, 203
imagination, 156, 271
incompatibilism about free will, 172, 186n1
individualism, 119, 296
infidelity, 74, 76, 262
instrumental value of guilt, 16, 127
integrity, 5–6, 131, 281–83, 290, 293–95, 302, 305
intentional objects, 30, 37, 46, 73, 77, 81, 84, 86–87, 90n28
internalization, 5, 6, 15, 61, 64–67, 114–15, 122, 124–27, 149, 150, 153, 155–62, 164–66, 213–14, 216, 236, 243, 275, 298, 299, 311n52;
    in the case of guilt, 155–60;
    of aggressive instincts as the key ingredient to guilt, 213;
    of external standards, 160
intrusive thoughts, 196–97, 199, 201–2, 204–6
irreversibility, 77, 79, 83–84, 88, 89n2

judgments, 43, 57, 66, 125, 156, 162, 183, 215, 228–29, 235, 244, 246–55, 258–63, 266n43, 278, 310n47
Jung, Carl, 235
justification, 72, 120–21, 154, 176, 217

Kant, Immanuel, 7–8, 229–33, 269–88, 295, 309n35

knowledge, 53–54, 67, 157, 198, 200, 227, 239, 244–47, 252–55, 260, 278–79;
    acting knowingly, 72, 74–75, 79, 101, 253, 261;
    self-knowledge, 276, 279–80

libertarianism about free will, 172
love, 19, 53, 56, 63, 155, 173, 218, 220, 241–42, 300;
    love of honor, 276, 285nn30–31;
    self-love, 230, 280, 283

means-end, 5, 118–20, 123–24
measuring guilt and shame, 1, 3, 13, 18–19, 21, 23–24, 33, 37, 39–41, 45–46, 48, 137–39, 154–55, 163–64, 182
mechanism, 17, 118, 124, 179, 188n35, 216
mental disorder, 48, 102
meta-cognition, 200–2, 204, 206
methodology, 2–3, 21, 33
mood, 30, 73
moral:
    development, 1, 3, 72, 92n43, 261, 275, 289, 290, 304–6;
    dilemmas, 17, 256–57, 261, 265n36;
    education, 45, 275, 309n35;
    emotions, 1, 3, 21, 33, 38, 42, 107n9, 113–15, 118–19, 121, 127, 131, 139–41, 289–94, 296–98, 300, 302–3;
    law, 243–44, 253, 255–56, 260–61, 269, 271, 274–75, 277–81;
    theory, 227–28, 244, 272–73, 281
motivation, 2, 16–17, 21, 37–38, 82, 92n43, 107n7, 119, 139, 151, 155–57, 177, 181–82, 189n49, 190n56, 245, 247, 249, 269, 277, 279, 281, 303–4

Nagel, Thomas, 91n40, 182, 184
narcissism, 271
natural selection, 119, 123

negative emotion, 7, 17, 23, 27, 31, 34n6, 38, 84, 114–16, 131–32, 137, 140, 149, 158, 165, 196, 198, 207
neuroses, 45, 53, 57, 132, 206, 308n27
Nietzsche, Friedrich:
   on bad conscience as a self-critical moral awareness, 239;
   on internalization, 213–14, 236;
   on the contingency of blame and guilt, 213–14;
   on the origin of conscience, 236–37;
   on the origin of guilt, 14;
   on the possibility of cultivating a culture without blame and guilt, 219–23;
   See also internalization
non-Western conceptions of guilt and shame, 166, 289–317
normativity, 8, 46, 81, 101, 183, 211–12, 224, 244, 249–51, 253, 257, 261–62, 281

Obsessive-Compulsive Disorder (OCD):
   defining, 196–97;
   metacognitive models of, 200;
   the fear of guilt experienced by patients with, 205;
   the guilt attitudes of patients with, 201–2
omission, 61, 72–73, 76–79, 83, 88, 195, 198, 201, 274

parenting, 20, 23, 56–57
Paul, Saint, 7, 227–42, 264n4
perception, 20, 119, 121, 203, 238, 245, 248–49, 259–60, 295
personality, 56, 65, 67, 68n9, 204–5, 279
phenomenology, 2, 4, 31, 37, 46–47, 72–73, 76–77, 79, 81–84, 87–88, 91n42, 98, 133–36, 138, 140, 149, 155, 181, 189n41, 207n3, 227, 232, 238, 258–59, 264
Plato, 68, 230, 270, 284n5, 296

post-traumatic stress disorder (PTSD), 102
practical reason, 183, 229, 244, 246–49, 252, 269, 272, 277
present-focused guilt, 77–79, 91n42
primitive emotions. *See* basic emotions
privacy
proneness, 4, 19–23, 39–40, 45, 59, 77, 113, 115–17, 126–27, 152–53, 155, 160, 173–74, 178, 182, 197, 206, 294
pro-social:
   behavior, 3, 20, 22, 23, 41, 46–47, 133–34, 137–39, 155, 166;
   feelings or emotions, 23, 155;
   nature of guilt, 23–24, 281
prototypicality, 38, 73, 124–26
psychoanalysis, 62–63
psychopathology, 15–16, 27, 38, 44–46, 67, 196, 206, 294
punishment, 14–17, 23, 25, 29, 55–59, 64–65, 69n15, 117–18, 120, 122, 124–25, 132–35, 141, 156, 158, 160, 213, 215–16, 222–23, 236, 248–49, 255, 263, 291, 298–99

reactive attitude, 6, 171–91, 270–71, 275, 281, 283
reciprocation, 66, 150, 162–65, 173, 178
recognition, 113, 116, 121, 178, 183, 213, 222–24, 235, 239–40, 276, 280
reconciliation, 115, 213, 295
reductionism, 72, 79, 84, 87–88, 91n42
regret, 7, 16–17, 23, 26, 46–47, 54, 63, 80–81, 133, 163, 190n56, 233, 240, 290, 293
religion, 24–26, 29, 34, 122, 196–97, 203, 213, 222, 237
remorse, 16–17, 29, 33, 133–34, 157, 163, 173, 177, 213, 222, 227, 233, 235, 249, 255, 262 reparation, 21, 23, 38, 40, 45–48, 62–64, 98, 101, 135–36, 139–40

repression, 53, 57, 68n8, 236–38, 292
reparative behavior, 21, 40, 45, 47, 48, 62, 64, 98, 135, 136, 139, 140, 177;
 as a sign of feeling of guilt, 62–63, 98, 140
resentment, 6, 16–17, 25, 38, 172, 174–77, 179–80, 182–85, 188n33, 213, 220
respect, 42, 64, 73, 82, 87, 96, 100–2, 150, 217, 233, 269, 276–79, 283;
 self-respect, 232, 299
responsibility, 6, 21, 26, 39–41, 44, 62, 77, 89n1, 98, 101–2, 114, 119, 133, 135–36, 157, 171–72, 179, 182, 185, 201–2, 217–18, 235
retreat, 38–39, 41–42, 47–48
retrospective guilt, 4, 71–93
role-reversal, 184
Rousseau, Jean-Jacques, 237
rule-breaking, 123, 204

self. *See* identity; identification
self-conscious emotions, 38, 113–14, 121, 131, 294, 303, 311n50
self-control, 5, 150–1, 154–56, 161–66
self-cultivation, 301, 304
self-esteem, 39–40, 42, 276
self-improvement, 132, 140–41, 182
self-interest, 118–19, 122, 124, 126–27, 150, 152–53, 291–92, 294–96
sensitivity, 43, 78, 201–2, 224, 282, 294, 297
shamelessness, 269, 293
Shadow of Doubt (Hitchcock), 54
Shakespeare, William, 54, 97, 103
shame:
 Aristotelian, 293–95;
 as a heteronomous emotion, 42;
 as a motivator of reparative behavior, 46;
 as a negative and stressful feeling, 291–93;
 as a relational moral sense, 295–97;
 Confucian, 289, 297–306;
 culture, 38, 41, 153;
 in personal self-control situations, 162;
 in relation to anger and blame, 41;
 in relation to honor, 39;
 in relation to social retreat, 47;
 phenomenology of, 47;
 Williams's account of the phenomenology of, 181;
 See also reparative behavior
shaming practices, positive functions of, 43
shame-proneness, 19, 22, 39, 40, 113, 182, 206
simulation, 73, 84–85, 87, 92n43, 106
sin, 213, 234, 241, 254–56, 261
social emotions, 38, 131, 139–40, 153, 155, 160, 162, 294, 306, 310n49
social functioning, 5–6, 48, 149, 155–56, 160
social norms, 98, 103, 114, 117, 123–24, 127
social psychology, 42, 60
social sanctions, 119, 165
social status, 47, 125, 276, 294
society, 14, 21, 43–44, 65–66, 114, 187n20, 212–14, 217–18, 221–22, 236–38, 254, 276, 292, 299
socioeconomic status, 125
sociopathy, 39, 204
Socrates, 68, 304
stoicism, 90, 244, 299
St. Paul, 233–34
Strawson, P. F., 6, 171–78, 180, 183–86, 188nn34–35, 189n36, 190n56, 225n2
submission, 46–47, 64, 119, 297, 300
survivor's guilt, 17, 24–26, 29, 31, 33, 101–2, 179
sympathy, 60, 175, 190n66, 240n4, 300

Tangney, June, 18, 19, 21, 22, 25, 38–42, 46, 47, 113–15, 132, 133, 135, 136, 141, 151, 154, 199, 205–7, 291, 292, 306n1,
temporality, 71–73, 79–81, 88

Test of Self-Conscious Affect (TOSCA), 21–24, 39–41, 45–46, 155
The Conscience Principle (CP), 243, 250, 252, 253, 255, 257, 259, 263, 265n34, 266n37
The Silence of the Lambs (Demme), 66, 106
theology, 230, 234, 244–45
transgression, 2, 5, 14, 19, 21, 28–29, 38, 42–48, 113–21, 127, 131–42, 153–54, 177, 198, 203–4, 206–7, 245, 274–75, 289
trust, 17, 22, 25–26, 64–65, 67–68, 81, 156, 182, 205
trauma, 102, 232–33
types of emotion freedom, 172, 214, 222, 229, 292, 295–96
types of guilt, 24–29, 76

unfittingness, 100–6
universality of emotions, 113, 173, 213, 303
Utilitarianism, 228–29, 241n4, 270, 281

vengeance, 217–18, 275
Vertigo (Hitchcock), 53
victims, 5, 23, 38–39, 45, 58, 63, 66, 101–2, 132–41, 179, 184, 271
virtue and virtue ethics, 228–29, 239–40, 244, 247, 249, 261–64, 269, 276, 285n30, 293–94, 297–99, 300–6

warrant, 16–17, 25, 58, 83, 100–3, 176, 215
Wallace, R. Jay, 174, 180, 183, 184
weakness of will, 4, 74, 76–78, 88, 247, 249–53, 256–57, 263, 265n21, 265n26, 236
well-being, 5, 38, 48, 61, 63, 73, 101, 122, 133, 139–40, 217
Williams, Bernard, 273–76, 281
wrongdoing, 2, 53–55, 57–59, 61, 63–65, 67, 82, 98, 116, 158, 179, 183, 207n3, 233, 244, 248–49, 255–56, 261, 263, 271

About the Contributors

Reid Blackman received his B.A. from Cornell University, his M.A. from Northwestern University, and his Ph.D. from The University of Texas in Austin. He was a fellow at the Parr Center for Ethics at The University of North Carolina, Chapel Hill, and an assistant professor of philosophy at Colgate University. He has published on metaethics, free will, Nietzsche, and the emotions. He recently left academia and founded Virtue, an ethics consultancy.

Bradford Cokelet is an assistant professor at the University of Kansas. His research focuses on the nature and value of character, virtue, and human flourishing. He teaches and writes about these topics from normative, empirical, and cross-cultural perspectives. He is currently completing his book *Buddhism, Ethics, and the Good Life,* which is under contract with Routledge.

Sophie-Grace Chappell is professor of philosophy at the Open University, UK, Leverhulme Major Research Fellow 2017–2020, visiting fellow in the Department of Philosophy, St. Andrews 2017–2020, and Erskine research fellow, University of Canterbury, NZ, Spring 2020. She was educated at Magdalen College, Oxford, and Edinburgh University. She was director of the Scots Philosophical Association, 2003–2006. Since 2000 she has been reviews editor of *The Philosophical Quarterly* and treasurer of the Mind Association. In 2021 she will be a REF sub-panelist for philosophy. She has held visiting appointments in the Universities of Edinburgh, Glasgow, British Columbia, Stirling, Reykjavik, and Oslo. She has published over a hundred articles on ethics, moral psychology, epistemology, ancient philosophy, and the philosophy of religion. Her books include *Aristotle and Augustine on Freedom* (Macmillan, 1995), *Understanding Human Goods* (Edinburgh University Press, 2003), *The Inescapable Self: An Introduction to Philosophy*

(Orion, 2005), *Reading Plato's Theaetetus* (Hackett, 2005), *Ethics and Experience* (Acumen, 2009), and *Knowing What to Do: Imagination, Virtue, and Platonism in Ethics* (Oxford University Press, 2014). She has also edited or co-edited five collections of essays in ethics, most recently *The Problem of Moral Demandingness* (Routledge 2011), *Intuition, Theory, and Anti-Theory in Ethics* (Oxford University Press, 2015), and *Ethics beyond the Limits: Essays on Bernard Williams' Ethics and the Limits of Philosophy* (Routledge, 2019). Her main current research is about epiphanies, immediate and revelatory encounters with value, and their place in our experience and our philosophical ethics. She was a governor of the British Association of Counsellors and Psychotherapists from 2012 to 2018. She is a member of the Scottish Mountaineering Club (climbing new winter routes up to grade VII,7), an active poet and translator of the classical Greek dramatists, and an untalented but keen cyclist and pianist. She is the UK's first openly transgender philosophy academic, having transitioned in 2014, and campaigns actively on feminist and transgender issues. She lives with her family in Dundee.

John Deigh is professor of law and philosophy at the University of Texas at Austin. He is the author of *The Sources of Moral Agency* (CUP, 1996), *Emotions and the Law* (OUP, 2008), and *From Psychology to Morality* (OUP, 2018). He was the editor of *Ethics* from 1997 to 2008.

Julien Deonna is associate professor in philosophy at the University of Geneva and project leader at the Swiss Centre in Affective Sciences. He is the author of many articles in the philosophy of emotions and moral psychology and co-author of two books: *In Defense of Shame* (OUP, 2011) and *The Emotions: a Philosophical Introduction* (Routledge, 2012). He is co-director of Thumos, the Genevan Research Group on Emotions, Values and Norms.

Blaine J. Fowers is professor of counseling psychology at the University of Miami. He conducts theoretical and empirical investigations of virtue and flourishing. Fowers is the author of *The Evolution of Ethics: Human Sociality and the Emergence of Ethical Mindedness* (2015, Palgrave Macmillan), *Virtue and Psychology* (2005, APA), and *Beyond the Myth of Marital Happiness* (2000, Jossey Bass), and a co-author of *Re-Envisioning Psychology* (1999, Jossey Bass) and *Frailty, Suffering, and Vice: Flourishing in the Face of Human Limitations* (2017, APA). He is a fellow of the American Psychological Association and a recipient of the Joseph B. Gittler award for contributions to the philosophical foundations of psychology.

Roger Giner-Sorolla is professor of social psychology at the University of Kent. He received his Ph.D. from New York University in 1996 and became interested in study moral emotions as a postdoctoral fellow of the University of Virginia. His main research interests are in anger, disgust, guilt, and shame, and in 2012 he published a monograph on moral emotions, *Judging Passions: Moral Emotions in Persons and Groups*. In addition to being an advocate for open science and replicability in research, he has been the editor in chief of the *Journal of Experimental Social Psychology* since 2016.

Gilbert Harman is the James S. McDonnell Distinguished University Professor of Philosophy, Emeritus, at Princeton University. Over the course of his career, he has authored nine monographs and published more than 180 articles. He is a fellow of the Cognitive Science Society, the American Psychological Society, and the American Academy of Arts and Sciences, and he won the Jean Nicod Prize in 2005. He lives in Princeton, New Jersey.

Ilona E. de Hooge is assistant professor of marketing and consumer behaviour at the Wageningen University, The Netherlands. She received her PhD from Tilburg University in 2008 with a dissertation examining the consequences of the emotions guilt and shame, and she continued her career as assistant professor at the Marketing Management Department of the Rotterdam School of Management (Erasmus University; 2008–2014). Ilona currently examines the role of emotions in a wide array of (consumer and marketing) behaviors, including pro-social behavior, gift-giving, advice-taking, e-commerce, and food waste. Her research has been published in *Journal of Personality and Social Psychology, Cognition and Emotion, Food Quality and Preference, Journal of Cleaner Production, International Journal of Research in Marketing, Journal of Advertising, Journal of Consumer Psychology, Journal of Behavioral Decision Making*, and in multiple book chapters. Moreover, her research has been presented at more than forty international conferences (e.g., Association for Consumer Research, Society for Consumer Psychology, Consortium of European Researchers on Emotions, International Society for Research on Emotion, European Association for Experimental Social Psychology, and Subjective Probability, Utility, and Decision Making), and at multiple professional conferences.

Anne Jeffrey is an assistant professor of philosophy at Baylor University. She works primarily in metaethics, normative ethics, and bioethics with a focus on the virtue tradition. She has recently published a monograph, *God and Morality* (Cambridge University Press), on the intersection between metaethics and philosophy of religion. Before coming to Baylor, she was an assistant professor of philosophy and director of the bioethics curriculum in the College of Medicine at the University of South Alabama. She worked as a postdoctoral researcher at the University of Notre Dame on the Hope and

Optimism project from 2015–2016, and she earned her Ph.D. in philosophy from Georgetown University in 2015.

Alison Duncan Kerr (PhD, OSU) is a research fellow in the Department of Philosophy and member of the Arché Philosophical Research Centre at the University of St. Andrews. Her research focuses on rationality and emotion as topics in philosophy of mind and philosophy of psychology. She instituted the Scottish Emotion Network, which brings together academics working on emotion from across Scotland. Dr. Kerr also founded and is currently the director of the St. Andrews Institute for Gender Studies—an institute with over a hundred academics spanning from twenty-two different departments, including a deeply interdisciplinary MLitt programme in gender studies that focuses on philosophical and theoretical approaches to understanding gender from an intersectional point of view.

Heidi L. Maibom is professor of philosophy at University of Cincinnati. She received her Cand.Phil. from the University of Copenhagen, and her Ph.D. from University College London. She studies all aspects of empathy, and also responsibility, emotions, moral psychology, and psychopathy. She is the editor of *The Routledge Handbook of the Philosophy of Empathy* (2017), *Empathy and Morality* (Oxford 2014), and *Neurofeminism* (w. Jacobson and Bluhm, 2012), and is currently writing an introductory book on empathy, and another on the nature and use of perspective taking.

Corey J. Maley is associate professor of philosophy at the University of Kansas. He earned his Ph.D. from Princeton University in 2015, where he wrote a dissertation on the nature of guilt and shame. In addition to philosophical questions about emotions, he is interested in how to understand computation, particularly as it is used to explain the mind and brain. He lives in Lawrence, Kansas, with his wife, Sarah, and son, Max.

Darren McGee received his M.A. in psychology from Durham University in 2012 and his Ph.D. from the University of Kent in 2017. His Ph.D. thesis examined the antecedents of shame and guilt in situations of self-control and interpersonal harm. His main research interests focus on moral emotions, specifically shame and guilt.

Heidy Meriste is a Ph.D. candidate in philosophy at the University of Tartu. Her research is focused on emotions and their role in morality and the good life. In particular, she has been working on, and taught courses on emotions like contempt, pride, shame, and guilt.

Laura Papish is an assistant professor of philosophy at The George Washington University, having received her Ph.D. from Northwestern University in 2011. Her main research areas are Kant's moral theory, the history of ethics, and contemporary ethics. Her articles have appeared in (among others) *Kantian Review*, *Social Theory and Practice*, *Ergo*, and *Ethical Theory and Moral Practice*. Her first book, *Kant on Evil, Self-Deception, and Moral Reform*, was published by Oxford University Press in 2018.

Nicholas Sars is a Ph.D. candidate at Tulane University and research assistant in the Center for Ethics and Public Affairs at The Murphy Institute. His dissertation focuses on attitudinal approaches to moral responsibility. His broader research interests include the overlap of moral, political, and legal philosophy.

Bongrae Seok is associate professor of philosophy at Alvernia University in Reading, Pennsylvania. He received his B.A. from Seoul National University (South Korea) and his M.A. and Ph.D. from the University of Arizona, where he studied philosophy and cognitive science. He researched the functional specialization of the prefrontal cortex as a postdoctoral fellow in a neuroscience research lab at the University of Arizona. Currently, he is the chair of the leadership studies department and the associate director of O'Pake center for ethics and leadership at Alvernia University. He is the president of ACPA (Association of Chinese Philosophers in America) and the executive board member of NAKPA (North American Korean Philosophy Association). He is also a recipient of the Neag Professorship (2014–2016). His primary research interest lies in the interdisciplinary and comparative studies of moral psychology and cognitive neuroscience that interface with the concepts of the mind, moral agency, moral emotion, and moral knowledge discussed in Asian philosophical traditions such as Confucianism and Buddhism. In his recent books (*Embodied Moral Psychology and Confucian Philosophy* [2013] and *Moral Psychology of Confucian Shame* [2016]), he discusses how embodied cognition explains the moral mind of Confucianism and how the self-critical emotion of shame can integrate social cognition and moral virtue in Confucian tradition. His recent articles ("David Wong's Interpretation of Confucian Moral Psychology" [2017] and "Neuroscience, Moral Sentimentalism, and Confucian Philosophy: Moral Psychology of the Body and Emotion" [2013]) and book chapters "Mencius's *Ceyinzhixin* and Nociceptive Mirror Emotion" (2015) and "The Four Seven Debate of Korean Neo-Confucianism and the Moral Psychological and Theistic Turn in Korean Philosophy" (2018) show his comparative and interdisciplinary integration of cognitive science and Confucian moral psychology. He also published articles and chapters on the phenomenological and cognitive embodiment in neuroaesthetics and spatial perception.

Juliette Vazard is currently doing a joint Ph.D. at the Swiss Center for Affective Sciences, University of Geneva, under the supervision of Fabrice Teroni, and at the Institut Jean Nicod under the supervision of Jérôme Dokic. Her project concerns the values of negative emotions, and her current focus is on the epistemic value of anxiety and its role in our inclinations to doubt.

www.ingramcontent.com/pod-product-compliance
Lightning Source LLC
Chambersburg PA
CBHW031544300426
44111CB00006BA/171